Kaplan Publishing are constantly finding new ways to make a difference to your studies and our exciting online resources really do offer something different to students looking for exam success.

This book comes with free MyKaplan online resources so that you can study anytime, anywhere. **This free online resource is not sold separately and is included in the price of the book.**

Having purchased this book, you have access to the following online study materials:

CONTENT	ACCA (including FBT, FMA, FFA)		FIA (excluding FBT, FMA, FFA)	
	Text	Kit	Text	Kit
Electronic version of the book	✓	✓	✓	✓
Knowledge checks with instant answers	✓		✓	
Material updates	✓	✓	✓	✓
Latest official ACCA exam questions*		✓		
Pocket Notes (digital copy)	✓		✓	
Study Planner	✓			
Progress Test including questions and answers	✓		✓	
Syllabus recap Videos		✓		✓
Revision Planner		✓		✓
Question Debrief and Walkthrough Videos		✓		
Mock Exam including questions and answers		✓		

* Excludes BT, MA, FA, FBT, FMA, FFA; for all other papers includes a selection of questions, as released by ACCA

How to access your online resources

Received this book as part of your Kaplan course?
If you have a MyKaplan account, your full online resources will be added automatically, in line with the information in your course confirmation email. If you've not used MyKaplan before, you'll be sent an activation email once your resources are ready.

Bought your book from Kaplan?
We'll automatically add your online resources to your MyKaplan account. If you've not used MyKaplan before, you'll be sent an activation email.

Bought your book from elsewhere?
Go to **www.mykaplan.co.uk/add-online-resources**
Enter the ISBN number found on the title page and back cover of this book.
Add the unique pass key number contained in the scratch panel below.
You may be required to enter additional information during this process to set up or confirm your account details.

This code can only be used once for the registration of this book online. This registration and your online content will expire when the examinations covered by this book have taken place. Please allow one hour from the time you submit your book details for us to process your request.

Please scratch the film to access your unique code.

Please be aware that this code is case-sensitive and you will need to include the dashes within the passcode, but not when entering the ISBN.

AF874508

KAPLAN PUBLISHING

ACCA

Applied Knowledge

ACCA Diploma in Accounting and Business (RQF Level 4)

Management Accounting (MA/FMA)

Study Text

British library cataloguing-in-publication data

A catalogue record for this book is available from the British Library.

Published by:

Kaplan Publishing UK
179 – 191 Borough High Street
London
SE1 1HR

ISBN 978-1-83735-244-9

Printed and bound in Great Britain

Acknowledgements

We are grateful to the Association of Chartered Certified Accountants and the Chartered Institute of Management Accountants for permission to reproduce past examination questions. The answers have been prepared by Kaplan Publishing.

Contents

Introduction

How to use the Materials

These Kaplan Publishing learning materials have been carefully designed to make your learning experience as easy as possible and to give you the best chances of success in your examinations.

The product range contains a number of features to help you in the study process. They include:

1 Detailed study guide and syllabus objectives

2 Description of the examination

3 Study skills and revision guidance

4 Study text

5 Question practice

The sections on the study guide, the syllabus objectives, the examination and study skills should all be read before you commence your studies. They are designed to familiarise you with the nature and content of the examination and give you tips on how to best to approach your learning.

The **Study Text** comprises the main learning materials and gives guidance as to the importance of topics and where other related resources can be found. Each chapter includes:

- The **learning objectives** contained in each chapter, which have been carefully mapped to the examining body's own syllabus learning objectives or outcomes. You should use these to check you have a clear understanding of all the topics on which you might be assessed in the examination.
- The **chapter diagram** provides a visual reference for the content in the chapter, giving an overview of the topics and how they link together.
- The **content** for each topic area commences with a brief explanation or definition to put the topic into context before covering the topic in detail. You should follow your studying of the content with a review of the illustration/s. These are worked examples which will help you to understand better how to apply the content for the topic.
- **Test your understanding** sections provide an opportunity to assess your understanding of the key topics by applying what you have learned to short questions. Answers can be found at the back of each chapter.
- **Summary diagrams** complete each chapter to show the important links between topics and the overall content of the examination. These diagrams should be used to check that you have covered and understood the core topics before moving on.
- **Question practice** is provided at the back of each text.

Quality and accuracy are of the utmost importance to us so if you spot an error in any of our products, please send an email to mykaplanreporting@kaplan.com with full details, or follow the link to the feedback form in MyKaplan.

Our Quality Coordinator will work with our technical team to verify the error and take action to ensure it is corrected in future editions.

Icon Explanations

Definition – Key definitions that you will need to learn from the core content.

Key point – Identifies topics that are key to success and are often examined.

Illustration – Worked examples help you understand the core content better.

Test your understanding – Exercises for you to complete to ensure that you have understood the topics just learned.

Supplementary reading – These sections will help to provide a deeper understanding of core areas. The supplementary reading is NOT optional reading. It is vital to provide you with the breadth of knowledge you will need to address the wide range of topics within your syllabus that could feature in an exam question. **Reference to this text is vital when self-studying.**

On-line subscribers

Our on-line resources are designed to increase the flexibility of your learning materials and provide you with immediate feedback on how your studies are progressing.

If you are subscribed to our on-line resources you will find:

1 On-line reference ware: reproduces your Study Text on-line, giving you anytime, anywhere access.

2 On-line testing: provides you with additional on-line objective testing so you can practice what you have learned further.

3 On-line performance management: immediate access to your on-line testing results. Review your performance by key topics and chart your achievement through the course relative to your peer group.

Syllabus introduction

Syllabus background

The aim of ACCA **Management Accounting (MA)**/FIA Diploma in Accounting and Business is to develop knowledge and understanding of management accounting techniques to support management in planning, controlling and monitoring performance in a variety of business context.

Objectives of the syllabus

- Explain the nature, source and purpose of management information.
- Explain and apply data analysis and statistical techniques.
- Explain and apply cost accounting techniques.
- Prepare budgets for planning and control.
- Compare actual costs with standard costs and analyse any variances.
- Explain and apply performance measurements and monitor business performance.

Core areas of the syllabus

- The nature, source and purpose of management information
- Data analysis and statistical techniques
- Cost accounting techniques
- Budgeting
- Standard costing
- Performance measurement.

ACCA Performance Objectives

In order to become a member of the ACCA, as a trainee accountant you will need to demonstrate that you have achieved nine performance objectives. Performance objectives are indicators of effective performance and set the minimum standard of work that trainees are expected to achieve and demonstrate in the workplace. They are divided into key areas of knowledge which are closely linked to the exam syllabus.

There are five Essential performance objectives and a choice of fifteen Technical performance objectives which are divided into five areas.

The performance objectives which link to this exam are:

1 Ethics and professionalism PO1 (Essential)

2 Evaluate management accounting systems PO12 (Technical)

3 Plan and control performance PO13 (Technical)

4 Monitor performance PO14 (Technical)

The following link provides an in depth insight into all of the performance objectives:

https://www.accaglobal.com/content/dam/ACCA_Global/Students/per/PER-Performance-objectives-achieve.pdf

Progression

There are two elements of progression that we can measure: first how quickly students move through individual topics within a subject; and second how quickly they move from one course to the next. We know that there is an optimum for both, but it can vary from subject to subject and from student to student. However, using data and our experience of student performance over many years, we can make some generalisations.

A fixed period of study set out at the start of a course with key milestones is important. This can be within a subject, for example 'I will finish this topic by 30 June', or for overall achievement, such as 'I want to be qualified by the end of next year'.

Your qualification is cumulative, as earlier papers provide a foundation for your subsequent studies, so do not allow there to be too big a gap between one subject and another. We know that exams encourage techniques that lead to some degree of short term retention, the result being that you will simply forget much of what you have already learned unless it is refreshed (look up Ebbinghaus Forgetting Curve for more details on this). This makes it more difficult as you move from one subject to another: not only will you have to learn the new subject, you will also have to relearn all the underpinning knowledge as well. This is very inefficient and slows down your overall progression which makes it more likely you may not succeed at all.

In addition, delaying your studies slows your path to qualification which can have negative impacts on your career, postponing the opportunity to apply for higher level positions and therefore higher pay.

You can use the following diagram showing the whole structure of your qualification to help you keep track of your progress.

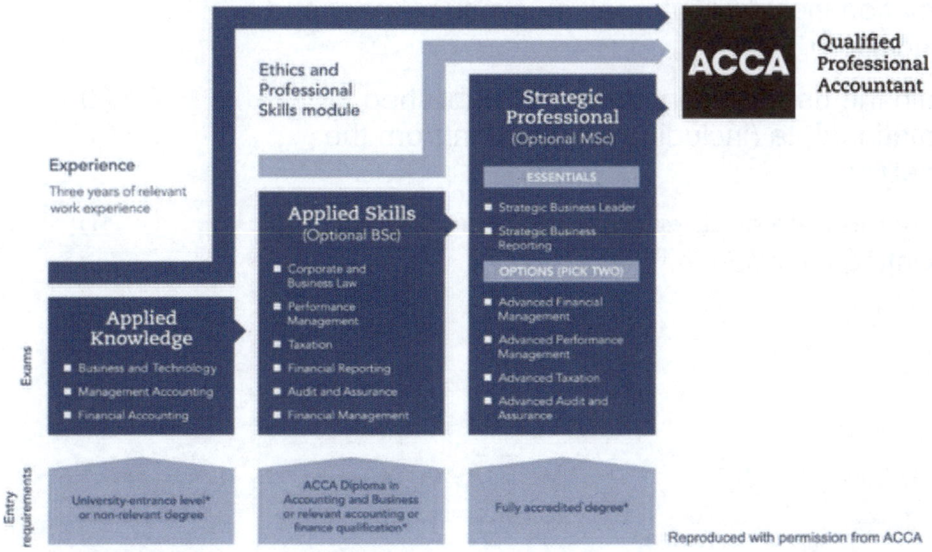

Reproduced with permission from ACCA

Syllabus objectives

We have reproduced the ACCA's syllabus below, showing where the objectives are explored within this book. Within the chapters, we have broken down the extensive information found in the syllabus into easily digestible and relevant sections, called Content Objectives. These correspond to the objectives at the beginning of each chapter.

Syllabus learning objective			Chapter reference
A	**THE NATURE, SOURCE AND PURPOSE OF MANAGEMENT INFORMATION**		
1	**Accounting for management**		
	(a)	Describe the purpose and role of cost and management accounting within an organisation.[k]	1
	(b)	Compare and contrast financial accounting with cost and management accounting.[k]	1
	(c)	Outline the managerial processes of planning, decision making and control.[k]	1
	(d)	Explain the difference between strategic, tactical and operational planning.[k]	1
	(e)	Distinguish between data and information.[k]	1
	(f)	Identify and explain the attributes of good information.[k]	1
	(g)	Explain the limitations of management information in providing guidance for managerial decision-making.[k]	1
2	**Sources of data**		
	(a)	Describe the three main data sources: machine/sensor, transactional and human/social.[k]	10
	(b)	Describe and identify sources and categories of information including internal, external, primary and secondary. [k]	10
	(c)	Explain the uses and limitations of published information/data (including information from the internet).[k]	10
	(d)	Identify the data capture costs of management accounting information.[k]	10

3	**Cost classification**		
	(a)	Explain and illustrate production and non-production costs.[k]	2
	(b)	Describe the different elements of non-production costs – administrative, selling, distribution and finance.[k]	2
	(c)	Describe the different elements of production cost – materials, labour and overheads.[k]	2
	(d)	Explain the importance of the distinction between production and non-production costs when valuing output and inventories.[k]	2
	(e)	Explain and illustrate with examples classifications used in the analysis of the product/service costs including by function, direct and indirect, fixed and variable, stepped fixed and semi variable costs.[s]	2
	(f)	Explain and illustrate the use of codes in categorising transaction.[k]	2
	(g)	Identify and interpret graphical representations of different types of cost behaviour.[s]	2
	(h)	Explain and illustrate the concept of cost objects, cost units and cost centres.[s]	2
	(i)	Distinguish between cost, profit, investment and revenue centres.[k]	2
	(j)	Describe the differing needs for information of cost, profit, investment and revenue centre managers.[k]	2
4	**Presenting information**		
	(a)	Prepare written reports representing management information in suitable formats according to purpose.[s]	17
	(b)	Use data visualisation to present information using table, charts and graphs (bar charts, line graphs, pie charts and scatter graphs).[s]	17
	(c)	Interpret information (including the tables, charts and graphs) presented in management reports.[s]	17

B DATA ANALYSIS AND STATISTICAL TECHNIQUES

1 Sampling methods

(a)	Explain sampling techniques (random, systematic, stratified, multistage, cluster and quota).[k]	10
(b)	Choose an appropriate sampling method in a specific situation. (Note: Derivation of random samples will not be examined).[s]	10

2 Analytical techniques in budgeting and forecasting

(a)	Explain the structure of linear functions and equations.[s]	2
(b)	Use high low analysis to separate the fixed and variable elements of total costs including situations involving semi variable and stepped fixed costs and changes in the variable cost per unit.[s]	2
(c)	Explain the advantages and disadvantages of using high low method to estimate the fixed and variable element of costing.[k]	2
(d)	Construct scatter diagrams and lines of best fit.[s]	17
(e)	Analysis of cost data.	12
	(i) Explain the concept of correlation coefficient and coefficient of determination.[k]	12
	(ii) Calculate and interpret correlation coefficient and coefficient of determination.[s]	12
	(iii) Establish a linear function using regression analysis and interpret the results.[s]	12
(f)	Use linear regression coefficients to make forecasts of costs and revenues.[s]	12
(g)	Adjust historical and forecast data for price movements.[s]	12
(h)	Explain the advantages and disadvantages of linear regression analysis.[k]	12
(i)	Explain the principles of time series analysis (cyclical, trend, seasonal variation and random elements).[k]	12
(j)	Calculate moving averages.[s]	12
(k)	Calculation of trend, including the use of regression coefficients.[s]	12
(l)	Use trend and seasonal variation (additive and multiplicative) to make budget forecasts.[s]	12
(m)	Explain the advantages and disadvantages of time series analysis.[k]	12
(n)	Explain the purpose of index numbers.[k]	12

	(o)	Calculate simple and multi-item (weighted) index numbers for one or more variables, including Laspeyre and Paasche indices.[s]	12
	(p)	Describe the product life cycle and explain its importance in forecasting.[k]	12
3	**Summarising and analysing data**		
	(a)	Describe the five characteristics of big data (volume, variety, velocity, value and veracity).[k]	10
	(b)	Explain the three types of big data: structured, semi-structured and unstructured.[k]	10
	(c)	Describe the main uses of big data and data analytics for organisations.[k]	10
	(d)	Describe the two types of data categorical (nominal and ordinal) and numerical (continuous and discrete).[s]	10
	(e)	Explain the terms descriptive analysis and inferential analysis.[k]	10
	(f)	Calculate the mean, mode and median for ungrouped data and the mean for grouped data.[s]	11
	(g)	Calculate measures of dispersion including the variance, standard deviation and coefficient of variation both grouped and ungrouped data.[s]	11
	(h)	Calculate expected values for use in decision-making.[s]	11
	(i)	Explain the properties of a normal distribution.[s]	11
	(j)	Interpret normal distribution graphs and tables.[s]	11
4	**Spreadsheets**		
	(a)	Explain the role and features of a computer spreadsheet system.[k]	18
	(b)	Identify applications for computer spreadsheets and their use in cost and management accounting.[s]	18
C	**COST ACCOUNTING TECHNIQUES**		
1	**Accounting for material, labour and overheads**		
	(a)	Accounting for materials	
		(i) Describe the systems necessary for the ordering, receiving and issuing of materials from inventory.[k]	3
		(ii) Describe the control procedures used to monitor physical and 'book' inventory and to minimise discrepancies and losses.[k]	3
		(iii) Interpret the entries and balances in the material inventory account.[s]	3

(iv)	Identify, explain and calculate the costs of ordering and holding inventory (including buffer inventory).[s]	3
(v)	Calculate and interpret optimal reorder quantities.[s]	3
(vi)	Calculate and interpret optimal reorder quantities when discounts apply.[s]	3
(vii)	Produce calculations to minimise inventory costs when inventory is gradually replenished.[s]	3
(viii)	Describe and apply appropriate methods for establishing reorder levels where demand in the lead time is constant.[s]	3
(ix)	Calculate the value of closing inventory and material issues using LIFO, FIFO and average methods.[s]	3
(x)	Explain Just in Time (JIT) as an inventory management approach.[k]	3

(b) Accounting for labour

(i)	Calculate direct and indirect costs of labour.[s]	4
(ii)	Explain the systems used to capture and record labour effort.[k]	4
(iii)	Prepare the journal and ledger entries to record labour cost inputs and outputs.[s]	4
(iv)	Describe different remuneration methods: time-based systems, piecework systems and individual and group incentive schemes.[k]	4
(v)	Calculate the level, and analyse the costs and causes of labour turnover.[s]	4
(vi)	Explain and calculate labour efficiency, capacity and production volume ratios.[s]	4
(vii)	Interpret the entries in the labour account.[s]	4

(c) Accounting for overheads

(i)	Explain the different treatment of direct and indirect expenses.[k]	5
(ii)	Describe the procedures involved in determining production overhead absorption rates.[k]	5
(iii)	Allocate and apportion production overheads to cost centres using an appropriate basis.[s]	5

		(iv)	Reapportion service cost centre costs to production cost centres (including using the reciprocal method where service cost centres work for each other).[s]	5
		(v)	Select, apply and discuss appropriate bases for absorption rates.[s]	5
		(vi)	Prepare journal and ledger entries for manufacturing overheads incurred and absorbed.[s]	5
		(vii)	Calculate and explain the under and over absorption of overheads.[s]	5
2	**Absorption and marginal costing**			
	(a)	Explain the importance of, and apply, the concept of contribution.[s]		6
	(b)	Demonstrate and discuss the effect of absorption and marginal costing on inventory valuation and profit determination.[s]		6
	(c)	Calculate profit or loss under absorption and marginal costing.[s]		6
	(d)	Reconcile the profits or losses calculated under absorption and marginal costing.[s]		6
	(e)	Describe the advantages and disadvantages of absorption and marginal costing.[k]		6
3	**Cost accounting methods**			
	(a)	Job and batch costing		
		(i)	Describe the characteristics of job and batch costing.[k]	7
		(ii)	Describe the situations where the use of job or batch costing would be appropriate.[k]	7
		(iii)	Prepare cost records and accounts in job and batch costing situations.[k]	7
		(iv)	Establish job and batch costs from given information.[s]	7
	(b)	Process costing		
		(i)	Describe the characteristics of process costing.[k]	7
		(ii)	Describe the situations where the use of process costing would be appropriate.[s]	7
		(iii)	Explain the concepts of normal and abnormal losses and abnormal gains.[k]	7

	(iv)	Distinguish between by-products and joint products.[k]	7
	(v)	Value by-products and joint products at the point of separation.[s]	7
	(vi)	Evaluate the benefit of further processing.[s]	7
(c)	Service/operation costing		
	(i)	Define the characteristics of service organisations.	8
	(ii)	Identify situations where the use of service/operation costing is appropriate.[k]	8
	(iii)	Illustrate suitable unit cost measures that may be used in different service/operation situations.[s]	8
	(iv)	Carry out service cost analysis in simple service industry situations.[s]	8

4 Alternative costing principles

(a)	Explain alternative cost management techniques (activity-based costing (ABC), target costing and life cycle costing).[k]	9
(b)	Differentiate alternative cost management techniques from the traditional costing techniques (note: calculations are not required).[k]	9

D BUDGETING

1 Nature and purpose of budgeting

(a)	Explain why organisations use budgeting.[k]	13
(b)	Describe the planning and control cycle in an organisation.[k]	13
(c)	Explain the administrative procedures used in the budgeting process.[k]	13
(d)	Describe the stages in the budgeting process (including sources of relevant data, planning and agreeing draft budgets and purpose of forecasting and how they link to budgeting).[k]	13

2 Budget preparation

(a)	Explain the importance of principal budget factor in constructing the budget.[k]	13
(b)	Prepare sales budgets.[s]	13
(c)	Prepare functional budgets (production, raw materials usage and purchases, labour, variable and fixed overheads).[s]	13

	(d)	Prepare cash budgets.[s]	13
	(e)	Prepare master budgets (statement of profit and loss and statement of financial position).[s]	13
	(f)	Explain and illustrate 'what if' analysis and scenario planning.[s]	13
	(g)	Describe the impact of the general economic environment on costs/revenue in budgeting.[k]	13
	(h)	Explain the importance of considering sustainability in budget preparation.	13
3	**Flexible budgets**		
	(a)	Explain the importance of flexible budgets in control.[k]	13
	(b)	Explain the disadvantage of fixed budgets in control.[k]	13
	(c)	Identify situations where fixed or flexible budgetary control would be appropriate.[k]	13
	(d)	Flex a budget to a given level of volume.[s]	13
4	**Asset budgeting and investment appraisal**		
	(a)	Discuss the importance of investment planning and control.[k]	14
	(b)	Define and distinguish between asset and expense items.[k]	14
	(c)	Outline the issues to consider and the steps involved in the preparation of an asset expenditure budget.[k]	14
	(d)	Explain and illustrate the difference between simple and compound interest, and between nominal and effective interest rates.[s]	14
	(e)	Explain and illustrate compounding and discounting.[s]	14
	(f)	Explain the distinction between cash flow and profit and the relevance of cash flow to investment appraisal.[k]	14
	(g)	Identify and evaluate relevant cash flows for individual investment decisions.[s]	14
	(h)	Explain and illustrate the net present value (NPV) and internal rate of return (IRR) methods of discounted cash flow.[s]	14
	(i)	Calculate present value using annuity and perpetuity formulae.[s]	14
	(j)	Calculate NPV, IRR and payback (discounted and non-discounted).[s]	14
	(k)	Interpret the results of NPV, IRR and payback calculations of investment viability.[s]	14

5	**Budgetary control and reporting**		
	(a)	Calculate simple variances between flexed budget, fixed budget and actual sales, costs and profits.[s]	13
	(b)	Discuss the relative significance of variances.[k]	15
	(c)	Explain potential action to eliminate variances.[k]	15
	(d)	Define the concept of responsibility accounting and its significance in control.[k]	13
	(e)	Explain the concept of controllable and uncontrollable costs.[k]	13
	(f)	Prepare control reports suitable for presentation to management (to include recommendation of appropriate control action).[s]	13
6	**Behavioural aspects of budgeting**		
	(a)	Explain the importance of motivation in performance management.[k]	13
	(b)	Identify factors in a budgetary planning and control system that influence motivation.[k]	13
	(c)	Explain the impact of targets upon motivation.[k]	13
	(d)	Discuss managerial incentive schemes.[k]	13
	(e)	Discuss the advantages and disadvantages of a participative approach to budgeting.[k]	13
	(f)	Explain top down, bottom up approaches to budgeting.[k]	13
E	**STANDARD COSTING**		
1	**Standard costing systems**		
	(a)	Explain the purpose and principles of standard costing.[k]	15
	(b)	Explain the difference between standard, marginal and absorption costing.[k]	15
	(c)	Establish the standard cost per unit under absorption and marginal costing.[k]	15
2	**Variance calculations and analysis**		
	(a)	Calculate sales price and volume variance.[s]	15
	(b)	Calculate materials total, price and usage variance.[s]	15
	(c)	Calculate labour total, rate and efficiency variance.[s]	15
	(d)	Calculate variable overhead total, expenditure and efficiency.[s]	15

	(e)	Calculate fixed overhead total, expenditure and, where appropriate, volume, capacity and efficiency.[s]	15
	(f)	Interpret the variances.[s]	15
	(g)	Explain factors to consider before investigating variances, explain possible causes of the variances and recommend control action.[s]	15
	(h)	Explain the interrelationships between the variances.[k]	15
	(i)	Calculate actual or standard figures where the variances are given.[k]	15
3	**Reconciliation of budgeted profit and actual profit**		
	(a)	Reconcile budgeted profit with actual profit under standard absorption costing.[s]	15
	(b)	Reconcile budgeted profit or contribution with actual profit or contribution under standard marginal costing.[s]	15
F	**PERFORMANCE MEASUREMENT**		
1	**Performance measurement overview**		
	(a)	Discuss the purpose of mission statements and their role in performance measurement.[k]	16
	(b)	Discuss the purpose of strategic and operational and tactical objectives and their role in performance measurement.[k]	16
	(c)	Discuss the impact of economic and market condition on performance measurement.[k]	16
	(d)	Explain the impact of government regulation on performance measurement.[k]	16
	(e)	Explain the impact of sustainability on performance measurement.[k]	16
2	**Performance measurement – application**		
	(a)	Discuss and calculate measures of financial performance (profitability, liquidity, efficiency and gearing) and non-financial measures.[s]	16
	(b)	Perspectives of the balance scorecard.	16
		(i) Discuss the advantages and limitations of the balance scorecard.[k]	16
		(ii) Describe performance indicators for financial, customer, internal business process and innovation and learning.[k]	16

	(iii)	Discuss critical success factors and key performance indicators and their link to objectives and mission statements.[k]	16
	(iv)	Establish critical success factors and key performance indicators in a specific situation.[s]	16
(c)		Economy, efficiency and effectiveness	16
	(i)	Explain the concepts of economy, efficiency and effectiveness.[k]	16
	(ii)	Describe performance indicators for economy, efficiency and effectiveness.[k]	16
	(iii)	Establish performance indicators for economy, efficiency and effectiveness in a specific situation.[s]	16
	(iv)	Discuss the meaning of each of the efficiency, capacity and activity ratios.[k]	16
	(v)	Calculate the efficiency, capacity and activity ratios in a specific situation.[s]	16
(d)		Resources utilisation	
	(i)	Describe measures of performance utilisation in service and manufacturing environments.[k]	16
	(ii)	Establish measures of resource utilisation in a specific situation.[s]	16
(e)		Profitability	
	(i)	Calculate return on investment and residual income.[s]	16
	(ii)	Explain the advantages and limitations of return on investment and residual income.[k]	16
(f)		Quality of service	16
	(i)	Distinguish performance measurement issues in service and manufacturing industries.[k]	16
	(ii)	Describe performance measures appropriate for service industries.[k]	16
	(iii)	Explain total quality management (TQM) as a quality management technique.[k]	16

3 Cost reductions and value enhancement

(a)	Compare cost control and cost reduction.[s]	16
(b)	Describe and evaluate cost reduction methods.[s]	16
(c)	Describe and evaluate value analysis.[s]	16

4 Monitoring performance and reporting

(a)	Discuss the importance of non-financial performance measures.[k]	16
(b)	Discuss the relationship between short-term and long-term performance.[k]	16
(c)	Discuss the measurement of performance in service industry situations.[k]	16
(d)	Discuss the measurement of performance in non-profit seeking and public sector organisations.[k]	16
(e)	Discuss measures that may be used to assess managerial performance and the practical problems involved.[k]	16
(f)	Discuss the role of benchmarking in performance measurement.[k]	16
(g)	Produce reports highlighting key areas for management attention and recommendations for improvement.[k]	16

The examination

Examination format

The syllabus is assessed by a two-hour computer-based examination. Questions will assess all parts of the syllabus and will contain both computational and non-computational elements:

	Number of marks
Section A 35 two mark objective questions	70
Section B 3 ten mark multi-task questions	30
	100

Section B will examine Budgeting, Standard costing and Performance measurement. Note: Budgeting MTQs in Section B can also include tasks from syllabus area B2 Analytical techniques in budgeting and forecasting. B4 Spreadsheets could be included in any of the MTQs, as either the basis for the presentation of information in the question scenario or as a task within the MTQ.

Total time allowed: 2 hours

Examination tips

Spend the first few minutes of the examination reviewing the format and content so that you understand what you need to do.

Divide the time you spend on questions in proportion to the marks on offer. One suggestion for **this exam** is to allocate 1 minute and 12 seconds to each mark available, so each 2-mark question should be completed in 2 minutes 24 seconds or approximately 2 and a half minutes.

Computer-based examination (CBE) tips

Be sure you understand how to use the software before you start the exam. If in doubt, ask the assessment centre staff to explain it to you.

Questions are **displayed on the screen** and answers are entered using keyboard and mouse. At the end of the exam, you are given a certificate showing the result you have achieved.

Do not attempt a CBE until you have **completed all study material** relating to it. **Do not skip any of the material** in the syllabus.

Read each question very carefully.

Double-check your answer before committing yourself to it.

Answer every question – if you do not know an answer, you don't lose anything by guessing. Think carefully before you **guess**.

The CBE question types are as follows:

- Multiple choice – where you are required to choose one answer from a list of options provided by clicking on the appropriate 'radio button'
- Multiple response – where you are required to select more than one response from the options provided by clicking on the appropriate tick boxes(typically choose two options from the available list
- Multiple response matching – where you are required to indicate a response to a number of related statements by clicking on the 'radio button' which corresponds to the appropriate response for each statement
- Number entry – where you are required to key in a response to a question shown on the screen.

With an objective test question, it may be possible to eliminate first those answers that you know are wrong. Then choose the most appropriate answer(s) as required from those that are left. This could be a single answer (e.g. multiple choice) or more than one response (e.g. multiple response and multiple response – matching).

After you have eliminated the ones that you know to be wrong, if you are still unsure, guess. But only do so after you have double-checked that you have only eliminated answers that are definitely wrong.

Don't panic if you realise you've answered a question incorrectly. Getting one question wrong will not mean the difference between passing and failing.

ACCA Support

For additional support with your studies please also refer to the ACCA Global website.

Study skills and revision guidance

This section aims to give guidance on how to study for your ACCA exams and to give ideas on how to improve your existing study techniques.

Preparing to study

Set your objectives

Before starting to study decide what you want to achieve – the type of pass you wish to obtain. This will decide the level of commitment and time you need to dedicate to your studies.

Devise a study plan

Determine which times of the week you will study.

Split these times into sessions of at least one hour for study of new material. Any shorter periods could be used for revision or practice.

Put the times you plan to study onto a study plan for the weeks from now until the exam and set yourself targets for each period of study – in your sessions make sure you cover the course, course assignments and revision.

If you are studying for more than one examination at a time, try to vary your subjects as this can help you to keep interested and see subjects as part of wider knowledge.

When working through your course, compare your progress with your plan and, if necessary, re-plan your work (perhaps including extra sessions) or, if you are ahead, do some extra revision/practice questions.

Effective studying

Active reading

You are not expected to learn the text by rote, rather, you must understand what you are reading and be able to use it to pass the exam and develop good practice. A good technique to use is SQ3Rs – Survey, Question, Read, Recall, Review:

1. **Survey the chapter** – look at the headings and read the introduction, summary and objectives, so as to get an overview of what the chapter deals with.
2. **Question** – whilst undertaking the survey, ask yourself the questions that you hope the chapter will answer for you.
3. **Read** through the chapter thoroughly, answering the questions and making sure you can meet the objectives. Attempt the exercises and activities in the text, and work through all the examples.
4. **Recall** – at the end of each section and at the end of the chapter, try to recall the main ideas of the section/chapter without referring to the text. This is best done after a short break of a couple of minutes after the reading stage.
5. **Review** – check that your recall notes are correct.

You may also find it helpful to re-read the chapter to try to see the topic(s) it deals with as a whole.

Note-taking

Taking notes is a useful way of learning, but do not simply copy out the text. The notes must:

- be in your own words
- be concise
- cover the key points
- be well-organised
- be modified as you study further chapters in this text or in related ones.

Trying to summarise a chapter without referring to the text can be a useful way of determining which areas you know and which you don't.

Three ways of taking notes:

Summarise the key points of a chapter.

Make linear notes – a list of headings, divided up with subheadings listing the key points. If you use linear notes, you can use different colours to highlight key points and keep topic areas together. Use plenty of space to make your notes easy to use.

Try a diagrammatic form – the most common of which is a mind-map. To make a mind-map, put the main heading in the centre of the paper and put a circle around it. Then draw short lines radiating from this to the main sub-headings, which again have circles around them. Then continue the process from the sub-headings to sub-sub-headings, advantages, disadvantages, etc.

Highlighting and underlining

You may find it useful to underline or highlight key points in your study text – but do be selective. You may also wish to make notes in the margins.

Revision

The best approach to revision is to revise the course as you work through it. Also try to leave four to six weeks before the exam for final revision. Make sure you cover the whole syllabus and pay special attention to those areas where your knowledge is weak. Here are some recommendations:

Read through the text and your notes again and condense your notes into key phrases. It may help to put key revision points onto index cards to look at when you have a few minutes to spare.

Review any assignments you have completed and look at where you lost marks – put more work into those areas where you were weak.

Practise exam standard questions under timed conditions. If you are short of time, list the points you would include or specify the calculations that you would include in your answer and then read the model answer, but do try to complete at least a few questions under exam conditions.

If you are stuck on a topic find somebody (e.g. your tutor or, where appropriate, a member of Kaplan's Academic Support team) to explain it to you.

Read good newspapers and professional journals, especially ACCA's Student Accountant – this can give you an advantage in the exam.

Ensure you **know the structure of the exam** – how many questions and of what type you will be expected to answer. During your revision attempt all the different styles of questions you may be asked.

Further reading

You can find further reading and technical articles under the student section of ACCA's website.

Technical update

This text has been updated to reflect Examinable Documents September 2023 to August 2024 issued by ACCA.

FORMULAE AND TABLES

Regression analysis

$$y = a + bx$$

$$a = \frac{\sum y}{n} - \frac{b\sum x}{n}$$

$$b = \frac{n\sum xy - \sum x \sum y}{n\sum x^2 - (\sum x)^2}$$

$$r = \frac{n\sum xy - \sum x \sum y}{\sqrt{(n\sum x^2 - (\sum x)^2)(n\sum y^2 - (\sum y)^2)}}$$

Economic order quantity

$$= \sqrt{\frac{2C_0D}{C_h}}$$

Economic batch quantity

$$= \sqrt{\frac{2C_0D}{C_h\left(1 - \frac{D}{R}\right)}}$$

Arithmetic mean

$$\bar{x} = \frac{\Sigma x}{n} \qquad \bar{x} = \frac{\Sigma fx}{\Sigma f} \text{ (frequency distribution)}$$

Standard deviation

$$\sigma = \sqrt{\frac{\Sigma(x - \bar{x})^2}{n}} \qquad \sigma = \sqrt{\frac{\Sigma fx^2}{\Sigma f} - \left(\frac{\Sigma fx}{\Sigma f}\right)^2} \text{ (frequency distribution)}$$

Variance

$$= \sigma^2$$

Co-efficient of variation

$$CV = \frac{\sigma}{\bar{x}}$$

Expected value

$$EV = \sum px$$

Present value table

Present value of 1, i.e. $(1 + r)^{-n}$

Where r = discount rate

n = number of periods until payment

Periods					Discount rate (r)					
(n)	1%	2%	3%	4%	5%	6%	7%	8%	9%	10%
1	0.990	0.980	0.971	0.962	0.952	0.943	0.935	0.926	0.917	0.909
2	0.980	0.961	0.943	0.925	0.907	0.890	0.873	0.857	0.842	0.826
3	0.971	0.942	0.915	0.889	0.864	0.840	0.816	0.794	0.772	0.751
4	0.961	0.924	0.888	0.855	0.823	0.792	0.763	0.735	0.708	0.683
5	0.951	0.906	0.863	0.822	0.784	0.747	0.713	0.681	0.650	0.621
6	0.942	0.888	0.837	0.790	0.746	0.705	0.666	0.630	0.596	0.564
7	0.933	0.871	0.813	0.760	0.711	0.665	0.623	0.583	0.547	0.513
8	0.923	0.853	0.789	0.731	0.677	0.627	0.582	0.540	0.502	0.467
9	0.914	0.837	0.766	0.703	0.645	0.592	0.544	0.500	0.460	0.424
10	0.905	0.820	0.744	0.676	0.614	0.558	0.508	0.463	0.422	0.386
11	0.896	0.804	0.722	0.650	0.585	0.527	0.475	0.429	0.388	0.350
12	0.887	0.788	0.701	0.625	0.557	0.497	0.444	0.397	0.356	0.319
13	0.879	0.773	0.681	0.601	0.530	0.469	0.415	0.368	0.326	0.290
14	0.870	0.758	0.661	0.577	0.505	0.442	0.388	0.340	0.299	0.263
15	0.861	0.743	0.642	0.555	0.481	0.417	0.362	0.315	0.275	0.239

(n)	11%	12%	13%	14%	15%	16%	17%	18%	19%	20%
1	0.901	0.893	0.885	0.877	0.870	0.862	0.855	0.847	0.840	0.833
2	0.812	0.797	0.783	0.769	0.756	0.743	0.731	0.718	0.706	0.694
3	0.731	0.712	0.693	0.675	0.658	0.641	0.624	0.609	0.593	0.579
4	0.659	0.636	0.613	0.592	0.572	0.552	0.534	0.516	0.499	0.482
5	0.593	0.567	0.543	0.519	0.497	0.476	0.456	0.437	0.419	0.402
6	0.535	0.507	0.480	0.456	0.432	0.410	0.390	0.370	0.352	0.335
7	0.482	0.452	0.425	0.400	0.376	0.354	0.333	0.314	0.296	0.279
8	0.434	0.404	0.376	0.351	0.327	0.305	0.285	0.266	0.249	0.233
9	0.391	0.361	0.333	0.308	0.284	0.263	0.243	0.225	0.209	0.194
10	0.352	0.322	0.295	0.270	0.247	0.227	0.208	0.191	0.176	0.162
11	0.317	0.287	0.261	0.237	0.215	0.195	0.178	0.162	0.148	0.135
12	0.286	0.257	0.231	0.208	0.187	0.168	0.152	0.137	0.124	0.112
13	0.258	0.229	0.204	0.182	0.163	0.145	0.130	0.116	0.104	0.093
14	0.232	0.205	0.181	0.160	0.141	0.125	0.111	0.099	0.088	0.078
15	0.209	0.183	0.160	0.140	0.123	0.108	0.095	0.084	0.074	0.065

Annuity table

Present value of an annuity of 1, i.e. $\frac{1-(1+r)^{-n}}{r}$

Where r = discount rate

n = number of periods

Periods					**Discount rate (r)**					
(n)	**1%**	**2%**	**3%**	**4%**	**5%**	**6%**	**7%**	**8%**	**9%**	**10%**
1	0.990	0.980	0.971	0.962	0.952	0.943	0.935	0.926	0.917	0.909
2	1.970	1.942	1.913	1.886	1.859	1.833	1.808	1.783	1.759	1.736
3	2.941	2.884	2.829	2.775	2.723	2.673	2.624	2.577	2.531	2.487
4	3.902	3.808	3.717	3.630	3.546	3.465	3.387	3.312	3.240	3.170
5	4.853	4.713	4.580	4.452	4.329	4.212	4.100	3.993	3.890	3.791
6	5.795	5.601	5.417	5.242	5.076	4.917	4.767	4.623	4.486	4.355
7	6.728	6.472	6.230	6.002	5.786	5.582	5.389	5.206	5.033	4.868
8	7.652	7.325	7.020	6.733	6.463	6.210	5.971	5.747	5.535	5.335
9	8.566	8.162	7.786	7.435	7.108	6.802	6.515	6.247	5.995	5.759
10	9.471	8.983	8.530	8.111	7.722	7.360	7.024	6.710	6.418	6.145
11	10.368	9.787	9.253	8.760	8.306	7.887	7.499	7.139	6.805	8.495
12	11.255	10.575	9.954	9.385	8.863	8.384	7.943	7.536	7.161	6.814
13	12.134	11.348	10.635	9.986	9.394	8.853	8.358	7.904	7.487	7.103
14	13.004	12.106	11.296	10.563	9.899	9.295	8.745	8.244	7.786	7.367
15	13.865	12.849	11.938	11.118	10.380	9.712	9.108	8.559	8.061	7.606

(n)	**11%**	**12%**	**13%**	**14%**	**15%**	**16%**	**17%**	**18%**	**19%**	**20%**
1	0.901	0.893	0.885	0.877	0.870	0.862	0.855	0.847	0.840	0.833
2	1.713	1.690	1.668	1.647	1.626	1.605	1.585	1.566	1.547	1.528
3	2.444	2.402	2.361	2.322	2.283	2.246	2.210	2.174	2.140	2.106
4	3.102	3.037	2.974	2.914	2.855	2.798	2.743	2.690	2.639	2.589
5	3.696	3.605	3.517	3.433	3.352	3.274	3.199	3.127	3.058	2.991
6	4.231	4.111	3.998	3.889	3.784	3.685	3.589	3.498	3.410	3.326
7	4.712	4.564	4.423	4.288	4.160	4.039	3.922	3.812	3.706	3.605
8	5.146	4.968	4.799	4.639	4.487	4.344	4.207	4.078	3.954	3.837
9	5.537	5.328	5.132	4.946	4.772	4.607	4.451	4.303	4.163	4.031
10	5.889	5.650	5.426	5.216	5.019	4.833	4.659	4.494	4.339	4.192
11	6.207	5.938	5.687	5.453	5.234	5.029	4.836	4.656	4.486	4.327
12	6.492	6.194	5.918	5.660	5.421	5.197	4.968	4.793	4.611	4.439
13	6.750	6.424	6.122	5.842	5.583	5.342	5.118	4.910	4.715	4.533
14	6.982	6.628	6.302	6.002	5.724	5.468	5.229	5.008	4.802	4.611
15	7.191	6.811	6.462	6.142	5.847	5.575	5.324	5.092	4.876	4.675

Standard normal distribution table

$$z = \frac{x - \mu}{\sigma}$$

	0.00	0.01	0.02	0.03	0.04	0.05	0.06	0.07	0.08	0.09
0.0	0.0000	0.0040	0.0080	0.0120	0.0160	0.0199	0.0239	0.0279	0.0319	0.0359
0.1	0.0398	0.0438	0.0478	0.0517	0.0557	0.0596	0.0636	0.0675	0.0714	0.0753
0.2	0.0793	0.0832	0.0871	0.0910	0.0948	0.0987	0.1026	0.1064	0.1103	0.1141
0.3	0.1179	0.1217	0.1255	0.1293	0.1331	0.1368	0.1406	0.1443	0.1480	0.1517
0.4	0.1554	0.1591	0.1628	0.1664	0.1700	0.1736	0.1772	0.1808	0.1844	0.1879
0.5	0.1915	0.1950	0.1985	0.2019	0.2054	0.2088	0.2123	0.2157	0.2190	0.2224
0.6	0.2257	0.2291	0.2324	0.2357	0.2389	0.2422	0.2454	0.2486	0.2517	0.2549
0.7	0.2580	0.2611	0.2642	0.2673	0.2704	0.2734	0.2764	0.2794	0.2823	0.2852
0.8	0.2881	0.2910	0.2939	0.2967	0.2995	0.3023	0.3051	0.3078	0.3106	0.3133
0.9	0.3159	0.3186	0.3212	0.3238	0.3264	0.3289	0.3315	0.3340	0.3365	0.3389
1.0	0.3413	0.3438	0.3461	0.3485	0.3508	0.3531	0.3554	0.3577	0.3599	0.3621
1.1	0.3643	0.3665	0.3686	0.3708	0.3729	0.3749	0.3770	0.3790	0.3810	0.3830
1.2	0.3849	0.3869	0.3888	0.3907	0.3925	0.3944	0.3962	0.3980	0.3997	0.4015
1.3	0.4032	0.4049	0.4066	0.4082	0.4099	0.4115	0.4131	0.4147	0.4162	0.4177
1.4	0.4192	0.4207	0.4222	0.4236	0.4251	0.4265	0.4279	0.4292	0.4306	0.4319
1.5	0.4332	0.4345	0.4357	0.4370	0.4382	0.4394	0.4406	0.4418	0.4429	0.4441
1.6	0.4452	0.4463	0.4474	0.4484	0.4495	0.4505	0.4515	0.4525	0.4535	0.4545
1.7	0.4554	0.4564	0.4573	0.4582	0.4591	0.4599	0.4608	0.4616	0.4625	0.4633
1.8	0.4641	0.4649	0.4656	0.4664	0.4671	0.4678	0.4686	0.4693	0.4699	0.4706
1.9	0.4713	0.4719	0.4726	0.4732	0.4738	0.4744	0.4750	0.4756	0.4761	0.4767
2.0	0.4772	0.4778	0.4783	0.4788	0.4793	0.4798	0.4803	0.4808	0.4812	0.4817
2.1	0.4821	0.4826	0.4830	0.4834	0.4838	0.4842	0.4846	0.4850	0.4854	0.4857
2.2	0.4861	0.4864	0.4868	0.4871	0.4875	0.4878	0.4881	0.4884	0.4887	0.4890
2.3	0.4893	0.4896	0.4898	0.4901	0.4904	0.4906	0.4909	0.4911	0.4913	0.4916
2.4	0.4918	0.4920	0.4922	0.4925	0.4927	0.4929	0.4931	0.4932	0.4934	0.4936
2.5	0.4938	0.4940	0.4941	0.4943	0.4945	0.4946	0.4948	0.4949	0.4951	0.4952
2.6	0.4953	0.4955	0.4956	0.4957	0.4959	0.4960	0.4961	0.4962	0.4963	0.4964
2.7	0.4965	0.4966	0.4967	0.4968	0.4969	0.4970	0.4971	0.4972	0.4973	0.4974
2.8	0.4974	0.4975	0.4976	0.4977	0.4977	0.4978	0.4979	0.4979	0.4980	0.4981
2.9	0.4981	0.4982	0.4982	0.4983	0.4984	0.4984	0.4985	0.4985	0.4986	0.4986
3.0	0.4987	0.4987	0.4987	0.4988	0.4988	0.4989	0.4989	0.4989	0.4990	0.4990

Chapter

1

Accounting for management

Chapter learning objectives

Upon completion of this chapter you will be able to:

- distinguish between data and information
- identify and explain the attributes of good information
- outline the managerial processes of planning, decision making and control
- explain the difference between strategic, tactical and operational planning
- describe the purpose and role of cost and management accounting within an organisation
- compare and contrast financial accounting with cost and management accounting
- explain the limitations of management information in providing guidance for managerial decision-making.

PER

One of the PER performance objectives (PO1) is to take into account all relevant information and use professional judgement, your personal values and scepticism to evaluate data and make decisions. You should identify right from wrong and escalate anything of concern. You also need to make sure that your skills, knowledge and behaviour are up-to-date and allow you to be effective in you role. Working through this chapter should help you understand how to demonstrate that objective.

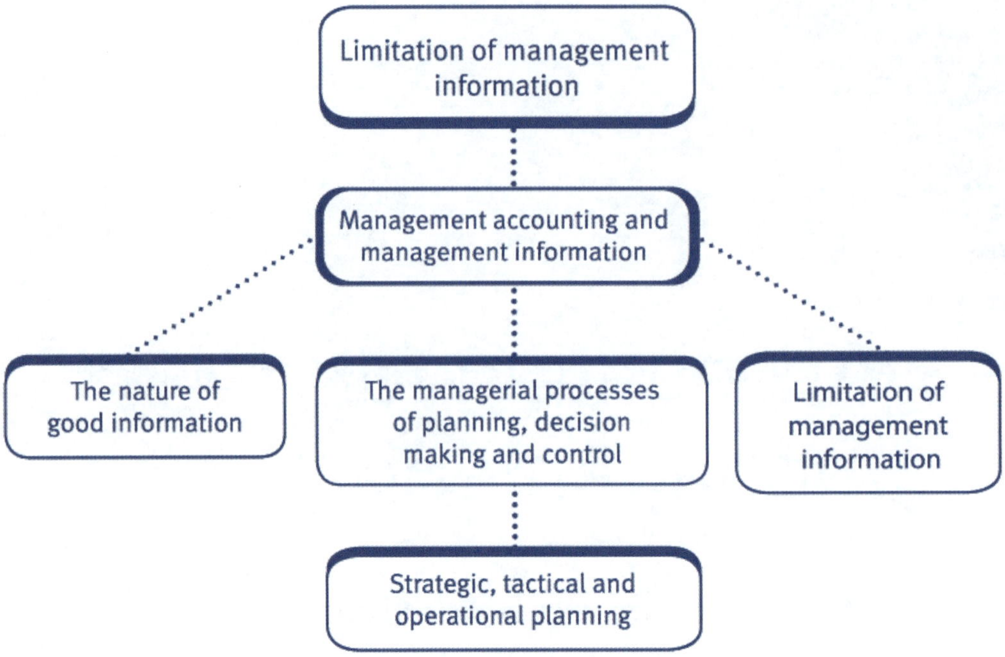

1 Management, Cost and Financial accounting

Management and Cost accounting

Managers usually want to know about the costs and the profits of individual products and services. In order to obtain this information, details are needed for each cost, revenue, profit and investment centre. Such information is provided by cost accounting and management accounting systems.

Cost accounting is a system for recording data and producing information about costs for the products produced by an organisation and/or the services it provides. It is also used to establish costs for particular activities or responsibility centres.

- Cost accounting involves a careful evaluation of the resources used within the enterprise.
- The techniques employed in cost accounting are designed to provide financial information about the performance of the enterprise and possibly the direction that future operations should take.
- The terms 'cost accounting' and 'management accounting' are often used to mean the same thing.
- Management accounting has cost accounting at its essential foundation.

Financial accounting

Financial accounting involves recording the financial transactions of an organisation and summarising them in periodic financial statements for external users who wish to analyse and interpret the financial position of the organisation.

- The main duties of the financial accountant include: maintaining the bookkeeping system of the nominal ledger, payables control account, receivables control account and so on and to prepare financial statements as required by law and accounting standards.
- Information produced by the financial accounting system is usually insufficient for the needs of management for decision making.

Differences between management accounting and financial accounting

The following illustration compares management accounting with financial accounting.

e.g

Illustration 1 – Management versus financial accounting

	Management accounting	**Financial accounting**
Information mainly produced for	Internal use e.g. managers and employees.	External use e.g. shareholders, payables, lenders, banks, government.
Purpose of information	To aid planning, controlling and decision making.	To record the financial performance in a period and the financial position at the end of that period.
Legal requirements	None.	Limited companies must produce financial accounts.
Formats	Management decide on the information they require and the most useful way of presenting it.	Format and content of financial accounts intending to give a true and fair view should follow accounting standards and company law.
Nature of information	Financial and non-financial.	Mostly financial.
Time period	Historical and forward-looking.	Mainly a historical record.

Test your understanding 1

The following assertions relate to management accounting:

(i) The purpose of management accounting is to provide accounting information to the managers of the business and other internal users.

(ii) Management accounts are only concerned with the cost of goods, services and operations.

Which of the following statements are true?

A Assertion (i) and (ii) are both correct

B Only assertion (i) is correct

C Only assertion (ii) is correct

D Neither assertion (i) or (ii) is correct

2 The nature of good information

Data and information

'Data' means facts. Data consists of numbers, letters, symbols, raw facts, events and transactions which have been recorded but not yet processed into a form suitable for use.

Information is data which has been processed in such a way that it is meaningful to the person who receives it (for making decisions).

- The terms data and information are often used interchangeably in everyday language.
- As data is converted into information, some of the detail of the data is eliminated and replaced by summaries which are easier to understand.

Test your understanding 2

What, if any, is the difference between data and information?

A They are the same

B Data can only be figures, whereas information can be facts or figures

C Information results from sorting and analysing data

D Data results from obtaining many individual pieces of information

Attributes of good information

Information is provided to management to assist them with planning, controlling operations and making decisions. Management decisions are improved when they are provided with better quality information.

The attributes of good information can be identified by the **'ACCURATE'** acronym as shown below:

Accurate

The degree of accuracy depends on the reason why the information is needed. For example:

- a report on the performance of different divisions of a business may show figures to the nearest dollar, or nearest thousand dollars.
- when calculating the cost of a unit of output, managers may want the cost to be accurate to the nearest cent.

Complete

Managers should be given all the information they need, but information should not be excessive. For example:

- a complete control report on variances should include all standard and actual costs necessary to aid understanding of the variance calculations.
- production managers will need the variance analysis relating to material usage where-as purchasing managers with need the variance analysis relating to material prices.

Cost-effective

The value of information should exceed the cost of producing it. Management information is valuable, because it assists decision making. If a decision backed by information is different from what it would have been without the information, the value of information equates to the amount of money saved as a result.

e.g

Illustration 2 – Marginal cost versus marginal benefit

Production costs in a factory can be reported with varying levels of frequency ranging from daily (365 times per year) to annually (once per year). Costs and benefits of reporting relate to the frequency of reporting.

- Information has to be gathered, collated and reported in proportion to frequency and costs will move in line with this.
- Initially, benefits increase sharply, but this increase starts to tail off. A point may come where 'information overload' sets in and benefits actually start to decline and even become negative. If managers are overwhelmed with information this can actually get in the way of completing a job.

This can be shown graphically:

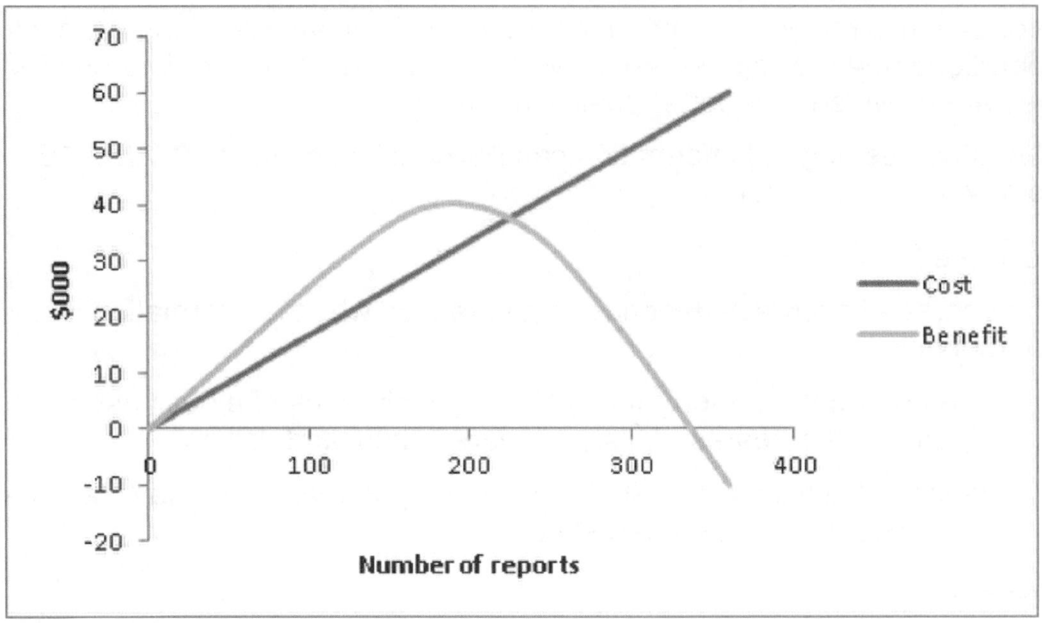

Understandable

Use of technical language or jargon must be limited. Accountants must always be careful about the way in which they present financial information to non-financial managers.

Relevant

The information contained within a report should be relevant to its purpose. Redundant parts should be removed. For example:

- the sales team may need to know the total cost of producing a unit to calculate the selling price but will not need to know the breakdown into material, labour and overhead costs.

Authoritative

Information should be trusted and provided from reliable sources so that the users can have confidence in their decision making.

Timely

Information should be provided to a manager in time for decisions to be made based on that information.

Easy to use

We must always think about the person using the information we provide and make sure the information meets their needs.

Data, Information, Knowledge and Wisdom

The arrival of the Internet has made it much easier for organisations and individuals to access data at the right time and the right place. However, at the same time the Internet has opened up questions about data being error free and about who can have access to it.

As well as the issue of data quality there is the question of how data, information and knowledge relate to one another. Russell Ackoff was one of the first people to speak of there being a hierarchy which he referred to as the Data Information Knowledge Wisdom (DIKW) Hierarchy. According to this model, data are simple facts or figures or maybe even a photograph or an illustration. In this form data is unstructured and uninterrupted. Information comes from processing or structuring data in a meaningful way. Another way of looking at this is that information is interpreted data. An interesting story is told by Joan Magretta in her book 'What Management is?' about Steve Jobs that clearly illustrates the difference between data and information.

Despite its small share of the total market for personal computers, Apple has long been a leader in sales to schools and universities. When CEO Steve Jobs learned that Apple's share of computer sales to schools was 12.5 per cent in 1999, he was dismayed, but unless you're an industry analyst who knows the numbers cold, you won't appreciate just how dismayed he was. That's because, in 1998, Apple was the segment leader with a market share of 14.6 per cent. And, while Apple slipped to the number two spot in 1999, Dell grew and took the lead with 15.1 per cent. Alone each number is meaningless. Together they spell trouble, if you're Steve Jobs, you see a trend that you'd better figure out how to reverse. This isn't number crunching, its sense making. (Magretta, 2003, p. 123)

In this example the 12.5 per cent was data and when it was seen in conjunction with the 15.1 per cent it became information.

Knowledge is again different to data and information. Knowledge is much more personal and the presence or absence of knowledge can normally only be seen through the actions of individuals. When knowledge is written down it effectively becomes information.

Finally with respect to wisdom it is difficult to define this concept. Wisdom has something to do with understanding or insight. It is to do with achieving a good long-term outcome in relation to the circumstances you are in.

3 Mission statements

Before any planning can take place the **mission** of the business needs to be established.

The mission statement is a statement in writing that describes the overall aims of an organisation, that is, what it is trying to accomplish. In other words, it sets out the whole purpose of the business.

There are four key elements to a mission statement:

- **Purpose** – why does the business exist and who does it exist for?
- **Strategy** – what does the business provide and how is it provided?
- **Policies and culture** – how does the business expect its staff to act/behave?
- **Values** – What are the core principles of the business?

The mission should express what the business wants to achieve overall and the aims and objectives managers produce should all work towards achieving this.

Mission statements will have some or all of the following characteristics:

- Usually a brief statement of no more than a page in length
- Very general statement of entity culture
- States the aims of the organisation
- States the business areas in which the organisation intends to operate
- Open-ended (not in quantifiable terms)
- Does not include commercial terms, such as profit
- Not time-assigned
- Forms a basis of communication to the people inside the organisation and to people outside the organisation
- Used to formulate goal statements, objectives and short term targets
- Guides the direction of the entity's strategy and as such is part of management information.

Kaplan UK's mission statement is:

Kaplan helps individuals achieve their educational and career goals. We build futures one success story at a time.

Our core values define our company culture and provide the framework for what we deliver to our customers and employees each day.

- **Integrity** – We hold ourselves to the highest ethical standards in everything we do.
- **Knowledge** – We offer expert resources to help you achieve your academic and career best.
- **Support** – We give you the tools you need to succeed.
- **Opportunity** – We open doors and broaden access to education.
- **Results** – We're dedicated to helping you achieve your goals – we succeed when you succeed.

Examples of mission statements

Honda

Maintaining a global viewpoint, we are dedicated to supplying products of the highest quality, yet at a reasonable price for worldwide customer satisfaction.

The Walt Disney Company

The mission of The Walt Disney Company is to entertain, inform and inspire people around the globe through the power of unparalleled storytelling, reflecting the iconic brands, creative minds and innovative technologies that make ours the world's premier entertainment company.

Microsoft UK

To empower every person and every organization on the planet to achieve more.

Cadbury

Cadbury means quality; this is our promise. Our reputation is built upon quality; our commitment to continuous improvement will ensure that our promise is delivered.

Battersea Dogs' & Cats' Home

We aim to never turn away a dog or cat in need of help, caring for them until their owners or loving new homes can be found, no matter how long it takes. We are champions for, and supporters of, vulnerable dogs and cats, determined to create lasting changes for animals in our society.

4 Planning, decision making and control

The main functions that management are involved with are planning, decision making and control.

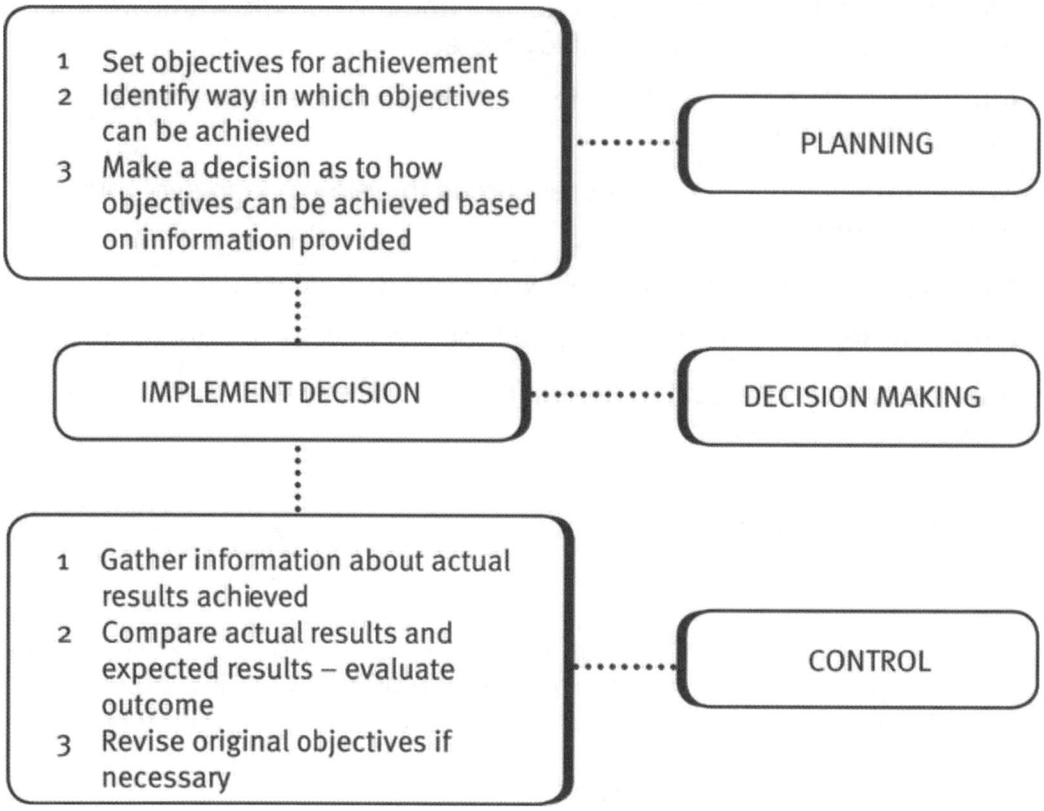

Planning

- Planning involves establishing the objectives of an organisation and formulating relevant strategies that can be used to achieve those objectives. In order to make plans, it helps to know what has happened in the past so that decisions about what is achievable in the future can be made. For example, if a manager is planning future sales volumes, he/she needs to know what the sales volumes have been in the past.
- Planning can be either short-term (tactical planning) or long-term (strategic planning).
- Planning is looked at in more detail in the next section of this chapter.

During the planning process the mission statement of a business is used to produce effective aims and objectives for employees and the company as a whole. Aims and objectives should be **SMART**:

- **Specific** – are the objectives well defined and understandable?
- **Measurable** – can achievement of the objectives be measured so that completion can be confirmed?
- **Attainable/Achievable** – can the objectives set be achieved with the resources and skills available?

- **Relevant** – are the objectives relevant for the people involved and to the mission of the business?
- **Timed** – are deadlines being set for the objectives that are achievable? Are there any stage reviews planned to monitor progress towards the objective?

By following the SMART hierarchy a business should be able to produce plans that lead to **goal congruence** throughout the departments, centres and/or regional offices (the whole business).

Levels of planning

There are three different levels of planning (known as 'planning horizons'). These three levels differ according to their time span and the seniority of the manager responsible for the tasks involved.

Strategic planning

'Strategic planning' can also be known as 'long-term planning' or 'corporate planning'. It considers:

- the longer term (five years plus)
- the whole organisation.

Senior managers formulate long-term objectives (goals) and plans (strategies) for an organisation as a whole. These objectives and plans should all be aiming to achieving the company's mission.

Tactical planning

Tactical planning takes the strategic plan and breaks it down into manageable chunks i.e. shorter term plans for individual areas of the business to enable the strategic plan to be achieved.

Senior and middle managers make short to medium term plans for the next year.

Operational planning

Operational planning involves making day-to-day decisions about what to do next and how to deal with problems as they arise.

All managers are involved in day to day decisions.

A simple hierarchy of management tasks can be presented as follows:

Strategic, tactical and operational planning

The table shown below illustrates the three different categories of planning.

	Private school (fees are charged to attend)	Profit-seeking business
Objective (mission)	To provide a high quality of education so that, within five years, 95% of pupils achieve grades A or B in their final examinations.	To achieve a 20% return on capital every year. To increase earnings per share by 10% every year for the next five years.
Strategic plans	Reduce class sizes. Raise new funds to invest $1 million in new equipment and facilities. Attract the highest quality of teacher by paying good salaries.	Cut costs by 15% in domestic markets. Expand into markets in Asia. Increase domestic market share by 10% in the next five years.

Tactical plans	Set a target for this year for examination results. Increase the number of teachers by 10% by the end of the year. Plan the launch of a fund-raising campaign.	Carry out a cost reduction program next year. Establish business relationships with customers in Asia and carry out market research. Increase the size of the work force in order to improve total sales.
Operational plans	Prepare teaching schedules for the next term. Monitor the marks gained by students in mock examinations. Provide whiteboard training to teaching staff.	Obtain prices from more than one supplier before purchasing materials. Offer a bulk purchase discount of 10% to a major customer.

Test your understanding 3

The Management Accountant has communicated a detailed budget to ensure that cost savings targets are achieved in the forthcoming period.

This is an example of:

A Operational planning

B Tactical planning

C Strategic planning

D Business planning

Decision making

Decision making involves considering information that has been provided and making an informed decision.

- In most situations, decision making involves making a choice between two or more alternatives. Managers need reliable information to compare the different courses of action available and understand what the consequences might be of choosing each of them.
- The first part of the decision-making process is planning, the second part is control.

Control

Information relating to the actual results of an organisation is reported to managers.

- Managers use the information relating to actual results to take control measures and to re-assess and amend their original budgets or plans.
- Internally-sourced information, produced largely for control purposes, is called feedback.
- The 'feedback loop' is demonstrated in the following illustration.

e.g

Illustration 3 – Planning, decision making and control

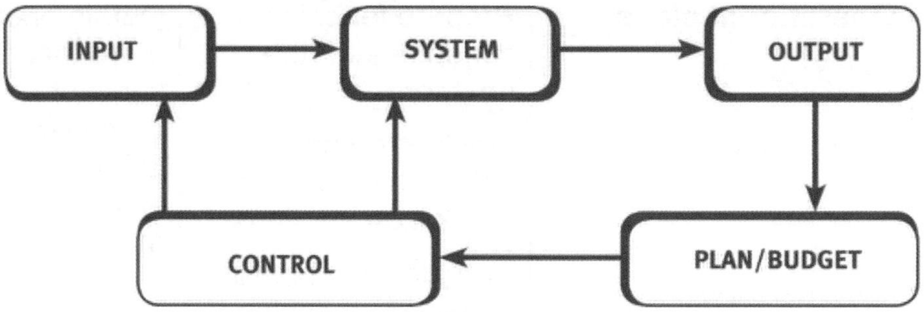

Here, management prepare a **plan**, which is put into action by the managers with **control** over the input resources (labour, money, materials, equipment and so on). Output from operations is measured and reported ('fed back') to management, and actual results are compared against the plan in control reports. Managers take corrective **action** where appropriate, especially in the case of exceptionally bad or good performance. Feedback can also be used to revise plans or prepare the plan for the next period.

Test your understanding 4

Required:

Complete the table identifying each function as planning, decision making and/or control.

	Planning	Control	Decision making
Preparation of the annual budget for a cost centre			
Revise budgets for next period for a cost centre			
Implement decisions based on information provided			
Set organisation's objectives for next period			
Compare actual and expected results for a period			

Information systems at different business levels

A modern organisation needs a wide range of systems to process, analyse and hold information. The different management decision-making levels within an organisation need different types of information:

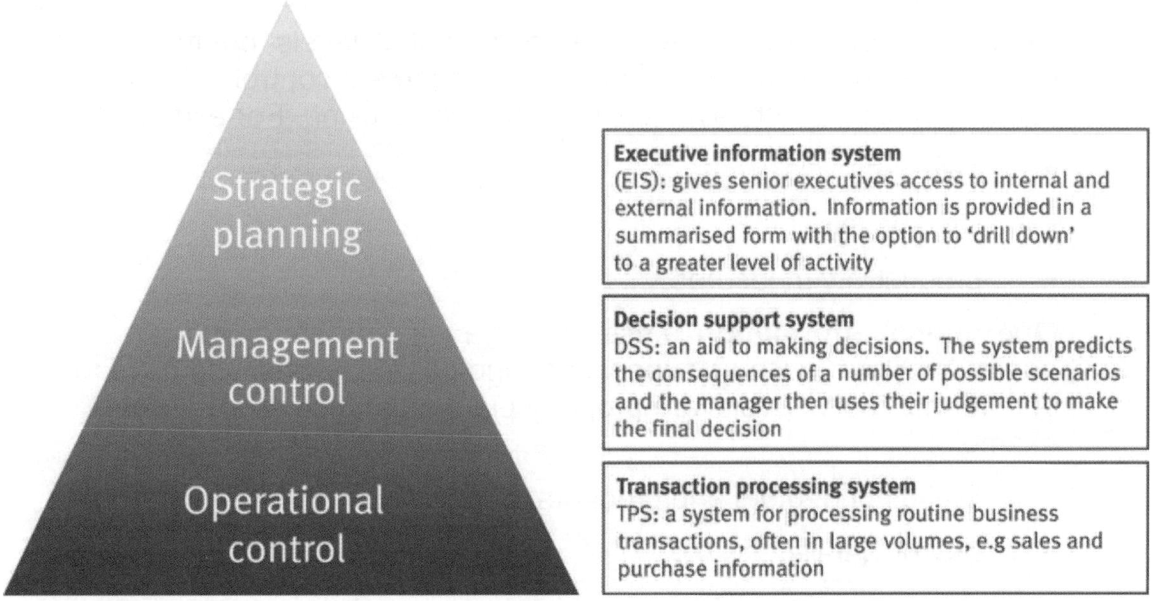

As a basic idea, the systems towards the top of the pyramid will support the strategic decisions and they will use data from systems in the levels below.

Levels of information

Decision making is an important aspect of any organisation.

Three levels of decision making are normally identified; strategic, tactical and operational. Each level has different information requirements.

Strategic decisions are long-term, complex decisions made by senior management. For example, a UK based supermarket chain may put a strategic plan in place outlining its aim to be the market leader. This plan is a long-term plan and the achievement of this aim will have far reaching implications for the whole organisation.

Tactical decisions are medium term, less complex decisions made by middle management. They follow on from strategic decisions. For example, in order to become the market leader the supermarket chain may have to launch new products/services or open new branches.

Operational decisions are day-to-day decisions made by junior managers, e.g. the ordering of supplies to ensure the new product lines are stocked.

Within an organisation, management information requirements can be classified into three different levels: strategic, tactical and operational.

Strategic information is mainly used by directors and senior managers to choose between alternative courses of action, to plan the organisation's overall objectives and strategy and to measure whether these are being achieved. For example:

- profitability of main business segments
- prospects for present and potential markets.

Tactical information is used by managers at all levels, but mainly at the middle level for tactical planning and management control activities, such as pricing, purchasing, distribution and stocking. For example:

- sales analysis
- stock levels
- productivity measures.

Operational information is used mainly by managers on the operational level such as supervisors and section heads who have to ensure that routine tasks are properly planned and controlled. For example:

- listings of debtors and creditors
- payroll details
- raw materials requirements and usage.

The role of management accounting within an organisation's management information system

The management information system of an organisation is likely to be able to prepare the following:

- annual statutory accounts
- budgets and forecasts
- product profitability reports
- cash flow reports
- investment appraisal reports
- standard cost and variance analysis reports
- returns to government departments, e.g. Sales Tax returns.

Management information is generally supplied to management in the form of reports. Reports may be routine reports prepared on a regular basis (e.g. monthly) or they may be prepared for a special purpose (e.g. ad hoc report).

5 The limitations of management information

There are a number of respects in which management accounting information may fail to meet its objective of assisting management in the decision making process.

These can be summarised as follows:

Failure to comply with the qualities of useful information

If information supplied to managers is deficient in any of these respects then inappropriate management decisions may be made. Consider the following:

- **Accuracy** – overestimating costs may result in a decision not to produce a product which in fact is profitable; on the other hand, overestimating the price at which the output can be sold may result in the organisation producing output which cannot be sold in sufficient volume to be profitable.
- **Timeliness** – if a business is considering closing a division or department information must be presented to management before a decision is been made to lay off staff that could have been profitably employed in other divisions or activities. The business would incur unnecessary redundancy costs, lose possible future revenues and demotivate the remaining employees if premature redundancies are made.
- **Understandable** – excessive focus by management accountants on more complex techniques of which general management have little or no knowledge or understanding may mean that the accountant's advice will be ignored. There is significant attention being given to the role of the management accountant as an educator within the organisation – explaining the information and training general management to help them to understand the information better.

Relevant costs and revenues

Not all information produced by an accounting system is relevant to the decisions made by management. In particular, information produced mainly for financial reporting purposes and then taken as the basis for management decisions will often need significant modification to be useful to management. The principle here is that the figures presented to assist in management decision-making are those that will be affected by the decision, i.e. they should be:

- **Future** – costs and revenues that are going to be incurred sometime in the future. Costs and revenues that have already been incurred are known as sunk costs and are not relevant to the decision to be made.
- **Incremental** – the **extra** cost or revenue that is created as a result of a decision taken.
- **Cash flows** – actual cash being spent or received not monetary items that are produced via accounting convention e.g. book or carrying values, depreciation charges.

Non-financial information

Managers will not always be guided by the sort of financial and other (hard) information supplied by the management accounting system. They will also look at qualitative, behavioural, motivational, even environmental factors. These non-financial factors can be just as important in relation to a decision as financial information – but they are often more difficult to estimate and quantify.

e.g

Illustration 4 – Non-financial factors

A processing company needs to increase its output in order to take advantage of an increase in the total market for its product.

Alternative A

To provide additional production capacity a new factory extension could be built. However, there is a danger that the extension will be seen by the local council and by residents as an eyesore. Some landscaping and re-design work may be carried out at extra cost to company to make the extension more environmentally acceptable.

Alternative B

This entails keeping the factory at its current size but increasing the working hours per week for all production staff by 20%. The latter may be a cheaper solution in financial terms but may have an adverse impact on staff morale and result in a significant increase in staff turnover.

It is not easy for the company to build the non-financial costs into its decision making process as they are often difficult to quantify.

Non-financial information

Information provided by cost accounting systems is financial in nature. Financial information is important for management because many objectives of an organisation are financial in nature, such as making profits and avoiding insolvency. Managers also need information of a non-financial nature.

- At a strategic level, management need to know about developments in their markets and in the economic situation. They also need to know about any new technology that emerges, and about the activities of competitors.
- At a tactical level, they might want to know about issues such as product or service quality, speed of handling customer complaints, customer satisfaction levels, employee skills levels and employee morale.
- At an operational level, they may want to know about the number of rejects per machine, the lead time for delivering materials and the number of labour and machine hours available.

The management accounting systems in many organisations are able to obtain non-financial as well as financial information for reporting to management. The importance of non-financial information within the reporting system should not be forgotten.

External information

The environment refers to all of the external factors that affect a company and includes government actions, competitor actions, customer demands and other factors for example the weather.

Conventional accounting systems focus entirely on internal information such as production costs and volume of output produced. Companies and organisations do not, of course exist in a vacuum – they live in an environment in which they are influenced by a number of other organisations and forces arising from outside the organisation itself. This leads into an area of study often referred to as environmental analysis.

We do not need to go into this area in detail here, but, as with the non-financial factors referred to above, you should be aware that the environment (this is simply the external circumstances in which the company operates) will have an influence on a company's actions which should be reflected in its decision making processes.

It follows from this that an organisation should have information on its environment available to it within its accounting information systems – the organisation needs external information as well as internal information.

6 Chapter summary

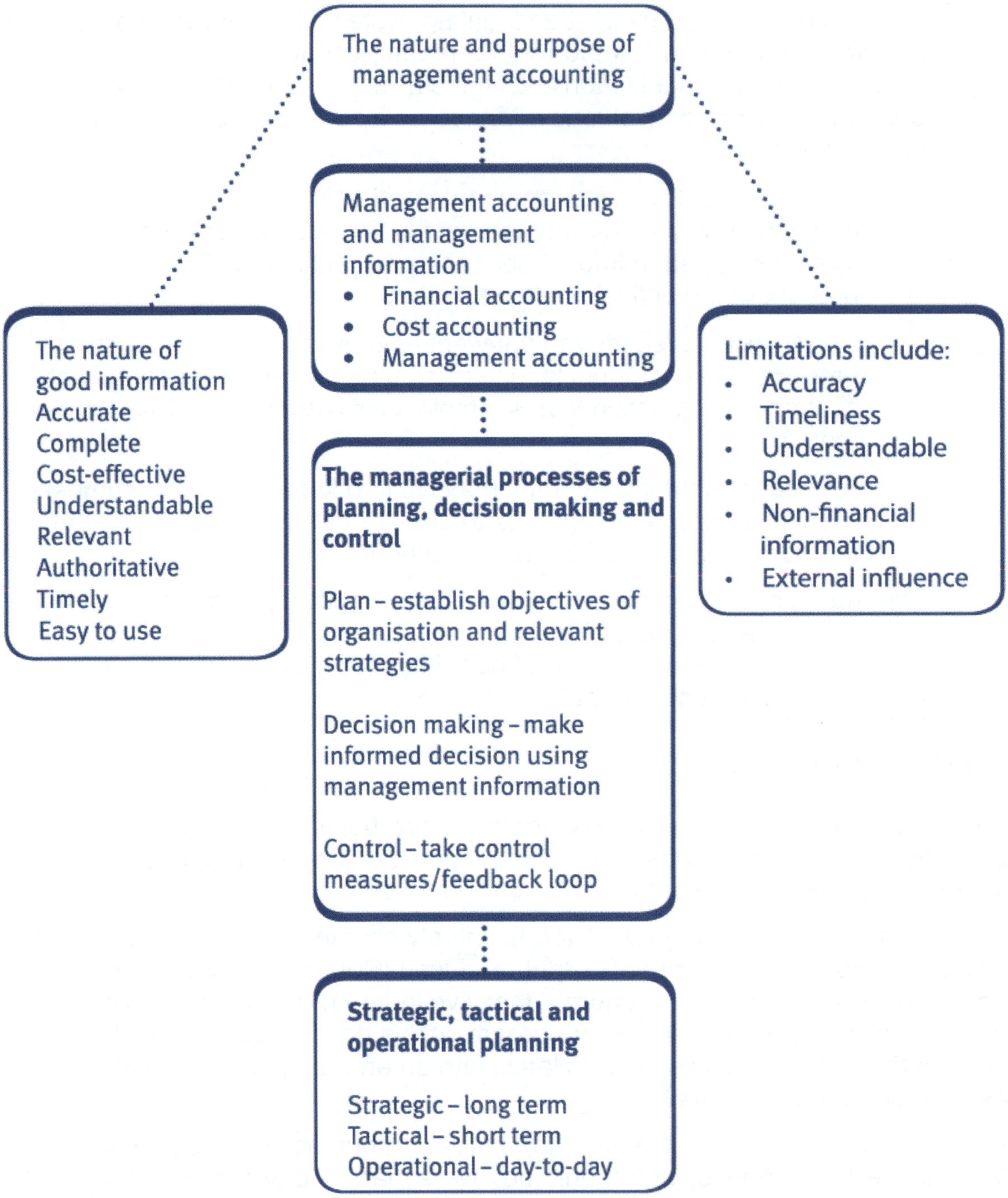

Test your understanding answers

Test your understanding 1

B

Management accounting provides managers and internal users with information to make decisions. Management accounts are concerned with more than only the cost of goods, services and operations such as quality and use of resources.

Test your understanding 2

C

The two terms are frequently used synonymously but strictly speaking they mean different things. Data is obtained from a survey and is turned into information by sorting and analysis. Both data and information can comprise either facts or figures.

Test your understanding 3

B

The management accountant is providing a new budget for the forthcoming period – i.e. a senior manager making a short term plan.

Test your understanding 4

	Planning	Control	Decision making
Preparation of the annual budget for a cost centre	✓		✓
Revise budgets for next period for a cost centre		✓	✓
Implement decisions based on information provided			✓
Set organisation's objectives for next period	✓		✓
Compare actual and expected results for a period		✓	✓

Note that all planning and control functions are part of the decision making process and are therefore identified as being both. The only exception is 'implement decisions based on information provided' which is not part of planning and control, but the one decision making task that there is.

Chapter

2

Cost classification

Chapter learning objectives

Upon completion of this chapter you will be able to:

- distinguish between cost, profit, investment and revenue centres
- describe the differing needs for information of cost, profit, investment and revenue centres managers
- explain and illustrate production and non-production costs
- describe the different elements of non-production cost – administrative, selling, distribution and finance
- describe the different elements of production cost – materials, labour and overheads
- explain the importance of the distinction between production and non-production costs when valuing output and inventories
- explain and illustrate with examples classifications used in the analysis of the product/service costs including by function, direct and indirect, fixed and variable, stepped fixed and semi variable costs
- identify and interpret graphical representations of different types of cost behaviour
- use high low analysis to separate the fixed and variable elements of total costs including situations involving semi variable and stepped fixed costs and changes in the variable cost per unit
- explain the advantages and disadvantages of using high low method to estimate the fixed and variable element of costing
- explain the structure of linear functions and equations

- explain and illustrate the concepts of cost objects, cost units and cost centres
- explain and illustrate the use of codes in categorising transaction.

PER

One of the PER performance objectives (PO12) is to apply different management accounting techniques is different business contexts to effectively manage and use resources. Working through this chapter should help you understand how to demonstrate that objective.

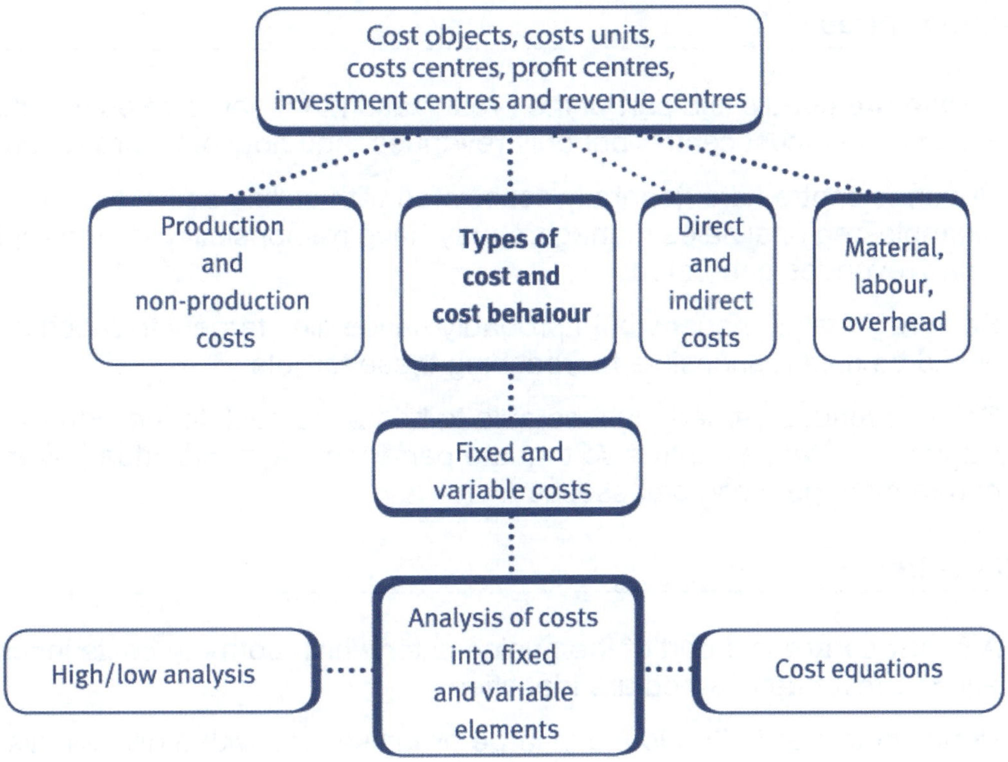

1 Analysing costs

Responsibility accounting

Responsibility accounting is based on identifying individual parts of a business that are the responsibility of a single manager.

A **responsibility centre** is an individual part of a business whose manager has personal responsibility for its performance.

Cost centres

A **cost centre** is a production or service location, function, activity or item of equipment whose costs are identified and recorded.

- For a paint manufacturer cost centres might be: mixing department; packaging department; administration; or marketing departments.
- For an accountancy firm, the cost centres might be: audit; taxation; accountancy; administration; canteen. Alternatively, they might be the various geographical locations, e.g. the London office, the Rome office, the Peru office.
- Cost centre managers need to have information about costs that are incurred and charged to their cost centres.
- The performance of a cost centre manager is judged on the extent to which cost targets have been achieved.

Revenue centres

A **revenue centre** is a part of the organisation that earns sales revenue. It is similar to a cost centre, but only revenues, and not costs, are recorded.

- Revenue centres are generally associated with selling activities, for example, regional sales managers may have responsibility for the regional sales revenues generated.
- Each regional manager would probably have sales targets to reach and would be held responsible for reaching these targets.
- Sales revenues earned must be able to be traced back to individual (regional) revenue centres so that the performance of individual revenue centre managers can be assessed.

Profit centres

A **profit centre** is a part of the business for which both the costs incurred and the revenues earned are identified.

- Profit centres are often found in large organisations with a divisionalised structure, and each division is treated as a profit centre.
- Within each profit centre, there could be several costs centres and revenue centres.
- The performance of a profit centre manager is measured in terms of the profit made by the centre.
- The manager must therefore be responsible for both costs and revenues and in a position to plan and control both.
- Data and information relating to both costs and revenues must be collected and allocated to the relevant profit centres.

Investment centres

Managers of investment centres are responsible for investment decisions as well as decisions affecting costs and revenues.

- Investment centre managers are therefore accountable for the performance of capital employed as well as profits (costs and revenues).
- The performance of investment centres is measured in terms of the profit earned relative to the capital invested (employed). This is known as the return on capital employed (ROCE).
- An example of an investment centres could be the UK and European divisions of a multinational company.

Cost objects

A cost object is any activity for which a separate measurement of cost is undertaken.

Examples of cost objects:

- cost of a product
- cost of a service
- cost of running a department
- cost of running a regional office.

Cost units

A cost unit is a unit of product or service in relation to which costs are ascertained.

Examples of cost units:

- a room (in a hotel)
- a litre of paint (paint manufacturers)
- in-patient (in a hospital).

Cost cards

A cost card is used to show the breakdown of the costs of producing output based on the classification of each cost. A cost card can be produced for one unit or a planned level of production.

The following costs are brought together and recorded on a cost card:

- direct materials
- direct labour
- direct expenses
- prime cost (total direct costs)
- variable production overheads
- fixed production overheads
- non-production overheads.

The terms used in the bullet points are explained in the rest of the chapter.

Illustration 1 – Cost card

A cost card for a hand-made wooden train set is shown below.

- The cutting and assembly department and the painting department are cost centres.
- One hand-made wooden train set is a cost unit (but may also be classed as a cost object).

		$ per unit
Direct materials:		
Wood	5m^2 @ $2.50 per m^2	12.50
Paint	0.1 litres at $10 per litre	1.00
Direct labour:		
Cutting and assembly department	0.5 hours at $6.00 per hour	3.00
Painting department	1.0 hours @ $7.00 per hour	7.00
Direct expenses:	Licence fee @ $2 per train set	2.00
PRIME COST		25.50
Variable production overheads:		
Power for electric saws	0.25 hours @ $2.00 per hour	0.50
TOTAL VARIABLE (MARGINAL) PRODUCTION COST		26.00
Fixed production overheads:		
	1.5 labour hours @ $10.00 per labour hour	15.00
TOTAL PRODUCTION (ABSORPTION) COST		41.00
Non-production overheads:		
Administration, selling and distribution	20% of total production cost	8.20
TOTAL COST		49.20

Once the total cost is calculated then the selling price of a product can be calculated using either a mark-up or a margin. The mark-up or margin will be the profit made on each unit.

Mark-up (based on cost being 100%)

There is to be a 20% mark-up applied when calculating the selling price:

Mark-up = $49.20/100 × 20 = $9.84

Selling price = $49.20 + $9.84 = $59.04

Margin (based on the selling price being 100%)

There is to be a margin of 10% applied when calculating the selling price:

Margin = $49.20/90 × 10 = $5.47

Selling price = $49.20 + $5.47 = $54.67

Management will require a variety of different cost summaries, including:

- costs for a particular product – a cost unit or cost object
- costs for use in the preparation of external financial reports
- costs for a particular department – a cost centre
- costs to be used for decision making
- costs that are useful for planning and control.

To be able to produce these summaries the type of cost and the cost behaviour will need to be analysed.

2 Classifying costs

Costs can be classified in a number of different ways.

- **Element** – classify costs as to whether they relate to material, labour or expenses. This is useful for cost control.
- **Nature** – classify costs as to how they relate to production. Are they directly involved in the production of the product/service or indirectly involved in production? This is useful for cost accounting.
- **Function** – classify costs based on whether they are production costs or non-production costs. This is useful for the financial accounts.
- **Behaviour** – classify costs based on how they change in relation to levels of output or activity. This is useful for budgeting and decision making.

Classification by element

To classify by element you need to decide if a cost is a material cost, a labour cost or a cost relating to something else – an expense.

- **Materials** – all costs of materials purchased for production or non-production activities. For example, raw materials, components, cleaning materials, maintenance materials and stationery.
- **Labour** – all staff costs relating to employees on the payroll of the organisation.
- **Expenses** – all other costs which are not materials or labour. This includes all bought-in services, for example, rent, telephone, sub-contractors and costs such as the depreciation of equipment.

Classification by nature

Direct costs

Direct costs are costs which can be directly identified with a specific cost unit or cost centre.

There are three main types of direct cost – direct material, direct labour and direct expenses. The direct costs associated with a shirt (cost unit) manufactured by a clothing company would be:

- direct materials – cloth for making shirts
- direct labour – the wages of the workers stitching the cloth to make the shirts
- direct expenses – the royalties paid to a designer.

The total of direct costs is known as the **prime cost**.

Indirect costs

Indirect costs are costs which cannot be directly identified with a specific cost unit or cost centre.

The indirect costs associated with a shirt (cost unit) manufactured by a clothing company would be:

- indirect materials – these include materials that cannot be traced to an individual item for example cleaning fluids for cleaning the machinery
- indirect labour – the cost of a supervisor who supervises the shirt makers
- indirect expenses – the cost of renting the factory where the shirts are manufactured.

The total of indirect costs is known as **overheads**.

Direct and indirect cost?

It is important to realise that a particular cost may sometimes be a direct cost and sometimes an indirect cost. It depends on the cost object we are trying to cost.

For example, the salary of the machining department supervisor is a direct cost of that department or cost centre because it can be specifically identified with the department. However, it is an indirect cost of each of the cost units processed in the machining department because it cannot be specifically identified with any particular cost unit.

Test your understanding 1

Identify whether the following costs are materials, labour or expenses and whether they are direct or indirect for the production of toy cars.

Cost	Materials, labour or expense	Direct or indirect?
The hire of specific tools or equipment		
Rent of the factory		
Supervisors' salaries		
Oil for lubricating machines		
Wages of factory workers involved in production		
Depreciation of equipment		

Test your understanding 2

(a) Which of the following would be classed as indirect labour?

A Assembly workers

B A stores assistant in a factory storeroom

C Plasterers in a building company

D An audit clerk in an accountancy firm

(b) Direct costs are:

A costs which can be identified with a cost centre but not a single cost unit

B costs which can be identified with a single cost unit or cost centre

C costs which can be attributed to an accounting period

D none of the above

Classification by function

Production costs

Production costs are costs that relate to the manufacture of a product or provision of a service. These costs are found in the cost of sales section of the statement of profit or loss.

Production costs, such as direct materials, direct labour, direct expenses and production overheads, **are** included in the **valuation of inventory**.

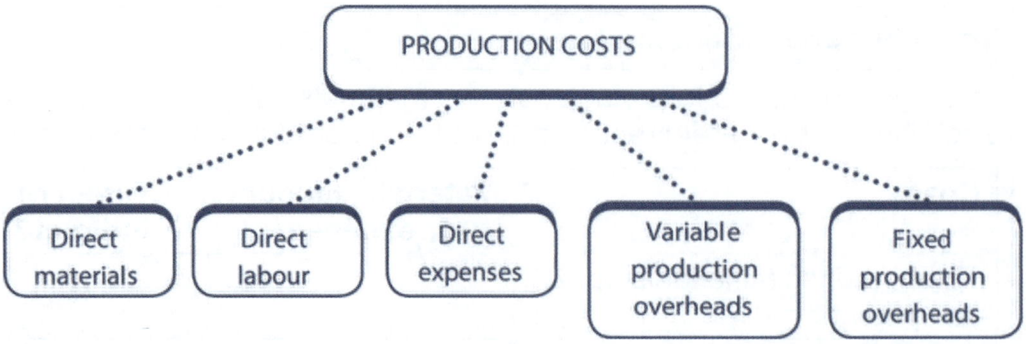

Examples of production costs

Examples of production costs for a construction company

- Direct materials – bricks, cement
- Direct labour – builders, plasterers, electricians
- Direct expenses – the cost of a subcontracted crane and driver
- Variable production overheads – electricity
- Fixed production overheads – site managers salary.

Non-production costs

Non-production costs are costs that are not directly associated with the production of the businesses output.

Non-production costs, such as administrative costs, selling costs and finance costs, are charged to the statement of profit or loss as expenses for the period in which they are incurred. Non-production costs **are not** included in the **valuation of inventory**.

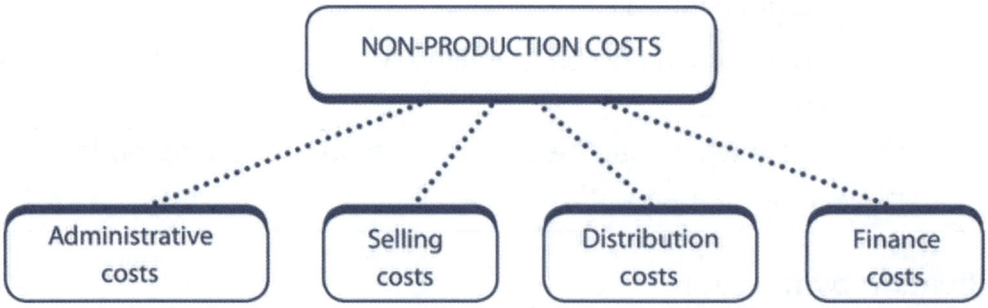

Examples of non-production costs

- Administrative costs – the costs involved in running the general administration departments of an organisation, for example, the accounts department.
- Selling costs – costs associated with taking orders from customers who wish to buy an organisation's products (sales department costs) and also marketing costs.
- Distribution costs – the costs involved in distributing an organisation's finished products, such as the cost of running the warehouse or delivery costs.
- Finance costs – the costs that are incurred in order to finance an organisation, for example, loan interest.

Test your understanding 3

Complete the following table by classifying each expense correctly.

Classifications

1 = Production

2 = Selling

3 = Distribution

4 = Administrative

5 = Finance

Cost	**Classification**
Overalls for machine workers	
Cost of printer cartridges in general office	
Salary of factory supervisor	
Salary of payroll supervisor	
Rent of warehouse for storing goods ready for sale	
Loan interest	
Salary of factory security guard	
Early settlement discounts for customers who pay early	
Salary of the Chairman's PA	
Road tax licence for delivery vehicles	
Bank overdraft fee	
Salesmen's commissions	

3 Classification by behaviour

Costs may be classified according to the way that they behave in relation to changes in levels of activity. Cost behaviour classifies costs as one of the following:

- variable cost
- fixed cost
- stepped fixed cost
- semi-variable cost.

Variable costs

Variable costs are costs that vary in direct proportion with the level of activity. As activity levels increase then total variable costs will also increase.

Variable costs can be shown graphically as follows:

GRAPH 1

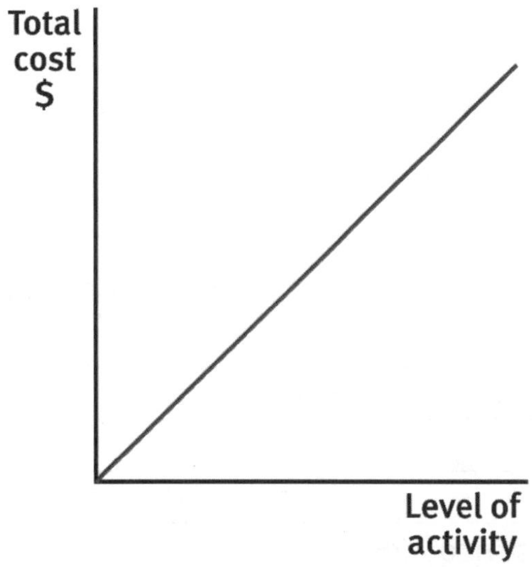

GRAPH 2

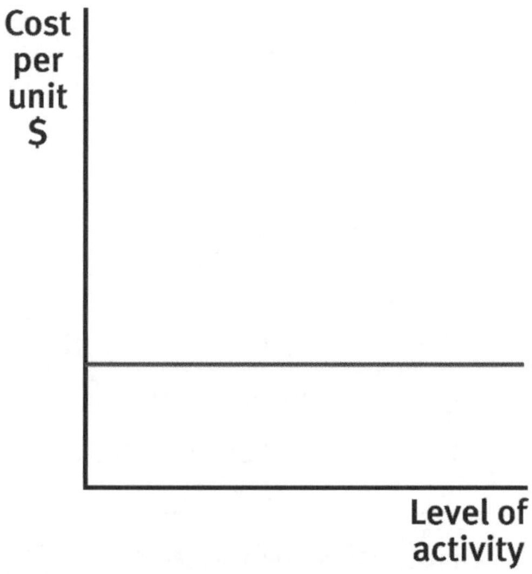

- Note that as total costs increase with activity levels, the cost per unit of variable costs remains constant.
- Examples of variable costs include direct costs such as raw materials and direct labour.

Numerical example of variable costs

- A factory is producing widgets. It takes $4m^2$ to make one widget and it costs $2 per square metre. If the factory makes 50 widgets it costs $400, if the factory makes 100 widgets it costs $800. The cost incurred increases in line with the volume being produced – graph 1 demonstrates this.
- The material for each widget costs 4 × $2 = $8 and it does not change if more or less widgets are made. The variable cost per unit remains constant – graph 2 demonstrates this.

Material cost and discounts

Direct material costs are assumed to have a variable cost behaviour but sometimes quantity discounts are available when purchases exceed a certain order size.

There are two main scenarios:

1 Discounts are received on additional purchases of material above a set order quantity and the discount only applies to the extra units.

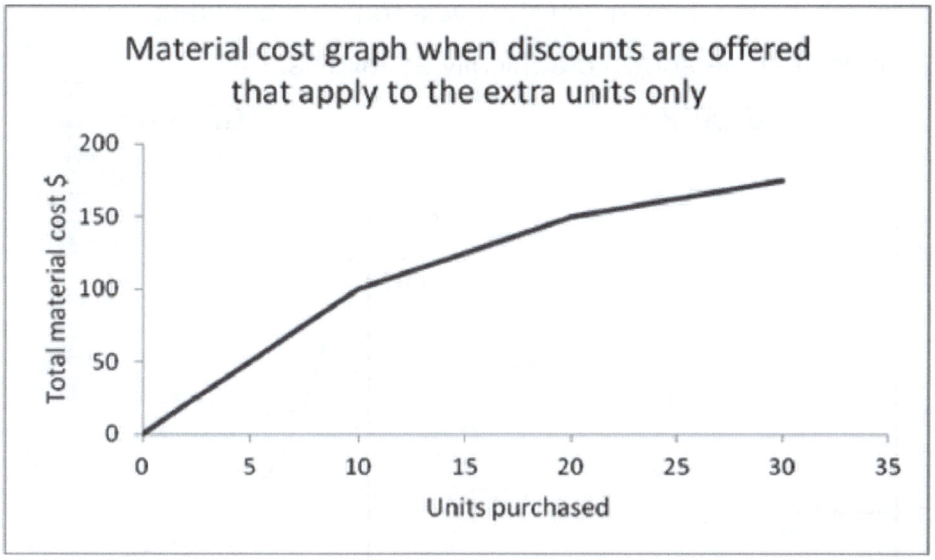

2 Discounts are received when total purchases exceed a certain level and all units purchased are invoiced at a lower cost per unit. Note: the data line will always return to the origin.

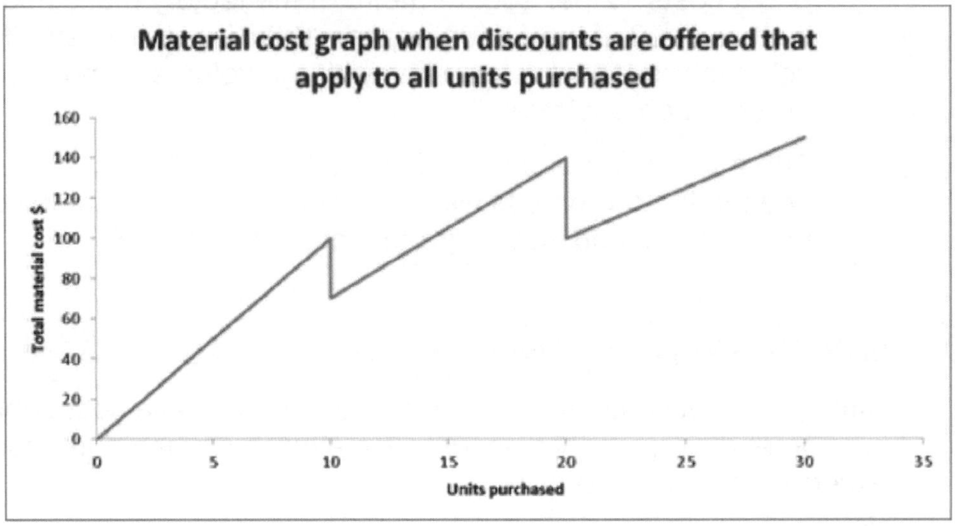

Fixed costs

A fixed cost is a cost which is incurred for an accounting period, and which, within certain activity levels remains constant.

Fixed costs can be shown graphically as follows:

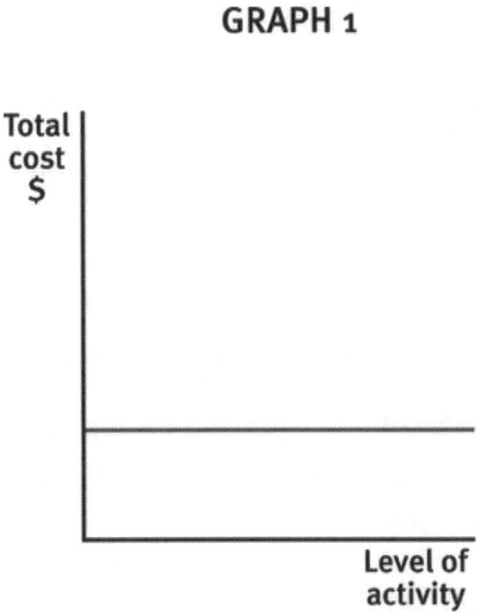

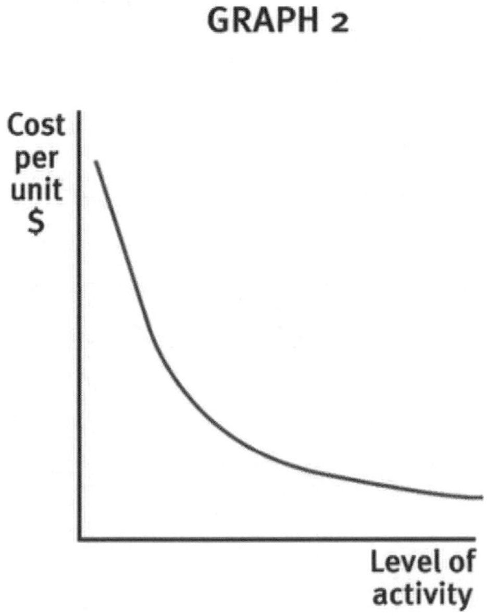

- Note that the total cost remains constant over a given level of activity but that the cost per unit falls as the level of activity increases.
- Examples of fixed costs:
  - rent
  - business rates
  - executive salaries.

Numerical example of fixed costs

- If factory rent is $5,000 per month, this cost will be incurred whether 2 widgets are made, or 200 widgets are made – graph 1 demonstrates this.
- If 2 widgets are made the fixed cost per unit is $5,000 ÷ 2, i.e. $2,500 per widget.
- If 200 widgets are made the fixed cost per unit is $5,000 ÷ 200, i.e. $25 per widget.
- Therefore, the fixed cost per unit falls at a reducing rate but never reaches zero – graph 2 demonstrates this.

Test your understanding 4

ILCB has the following information relating to one of its products:

- Direct material cost per unit $1
- Direct labour cost per unit $3
- Variable production cost per unit $3
- Fixed production overhead $30,000 per month
- Budgeted production 15,000 units per month

Required:

Calculate the cost per unit and the total cost of the budgeted monthly production?

Stepped fixed costs

This is a type of fixed cost that is only fixed within certain levels of activity. Once the upper limit of an activity level is reached then a new higher level of fixed cost becomes relevant.

Stepped fixed costs can be shown graphically as follows:

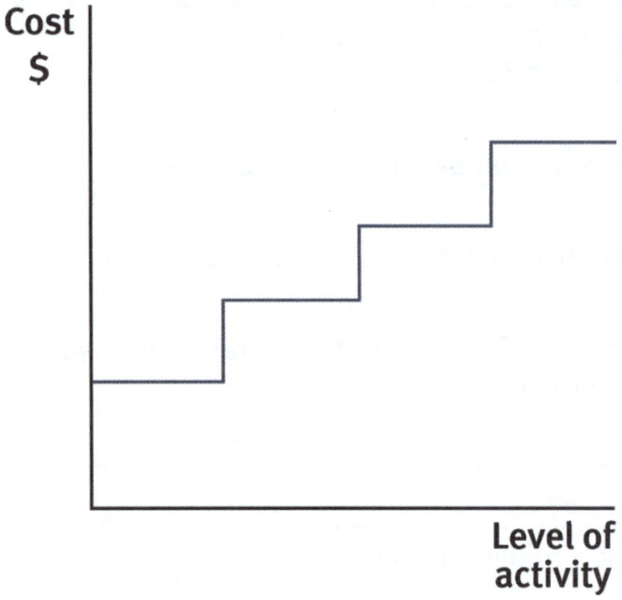

- Examples of stepped fixed costs:
  - warehousing costs (as more space is required, more warehouses must be purchased or rented)
  - supervisors' wages (as the number of employees increases, more supervisors are required).

Numerical example of stepped costs

- For production of up to 50 widgets, only one supervisor is required but if production is between 50 and 100 widgets, two supervisors are required.
- The cost of one supervisor is $18,000 per annum and the cost of two supervisors is therefore $36,000.
- The fixed costs therefore increase in steps.

Semi-variable costs

Semi-variable costs contain both fixed and variable cost elements and are therefore partly affected by changes in the level of activity.

Semi-variable costs can be shown graphically as follows:

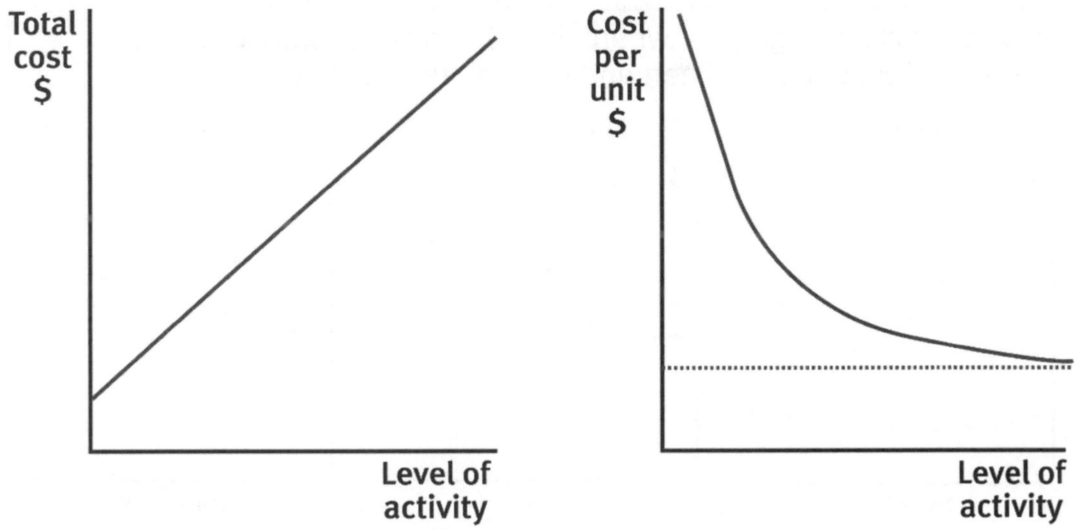

- Examples of semi-variable costs:
  - electricity bills (fixed standing charge plus variable cost per unit of electricity consumed)
  - telephone bills (fixed line rental plus variable cost per call).

Test your understanding 5

Classify the following items of expenditure according to their behaviour i.e. as fixed, variable, semi-variable or stepped fixed costs.

1	Monthly rent	5	Telephone bill
2	Council tax charge	6	Annual salary
3	Production line workers wages	7	Depreciation of 1, 2 or 3 machines
4	Electricity bill	8	Raw materials

Test your understanding 6

Study the following graphs, where the vertical axis represents 'Total Costs' or 'Cost per unit'. Then answer the questions shown below.

Graph 1

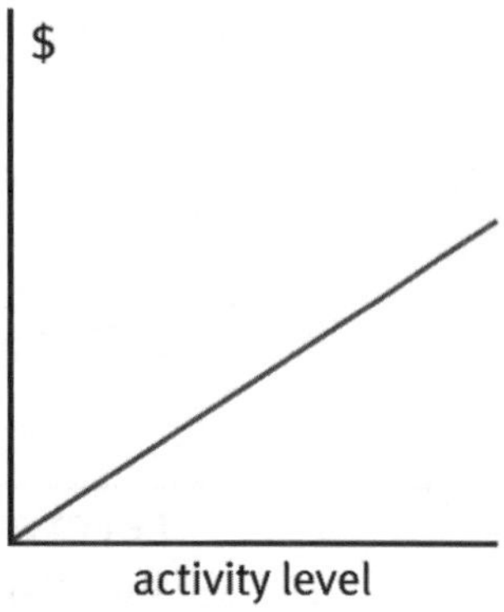

Graph 2

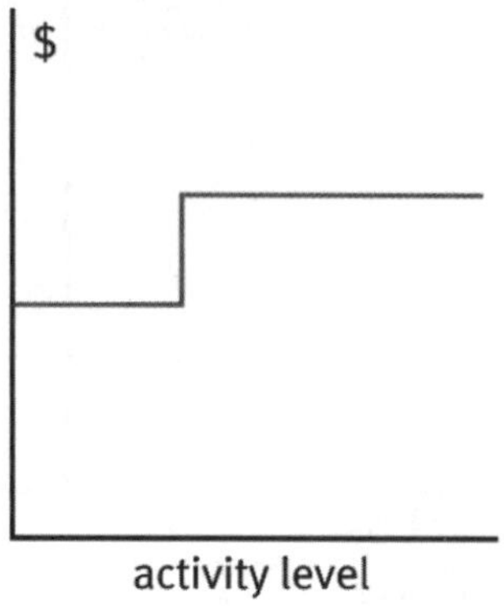

Graph 3

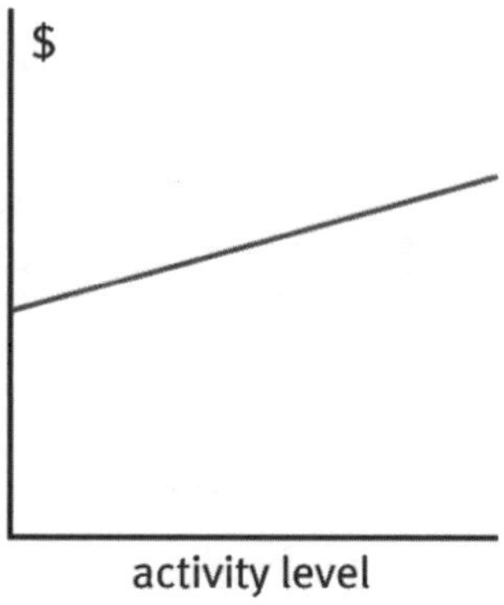

Graph 4

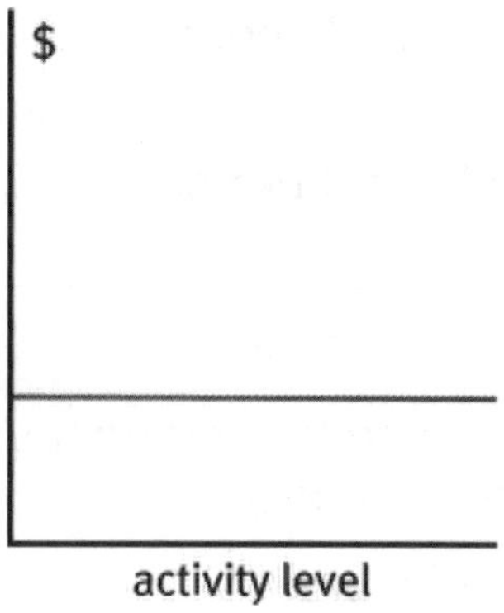

Graph 5

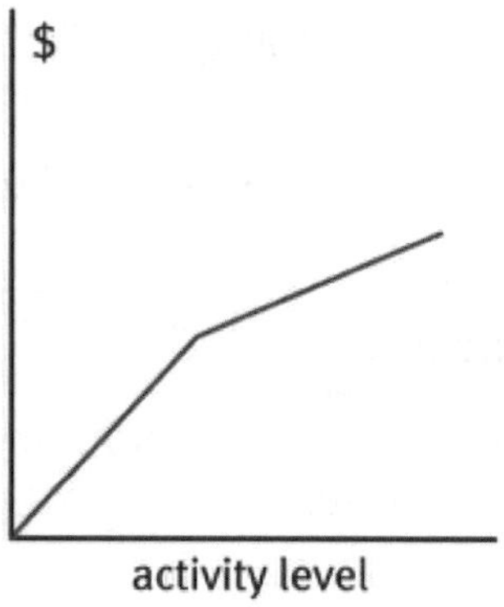

Graph 6

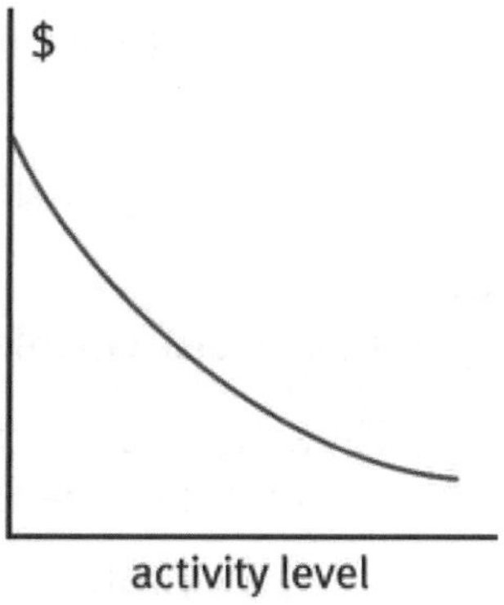

Total fixed cost is shown in graph	
Total variable cost is shown in graph	
Total semi-variable cost is shown in graph	
Fixed cost per unit is shown in graph	
Variable cost per unit is shown in graph	
A stepped fixed cost is shown in graph	

4 Identifying cost behaviours

The behavioural characteristics of costs are used when planning or forecasting costs at different levels of production or activity. When producing a forecast it may be necessary to identify the type of behaviour a cost is exhibiting. It is useful to remember the following:

- Fixed costs are constant in total
- Variable costs are constant per unit
- Semi-variable costs are neither constant in total nor constant per unit
- Stepped fixed costs will be constant in total within a certain range.

e.g

Illustration 2 – Identifying cost behaviours

A company has a mix of variable, semi variable, fixed and stepped fixed costs.

Total cost at different activity levels:

Cost	1,000 units	3,000 units	5,000 units	7,000 units
1	$19,000	$33,000	$47,000	$61,000
2	$1,920	$5,760	$9,600	$13,440
3	$7,000	$7,000	$7,000	$7,000
4	$12,500	$12,500	$17,000	$17,000

Cost per unit at different activity levels:

Cost	1,000 units	3,000 units	5,000 units	7,000 units
1	$19.00	$11.00	$9.40	$8.71
2	$1.92	$1.92	$1.92	$1.92
3	$7.00	$2.33	$1.40	$1.00
4	$12.50	$4.17	$3.40	$2.43

Identify the behaviour for each of the costs

- Cost 1 is a semi-variable cost as the total cost changes when activity level change and the cost per unit also changes at the different activity levels
- Cost 2 is a variable cost as the cost per unit is constant at each activity level
- Cost 3 is a fixed cost as the total cost does not change as activity level changes
- Cost 4 is a stepped fixed cost as the total cost is constant then increases to a new constant level and the cost per unit is changing at each activity level

5 The high low method used for separating a semi-variable cost

The total cost of a semi-variable cost is:

Total costs = Total fixed costs + (Variable cost per unit × Activity level)

To be able to predict costs at different activity levels it is necessary to separate the fixed cost element from the variable cost element. The high low method can be used to **approximate** the variable cost per unit and the total fixed cost.

The high low method

Step 1

Select the highest and lowest **activity levels**, and their associated costs.

Step 2

Calculate the variable cost (VC) per unit:

$$\text{VC per unit} = \frac{\text{Cost at high level of activity} - \text{cost at low level of activity}}{\text{High level of activity} - \text{low level of activity}}$$

Step 3

Calculate the fixed cost by substitution, using either the high or low activity level:

Fixed cost = Total cost at activity level – (Variable cost per unit × Activity level)

Step 4

Use the total fixed cost and the variable cost per unit values from steps 2 and 3 to calculate the estimated cost at different activity levels:

Total costs = Total fixed costs + (Variable cost per unit × Activity level)

Assumption underlying the high low method

Assumptions of the high low method are as follows:

- the only thing causing any change in cost is the change in activity
- the cost under consideration is potentially semi-variable (i.e. it has both fixed and variable elements)
- the linear model of cost behaviour is valid i.e. y = a + bx (we will study this in more detail later on in this chapter).

Illustration 3 – The high low method

Output (units)	**Total cost** ($)
200	7,000
300	8,000
400	9,000

Required:

(a) Calculate the variable cost per unit.

(b) Calculate the total fixed cost.

(c) Estimate the total cost if output is 350 units.

(d) Estimate the total cost if output is 600 units.

Solution

(a) Variable cost per unit = ($9,000 – $7,000)/(400 – 200) = $2,000/200 = $10 per unit

(b) Total fixed cost by substituting at high activity level:

Total cost	=	$9,000
Total variable cost	= 400 × $10	$4,000
Therefore fixed cost	=	$5,000

(c) If output is 350units

Variable cost	= 350 × $10 =	$3,500
Fixed cost	=	$5,000
Total cost	=	$8,500

(d) If output is 600 units:

Variable cost	= 600 × $10 =	$6,000
Fixed cost	=	$5,000
Total cost	=	$11,000

Test your understanding 7

The total costs incurred at various output levels in a factory have been measured as follows:

Output (units)	**Total cost** ($)
26	6,566
30	6,510
33	6,800
44	6,985
48	7,380
50	7,310

Required:

Using the high low method, analyse the total cost into fixed and variable components.

High low method with stepped fixed costs

Sometimes fixed costs are only fixed within certain levels of activity (stepped fixed costs). The high low method can still be used to estimate fixed and variable costs.

- Choose the two activity levels where the fixed costs remain unchanged and calculate the variable cost per unit and the total fixed cost using the high low technique.
- Adjustments may need to be made to the fixed costs when calculating the total cost for a new activity level.

Illustration 4 – the high low method with stepped fixed costs

An organisation has the following total costs at three activity levels

Activity level (units)	4,000	6,000	7,500
Total cost	$40,800	$50,000	$54,800

Variable cost per unit is constant within this activity range and there is a step up of 10% in the total fixed costs when the activity level exceeds 5,500 units.

What is the total cost at an activity level of 5,000 units?

A $44,000

B $44,800

C $45,400

D $46,800

Solution

A

Calculate the variable cost per unit by comparing two output levels where fixed costs will be the same:

Variable cost per unit = [(54,800 – 50,000) ÷ (7,500 – 6,000)] = $3.20

Total fixed cost above 5,500 units = [54,800 – (7,500 × 3.20)] = $30,800

Total fixed cost below 5,500 units = 30,800/110 × 100 = $28,000

Total cost for 5,000 units = [(5,000 × 3.20) + 28,000] = $44,000

High low method with changes in the variable cost per unit

Sometimes there may be changes in the variable cost per unit, and the high low method can still be used to determine the fixed and variable elements of semi-variable costs. As with the stepped fixed costs – choose activity levels where the variable costs per unit remain unchanged.

e.g

Illustration 5 – The high low method with changing variable costs

The following information relates to the manufacture of Product LL:

Output (units)	**Total cost** ($)
200	7,000
300	8,000
400	8,600

For output volumes above 350 units the variable cost per unit falls by 10%. (Note: this fall applies to all units – not just the excess above 350).

Required:

Estimate the cost of producing 450 units of Product LL.

Solution

$$\text{Variable cost per unit } (<350) = \frac{\$8{,}000 - \$7{,}000}{300 - 200} = \frac{\$1{,}000}{100} = \$10 \text{ per unit}$$

Total cost at 300 units	=		$8,000
Total variable cost	=	300 × $10	$3,000
Therefore fixed cost	=		$5,000

If output is 450 units:

Variable cost	= 450 × $10 × 90%	$4,050
Fixed cost	=	$5,000
Total cost	=	$9,050

Test your understanding 8

The total costs incurred in 20X3 at various output levels in a factory have been measured as follows:

Output (units)	**Total cost** ($)
26	6,566
30	6,510
33	6,800
44	6,985
48	7,380
50	7,310

When output is 80 units or more, another factory unit must be rented and fixed costs therefore increase by 100%.

Variable cost per unit is forecast to rise by 10% in 20X4.

Required:

Calculate the estimated total costs of producing 100 units in 20X4.

Advantages and limitations of the high low method

The main advantage of the high low method is that it is easy to understand and easy to use.

The limitations of the high low method are as follows:

- it relies on historical cost data and assumes this data can reliably predict future costs
- it assumes that activity levels are the only factor affecting costs
- it uses only two values (highest and lowest) to predict future costs and these results may be distorted because of random variations which may have occurred
- bulk discounts may be available for purchasing resources in large quantities.

6 Cost equations

Cost equations are derived from historical cost data. Once a cost equation has been established, for example distinguishing the fixed and variable costs using the high low method, it can be used to estimate future costs. Cost equations are assumed to have a linear function and therefore the equation of a straight line can be applied:

$y = a + bx$

Where:

- 'a' is the intercept, i.e. the point at which the line $y = a + bx$ cuts the y axis (the value of y when $x = 0$).
- 'b' is the gradient/slope of the line $y = a + bx$ (the change in y when x increases by one unit).
- 'x' = independent variable.
- 'y' = dependent variable (its value depends on the value of 'x').

This formula can be related to the results of the high low calculation as follows:

- 'a' is the fixed cost per period (the intercept)
- 'b' is the variable cost per unit (the gradient)
- 'x' is the activity level (the independent variable)
- 'y' is the total cost = fixed cost + variable cost (dependent on the activity level)

Suppose a cost has a cost equation of y = $5,000 + 10x, this can be shown graphically as follows:

Graph of cost equation y = 5,000 + 10x

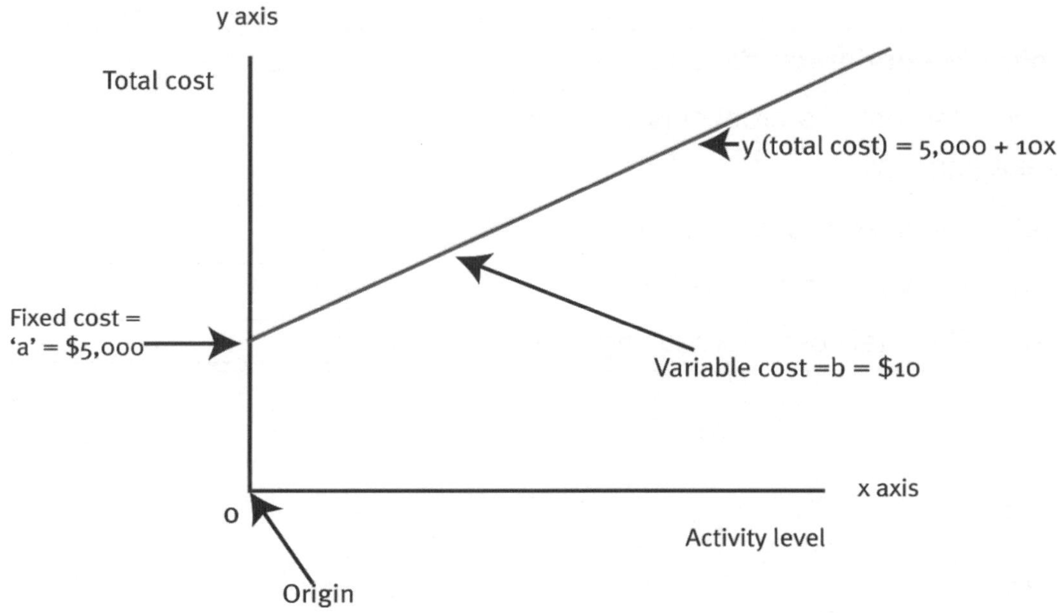

Illustration 6 – Cost equations

If y = 8,000 + 40x

(a)	Fixed cost = $	
(b)	Variable cost per unit = $	
(c)	Total cost for 200 units = $	

Solution

(a)	Fixed cost = $	8,000
(b)	Variable cost per unit = $	40
(c)	Total cost for 200 units = $	16,000

Working

Fixed cost = $8,000

Variable cost = 200 × $40 = $8,000

Total cost = fixed cost + variable cost = $8,000 + $8,000 = $16,000

Test your understanding 9

Consider the linear function y = 1,488 + 20x and answer the following questions.

(a)	The line would cross the y axis at the point	
(b)	The gradient of the line is	
(c)	The independent variable is	
(d)	The dependent variable is	

Test your understanding 10

If the total cost of a product is given as:

Y = 4,800 + 8x

(a)	The fixed cost is $	
(b)	The variable cost per unit is $	
(c)	The total cost of producing 100 units is $	

7 Cost codes

A code is a system of symbols designed to be applied to a classified set of items, to give a brief accurate reference, which helps entry into the records, collation and analysis.

A cost code is a code used in a costing system.

The first step in creating a cost code will be to determine the cost centre to which the cost relates and then to allocate the correct cost centre code.

Illustration 7 – Cost code example

If a cost relates to Machine Group 7 the cost centre code might be 07. If the cost relates to the canteen the cost centre code might be 16.

Generic or functional codes

Once a cost has been allocated its correct cost centre code then it may also be useful to know the particular type of expense involved. Therefore some more digits might be added to the cost centre code to represent the precise type of cost.

Illustration 8 – Generic or functional codes

If an expense for Machine Group 7 is for oil then its code might be 07 (for its cost centre) followed by 23 to represent indirect materials.

If an expense of the canteen is identified as frozen peas then its cost code might be 16 (its cost centre) followed by 02 to represent food purchases.

Specific codes

Finally it may be necessary for cost allocation, decision making or accounting purposes to allocate a code which specifically identifies the item of cost.

Illustration 9 – Specific codes example

The oil for Machine Group 7 might eventually be coded as 072304. This represents Machine Group 7 (07) indirect material use (23) of oil (04).

The frozen peas for the canteen might be coded as 160219. This represents canteen (16) food purchases (02) of frozen peas (19).

A cost code is designed to analyse and classify the costs of an organisation in the most appropriate manner for that organisation. Therefore there are no set methods of designing a cost code and the cost code of a particular organisation will be that which best suits the operations and costs of that business.

Test your understanding 11

A cost coding system is such that the first two letters of the code represent the cost centre, the third letter the type of expense and the fourth letter the detail of the expense.

Codes are as follows:

- S = Sales representative's expenses
- ED = Eastern Division
- P = Petrol

What is the correct code for an Eastern Division's sales representative's petrol expenses?

Coding systems

There are many ways to code costs. Here are some of the more popular methods:

Sequential code

This is the most basic type of code. It simply means that each code follows a numerical or alphabetical sequence. Planning is needed to determine how many codes might be needed in total.

For example, let's assume we are making a coding list for different types of expenses. We could give our first category, say Motor Expenses, code 001. Our next type of expense, say Electricity, would get code 002. Each expense would then follow in sequence. This allows us to have as many as 999 different types of expenses as we are using a three digit sequential code.

Block code

Block codes are often used to categorise sequential codes together. For example, an accounting system might have the following block codes:

Code	Item
0000	Expenses
1000	Revenue
2000	Non-current assets
3000	Current assets
4000	Long term liability
5000	Equity

The 3000 "Block" is allocated to Current assets. This means that it is possible to classify up to 1,000 different current assets (such as different types of inventories and bank accounts) using this block.

Hierarchical code

Each digit in the code represents a classification. As the code progresses from left to right each digit represents a smaller subset. For example, codes for sales for an international electronics retailer could have the hierarchy:

1 represents revenue

1.1 Revenue from the UK (.1)

1.2 Revenue from the USA (.2)

1.3 Revenue from China (.3)

This allows for infinite expandability. For example, it can be expanded as:

1.1.1 Revenue in the UK from laptop sales (.1)

1.1.2 Revenue in the UK from photocopier sales (.2)

1.2.1 Revenue in the USA from laptop sales (.1)

1.3.2 Revenue in China from photocopier sales (.2)

Each sub-category simply gets a further decimal coding.

Significant digit code

A significant digit code is a code that contains individual digits and letters that are used to represent features of the coded item. The example given is one used to describe packs of paper file dividers:

Code	Item
2000	Paper file dividers
2010	10 pack of paper file dividers
2020	20 pack of paper file dividers
2030	30 pack of paper file dividers

2000 is the code for the dividers and then the 10, 20, 30 represents the number of dividers in a pack.

Faceted code

A faceted code is one that is broken down into a number of facets or fields, each of which signifies a unit of information.

Consider the following simplified table which has been extracted as a sample from the faceted code used by a large international manufacturer:

Region	Code	Department	Code	Expense	Code
Europe	01	Sales	01	Salaries	0244
Asia	02	Production	02	National Insurance	0245
USA	03	Personnel and Finance	03	Pension contribution	0246
Africa	04	Administration	04	Bonus payments	0247

In this example, there are three facets, or fields, to the code:

Facet 1 is the region, and is 2 digits long

Facet 2 is the department, and is 2 digits long

Facet 3 is the type of expense, and is 4 digits long

If we wanted to post an expense for a bonus paid to the production department of the USA region, the code would be 03020247. That is: 03 (for USA), 02 (for Production) and 0247 (for Bonus payments).

It can be seen that a faceted system is a complicated one and requires lots of training and possibly a table such as the one above to be used for interpretation of codes. But it does allow for more sub-divisions and a greater number of codes.

Mnemonic code

Mnemonic means something that aids the memory or understanding. This uses an alphabetical coding rather than a numerical coding system. It is often used to abbreviate or simplify information.

For example, in accounting we might use:

Code	Meaning
NCA	Non-current assets
EXP	Expenses
REV	Revenue

Mnemonic codes are a way of quickly expressing information and making that information easily understood. However, this coding method makes it very difficult to use sub-categories or to have too much information. Mnemonic coding is likely to struggle to categorise 999 different types of expenses.

Test your understanding 12

Explain the following types of coding systems:

(a) sequence codes

(b) block codes

(c) significant digit codes

(d) faceted codes

Test your understanding 13

A company operates from three main sites. In analysing its overhead costs it uses a nine-digit coding system. A sample from the coding manual shows:

Site	Code	Expenditure days	Code	Function	Code
Whitby	100	Rent	410	Purchasing	600
Scarborough	200	Power	420	Finance	610
York	300	Heat and light	430	Production	620
		Travel costs	500	Sales	630
		Telephone and postage	520		

The order of coding is: site/expense/function

An invoice for the York site for travel costs incurred by a sales representative would be coded as:

A 300/500/600

B 300/500/630

C 300/500/610

D 300/500/620

Test your understanding 14

The accounting system can contain codes to identify:

(i) the type of cost

(ii) the responsibility centre

(iii) the supplier.

Which of these options are correct?

A (i) only

B (ii) only

C (i) and (ii)

D (i), (ii) and (iii)

Test your understanding 15

An indirect cost should:

A be coded to a cost unit

B be coded to the different costs centres that incur the cost

C be coded to an overhead cost centre

D not be coded at all

8 Chapter summary

Cost object, cost unit and cost centre

Cost object – activity for which costs can be separately measured

Cost unit – unit of product or service in relation to which costs are ascertained

Cost centre – production or service location, function, activity or item of equipment for which costs can be ascertained

Profit centres – cost and revenues indentified

Investment centres – profit centre with responsibility for investment

Revenue centre – accountable for revenues only

Production and non-production costs

Production costs = prime cost (total direct costs) plus overheads

Non-production costs = admin, selling, distribution and finance

Types of cost behaviour

Direct and indirect costs

Direct costs – directly involved in production

Indirect costs – not directly involved in production

Material, labour, overhead

Fixed and variable costs

Fixed – do not vary with level of activity

Variable – vary with level of activity

Analysis of semi-variable costs into fixed and variable elements

Cost equations (linear function) y =a + bx

High/low analysis

Variable cost per unit = $\frac{\text{Cost at high level of activity} - \text{Cost at low level of activity}}{\text{High level of activity} - \text{Low level of activity}}$

Fixed cost = Total cost at activity level – Total variable cost

Test your understanding answers

Test your understanding 1

Cost	Materials, labour or expense	Direct or indirect
The hire of tools or equipment	Expense	Direct
Rent of a factory	Expense	Indirect
Supervisors' salaries	Labour	Indirect
Oil for lubricating machines	Material	Indirect
Wages of factory workers involved in production	Labour	Direct
Depreciation of equipment	Expense	Indirect

Test your understanding 2

(a) **B**

Store assistants are not directly involved in producing the output (goods or services) of an organisation.

(b) **B**

This is a basic definition question. Direct costs are costs which can be identified with a single cost unit, or cost centre.

Test your understanding 3

Cost	**Classification**
Overalls for machine workers	1
Cost of printer cartridges in general office	4
Salary of factory supervisor	1
Salary of payroll supervisor	4
Rent of warehouse for storing goods ready for sale	3
Loan interest	5
Salary of factory security guard	1
Early settlement discounts for customers who pay early	2
Salary of the Chairman's PA	4
Road tax licence for delivery vehicles	3
Bank overdraft fee	5
Salesmen's commissions	2

Test your understanding 4

The production cost includes:

	Per unit	Total
	$	$
Direct material cost	1	15,000
Direct labour cost	3	45,000
Variable production cost	3	45,000
Fixed production cost	2	30,000
	9	135,000

Test your understanding 5

The items of expenditure would be analysed as follows.

1	Fixed	5	Semi-variable
2	Fixed	6	Fixed
3	Variable	7	Stepped fixed
4	Semi-variable	8	Variable

Note: the depreciation charge for the factory machines (7) is a stepped fixed cost – when activity increases to such a level that a second and third machine is required, the fixed cost will step up.

Test your understanding 6

Total fixed cost is shown in graph	4
Total variable cost is shown in graph	1
Total semi-variable cost is shown in graph	3
Fixed cost per unit is shown in graph	6
Variable cost per unit is shown in graph	4
A stepped fixed cost is shown in graph	2

Test your understanding 7

Variable cost per unit = $\frac{\$7,310 - \$6,566}{50 - 26} = \frac{\$744}{24}$ = \$31 per unit

Substituting at high activity level:

Total cost	=	\$7,310
Total variable cost	= 50 × \$31	\$1,550
Therefore fixed cost	=	\$5,760

Test your understanding 8

Variable cost per unit (20X3) = $\frac{\$7,310 - \$6,566}{50 - 26} = \frac{\$744}{24}$ = \$31 per unit

Substituting at high activity level:

Total cost	=	\$7,310
Total variable cost	= 50 × \$31	\$1,550
Therefore fixed cost	=	\$5,760

Estimated total costs of producing 100 units in 20X4:

Variable cost	= 100 × \$31 × 1.1	\$3,410
Fixed cost	= \$5,760 × 2	\$11,520
Total cost	=	\$14,930

Test your understanding 9

(a)	The line would cross the y axis at the point	1,488
(b)	The gradient of the line is	20
(c)	The independent variable is	x
(d)	The dependent variable is	y

Test your understanding 10

(a)	The fixed cost is $	4,800
(b)	The variable cost per unit is $	8
(c)	The total cost of producing 100 units is $	5,600

Working

Fixed cost = $4,800

Variable cost = 100 × $8 = $800

Total cost = fixed cost + variable cost = $4,800 + $800 = $5,600

Test your understanding 11

The code is:

EDSP

Test your understanding 12

(a) Sequence codes allocate a number, or a letter, to items in a simple list. Their main advantage lies in simplicity of allocation, but they provide no correlation between the items and their code numbers, and insertions and deletions are not so easily handled. It is much better to have the code progressing in groups of say 10 so that room is left for insertions.

(b) Block codes allocate bands of numbers to particular categories. With each category there is usually a limited amount of possible expansion. They have the merit of simplicity and give a more direct relationship between items and codes, which may help with indexing or information retrieval.

(c) Significant digit codes are when individual digits and letters are used to represent features of the coded item.

(d) Faceted codes are when the digits of the code are divided into facets of several digits and each facet represents some attribute of the item being coded. These codes are similar to significant digit codes but are purely numerical, which may be preferable in computer systems.

Test your understanding 13

B

300 for York followed by 500 for travel costs followed by 630 for the sales function.

Test your understanding 14

D

Codes representing the type of cost and responsibility centre will be used in the main ledger. The purchase ledger will contain codes representing individual suppliers so that details of supplier invoices and payments made to suppliers can be quickly accessed.

Test your understanding 15

C

It is more usual to code overhead costs to an overhead cost centre before sharing the costs to the cost centres that incur the cost.

Chapter

3

Accounting for materials

Chapter learning objectives

Upon completion of this chapter you will be able to:

- describe the systems necessary for the ordering, receiving and issuing of materials from inventory
- identify, explain and calculate the costs of ordering and holding inventory (including buffer inventory)
- describe and apply appropriate methods for establishing reorder levels where demand in the lead time is constant
- calculate and interpret the optimal reorder quantities
- calculate and interpret the optimal reorder quantities when discounts apply
- produce calculations to minimise inventory costs when inventory is gradually replenished
- calculate the value of closing inventory and material issues using LIFO, FIFO and average methods
- describe the control procedures used to monitor physical and 'book' inventory and to minimise discrepancies and losses
- interpret the entries and balances in the material inventory account
- explain Just in Time (JIT) as an inventory management approach.

PER

One of the PER performance objectives (PO1) is to take into account all relevant information and use professional judgement, your personal values and scepticism to evaluate data and make decisions. You should identify right from wrong and escalate anything of concern. You also need to make sure that your skills, knowledge and behaviour are up-to-date and allow you to be effective in your role. Working through this chapter should help you understand how to demonstrate that objective.

PER

One of the PER performance objectives (PO12) is to apply different management accounting techniques is different business contexts to effectively manage and use resources. Working through this chapter should help you understand how to demonstrate that objective.

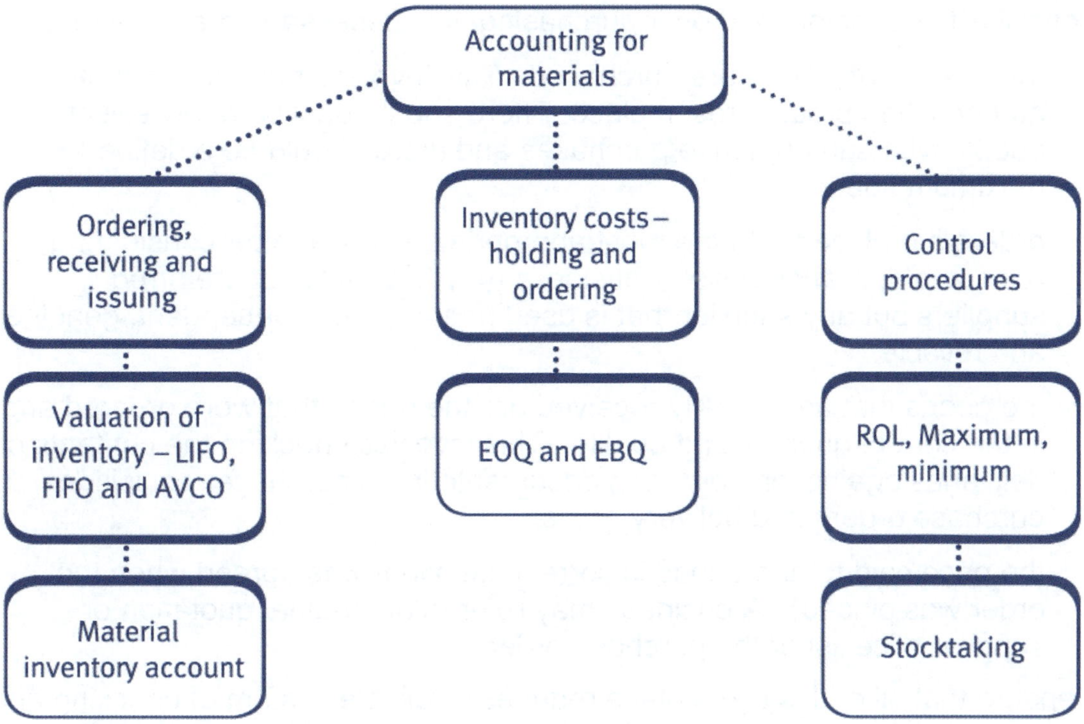

1 Inventory control

In a manufacturing business inventory (materials) may be the largest item of cost. The principal reasons why a business needs inventory are as follows:

- It acts as a buffer in times when there is an unusually high rate of consumption.
- It enables the business to take advantage of quantity discounts by buying in bulk.
- The business can take advantage of seasonal and other price fluctuations (e.g. an end of season sale).
- Any delay in production caused by lack of parts is kept to a minimum, so production processes will flow smoothly and efficiently.
- It may be necessary to hold inventory for a technical reason, for example, some food items need to 'mature'.

It is essential that the material purchased is the most suitable for the intended purpose. When material is required it must be ordered, received by the stores department, recorded, issued to the production department that requires it and eventually paid for. This process needs a great deal of organisation and strict internal controls.

If control is to be maintained over purchasing, it is necessary to ensure that:

- only necessary items are purchased. This involves have appropriate authorisation procedures in place. There should only be a few select people who can authorise purchases and there should be a defined maximum spend.
- orders are placed with the most appropriate supplier after considering price and delivery details. A business may have a list of preferred suppliers but any supplier that is used needs to be independent, genuine and reliable.
- the goods that are actually received are the goods that were ordered and in the correct quantity and quality. This involves checking the contents of deliveries against any ordering documentation – purchase requisitions, purchase orders and delivery notes.
- the price paid for the goods is correct (i.e. what was agreed when the order was placed). A business may refer to an original quotation or supplier price list or the purchase order.

To ensure that all of this takes place requires a reliable system of checking and control. Internal control consists of full documentation and appropriate authorisation of all transactions, movements of materials and of all requisitions, orders, receipts and payments. This used to be completed via various paper documents but is now mostly computerised.

Ordering, purchasing and receiving materials – documentation

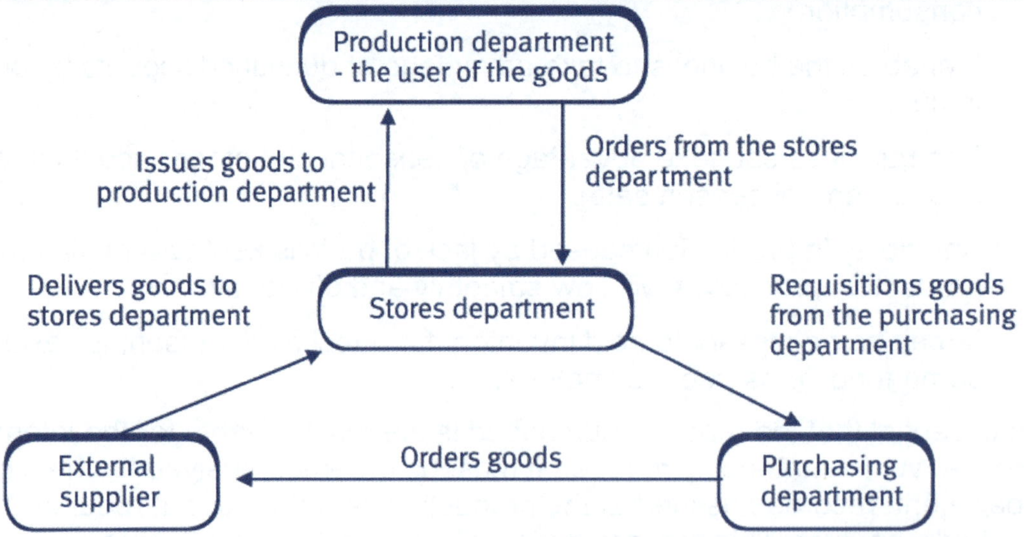

- **Materials requisitions** are issued by production departments. Their purpose is to authorise the stores department, or equivalent, to release the goods that have been requested. They may be used to update the stores records if the material is available for instant release.

- A **purchase requisition** is completed by the stores department, it must be authorised by the relevant manager and is sent to the purchasing department to request goods be ordered.
- On receipt of a properly authorised requisition, the purchasing department will select a supplier and create an order on a **purchase order** form.
- The purchase order form is sent to the supplier and copies are sent to the accounts department and the stores department.
- On receipt of the goods, the stores department will check the goods against the relevant purchase order, and check the **delivery note** that accompanies the goods.
- The supplier will send an **invoice** that details that money due to be paid for the goods that have been received.

Other documentation a business may encounter include:

- **Quotations** will be received from the supplier detailing the cost of goods to be ordered.
- **Material returns** are used to record any unused materials that are returned to stores from production or from the business to the supplier.
- **Goods returned notes** used to detail what is being returned to the supplier. The goods may be damaged or not as ordered.
- **Credit notes** are received if goods have been returned to the supplier or there is a fault with the invoice.

Computerised inventory control systems

Depending on the size of the businesses, there could be differing procedures for ordering, controlling and monitoring inventory levels.

The majority of large businesses will have some form of computerised system in place, so levels can be checked constantly and orders can be placed at an appropriate point or 'at the click of a button'. Smaller businesses may use paper records but that is becoming less common.

The computerised inventory control may fall into one or more of the categories below:

Extranet

An extranet is a controlled private network that allows access to partners, vendors and suppliers and authorised customers to access information from an organisation's intranet. An extranet provides access to needed services for authorised parties, without granting access to an organisation's entire network.

Examples of extranets

- A distribution network to maintain communication between suppliers and distributors.
- Ecommerce site integration to exchange inventory data via a secure network.

Advantages of extranets

- They can be used to share product catalogues exclusively with trade partners.
- They can improve efficiency through direct connection with customers and suppliers.

Disadvantages of extranets

- Extranets can be expensive to implement and maintain within an organisation (e.g., hardware, software, employee training costs), if hosted internally rather than by an application service provider.
- Security of extranets can be a concern when hosting valuable or personal information.

Transaction Processing Systems (TPS)

A TPS records historic information and represents the simple automation of previously manual systems.

For example, a TPS could be used to record the sales for a bookstore. At the end of each day, it could produce a summary of how many of each type of book has been sold. This would allow the operational managers to decide which books they need to order from their suppliers and how many books they need to buy in order to replenish their inventory.

A TPS routinely captures, processes, stores and outputs the low-level transaction data. This system is very important if data is input incorrectly it will affect every report produced using it, giving management misinformation and hence they may make poor decisions.

A TPS records all the daily transactions of the organisation and summarises them so they can be reported on a routine basis.

Transaction processing systems are used mainly by operational managers to make basic decisions.

Examples include:

- Sales/marketing systems – recording sales transactions and providing details on marketing and promotional activities.
- Manufacturing production systems – recording details of purchases, production and shipping of goods.
- Finance and accounting systems – maintenance of financial data in an organisation. The purchase ledger, sales ledger and payroll systems are all examples of a TPS system.

Management information systems (MIS)

A management information system (MIS) converts internal and external data into useful information that is then communicated to managers at all levels and across all functions to enable them to make timely and effective decisions for planning and controlling activities.

MIS provide information to all levels of management to enable them to make timely and effective decisions for planning and controlling the activities for which they are responsible. Middle managers will find these systems particularly useful:

- A MIS will collate information from individual transactions recorded in the accounting system to allow middle managers to control the business.
- Customer purchases are summarised into reports to identify the products and customers providing the most revenue.

Examples

Management information systems can be found in almost any organisation above a small size. For example:

- Car manufacturing systems – summarise sales of motor vehicles, in order to assist in trend analysis and purchase/production of components.
- Firm of accountants – summarising work performed on different audit engagements to assist in fee negotiation.
- Training company – provision of details of students booked on to different courses to indicate the size of lecture rooms required and volume of study material needed.
- Manufacturing company – provision of inventory ageing analysis to determine the amount of inventory provision in the financial statements.

Features of a management information system

Management information systems can be distinguished from other information systems within an organisation:

- They provide support for structured decision making at all management levels.
- They provide on-line access to the transaction processing systems of the organisation, to give summary information on the performance of the organisation.
- They provide an internal rather than external focus, with detail being provided internally about the organisation itself, rather than externally generated information about competitors or the overall economic environment.
- If required, they can provide more detailed information about the organisation's operations, or individual transactions, through a 'drill down' facility.
- An MIS produces relatively simple summary reports and comparisons, and does not contain the more detailed mathematical models or statistical techniques found in some other systems.

Illustration 1 – MIS

A company that operates a national chain of car showrooms could use an MIS for performance measurement.

The MIS could use the information from the sales TPS to generate reports such as:

- total sales for each type of car
- total sales made by each salesperson
- total sales by showroom or by geographic area.

This information could be extremely useful for control and performance appraisal purposes.

2 Inventory holding and ordering costs

Most businesses, whatever their size, will be concerned with the problem of which items to have in inventory and how much of each item should be kept.

Costs of carrying inventory

Irrespective of the nature of the business, a certain amount of inventory will need to be held.

However, holding inventory costs money and the principal 'trade-off' in an inventory holding situation is between the costs of acquiring and storing inventory and the level of service that the company wishes to provide.

The total cost of having inventory consists of the following:

- Purchase price
- Holding costs:
  - the opportunity cost of capital tied up
  - insurance
  - deterioration
  - obsolescence
  - damage and pilferage
  - warehouse upkeep
  - stores labour and administration costs.
- Ordering costs:
  - clerical and administrative costs – the total administrative costs of placing orders will increase in proportion to the number of orders placed. They therefore exhibit the behaviour of variable costs.
  - transport costs.

- Stock-out costs (items of required inventory are not available):
  - loss of sales
  - long-term damage to the business through loss of goodwill
  - production stoppages caused by a shortage of raw materials
  - extra costs caused by the need for emergency orders.
- Inventory recording systems costs:
  - maintaining the stores record card.

Costs of holding inventory

Holding costs can be distinguished between fixed holding costs and variable holding costs:

- Fixed holding costs include the cost of storage space and the cost of insurance. Note that the cost of storage space may be a stepped fixed cost if increased warehousing is needed when higher volumes of inventory are held.
- Variable holding costs include interest on capital tied up in inventory. The more inventory that is held, the more capital that is tied up.

Holding costs can be calculated as follows:

Total annual holding cost = holding cost per unit of inventory (Ch) × average inventory (Q/2).

Where average inventory held is equal to half of the order quantity Q.

Costs of ordering inventory

Ordering costs can be calculated as follows:

Total annual ordering cost = cost of placing an order (Co) × number of orders (D/Q).

Where the expected number of orders in a year (annual demand) D is divided by the order quantity Q.

Total annual cost of inventory

The Total Annual Costs (TAC) is the total of purchasing costs P multiplied by annual demand D plus total ordering costs (Co × D/Q) and total holding costs (Ch × Q/2):

Total annual cost = PD + (Co × D/Q) + (Ch × Q/2)

Costs of carrying buffer inventory

Buffer or safety inventory allows you to meet unpredictable peaks in demand, and it allows you to protect your customers from production breakdowns, supplier failures, or delays in deliveries from suppliers. It can also reduce the cost of purchasing as inventory levels should never get to a critical level.

However, buffer inventory ties up cash that could be better invested in other parts of the business. It costs money in terms of the opportunity cost (what else the cash could be being used for), the cost to insure the inventory, the cost to store the product, and the cost of theft or damage.

Buffer inventory could also end up being a huge liability if the demand falls or the product becomes obsolete before you can use the inventory.

Disadvantages of low and high inventory levels

Disadvantages of low inventory levels

To keep the holding costs low it may be possible to reduce the volume of inventory that is kept but this can cause some problems:

- Customer demand cannot always be satisfied; this may lead to loss of business if customers become dissatisfied.
- In order to fulfil commitments to important customers, costly emergency procedures (e.g. special production runs) may become necessary in an attempt to maintain customer goodwill.
- It will be necessary to place replenishment orders more frequently than if higher inventories were held, in order to maintain a reasonable service. This will result in higher ordering costs being incurred.

Disadvantages of high inventory levels

To reduce the problems mentioned above management may consider holding high levels of inventory but again this can have issues:

- Storage or holding costs are very high; such costs will usually include rates, rent, labour, heating, deterioration, etc.
- The cost of the capital tied up in inventories, i.e. the cash spent to buy the inventory is not available to pay other bills.
- If the stored product becomes obsolete, a large inventory holding of that item could, at worst, represent a large capital investment in an unsaleable product whose cash value is only that of scrap.
- If a great deal of capital is invested in inventory, there will be proportionately less money available for other requirements such as improvement of existing production facilities, or the introduction of new products.

- When a high inventory level of a raw material is held, a sudden drop in the market price of that material represents a cash loss to the business for having bought at the higher price. It follows that it would seem sensible to hold higher inventories during an inflationary period and lower inventories during a period of deflation.

e.g

Illustration 2 – The cost of holding inventory

A company uses components at the rate of 6,000 units per year, which are bought in at a cost of $1.20 each from the supplier. The company orders 1,000 units each time it places an order and the average inventory held is 500 units. It costs $20 each time to place an order, regardless of the quantity ordered.

The total holding cost is 20% per annum of the average inventory held.

Required:

Calculate the annual ordering and holding costs.

Solution

$$\text{Annual ordering cost} = \frac{\text{Annual usage}}{\text{Order size}} \times \$20$$

$$= \frac{6{,}000}{1{,}000} \times \$20$$

$$= \$120$$

Annual holding cost

= average inventory held × cost per unit × 20%

= 500 units × $1.20 × 20%

= $120

Test your understanding 1

A company has recorded the following details for Component 427 which is sold in boxes of 10 components.

Ordering cost	$32 per order placed
Purchase price	$20 per box of 10 components
Holding cost	10% of purchase price
Monthly demand	1,500 components

Component 427 is currently ordered in batches of 240 boxes at a time. The average inventory held is 120 boxes.

Required:

Calculate the annual holding cost and the annual ordering cost for Component 427.

3 Systems of inventory control

Reorder level

The reorder level is the quantity of inventory in hand when a replenishment order should be placed. It is calculated with reference to the time it will take to receive the order (the lead time) and the possible requirements during that time.

If the demand in the lead time is constant, the reorder level is calculated as follows:

Reorder level = Maximum usage × Maximum lead time

e.g

Illustration 3 – Reorder levels

A company uses Component M at the rate of 1,500 per week. The time between placing an order and receiving the components is five weeks. The reorder quantity is 12,000 units.

Required:

Calculate the reorder level.

Solution

Reorder level	= Usage × Lead time
	= 1,500 units × 5 weeks = 7,500 units

Test your understanding 2

A national chain of tyre fitters stocks a popular tyre for which the following information is available:

Usage – 175 tyres per day

Lead time – 16 days

Reorder quantity – 3,000 tyres

Based on the data above, at what level of inventory should a replenishment order be issued in order to ensure that there are no stock-outs?

A 2,240

B 2,800

C 3,000

D 5,740

The economic order quantity (EOQ)

The EOQ is the reorder quantity which minimises the total costs associated with holding and ordering inventory (i.e. holding costs + ordering costs) are at a minimum.

We can estimate the EOQ graphically by plotting holding costs, ordering costs and total costs against different levels of re-order quantities.

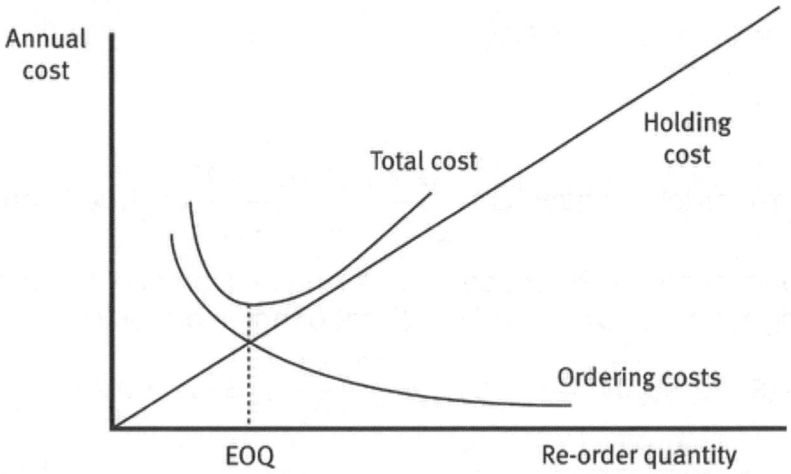

EOQ formula

The formula for the EOQ (or Q) is as follows:

$$Q = EOQ = \sqrt{\frac{2C_OD}{C_h}}$$ GIVEN

Where:

D = Demand per **annum**

C_o = Cost of placing **one** order

C_h = Cost of holding **one** unit for **one** year

Note that the formula for the EOQ is provided in your exam. You must make sure that you know what the different symbols represent so that you can use the formula correctly.

EOQ assumptions

There are a number of important assumptions related to the EOQ that you should note:

- Demand and lead time are constant and known
- Purchase price is constant
- No buffer inventory is held.

e.g

Illustration 4 – The economic order quantity (EOQ)

A company uses components at the rate of 500 units per month, which are bought in at a cost of $1.20 each from the supplier. It costs $20 each time to place an order, regardless of the quantity ordered.

The total holding cost is 20% per annum of the value of inventory held.

Required:

Calculate the EOQ and TAC

Solution

$$\text{Economic order quantity (Q)} = \sqrt{\frac{2 \times 20 \times 500 \times 12}{0.2 \times 1.2}} = 1{,}000 \text{ components}$$

Total annual cost = Purchase price × Annual Demand + (Cost of ordering × Annual Demand/Q) + (Cost of holding × Q/2)

$$\text{TAC} = (\$1.20 \times 500 \times 12) + \left(\$20 \times \frac{500 \times 12}{1{,}000}\right) + \left(\$1.20 \times 0.2 \times \frac{1{,}000}{2}\right) = \$7{,}440$$

Test your understanding 3

A company is planning to purchase 90,800 units of a particular item in the year ahead. The item is purchased in boxes each containing 10 units of the item, at a price of $200 per box. A safety inventory of 250 boxes is kept.

The cost of holding an item in inventory for a year (including insurance, interest and space costs) is 15% of the purchase price. The cost of placing and receiving orders is to be estimated from cost data collected relating to similar orders, where costs of $5,910 were incurred on 30 orders. It should be assumed that ordering costs change in proportion to the number of orders placed. 2% should be added to the above ordering costs to allow for inflation. Assume that usage of the item will be even over the year.

The order quantity which minimises total costs is [ ] boxes

The EOQ with discounts

Quantity discounts

It is often possible to negotiate a quantity discount on a purchase price offered by a supplier if bulk orders are placed.

If a quantity discount is accepted this will have the following effects:

- The annual purchase price will decrease.
- The annual holding cost will increase.
- The annual ordering cost will decrease.

EOQ when quantity discounts are available

The steps involved in calculating the EOQ when quantity discounts are available are as follows:

- calculate the EOQ, ignoring discounts.

  If the EOQ is smaller than the minimum purchase quantity to obtain a bulk discount:

- calculate the total of the annual inventory holding costs, inventory ordering costs and inventory purchase costs at the EOQ.
- calculate the annual inventory holding costs, inventory ordering costs and inventory purchase costs quantity that qualifies for the bulk discount.
- compare the total costs and select the minimum cost alternative.
- if there is a further discount available for an even larger order size, repeat the same calculations for the higher discount level.

e.g

Illustration 5 – The EOQ with discounts

A company uses components at the rate of 500 units per month, which are bought in at a cost of $1.20 each from the supplier. It costs $20 each time to place an order, regardless of the quantity ordered.

The supplier offers a 5% discount on the purchase price for order quantities of 2,000 items or more. The current EOQ is 1,000 units.

The total holding cost is 20% per annum of the value of inventory held.

Required:

Should the discount be accepted?

Solution

Order quantity =	**1,000**		**2,000**
	$		$
Order cost			
(6,000/1,000 × $20)	120	(6,000/2,000 × $20) =	60
Holding cost			
(20% × $1.20 × 1,000/2)	120	($0.24 × 0.95 × 2,000/2) =	228
Purchase cost			
(6,000 × $1.20)	7,200	(6,000 × $1.20 × 0.95) =	6,840
Total annual costs	7,440		7,128

The discount should be accepted because it saves the company $312 ($7,440 – $7,128).

Test your understanding 4

Watton Ltd is a retailer of beer barrels. The company has an annual demand of 36,750 barrels. The barrels cost $12 each. Fresh supplies can be obtained immediately, but ordering costs and the cost of carriage inwards are $200 per order. The annual cost of holding one barrel in inventory is estimated to be $1.20. The economic order quantity has been calculated to be 3,500 barrels.

The suppliers introduce a quantity discount of 2% on orders of at least 5,000 barrels and 2.5% on orders of at least 7,500 barrels.

Required:

Determine whether the least-cost order quantity is still the EOQ of 3,500 barrels.

Economic batch quantity (EBQ)

Organisations who replenish inventory levels gradually by manufacturing their own products internally also need to calculate the most economical batch size to produce:

- The decisions faced by organisations that manufacture and store their own products involve deciding whether to produce large batches at long intervals OR produce small batches at short intervals.
- An amended EOQ model is used to help organisations to decide which course of action to take.
- The amended EOQ model is known as the Economic Batch Quantity (EBQ) model.
- As the items are being produced, there is a machine setup cost. This replaces the ordering cost of the EOQ.
- In the EOQ, inventory is replenished instantaneously whereas here, it is replenished over a period of time.
- Depending on the demand rate, part of the batch will be sold or used while the remainder is still being produced.

Large or small batches

- Producing large batches at long intervals will lead to low machine setup costs (as fewer machine setups will be needed) and high holding costs (high average inventory levels as more inventory held).
- Producing small batches at short intervals will lead to high machine setup costs (as more machine setups will be needed) and low holding costs (low average inventory levels as less inventory held).

The EBQ model is primarily concerned with determining the number of items that should be produced in a batch (compared to the size of an order with the EOQ).

The formula for the EBQ is as follows:

Economic batch quantity = $\sqrt{\dfrac{2C_oD}{C_h\left(1-\frac{D}{R}\right)}}$ GIVEN

Where:

Q = Batch size

D = Demand per **annum**

C_h = Cost of holding **one** unit for **one** year

C_o = Cost of setting up **one** batch ready to be produced

R = **Annual** replenishment rate

e.g

Illustration 6 – Gradual replenishment of inventory

The following is relevant for Item X:

- Production is at a rate of 500 units per week.
- Demand is 10,000 units per annum; evenly spread over 50 working weeks.
- Setup cost is $2,700 per batch.
- Storage cost is $2.50 per unit for a year.

Required:

Calculate the economic batch quantity (EBQ) for Item X.

Solution

Annual production rate, R = 500 × 50 = 25,000 units

Annual demand rate = 10,000 units

Cost per setup, C_o = $2,700

Cost of holding one item in inventory per year, C_h = $2.50

$$\text{EBQ} = \sqrt{\frac{2C_oD}{C_h\left(1-\left(\frac{D}{R}\right)\right)}} = \sqrt{\frac{2 \times 2{,}700 \times 10{,}000}{2.5\left(1-\frac{10{,}000}{25{,}000}\right)}} = 6{,}000 \text{ units}$$

Test your understanding 5

AB Ltd makes a component for one of the engines that it builds. It uses, on average, 2,000 of these components, steadily throughout the year. The component costs $16 per unit to make and it costs an additional $320 to setup the production process each time a batch of components is made. The holding cost per unit is 10% of the unit production cost.

The company makes these components at a rate of 200 per week, and the factory is open for 50 weeks per annum.

Required:

Calculate the EBQ.

Maximum and minimum inventory

Many inventory systems will also incorporate maximum and minimum inventory 'warning' levels, above or below which (respectively) inventory should not be allowed to rise or fall.

In practice, the maximum inventory level is fixed by taking into account:

- rate of consumption of the material
- time needed to obtain new supplies
- financial considerations due to high inventories tying up capital
- storage space with regard to the provision of space and maintenance costs
- extent to which price fluctuates
- risks of changing specifications
- possibility of loss by evaporation, deterioration, etc
- seasonal considerations as to both price and availability
- economic order quantities.

The minimum inventory level is fixed by taking into account:

- rate of consumption
- time needed to obtain delivery of supplies
- the costs and other consequences of stock-outs.

A simplified method of determining these control levels is by reference to the re-order level, re-order quantity and estimates of possible lead times and usage rates, as follows:

Minimum level = Re-order level – (Average usage × Average lead time)

Maximum level = Re-order level + Re-order quantity – (Minimum usage × Minimum lead time)

If at any time inventories fall below the minimum level, this is a warning that usage or lead time are above average. Thus the storekeeper will need to keep an eye on inventory levels and be prepared to place an emergency order if inventories get too low.

If inventories rise above the maximum level, then usage or lead time have actually been lower than the expected minimum. If it is usage, this may indicate a general decline in the demand for the inventory and the order quantity (and possibly the re-order level) should be reviewed to avoid holding excess inventory with associated holding costs.

Control procedures to minimise discrepancies and losses

The level of investment in inventory and the labour costs of handling and recording or controlling them is considerable in many organisations. It is for this reason that organisations must have control procedures in place in order to minimise discrepancies and losses.

Stocktaking

The process of stocktaking involves checking the physical quantity of inventory held on a certain date and then checking this balance against the balances on the stores ledger (record) cards or bin cards. Stocktaking can be carried out on a **periodic basis** or a **continuous basis**.

- **Periodic stocktaking** involves checking the balance of every item of inventory on the same date, usually at the end of an accounting period.
- **Continuous stocktaking** involves counting and valuing selected items of inventory on a rotating basis. Specialist teams count and check certain items of inventory on each day. Each item is checked at least once a year with valuable items being checked more frequently.
- Any differences (or discrepancies) which arise between 'book' inventory and physical inventory must be investigated.
- In theory any differences, as recorded in the stores ledger or the bin card, must have arisen through faulty recording.
- Once the discrepancy has been identified, the stores ledger card is adjusted in order that it reflects the true physical inventory count.
- Any items which are identified as being **slow-moving** or **obsolete** should be brought to the attention of management as soon as possible.
- Management will then decide whether these items should be disposed of and written off to the statement of profit or loss.
- Slow-moving items are those inventory items which take a long time to be used up.
- Obsolete items are those items of inventory which have become out of date and are no longer required.

Examples of other issues and controls

Issue	Control procedure
Ordering goods at inflated prices	• Use of standard costs for purchases • Quotation for special items
Fake purchases	• Separation of ordering and purchasing • Physical controls over materials receipts, usage and inventory
Shortages on receipts	• Checking in all goods inwards at gate • Delivery signatures
Losses from inventory	• Regular stocktaking • Physical security procedures
Writing off obsolete or damaged inventory which is good	• Control of responsible official over all write-offs
Losses after issue to production	• Records of all issues • Standard usage allowance

Inventory losses and waste

- Inventory losses may be quantified by comparing the physical quantity of an item held with the balance quantity recorded on the bin card and/or stores ledger card.
- There are two categories of loss: those which occur because of theft, pilferage, damage or similar means and those which occur because of the breaking of bulk receipts into smaller quantities.
- It is the second of these which are more commonly referred to as waste.
- Inventory losses must be written off against profits as soon as they occur. If the value to be written off is significant then an investigation should be made of the cause.
- When waste occurs as a result of breaking up bulk receipts, it is reasonable to expect that the extent of such wastage could be estimated in advance based upon past records. Either of two accounting treatments could then be used:
  - Issues continue to be made and priced without any adjustment and the difference at the end of the period is written off.
  - Alternatively, the issue price is increased to compensate for the expected waste.

- Suppose that a 100 metre length of copper is bought for $99. The estimated loss caused by cutting into shorter lengths as required is 1%.
- The issue price could be based on the expected issues of 99 metres, i.e. $1 per metre rather than pricing the copper at:

  Issue price= $\frac{\$99}{100}$ = $0.99/metre

4 Valuing inventory

Perpetual inventory

Perpetual inventory is the recording as they occur of receipts, issues and the resulting balances of individual items of inventory in either quantity or quantity and value.

- The majority of companies will now have automated/computerised stores ledger cards to record the inflow (receipts) and outflow (issues) of inventory.
- An example of a stores ledger card is shown below.

STORES LEDGER CARD

Description: .... Unit: .... Location: .... Code: ....

Maximum: .... Minimum: .... Reorder level: .... Reorder quantity: ....

Receipts			Issues			On order		
Date/ref	Quantity	$	Date/ref	Quantity	$	Date/ref	Quantity	$

Inventory valuation is important for:

- Financial reporting
  - for inclusion in the financial statements of a business
- Costing
  - to calculate how much to charge for a product based on the amount of inventory consumed.

To charge units of inventory with an appropriate value the business will consistently use an appropriate basis:

- FIFO (First In First Out)
- LIFO (Last In First Out)
- AVCO or WACO (Weighted Average Cost)

All will be illustrated using following information.

Illustration 7 – Inventory valuation

M Ltd had the following material transactions during the first week in March.

		Quantity (units)	Unit cost ($)
Opening balance	1st March	10	2.00
Receipts	2nd March	70	2.20
Issues	3rd March	40	
Receipts	4th March	50	2.30
Issues	5th March	70	

Note: per unit prices are rounded to 2 decimal places and total figures are to the nearest whole number.

FIFO

- Assumes that materials are issued out of inventory in the order in which they were delivered into inventory.
- Appropriate for many businesses (e.g. retailer selling fresh food using sell-by date rotation techniques).

Illustration 8 – FIFO inventory valuation

Date	Receipts			Issues			Balance		
	Units	Unit cost ($)	Total cost ($)	Units	Unit cost ($)	Total cost ($)	Units	Unit cost ($)	Total cost ($)
Op/Bal							10	2.00	20
2nd Mar	70	2.20	154				10	2.00	20
							70	2.20	154
									174
3rd Mar				10	2.00	20	40	2.20	88
				30	2.20	66			
				40		86			
4th Mar	50	2.30	115				40	2.20	88
							50	2.30	115
									203
5th Mar				40	2.20	88	20	2.30	46
				30	2.30	69			
				70		157			

- Closing inventory valuation = Opening inventory + receipts – issues

  = $20 + ($154 + $115) – ($86 + $157) = $46

Features of FIFO

Advantages:	Disadvantages:
• Logical – reflects the most likely physical flow. • Easily understood. • Inventory values at up-to-date prices. • Acceptable to HM Revenue and Customs and IAS2.	• Issues may be at out-of-date prices. • In times of rising prices reported profits are high ('high' closing inventory valuations). • Cost comparisons between jobs are difficult.

LIFO

- Assumes that materials are issued out of inventory in the reverse order to which they were delivered. An uncommon method which is only appropriate for a few businesses
  - e.g. a coal merchant who stores coal inventories in a large 'bin'.

e.g **Illustration 9 – LIFO inventory valuation**

Date	Receipts			Issues			Balance		
	Units	Unit cost ($)	Total cost ($)	Units	Unit cost ($)	Total cost ($)	Units	Unit cost ($)	Total cost ($)
Op/Bal							10	2.00	20
2nd Mar	70	2.20	154				10	2.00	20
							70	2.20	154
									174
3rd Mar				40	2.20	88	10	2.00	20
							30	2.20	66
									86
4th Mar	50	2.30	115				10	2.00	20
							30	2.20	66
							50	2.30	115
									201

5th Mar				50	2.30	115	10	2.00	20
				20	2.20	44	10	2.20	22
				——		——			——
				70		159			42

- Closing inventory valuation = Opening inventory + receipts – issues $20 + ($154 + $115) – ($88 + $159) = $42

Features of LIFO

Advantages:	**Disadvantages:**
• Issue prices are up-to-date. • In times of rising prices, reported profits are reduced (as in this example where closing inventory is valued at 'lower' cost).	• Not usually acceptable to the HM Revenue & Customs and accounting standards. • Inventory values may become very out-of-date. • Cost comparisons between jobs are difficult.

AVCO

- All issues and inventory are valued at an average price.
- The average price is recalculated after each receipt.
- Cumulative weighted average price = $\frac{\text{Total costs before issue}}{\text{Total number of units before issue}}$
- Could be appropriate for businesses such as an oil merchant, where deliveries are fully mixed in with existing inventory.

e.g. Illustration 10 – AVCO inventory valuation

Date	**Receipts**			**Issues**			**Balance**		
	Units	**Unit cost** ($)	**Total cost** ($)	**Units**	**Unit cost** ($)	**Total cost** ($)	**Units**	**Unit cost** ($)	**Total cost** ($)
Op/Ball							10	2.00	20
2nd Mar	70	2.20	154				80	2.18	174
3rd Mar				40	2.18	87	40		87

4th Mar	50	2.30	115				90	2.24	202
5th Mar				70	2.24	157	20		45

- AVCO price after 2nd March delivery
  = ($20 + $154)/(10 + 70) = $174/80 = $2.18 per unit
- Closing inventory valuation = Opening inventory + receipts – issues
  = $20 + ($154 + $115) – ($87 + $157) = $45

Features of AVCO

Advantages:	**Disadvantages:**
• Acceptable to Accounting Standards and HM Revenue & Customs. • Logical because units all have the same value.	• Issue prices and inventory values may not be an actual purchase price (as in above example). • Inventory values and issue prices may both lag behind current values (e.g. issue on 5 March is at $2.244/unit whereas most recent purchase price = $2.30/unit).

The following information relates to TYUs 6 to 9.

A business had opening inventory of 300 units valued at $4.50 per unit on 1 May. The following receipts and issues were recorded in May:

2 May	Issue	200 units
7 May	Receipt	500 units @ $4.80 per unit
13 May	Issue	400 units
20 May	Receipt	500 units @ $5.00 per unit
28 May	Issue	450 units

Test your understanding 6

What is the value of issues during the month using the FIFO method?

A $4,750

B $5,000

C $5,030

D $5,080

Test your understanding 7

What is the value of issues during the month using the LIFO method?

A $4,750

B $5,000

C $5,030

D $5,070

Test your understanding 8

What is the value of closing inventory?

	FIFO method	LIFO method
A	$1,180	$1,250
B	$1,250	$1,180
C	$1,250	$730
D	$1,180	$730

Test your understanding 9

What is the value of closing inventory using the AVCO method? (per unit values to 2 decimal places)

A $1,180

B $1,231

C $1,250

D $1,282

5 Just in time (JIT)

Just in time is an approach based on the idea that goods and services should be produced only when they are needed. JIT aims to have zero inventories of raw materials, work in progress or finished goods.

JIT **production** is defined as:

A production system which is driven by demand for finished products whereby each component on a production line is produced only when needed for the next stage.

JIT **purchasing** is defined as:

A purchasing system in which material purchases are contracted so that the receipt and usage of material, to the maximum extent possible, coincide.

These definitions give JIT the appearance of being merely an alternative production management system. However, JIT is better described as a philosophy, or approach to management, as it encompasses a commitment to continuous improvement and the pursuit of excellence in the design and operation of the production management system.

The JIT philosophy is based on:

- Continuous improvement ('kaizen') – doing things well and gradually doing them better
- The elimination of waste – overproduction of goods, waste in the process, holding inventory, defective goods.

To be able to operate a JIT system there are a number of requirements:

- High quality – materials and the production system must be reliable
- Speed – the production system must be fast to enable customer orders to be met when placed
- Flexibility – the production system must be able to respond immediately to customer orders and be flexible to order size.

The benefits of a JIT system include:

- Less cash tied up in inventory
- Less storage space needed
- Better quality output
- More flexible production and better co-ordination
- Reliable and supportive suppliers.

The problems with JIT:

- requires predictable demand, flexible suppliers and a flexible workforce to be successful
- no fall-back position (buffer) if production is disrupted.

e.g

Toyota

Organisations in the West have traditionally used a 'push' production flow system. This system has the following stages:

1 Buy raw materials and put them into inventory.

2 Produce a production schedule based on sales forecasts.

3 Withdraw goods from inventory and make products according to the production schedule.

4 Put completed units into finished goods store.

5 Sell from finished goods store when customers request products.

Work in progress (WIP) is an unavoidable feature of such a system.

Toyota developed a different system known as JIT. This system is not a 'push' system but a 'pull' system. A product is not 'made' until the customer requests it, and components are not made until they are required by the next production stage. In a full JIT system, virtually no inventory is held, that is no raw material inventory and no finished goods inventory is held, but there will be a small amount of WIP, say one-tenth of a day's production. The system works by the customer triggering the final stage of production, the assembly. As the product is assembled, components are used and this in turn triggers the component stage of production and a small amount of WIP is made ready for the next product. So the cycle goes on until the final trigger requests more raw material from the supplier.

A 'push' system

A 'pull' system

If a JIT system is to work satisfactorily, suppliers must deliver several times a day and so when the raw material arrives it may go straight into the factory and be used immediately. This means that the production lead-time (i.e. the time from raw materials entering production to the finished goods emerging) should equal the processing time. In many Western organisations in the past it took several months to make a product from start to finish, despite the fact that if worked on continuously it could be made in, say, two days. The difference in time is largely due to WIP waiting to be used in the next process.

It will be apparent that value is only added to the product during the actual processing stages. These have been estimated to represent as little as 10 per cent of the total manufacturing lead-time in many companies, and thus up to 90 per cent of production time adds costs but no value.

JIT requires the following:

1 The **labour force must be versatile** so that they can perform any job within reason to keep production flowing as required. Workers in a JIT cell are trained to operate all the machines within it, and perform routine preventive maintenance on them.

2 Production processes must be **grouped by product line,** rather than by function in order to eliminate inventory movements between workstations and to speed flow.

3 A simple, **infallible information system**. Originally the Japanese used a system based on cards which were called Kanban. There would be a small container of components (WIP) between each workstation with a Kanban resting on top. When the container was taken for use by the following workstation the card would be taken off and left behind. This would act as a trigger for the previous workstation to produce another container of that component. Nowadays computer systems are likely to be used instead of cards but the basic simplicity of the system should not change.

4 A **'get it right first time'** approach and an aim of 'zero defects'. Defects cause breakdowns in the value chain: they stop the flow of production, create expensive rework and lead to late deliveries to customers.

5 **Strong supplier relationships**. Suppliers must take responsibility for the quality of their goods; the onus is on the supplier to inspect the parts or materials before delivery and guarantee their quality. The considerable savings in inspection costs go happily with the benefits of increased quality to achieve cost reduction – another facet of continuous improvement. This enhanced level of service is obtained by reducing the number of suppliers and increasing the business given to each of them. Longer-term commitments are entered into, assuring the supplier of continuity of demand, and enabling the supplier to plan to meet customers' production schedules. In essence the supplier becomes a key part of the value chain.

An important consequence of the 'pull' system, is that problems in any part of the system will immediately halt the production line, as earlier workstations will not receive the 'pull' signal and later stations will not have their own 'pull' signals answered.

This has the powerful effect of concentrating all minds on finding a long-term solution to the problem. JIT exposes problems within a plant, and forces management to address problems and rectify them, rather than simply burying them by holding excess inventory.

The aims of JIT are to produce the required items, at the required quality and in the required quantities, at the precise time they are required.

6 Accounting for inventory – the material inventory account

Material inventory account

Materials held in stores are an asset and are recorded as inventory in the statement of financial position of a company.

Accounting transactions relating to materials are recorded in the material inventory account.

Material inventory account

Debit entries reflect an **increase** in inventory	Credit entries reflect a **decrease** in inventory
• purchases	• issues to production
• returns to stores	• returns to suppliers

e.g

Illustration 11 – Accounting for inventory

Material inventory account

	$000		$000
Opening balance (1)	33	Work-in-progress (4)	137
Payables (2)	146	Materials returned to suppliers (5)	2
		Production overhead account (6)	4
Materials returned to stores (3)	4		
		Statement of profit or loss (7)	3
		Closing balance (8)	37
	183		183

1 The opening balance of materials held in inventory at the beginning of a period is shown as a debit in the material inventory account.

2 Materials purchased on credit are debited to the material inventory account.

3 Materials returned to stores cause inventory to increase and so are debited to the material inventory account.

4 **Direct** materials used in production are transferred to the **work-in-progress** account by crediting the material inventory account.

5	Materials returned to suppliers cause inventory levels to fall and are therefore 'credited out' of the material inventory account.
6	**Indirect** materials are not a direct cost of manufacture and are treated as **overheads**. They are therefore transferred to the production overhead account by way of a credit to the material inventory account.
7	Any material write-offs are 'credited out' of the material inventory account and transferred to the statement of profit or loss where they are written off.
8	The balancing figure on the material inventory account is the closing balance of material inventory at the end of a period. It is also the opening balance at the beginning of the next period.

Test your understanding 10

Transaction	Debit which account?	Credit which account?
Issue materials to production.		
Purchase new materials on credit.		
Materials returned to store from production.		
Materials written off.		
Indirect materials transferred to production overheads.		

7 Chapter summary

Accounting for materials

Computerised inventory control

- Extranet
- TPS
- MIS

Valuation of inventory:

- LIFO
- FIFO
- AVCO

Material inventory account:

- Dr when material enters stores
- Cr when material leaves stores

Inventory costs

Holding costs:

- Interest on capital
- Storage
- Insurance
- Stock outs

Ordering:

- Administrative
- Clerical
- Delivery

EOQ and EBQ

$$EOQ = \sqrt{\frac{2 \times C_o \times D}{C_h}}$$

$$EBQ = \sqrt{\frac{2C_oD}{C_h(1-D/R)}}$$

Control procedures

- Re-order level
- Maximum and minimum inventory levels

Stocktaking:

- Periodic
- Continuous

Just in Time (JIT)

- Continuous improvement
- Elimination of waste
- High quality
- Speed
- Flexibility

Test your understanding answers

Test your understanding 1

Annual holding cost = average inventory held × cost per box × 10%

= 120 × $20 × 10% = $240

Annual usage (in boxes) = $\frac{1,500}{10}$ × 12 months = 1,800 boxes

Annual ordering cost = $\frac{\text{Annual usage}}{\text{Order size}}$ × $32

= $\frac{1,800}{240}$ × $32

= $240

Test your understanding 2

B

Reorder level = Usage × Lead time

= 175 × 16

= 2,800 units

Test your understanding 3

The order quantity which minimises total costs is **349 boxes**

Working

To avoid confusion this question is best tackled by working in boxes not units.

C_o =	5,910/30	× 1.02	= $200.94
C_h =	0.15	× $200	= $30 per box
D =	90,800/10		= 9,080 boxes
EOQ	$\sqrt{(2 \times 200.94 \times 9,080/30)}$		= 349 boxes

Test your understanding 4

Order size	3,500 barrels	5,000 barrels	7,500 barrels
Purchase cost	36,750 × \$12 = \$441,000	36,750 × \$12 × 98% = \$432,180	36,750 × \$12 × 97.5% = \$429,975
Holding cost	\$1.20 × 3,500/2 = \$2,100	\$1.20 × 5,000/2 = \$3,000	\$1.20 × 7,500/2 = \$4,500
Ordering cost	\$200 × 36,750/3,500 = \$2,100	\$200 × 36,750/5,000 = \$1,470	\$200 × 36,750/7,500 = \$980
Total cost	\$445,200	\$436,650	\$435,455

Total costs are minimised with an order size of 7,500 barrels.

Test your understanding 5

D		= 2,000 units
R	= 200 × 50	= 10,000 units
C_o		= \$320
C_h	= 10% of \$16	= \$1.60

$$EBQ = \sqrt{\frac{2C_oD}{C_h\left(1-\frac{D}{R}\right)}} = \sqrt{\frac{2 \times 320 \times 2{,}000}{1.60\ (1-2{,}000/10{,}000)}} = 1{,}000 \text{ units}$$

Test your understanding 6, 7 and 8

TYU 6 B, TYU 7 D, TYU 8 B

Workings

FIFO

Date	Receipts			Issues			Balance		
	Units	Unit cost (\$)	Total cost (\$)	Units	Unit cost (\$)	Total cost (\$)	Units	Unit cost (\$)	Total cost (\$)
Op/Ball							300	4.50	1,350
2nd May				200	4.50	900	100	4.50	450
7th May	500	4.80	2,400				100	4.50	450
							500	4.80	2,400
							600		2,850

13th May				100 300 —— 400	4.50 4.80	450 1,440 —— 1,890	200	4.80	960
20th May	500	5.00	2,500				200 500 —— 700	4.80 5.50	960 2,500 —— 3,460
28th May				200 250 —— 450	4.80 5.00	960 1,250 —— 2,210	250	5.00	**1,250**

Total cost of FIFO issues = $900 + $1,890 + $2,210 = $5,000

LIFO

Date	Receipts			Issues			Balance		
	Units	**Unit cost** ($)	**Total cost** ($)	**Units**	**Unit cost** ($)	**Total cost** ($)	**Units**	**Unit cost** ($)	**Total cost** ($)
Op/Ball							300	4.50	1,350
2nd May				200	4.50	900	100	4.50	450
7th May	500	4.80	2,400				100 500 —— 600	4.50 4.80	450 2,400 —— 2,850
13th May				400	4.80	1,920	100 100 —— 200	4.50 4.80	450 480 —— 930
20th May	500	5.00	2,500				100 100 500 —— 700	4.50 4.80 5.50	450 480 2,500 —— 3,430
28th May				450	5.00	2,250	100 100 50 —— 250	4.50 4.80 5.00	450 480 250 —— **1,180**

Total cost of LIFO issues = $900 + $1,920 + $2,250 = $5,070

Test your understanding 9

B

Date	Receipts			Issues			Balance		
	Units	Unit cost ($)	Total cost ($)	Units	Unit cost ($)	Total cost ($)	Units	Unit cost ($)	Total cost ($)
Op/Ball							300	4.50	1,350
2nd May				200	4.50	900	100	4.50	450
7th May	500	4.80	2,400				100	4.50	450
							500	4.80	2,400
							600		2,850
13th May				400	4.75	1,900	200		950
20th May	500	5.00	2,500				200		950
							500	5.00	2,500
							700		3,450
28th May				450	4.93	2,219	250	5.00	**1,231**

Test your understanding 10

Transaction	Debit which account?	Credit which account?
Issue materials to production.	Work-in-progress.	Material inventory account.
Purchase new materials on credit.	Material inventory account.	Payables.
Materials returned to store from production.	Material inventory account.	Work-in-progress account.
Materials written off.	Statement of profit or loss.	Material inventory account.
Indirect materials transferred to production overheads.	Production overhead account.	Material inventory account.

Chapter

4

Accounting for labour

Chapter learning objectives

Upon completion of this chapter you will be able to:

- calculate direct and indirect costs of labour
- explain the systems used to capture and record labour effort
- prepare the journal and ledger entries to record labour costs inputs and outputs
- interpret entries in the labour account
- describe different remuneration methods: time-based systems; piecework systems and individual and group incentive schemes
- calculate the level, and analyse the costs and causes of labour turnover
- explain and calculate labour efficiency, capacity and production volume ratios.

PER

One of the PER performance objectives (PO12) is to apply different management accounting techniques is different business contexts to effectively manage and use resources. Working through this chapter should help you understand how to demonstrate that objective.

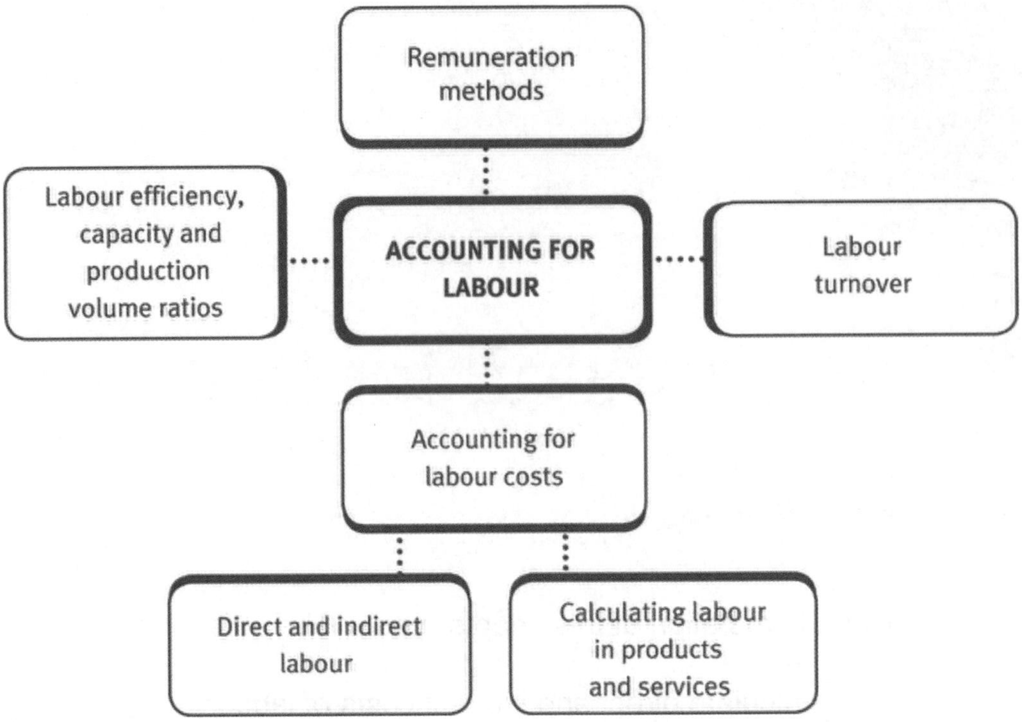

1 Remuneration systems

Payroll department

The payroll department is involved in carrying out functions that relate input labour costs to the work done.

- Preparation of the payroll involves calculating gross wages from time and activity records.
- The payroll department also calculates net wages after deductions from payroll.
- The payroll department also carries out an analysis of direct wages, indirect wages, and cash required for payment.

Time-related systems

The most common remuneration method is to calculate pay or wages based on the number of hours an employee works.

- Employees are paid a basic rate per hour, day, week or month.
- Time-based systems do not overall provide any incentive for employees to improve productivity and close supervision is often necessary.
- Overtime can be paid at a premium if any extra hours are worked. Overtime is looked at in more detail in section 3.
- The formula for a time-based system is as follows.

Total wages = (total hours worked × basic rate of pay per hour) + (overtime hours worked × overtime premium per hour)

- A guaranteed minimum wage is often required due to minimum wage requirements.

Time records

It is essential that organisations employ relevant methods in both manufacturing and service industries to relate the labour costs incurred to the work done. One of the ways in which this can be done is to make records of the time spent by employees doing jobs.

- Time recording is required both for payment purposes and also for determining the costs to be charged to specific jobs.
- In many manufacturing industries employees used to be supplied with an attendance record on which to record their time of arrival and departure from the factory. Such records are known as time cards (gate or clock cards) and are used to calculate wages and rates of pay. There has been a move to plastic 'swipe' cards directly linked to a central computer as technology has improved.

Output related systems

A **piecework** system pays a fixed amount per unit produced. The formula for a piecework system is as follows.

Total wages = (units produced × rate of pay per unit)

- A guaranteed minimum wage is often required due to minimum wage requirements.
- Piecework is often combined with a time-based system to provide an added incentive to employees.

Types of piecework system

There are two main piecework systems that you need to know about:

- **Straight piecework systems** – the same rate per unit is paid no matter how many units are produced. These systems are almost extinct today as employees are more likely to be paid a guaranteed minimum wage within a straight piecework system.
- **Differential piecework systems** – these systems are the most widely used piecework systems and involve different piece rates for different levels of production.

Illustration 1 – Piecework schemes

A company operates a piecework system of remuneration, but also guarantees its employees 75% of a time-based rate of pay which is based on $19 per hour for an eight hour working day. Each unit should take 3 minutes to produce (standard time). Employees are paid based on the number of hours their output should have taken (standard hours). Piecework is paid at the rate of $18 per standard hour.

If an employee produces 200 units in eight hours on a particular day, what is the employee gross pay for that day?

Solution

200 units × standard time of 3 minutes per unit = 600 minutes, or 10 hours.

Employee gross pay = 10 hours × $18 = $180

Guaranteed ($19 × 8 hours) × 75% = $152 × 75% = $114

As gross pay exceeds the guaranteed amount, the answer is $180.

Test your understanding 1

The following graph shows the wages earned by an employee during a single day.

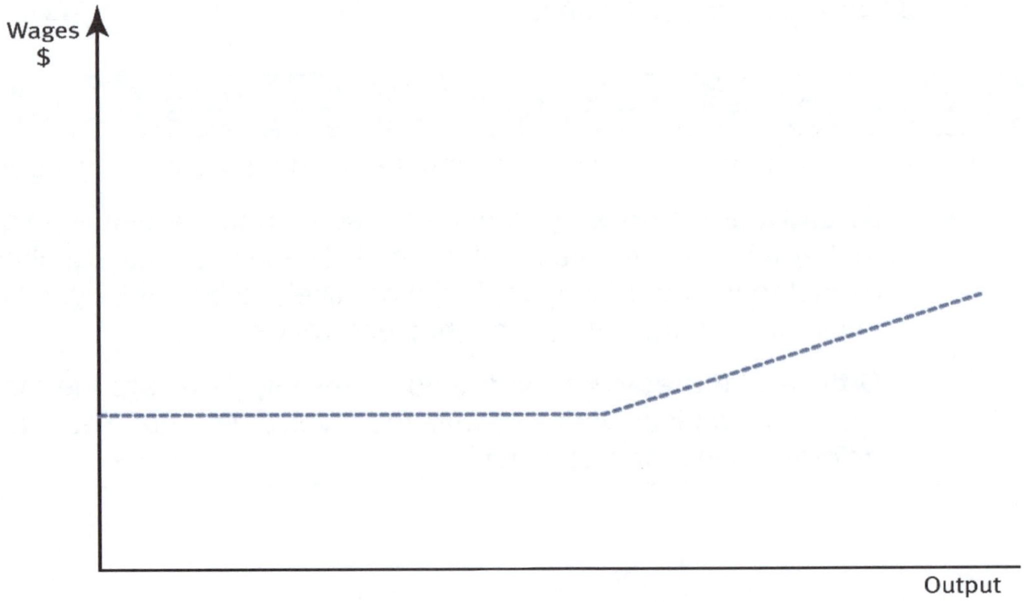

Which one of the following remuneration systems does the graph represent?

A Differential piecework

B A flat rate per hour with a premium for overtime working

C Straight piecework

D Piecework with a guaranteed minimum daily wage

Activity time records

Another method of relating work done to costs incurred is by the use of activity time records. Activity time records may be either period related or task related.

- Period-related timesheets are commonly used in service industries, for example in accountancy firms where time spent working for different clients is analysed, often to the nearest 15 minutes. Management information systems (MIS) can be used to log and record the time taken and this will feed directly into the invoicing system.
- Period-related timesheets are records that may cover days, weeks or sometimes longer periods.
- Task-related activity time records are known as job sheets, operations charts or piecework tickets.

There are two basic approaches to remuneration – time-related or output-related.

Overtime and overtime premiums

If employees are entitled to extra pay when hours in excess of contracted hours are worked then they will be paid for **overtime**. When employees work overtime, they receive an **overtime payment** which includes a **basic pay** element and an **overtime premium**.

- For example, if Fred is paid a basic wage of \$8 per hour and overtime is paid at time and a half, when Fred works overtime, he will receive an overtime payment of \$12 per hour (\$8 basic + \$4 premium (50% × \$8)).

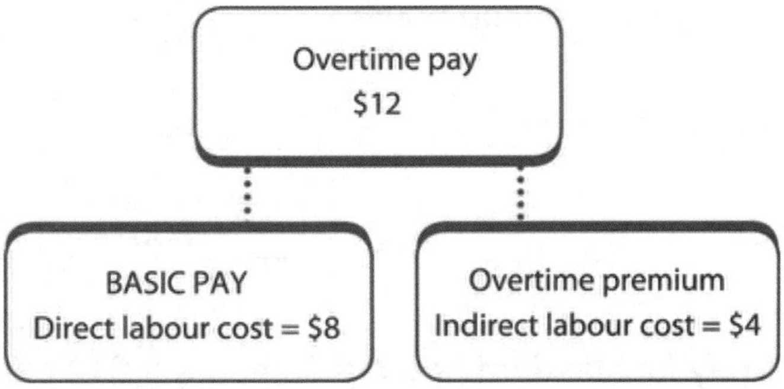

It is important that the overtime payment is analysed correctly into direct and indirect labour costs.

- Basic pay (whether it relates to overtime or normal working hours) is always classified as a direct labour cost for direct labour workers.
- Overtime premiums are usually classified as an indirect labour cost but if the extra hours are at the **specific request of a customer** because they want a job to be finished as soon as possible they can be classified as direct labour.
- Employees who work night shifts, or other anti-social hours may be entitled to a shift allowance or shift premium. Shift premiums are similar to overtime premiums where the extra amount paid above the basic rate is treated as an indirect labour cost.

Illustration 2 – Overtime

Vienna is a direct labour employee who works a standard 35 hours per week and is paid a basic rate of $12 per hour. Overtime is paid at time and a third. In week 8 she worked 42 hours and received a $50 bonus.

Required:

Calculate the following labour costs and state if it is a direct or indirect cost:

	Labour cost	Direct or Indirect
Basic pay for standard hours	$	
Basic pay for overtime hours	$	
Overtime premium	$	
Bonus	$	

Solution

		Labour cost	Direct or Indirect
1	Basic pay for standard hours	$420	Direct
2	Basic pay for overtime hours	$84	Direct
3	Overtime premium	$28	Indirect
4	Bonus	$50	Indirect

Workings

1 Basic pay for standard hours = 35 hours × $12 per hour = $420

Basic pay for standard hours is a **direct labour cost** because the work involved is directly attributable to production.

2 Basic pay for overtime hours = 7 hours × $12 = $84. This is also a **direct labour cost** because the **basic rate for overtime** is part of the direct labour cost. It is the **overtime premium** which is usually part of the indirect labour cost.

3 Overtime premium = 1/3 of $12 = $4

Total overtime premium = 7 hours × $4 = $28

Unless overtime is worked at the specific request of a customer, overtime premium is part of the **indirect labour costs** of an organisation.

Test your understanding 2

A company operates a factory which employed 40 direct workers throughout the four-week period just ended. Direct employees were paid at a basic rate of $4.00 per hour for a 38-hour week. Total hours of the direct workers in the four-week period were 6,528. Overtime, which is paid at a premium of 35%, is worked in order to meet general production requirements. Employee deductions total 30% of gross wages. 188 hours of direct workers' time were registered as idle.

Calculate the direct and indirect costs for the four-week period just ended.

Direct labour cost	$
Indirect labour cost	$

Incentive schemes

Incentive schemes can be aimed at individuals and/or groups.

- Many different systems exist in practice for calculating bonus schemes. General rules are as follows:
  - They should be closely related to the effort expended by employees.
  - They should be agreed by employers/employees before being implemented.
  - They should be easy to understand and simple to operate.
  - They must be beneficial to all of those employees taking part in the scheme.
- Most bonus schemes pay a basic time rate, plus a portion of the time saved as compared to some agreed allowed time. These bonus schemes are known as **premium bonus plans**. For example:
  - The employee receives 50% of the time saved.

$$\text{Bonus} = \frac{\text{Time allowed} - \text{Time taken}}{2} \times \text{Time rate}$$

  - The proportion paid to the employee is based on the ratio of time taken to time allowed.

$$\text{Bonus} = \frac{\text{Time taken}}{\text{Time allowed}} \times \text{Time rate} \times \text{Time saved}$$

- **Measured day work** – the concept of this approach is to pay a high time rate, but this rate is based on an analysis of past performance. Initially, work measurement is used to calculate the allowed time per unit. This allowed time is compared to the time actually taken in the past by the employee, and if this is better than the allowed time an incentive is agreed, e.g. suppose the allowed time is 1 hour per unit and that the average time taken by an employee over the last three months is 50 minutes. If the normal rate is $12/hour, then an agreed incentive rate of $14/hour could be used.
- **Share of production** – share of production plans are based on acceptance by both management and labour representatives of a constant share of value added for payroll. Thus, any gains in value added – whether by improved production performance or cost savings – are shared by employees in this ratio.

e.g

Illustration 3 – Incentive schemes

The following data relate to Job A.

Employee's basic rate = $4.80 per hour

Allowed time for Job A = 1 hour

Time taken for Job A = 36 minutes

The employee is paid the basic rate for the allowed time for the job and then the bonus based on any time saved. The bonus is calculated based on the following formula:

$$\text{Bonus} = \frac{\text{Time taken}}{\text{Time allowed}} \times \text{Time rate} \times \text{Time saved}$$

Required:

Calculate the total payment for Job A

Solution

			$
Bonus	=	$\frac{36}{60} \times \frac{\$4.80}{60} \times 24$	1.15
Basic rate	=		4.80
Total payment for Job A			5.95

Test your understanding 3

Ten employees work as a group. When production of the group exceeds the standard – 200 pieces per hour – each employee in the group is paid a bonus for the excess production in addition to wages at hourly rates.

The bonus is computed thus: the percentage of production in excess of the standard quantity is found, and one half of the percentage is regarded as the employees' share. Each employee in the group is paid as a bonus this percentage of a wage rate of $5.20 per hour. There is no relationship between the individual worker's hourly rate and the bonus rate.

The following is one week's record:

	Hours worked	Production
Monday	90	24,500
Tuesday	88	20,600
Wednesday	90	24,200
Thursday	84	20,100
Friday	88	20,400
Saturday	40	10,200
	480	120,000

During this week, Jones worked 42 hours and was paid $3 per hour basic.

Complete the following.

1 The bonus rate for the week was $ ______

2 The total bonus for the group for the week was $ ______

3 The total pay for Jones for the week was $ ______

In the examination you will be given clear instructions on any bonus scheme in operation. You should follow the instructions given carefully in order to calculate the bonus payable from the data supplied.

2 Direct and indirect labour

One of the most important distinctions of labour is between **direct** and **indirect** costs.

- Direct labour costs make up part of the prime cost of a product and include the basic pay of direct workers.
- Direct workers are those employees who are directly involved in producing the output of the business.
- Indirect labour costs make up part of the overheads (indirect costs) and include the basic pay of indirect workers.
- Indirect workers are those employees who are **not** directly involved in producing the output of the business, (for example, maintenance staff, factory supervisors and canteen staff).
- Indirect labour costs also include the following:
  - Bonus payments.
  - Benefit contributions.
  - Idle time (when workers are paid but are not making any products, for example when a machine breaks down).
  - Sick pay.
  - Time spent by direct workers doing 'indirect jobs' for example, cleaning or repairing machines.

Test your understanding 4

Which one of the following should be classified as direct labour?

A Supervisors' salaries in a factory

B Maintenance workers looking after equipment in a hospital

C Bricklayers in a house building company

D Wages of cleaning and housekeeping personnel

3 Accounting for labour costs

Labour costs are recorded in an organisation's statement of profit and loss. Accounting transactions relating to labour are recorded in the labour account.

- The labour account is debited with the labour costs incurred by an organisation. The total labour costs are then analysed into direct and indirect labour costs.
- **Direct labour costs** are credited from the labour account and debited in the work-in-progress (WIP) account. Remember, direct labour is directly involved in production and are therefore transferred to WIP before being transferred to finished goods and then cost of sales.
- **Indirect labour costs** are credited from the labour account and debited to the production overheads account. It is important that total labour costs are analysed into their direct and indirect elements.

Illustration 4 – Accounting for labour costs

Labour account

	$000		$000
Bank (1)	80	WIP (2)	60
		Production overheads (3)	
		Indirect labour	14
		Overtime premium	2
		Shift premium	2
		Sick pay	1
		Idle time	1
	80		80

1 Labour costs incurred are paid out of the bank before they are analysed further in the labour account.

2 The majority of the labour costs incurred by a manufacturing organisation are in respect of direct labour costs. Direct labour is directly involved in production and the cost incurred is transferred out of the labour account via a credit entry, to the WIP account.

3 Indirect labour costs include indirect labour (costs of indirect labour workers), overtime premium (unless overtime is worked at the specific request of a customer), shift premium, sick pay and idle time. All of these indirect labour costs are collected in the production overheads account. They are transferred there via a credit entry out of the labour account and then debited in the production overheads account.

Test your understanding 5

The following information is taken from the payroll records of a company.

	Direct workers	Indirect workers	Total
	$	$	$
Basic pay for basic hours	43,000	17,000	60,000
Overtime – basic pay	10,000	4,500	14,500
Overtime – premium	5,000	2,250	7,250
Training	2,500	1,250	3,750
Sick pay	750	250	1,000
Idle time	1,200	–	1,200

Required:

Using the information given, complete the labour account shown below:

Labour account

	$000		$000
	——		——
	——		——

4 Labour ratios

Labour turnover

Labour turnover is a measure of the proportion of people leaving relative to the average number of people employed.

- Management might wish to monitor labour turnover, so that control measures might be considered if the rate of turnover seems too high.
- Labour turnover is calculated for any given period of time using the following formula:

$$\frac{\textbf{Number of leavers who require replacement}}{\textbf{Average number of employees}} \times \mathbf{100}$$

e.g

Illustration 5 – Labour turnover

At 1 January a company employed 3,641 employees and at 31 December employee numbers were 3,735. During the year 624 employees chose to leave the company.

Required:

What was the labour turnover rate for the year?

Solution

$$\text{Labour turnover rate} = \frac{\text{Number of leavers who require replacement}}{\text{Average number of employees}} \times 100$$

Average number of employees in the year = (3,641 + 3,735) ÷ 2 = 3,688.

$$\text{Labour turnover rate} = \frac{624}{3{,}688} \times 100\% = 16.9\%$$

Test your understanding 6

A company had 4,000 staff at the beginning of 20X8. During the year, there was a major restructuring of the company and 1,500 staff were made redundant and 400 staff left the company to work for one of the company's main competitors. 400 new staff joined the company in the year to replace those who went to work for the competitor.

Required:

Calculate the labour turnover rate for 20X8.

Causes and costs of labour turnover

Causes

It is important to try to identify why people leave an organisation and to distinguish between avoidable and unavoidable causes of labour turnover.

- Causes of labour turnover – avoidable:
  - poor remuneration
  - poor working conditions
  - lack of training opportunities
  - lack of promotion prospects
  - bullying in the workplace.
- Causes of labour turnover – unavoidable:
  - retirement
  - illness/death
  - family reasons (e.g. pregnancy)
  - relocation.
- Efficient managers will investigate high levels of labour turnover and aim to keep that turnover rate at a minimum.

Costs

Every time an employee leaves, an organisation will incur costs that are associated with replacing the employee. These costs are known as replacement costs.

- Replacement costs include the following:
  - advertising costs
  - cost of selection (time spent interviewing etc.)
  - training new employees
  - reduced efficiency until the new employee reaches the required skill.

- A high labour turnover rate tends to lower the performance of employees who remain in the organisation. Such employees may become restless and resentful of the extra burden of training new members and of additional temporary duties imposed upon them.
- In order to keep the labour turnover rate to a minimum, organisations should aim to prevent employees from leaving. Such preventive measures come with their own costs, known as preventive costs.
- Preventive costs include the costs associated with escaping the avoidable causes of labour turnover:
  - pay competitive wages and salaries if remuneration is poor
  - improve poor working conditions
  - offer good training opportunities
  - make sure promotion prospects arise as necessary
  - stamp out bullying in the workplace
  - investigate high labour turnover rates objectively.

Labour efficiency ratio

Labour is a significant cost in many organisations and it is important to continually measure the efficiency of labour against pre-set targets.

- The labour efficiency ratio measures the performance of the workforce by comparing the actual time taken to do a job with the expected or standard time.
- The standard time is how long it should take to complete the actual output.
- The labour efficiency ratio is calculated using the following formula:

$$\frac{\textbf{Standard hours for actual output}}{\textbf{Actual hours worked to produce output}} \times 100$$

Idle time ratio

Sometimes the workforce is 'idle' through no fault of its own, and cannot get on with productive work. This happens if machines break down, or needs to be reset for a new production run. An idle time ratio can be calculated as follows:

$$\frac{\textbf{Idle hours}}{\textbf{Total hours}} \times 100$$

Labour capacity ratio

The labour capacity ratio measures the number of hours spent actively working as a percentage of the total hours available for work (full capacity or budgeted hours). The labour capacity ratio is calculated using the following formula:

$$\frac{\textbf{Actual hours worked to produce output}}{\textbf{Total budgeted hours}} \times 100$$

Labour production volume ratio ('activity' ratio)

- The labour production volume ratio compares the number of hours expected to be worked to produce actual output with the total hours available for work (full capacity or budgeted hours).
- The labour production volume ratio is calculated using the following formula:

$$\frac{\textbf{Standard hours for actual output}}{\textbf{Total budgeted hours}} \times 100$$

e.g

Illustration 6 – Labour efficiency, capacity and production volume ratios

A company budgets to make 800 units in 400 hours in a period.

Actual output during the period was 840 units which took 410 hours to make.

Required:

Calculate the labour efficiency, capacity and production volume ratios.

Solution

Standard hours = 400 hours/800 units = 0.5 hours per unit.

Standard hours for actual output = 840 units × 0.5 hours per unit = 420 standard hours

Labour efficiency ratio:

$$\frac{\text{Standard hours for actual output}}{\text{Actual hours worked to produce output}} \times 100\%$$

$$= 420/410 \times 100\% = 102\%$$

Labour capacity ratio:

$$\frac{\text{Actual hours worked to produce actual output}}{\text{Total budgeted hours}} \times 100\%$$

$$= 410/400 \times 100\% = 102.5\%$$

Production volume ratio:

$$\frac{\text{Standard hours for actual output}}{\text{Total budgeted hours}} \times 100\%$$

$$= 420/400 \times 100\% = 105\%$$

Test your understanding 7

A company budgets to make 40,000 units of Product DOY in 4,000 hours in a year.

Actual output during the year was 38,000 units which took 4,180 hours to make.

Required:

Calculate the labour efficiency, capacity and production volume ratios.

5 Chapter summary

ACCOUNTING FOR LABOUR

Remuneration methods

- Time-based systems
- Piecework systems
- Individual incentive schemes
- Group incentive schemes

Labour efficiency capacity and production volume ratios

Labour is significant cost in many organisations – important to use these ratios to continually 'measure' how it is doing by reference to effciency, capacity and production volume ratios

Accounting for labour costs

Debit labour account with labour costs incurred

Credit labour account with direct labour – transfer to WIP

Credit labour account with indirect labour – transfer to production overheads account

Labour turnover

Measure of proportion of employees leaving relative to the average number of people employed

Many causes and costs of labour turnover – both avoidable and unavoidable

Direct and indirect labour

Direct labour – makes up part of prime cost and includes basic pay of direct workers

Indirect labour – makes up part of overheads and includes basic pay of indirect workers

Overtime premiums are treated as overheads unless worked at specific request of customer when treated as direct cost

Calculating labour in products and services

- Swipe cards
- MIS

Test your understanding answers

Test your understanding 1

D

The graph represents a piecework system (as shown by the gentle upward-sloping line) with a guaranteed minimum daily wage (as shown by the horizontal line).

Test your understanding 2

Direct labour cost	$25,360
Indirect labour cost	$1,379.20

Workings

Basic time	= 40 workers × 38 hrs/week × 4 weeks	= 6,080 hrs
Overtime	= Total time – Basic time	
	= 6,528 – 6,080	= 448 hrs
Productive time	= Total time – Idle time	
	= 6,528 – 188	= 6,340 hrs
Direct labour	= 6,340 hours at $4.00 per hour	= $25,360
Indirect labour	= Overtime premium + Idle time costs	
	= (448 hours × $4.00 × 35%) + (188 hours × $4.00/hr)	= $1,379.20

Test your understanding 3

1	The bonus rate for the week was $	0.65
2	The total bonus for the week was $	312
3	The total pay for Jones for the week was $	153.30

Workings

Standard production for the week = 480 hours × 200 = 96,000 pieces

Actual production for the week = 120,000 pieces

Excess production = 120,000 – 96,000 = 24,000

1 Bonus rate = 24,000 ÷ 96,000 × 0.5 × $5.20

= $0.65 per hour

2	Total bonus	= 480 hours × $0.65
		= $312
3	Pay for Jones	= 42 × (3.00 + 0.65)
		= $153.30

Test your understanding 4

C

Test your understanding 5

Labour account

	$		$
Bank	87,700	WIP (43,000 + 10,000)	53,000
		Production overheads	
		Indirect labour	21,500
		(17,000 + 4,500)	
		Overtime premium	7,250
		Training	3,750
		Sick pay	1,000
		Idle time	1,200
	87,700		87,700

Test your understanding 6

Number of staff at beginning of year = 4,000

Number of staff at end of year = 4,000 – 1,500 – 400 + 400 = 2,500

Labour turnover rate =

$$\frac{\text{Number of leavers who require replacement}}{\text{Average number of employees}} \times 100$$

$$\text{Average number of employees in the year} = \frac{4,000 + 2,500}{2} = 3,250$$

$$\text{Labour turnover rate} = \frac{400}{3,250} \times 100\% = 12.3\%$$

Test your understanding 7

Standard hours for actual output = 38,000 × 0.1 hours = 3,800 standard hours.

Labour efficiency ratio:

$$\frac{\text{Standard hours for actual output}}{\text{Actual hours worked to produce output}} \times 100\%$$

$$= (3,800/4,180) \times 100\% = 91\%$$

Labour capacity ratio:

$$\frac{\text{Actual hours worked to produce output}}{\text{Total budgeted hours}} \times 100\%$$

$$= (4,180/4,000) \times 100\% = 104.5\%$$

Production volume ratio:

$$\frac{\text{Standard hours for actual output}}{\text{Total budgeted hours}} \times 100\%$$

$$= \frac{3,800}{4,000} \times 100\% = 95\%$$

Chapter

5

Accounting for overheads

Chapter learning objectives

Upon completion of this chapter you will be able to:

- explain the different treatment of direct and indirect expenses
- describe the procedures involved in determining production overhead absorption rates
- allocate and apportion production overheads to cost centres using an appropriate basis
- reapportion service cost centre costs to production cost centres (including using the reciprocal method where service cost centres work for each other)
- select, apply and discuss appropriate bases for absorption rates
- prepare journal and ledger entries for manufacturing overheads incurred and absorbed
- calculate and explain the under and over absorption of overheads.

PER

One of the PER performance objectives (PO12) is to apply different management accounting techniques is different business contexts to effectively manage and use resources. Working through this chapter should help you understand how to demonstrate that objective.

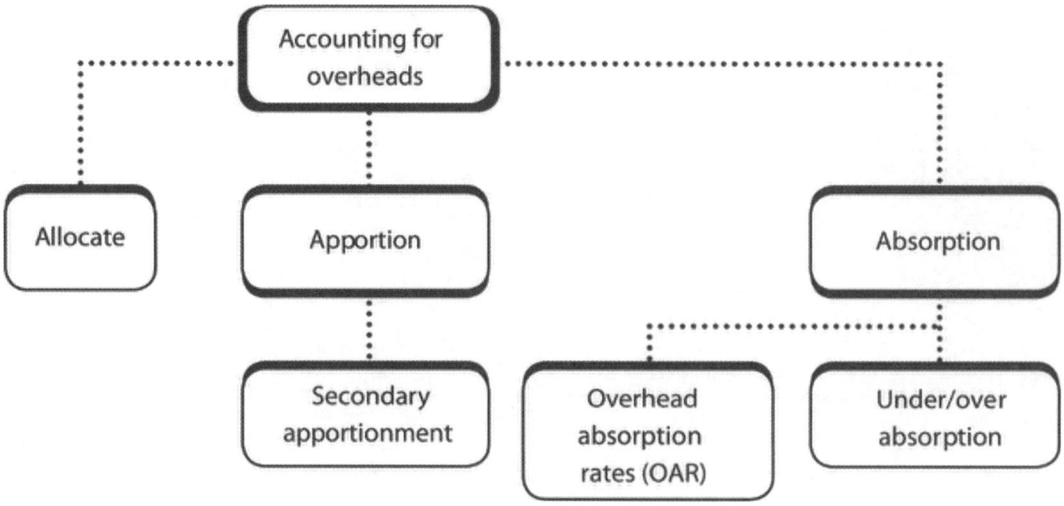

1 What are overheads?

Direct expenses are expenses that **can** be directly identified with a specific cost unit or cost centre.

- There are not many examples of direct expenses but royalties paid to a designer or fees paid to a subcontractor for a specific job could be classed as direct expenses.
- Direct expenses, direct materials and direct labour are the **prime** cost of a product.

Indirect expenses are expenses that **cannot** be directly identified with a specific cost unit or cost centre.

- The cost of renting a factory is classified as an indirect cost as the rent could be covering the manufacturing location of all products and also possibly other areas of the business such as the accounting department, a non-production location. It is not possible to relate the rent to a single products or location.
- Indirect expenses, indirect materials and indirect labour are the **overheads** of a business.

Production (manufacturing) overheads

Overheads can be grouped based on where in the business they are incurred:

- Production/manufacturing
- Administration
- Sales and distribution.

This chapter focuses on how production overheads are absorbed into the products being manufactured.

Production overheads of a factory can include the following costs:

- heating the factory
- lighting the factory
- renting the factory.

Production may take place over a number of different production cost centres and each cost centre should be assigned with its fair share of overhead cost. Examples of production cost centres include:

- Assembly
- Machining
- Finishing.

There may also be a number of production service cost centres that provide support to the production cost centres. Examples of production service cost centres include:

- Maintenance
- Canteen
- Stores.

Absorption costing

Production overheads are recovered by absorbing them into the cost of a product and this process is called absorption costing.

- The main aim of absorption costing is to recover overheads in a way that fairly reflects the amount of time and effort that has gone into making a product or service.
- Absorption costing involves the following stages:
  - allocation and apportionment of overheads to the different production cost centres
  - reapportionment of production service cost centre overheads to the production cost centres
  - absorption of overheads into the products.
- Absorption costing allows businesses to make decisions about pricing policies and value its inventory in accordance with IAS 2.

> **IAS 2**
>
> IAS 2 *Inventories* defines cost as comprising: 'all costs of purchase, costs of conversion and other costs incurred in bringing the inventories to their present location and condition'.
>
> Specifically excluded are:
>
> (a) abnormal amounts of wasted materials, labour and other production costs
>
> (b) storage costs, unless necessary in the production process before a further production stage
>
> (c) administrative overheads that do not contribute to bringing inventories to their present location and condition
>
> (d) selling costs.

2 Allocation and apportionment

Allocation and apportionment of overheads

The first stage of the absorption costing process involves the allocation and apportionment of overheads.

- Allocation involves charging overheads directly to specific cost centres (production and/or service).
- If overheads relate to more than one production or service cost centre, then they must be shared between these cost centres using a method known as apportionment.
- Overheads must be apportioned between different production and service cost centres on a fair basis.

Bases of apportionment

There are no hard and fast rules for which basis of apportionment to use except that whichever method is used to apportion overheads, it must be fair. Possible bases of apportionment include the following:

- floor area – for rent and rates overheads
- carrying amount of non-current assets – for depreciation and insurance of machinery
- number of employees – for canteen costs.

Illustration 1 – Allocation and apportionment

LS Ltd has two production cost centres (Assembly and Finishing) and two production service cost centres (Maintenance and Canteen).

The following are budgeted costs for the next period:

Indirect materials	– $20,000
Rent	– $15,000
Electricity	– $10,000
Machine depreciation	– $5,000
Indirect labour	– $16,520

The following information is available:

	Assembly	Finishing	Maintenance	Canteen	Total
Area (sq metres)	1,000	2,000	500	500	4,000
kW hours consumed	2,750	4,500	1,975	775	10,000
Machine value($)	45,000	35,000	11,000	9,000	100,000
Staff	18	30	12	2	62
Direct labour hours	3,175	3,800	–	–	6,975
Indirect materials budget ($)	7,000	8,000	3,000	2,000	20,000
Indirect labour budget ($)	1,600	2,220	11,200	1,500	16,520

Required:

Complete the extract from the overhead analysis sheet shown below.

Solution

(W1) Indirect materials are allocated directly to the relevant cost centres.

(W2) Rent is apportioned to all cost centres based on the area occupied.

Total rent cost	= $15,000
Total area occupied	= 4,000 sq metres
Apportioned to Assembly cost centre	= area of assembly/total area × cost = 1,000/4,000 × $15,000 = $3,750

(W3) Electricity is apportioned to all cost centres on the basis of kW hours.

Total electricity costs	= $10,000
Total kW hours consumed	= 10,000 kW hours
Apportioned to Finishing cost centre	= 4,500/10,000 × $10,000 = $4,500

(W4) Machine depreciation is apportioned to all cost centres on the basis of machine value.

Total machine depreciation costs	= $5,000
Total machine value	= $100,000
Apportioned to Maintenance cost centre	= 11,000/100,000 × $5,000 = $550

(W5) Indirect labour costs are allocated directly to all cost centres based on the indirect labour budget for each cost centre.

Overhead analysis sheet

Overhead	**Basis of apportionment**	**Assembly** $	**Finishing** $	**Mainten -ance** $	**Canteen** $	**Total** $
Indirect materials	Allocated (W1)	7,000	8,000	3,000	2,000	20,000
Rent	Area (W2)	3,750	7,500	1,875	1,875	15,000
Electricity	kW Hours (W3)	2,750	4,500	1,975	775	10,000
Machine depreciation	Machine value (W4)	2,250	1,750	550	450	5,000
Indirect labour	Allocated (W5)	1,600	2,220	11,200	1,500	16,520

3 Reapportionment

Production service cost centres are not directly involved in making products and therefore the production overheads of service cost centres must be shared out between the production cost centres using a suitable basis. This is known as reapportionment or secondary apportionment.

There are 3 methods that can be used:

- **Direct** method – the cost of each production service cost centre is reapportioned to the production cost centres only.
- **Step down** method – used when one production service cost centre works or provides a service for other production service cost centres as well as the production cost centres.
- **Reciprocal** reapportionment (or the repeated distribution method) – used where production service cost centres work for each other as well as provide a service for the production cost centres.

e.g

Illustration 2 – Direct reapportionment

The total overheads allocated and apportioned to the production and service cost centres of LS Ltd are as follows:

Assembly	= $17,350
Finishing	= $23,970
Maintenance	= $18,600
Canteen	= $6,600

The canteen feeds the staff that work for the company in Assembly and Finishing. The number of employees in each cost centre:

	Assembly	Finishing	Maintenance	Canteen
Number of employees	18	30	12	2

The amount of time spent by the maintenance cost centre servicing equipment in the Assembly and Finishing cost centres has been analysed as follows:

Assembly	60%
Finishing	40%

Required:

Complete the overhead analysis sheet.

Solution

(W1) Canteen overheads are reapportioned on the basis of number of employees that work in the cost centres it services.

Total employees that eat in the canteen = 18 + 30 = 48

Reapportioned to Assembly cost centre = 18/48 × $6,600 = $2,475

Reapportioned to Finishing cost centre = 30/48 × $6,600 = $4,125

(W2) Assembly = 60% × $18,600 = $11,160

Finishing = 40% × $18,600 = $7,440

Overhead	Basis of apportionment	Assembly $	Finishing $	Maintenance $	Canteen $	Total $
Total from above		17,350	23,970	18,600	6,600	66,520
Reapportion canteen	Employees (W1)	2,475	4,125	–	(6,600)	–
Reapportion maintenance	% time (W2)	11,160	7,440	(18,600)	–	–
Total		30,985	35,535	0	0	66,520

Illustration 3 – Step down reapportionment

The total overheads allocated and apportioned to the production and service cost centres of LS Ltd are as follows:

Assembly	= $17,350
Finishing	= $23,970
Maintenance	= $18,600
Canteen	= $6,600

The canteen feeds all the staff that work for the company in maintenance, finishing and assembly but the maintenance staff do not provide support for the canteen equipment.

The amount of time spent by the maintenance cost centre servicing equipment in the Assembly and Finishing cost centres has been analysed as follows:

Assembly	60%
Finishing	40%

The number of employees in each cost centre:

	Assembly	Finishing	Maintenance	Canteen
Number of employees	18	30	12	2

Required:

Complete the overhead analysis sheet.

Solution

Workings

(W1) Canteen overheads are reapportioned on the basis of the number of employees that work in the cost centres it serves

Total employees that eat in the canteen = 18 + 30 + 12 = 60

Reapportioned to Assembly department = 18/60 × $6,600 = $1,980

(W2) Assembly = 60% × $19,920 = $11,952

Finishing = 40% × $19,920 = $7,968

Overhead	Basis of apportionment	Assembly $	Finishing $	Maintenance $	Canteen $	Total $
Total from above		17,350	23,970	18,600	6,600	66,520
Reapportion canteen	Employees (W1)	1,980	3,300	1,320	(6,600)	–
Subtotal		19,330	27,270	19,920	0	66,520
Reapportion maintenance	% time (W2)	11,952	7,968	(19,920)	–	–
Total		31,282	35,238	0	0	66,520

Test your understanding 1

A manufacturing company runs two production cost centres C1 and C2, and two service cost centres S1 and S2. The total allocated and apportioned overheads for each is as follows:

C1	C2	S1	S2
$12,000	$17,000	$9,500	$8,000

It has been estimated that each service cost centre does work for other cost centres in the following proportions:

	C1	C2	S1	S2
Percentage of service cost centre S1 to:	60%	40%	–	–
Percentage of service cost centre S2 to:	35%	35%	30%	–

After the reapportionment of service cost centre costs has been carried out, what is the total overhead for production cost centre C1?

A $17,700

B $19,140

C $21,940

D $23,240

Illustration 4 – Reciprocal reapportionment

The total overheads allocated and apportioned to the production and service cost centres of LS Ltd are as follows.

Assembly	= $17,350
Finishing	= $23,970
Maintenance	= $18,600
Canteen	= $6,600

The maintenance costs are to be reapportioned on the basis of time spent servicing equipment:

	Assembly	Finishing	Maintenance	Canteen
Time spent	50%	40%	–	10%

The Canteen cost centre's overheads are to be reapportioned on the basis of the number of employees in the other three cost centres.

	Assembly	Finishing	Maintenance	Canteen
Number of employees	18	30	12	2

Required:

Complete the overhead analysis sheet below and reapportion the service cost centres' overheads to the production cost centres.

Solution

(W1) reapportioned canteen to assembly = 18/60 × 6,600 = 1,980

(W2) reapportioned maintenance to assembly = 50% × 19,920 = 9,960

(W3) reapportioned canteen to assembly = 18/60 × 1,992 = 598

(W4) reapportioned maintenance to assembly = 50% × 398 = 199

Overhead	Assembly $	Finishing $	Maintenance $	Canteen $	Total $
Total from above	17,350	23,970	18,600	6,600	66,520
Reapportion canteen **(W1)**	1,980	3,300	1,320	(6,600)	–
Reapportion maintenance **(W2)**	9,960	7,968	(19,920)	1,992	–
Reapportion canteen **(W3)**	598	996	398	(1,992)	–
Reapportion maintenance **(W4)**	199	159	(398)	40	–
Reapportion canteen	12	20	8	(40)	–
Reapportion maintenance	4	3	(8)	1	–
Reapportion canteen	0	1	–	(1)	–
Total	30,103	36,417	0	0	66,520

Solution – Using equations

There is another option for calculating the total overhead in each production cost centre. Some people will find it a quicker option but others prefer to reapportion as in the previous solution. Whichever you choose you should arrive at the same answer.

Often you will find that the data for reapportioning is given in percentages. The amount of time spent by the maintenance cost centre servicing equipment in the other three cost centres has been analysed as percentages.

Assembly	50%
Finishing	40%
Canteen	10%

In this illustration we need to convert the relevant number of employees into percentages.

	Assembly	Finishing	Maintenance
Number of employees	18	30	12
Number of employees as a %	18/60 × 100 = 30%	30/60 × 100 = 50%	12/60 × 100 = 20%

Now we can produce two calculations that show the relationship between Maintenance and Canteen – the two service cost centres.

Maintenance = $18,600 (overhead already apportioned) + 20% of the Canteen overhead

Canteen = $6,600 (overhead already apportioned) + 10% of the Maintenance overhead

These can be shortened to:

M = 18,600 + 20%C

C = 6,600 + 10%M

Currently each formula has 2 unknowns in them – M and C. We can substitute one of the formulae into the other to calculate the unknowns:

M = 18,600 + 20% (6,600 + 10%M)

M is the only unknown.

Change the % to decimals.

M = 18,600 + 0.2 (6,600 + 0.1 M)

Remove the brackets.

M = 18,600 + (0.2 × 6,600) + (0.2 × 0.1 M)

M = 18,600 + 1,320 + 0.02M

Put the 'unknowns' together.

M – 0.02M = 18,600 + 1,320 0.98M = 19,920

Therefore **M = 19,920/0.98 = $20,327**

We now know M so can substitute into the formula for C.

C = 6,600 + 10%M

C = 6,600 + 0.1 × 20,327

C = $8,633

Final step is to then relate these amounts to the production centres:

Assembly = 17,350 + 0.5M + 0.3C

Assembly = 17,350 + (0.5 × 20,327) + (0.3 × 8,633)

Assembly = $30,103

Finishing = 23,970 + 0.4M + 0.5C

Finishing = 23,970 + (0.4 × 20,327) + (0.5 × 8,633)

Finishing = $36,417

Test your understanding 2

A company has three production cost centres, Alpha, Beta and Gamma, and two service cost centres, Maintenance (M) and Payroll (P). The following table shows how costs have been allocated and the relative usage of each service cost centre by other cost centres.

	Production			**Service**	
Cost centre	**Alpha**	**Beta**	**Gamma**	**M**	**P**
Costs	$3,000	$4,000	$2,000	$2,500	$2,700
Proportion M (%)	20	30	25	–	25
Proportion P (%)	25	25	30	20	–

Required:

Complete the overhead analysis sheet below and reapportion the service cost centre overheads to the production cost centres using the reciprocal method.

Overhead	**Alpha** $	**Beta** $	**Gamma** $	**M** $	**P** $
Total overheads					
Reapportion M					
Reapportion P					
Reapportion M					
Reapportion P					
Reapportion M					
Reapportion P					
Total					

4 Absorption

Bases of absorption

Once the overheads are allocated, apportioned and reapportioned into the production cost centres the overheads need to be related to or absorbed into the units of product.

- Overheads can also be absorbed into cost units using the following absorption bases:
  - units produced
  - machine-hour rate (when production is machine intensive)
  - labour-hour rate (when production is labour intensive)
  - percentage of prime cost
  - percentage of direct wages.

- Production overheads are usually calculated at the beginning of an accounting period in order to determine how much cost to assign to a unit before calculating a selling price.
- The overhead absorption rate (OAR) is calculated as follows:

$$\textbf{OAR} = \frac{\textbf{Budgeted production overhead}}{\textbf{Budgeted total of absorption basis}}$$

- The absorption basis is most commonly units of a product, labour hours, or machine hours.

It is usual for a product to pass through more than one cost centre during the production process. Each cost centre will normally have a separate OAR.

- For example, a machining cost centre will probably use a machine-hour OAR.
- Similarly, a labour-intensive cost centre will probably use a labour-hour OAR.

An alternative to individual cost centre OAR is a blanket OAR. With blanket OARs, only one absorption rate is calculated for the entire factory regardless of the cost centres involved in production. Blanket OARs are also known as single factory-wide OARs.

e.g

Illustration 5 – OAR per unit

RS Ltd is a manufacturing company producing Product P, which has the following cost card.

		$
Direct labour	2 hrs @ $5 per hour	10
Direct materials	1 kg @ $5 per kg	5
Direct expenses		1
Prime cost		**16**

RS Ltd produces and sells 1,000 units in a month. RS absorbed overheads based on the number of units produced.

Based on past experience, RS Ltd estimates its monthly overheads will be as follows.

	$
Heating	3,000
Power	2,000
Maintenance	500
Total	5,500

Required:

Calculate the total cost of one unit of product P

Solution

	$
Prime cost	16.00
Overheads $5,500/1,000 units	5.50
Total	**21.50**

Illustration 6 – OAR per hour

Ballard Ltd makes three products A, B and C. Each passes through two cost centres: Machining and Assembly.

Budgeted production in each cost centre by each product

	Units	**Machining**	**Assembly**
Product A	1,000	1 hr	1 hr
Product B	2,000	2 hrs	1/2 hr
Product C	500	None	4 hrs

Overheads are budgeted as follows:

Machining	**Assembly**
$100,000	$150,000

Required:

(a) Calculate the OAR per hour for each cost centre and the overall blanket OAR per hour.

(b) Calculate the overhead absorbed by Product B based on the individual cost centre OAR per hour.

Solution

(a) **Machining**

Total hours = (1,000 × 1) + (2,000 × 2) = 5,000 hours

OAR = $100,000/5,000 hours = $20 per hour

Assembly

Total hours = (1,000 × 1) + (2,000 × 0.5) + (500 × 4) = 4,000 hours

OAR = $150,000/4,000 hours = $37.50

Blanket OAR = $250,000/9,000 hours = 27.78

(b) Overhead absorbed by Product B

= (2 hours × $20) + (0.5 hours × $37.50) = $58.75

Test your understanding 3

The Major Gnome Manufacturing Company has two cost centres – Moulding and Painting – and uses a single production OAR based on direct labour hours. The budget and actual data for Period 6 are given below:

	Direct wages $	Labour hours	Machine hours	Production overhead $
Budget				
Moulding	24,000	4,000	12,000	180,000
Painting	70,000	10,000	1,000	100,000
	94,000	14,000	13,000	280,000
Actual				
Moulding	30,000	5,000	14,000	200,000
Painting	59,500	8,500	800	95,000
	89,500	13,500	4,800	295,000

During Period 6, a batch of Pixie Gnomes was made, with the following costs and times:

	Direct wages $	Labour hours	Machine hours
Moulding	726	120	460
Painting	2,490	415	38
	3,216	535	498

The direct material cost of the batch was $890.

Complete the following.

(a) Using a single blanket OAR based on labour hours:

The cost of the batch of Pixie Gnomes is $

(b) It has been suggested that appropriate cost centre OARs may be more realistic. The OAR in:

(i) the moulding cost centre is $

(ii) the painting cost centre is $

(c) Using cost centre OARs:

The cost of the batch of Pixie Gnomes is $

5 Under- and over-absorption

If the estimates for the budgeted overheads and/or the budgeted level of activity are different from the actual results for the year then this will lead to one of the following:

- under-absorption (recovery) of overheads
- over-absorption (recovery) of overheads.

Calculating an under- or over-absorption

There is a three step procedure:

Step 1 – calculate the OAR (based on budget)

$$\text{OAR} = \frac{\textbf{Budgeted overheads}}{\textbf{Budgeted level of activity}}$$

Step 2 – calculate the overhead absorbed by actual activity

Overheads absorbed = OAR × actual level of activity

Step 3 – Compare absorbed to actual

If at the end of this period, the overheads **absorbed are greater than the actual** overheads, then there has been an **over-absorption** of overheads.

If the overheads **absorbed are less than the actual** overheads, then there has been an **under-absorption** of overheads.

e.g

Illustration 7 – Under- and over-absorption of overheads

The following data relate to Lola Ltd for Period 8.

	Budget	Actual
Overheads	$80,000	$90,000
Labour hours worked	20,000	22,000

Required:

Calculate the under or over absorption of overheads.

Solution

$$\text{OAR} = \frac{\$80{,}000}{20{,}000} = \$4 \text{ per labour hour worked}$$

Overhead absorbed = 22,000 × $4	= $88,000
Actual overhead	= $90,000
Under-absorbed overhead	= $2,000

Test your understanding 4

The following data relate to Lola Ltd for Period 9.

	Budget	Actual
Overheads	$148,750	$146,200
Machine hours	8,500	7,928

Overheads were under/over* absorbed by $

* delete as appropriate

Working backwards

Sometimes you may be given information relating to the actual under- or over-absorption in a period and be expected to calculate the budgeted overheads or the actual number of hours worked.

Approach to working backwards

- As long as you remember the basic calculation involved in identifying an under/over-absorption, you should not have any problems.
- The main thing to remember is that if actual overheads are greater than absorbed overheads then we have under-absorption and any under-absorption need to be deducted from actual overheads incurred in order to calculate the overheads absorbed.
- Similarly, if over-absorption occurs, the over-absorption needs to be added to actual overhead in order to calculate the overheads absorbed.

Illustration 8 – Under- and over-absorption of overheads

A business absorbs its fixed production overhead on the basis of direct labour hours. The budgeted direct labour hours for week 24 were 4,200. During that week 4,050 direct labour hours were worked and the production overhead incurred was $16,700. The overhead was under-absorbed by $1,310.

Required:

Calculate the budgeted fixed overhead for the week (to the nearest $10).

Solution

Actual overhead	\$16,700
Under-absorbed	\$(1,310)
Overhead absorbed	\$15,390

$$\text{OAR} = \frac{15{,}390}{4{,}050} = \$3.80 \text{ per hour}$$

Budgeted fixed overhead = 4,200 × \$3.80 = \$15,960

Test your understanding 5

A business absorbs its fixed overheads on the basis of machine hours worked. The following figures are available for the month of June:

Budgeted fixed overhead	\$45,000
Budgeted machine hours	30,000
Actual fixed overhead	\$49,000

If there was an over-absorption of overhead of \$3,500, how many machine hours were worked in the month?

A 30,334

B 32,667

C 35,000

D 49,000

Diagrams of under- and over-absorption

If we consider that the budgeted overhead cost is fixed (it is budgeted to be a set amount) and the actual overhead cost is also a fixed amount (it has actually been incurred and is not going to change), then we could also assume that the overhead that is being absorbed behaves like a variable cost – the more actual activity there is the more cost will be absorbed.

Under-absorbed overheads

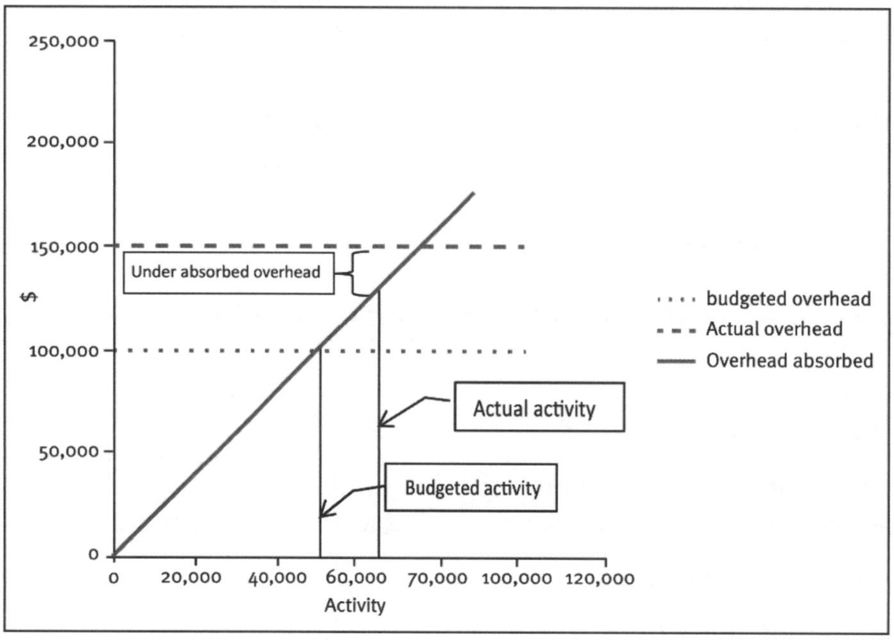

Over-absorbed overheads

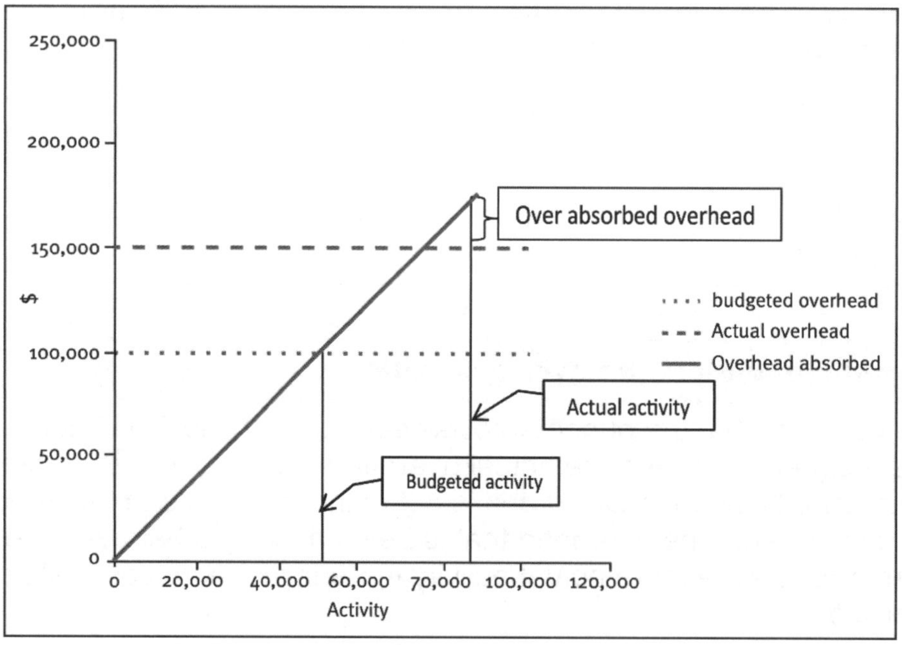

6 Accounting for production overheads

Production overheads account

Illustration 9 – Journal and ledger entries for manufacturing

Production overheads

	$000		$000
Indirect Labour (1)	20	WIP (2)	108
Indirect Expenses (1)	92	Under-absorption (Bal. figure) (3)	9
Indirect Material (1)	5		
	117		117

Over/under-absorption of overheads

	$000		$000
Production overheads (3)	9	Statement of profit or loss	9
	9		9

1 The production overheads account acts as a collecting place for all the indirect costs of a production process. All the costs are debited to this account.

2 Production overheads are absorbed into production on the basis of actual activity. The absorbed overheads are 'credited out' of the production overheads account and transferred to the WIP account where they are added to the cost of production, and hence the cost of sales.

3 The difference between the overheads absorbed and the overheads actually incurred is either an under- or over-absorption. This is the balancing figure and is transferred to the Over/under-absorption of overheads account. A debit balancing amount in the production overheads accounts is an over-absorption and a credit balancing amount is an under-absorption.

4 At the end of an accounting period, the balance on the over/under-absorption account is transferred to the statement of profit or loss where it is written off (under-absorbed overhead) or increases profit (over-absorbed overhead).

Test your understanding 6

Transaction	Debit which account?	Credit which account?
Indirect materials issued from stores		
Indirect wages analysed in the labour account		
Indirect expenses purchased (cash)		
Production overheads absorbed into the cost of production		
Direct materials issued from stores		

7 Chapter summary

Recap of direct and indirect expenses

- **Direct expenses are part of the prime cost of a product**
- **Indirect expenses are known as overheads**

Accounting for overheads

Journal and ledger entries for manufacturing overheads

Relating non-production overheads to cost units

Allocation and apportionment

- Allocation charges overheads directly to specific departments
- If overheads relate to more than one specific department they must be apportioned (shared) between departments
- Apportioned fixed production overheads include: rent, rates, heating and electricity costs

Reapportionment of service cost centre costs to production cost centres

Reapportionment involves sharing out the fixed production overheads of service cost centres between production cost centres

Basic method – one service department does work for another, but not vice versa

Production overhead absorption

Reciprocal method – both service departments do work for each other

Appropriate bases for absorption

- Machine-hour rate
- Labour-hour rate
- Percentage of prime cost
- Percentage of direct wages

Under- and over-absorption of overheads

If either or both of the estimates for budgeted overheads or budgeted level of activity are different from actual results then this will lead to under-or-over-absorption (recovery) of overheads

Test your understanding answers

Test your understanding 1

C

Allocated and apportioned overheads $12,000

Add: reapportionment of S1: 60% × $9,500 = $5,700

Add: reapportionment of S2 overhead apportioned to S1: $8000 × 30% × 60% = $1,440

Add: reapportionment of S2: 35% × $8,000 = $2,800

Total = $21,940

Test your understanding 2

Overhead	Alpha $	Beta $	Gamma $	M $	P $
Total overheads	3,000	4,000	2,000	2,500	2,700
Reapportion M	500	750	625	(2,500)	625
	(20%)	(30%)	(25%)		(25%)
Reapportion P	831	831	998	665	(3,325)
	(25%)	(25%)	(30%)	(20%)	
Reapportion M	133	200	166	(665)	166
	(20%)	(30%)	(25%)		(25%)
Reapportion P	41	42	50	33	(166)
	(25%)	(25%)	(30%)	(20%)	
Reapportion M	7	10	8	(33)	8
	(20%)	(30%)	(25%)		(25%)
Reapportion P	3	2	3		(8)
	(25%)	(25%)	(30%)		
Total	4,515	5,835	3,850		

Alternative answer (using equations)

M = 2,500 + 20% P

and

P = 2,700 + 25% M

Substitute the equation for P into the equation for M to have one unknown:

M = 2,500 + 20% (2,700 + 25% M)

Turn the percentages to decimals and multiply out the brackets:

M = 2,500 + (0.2 × 2,700) + (0.2 × 0.25M)
M = 2,500 + 540 + 0.05M

Put the unknowns together:

M – 0.05M = 2,500 + 540
0.95M = 3,040

Calculate was M equals:

M = 3,040/0.95
M = 3,200

Go to original equations to calculate P:

P = 2,700 + 25% M
P = 2,700 + 0.25 × 3,200
P = 3,500

Using the percentages in the original data for Alpha, Beta and Gamma we can calculate how much overhead each cost centre receives:

Alpha = 3,000 + (20% × 3,200) + (25% × 3,500)
Alpha = $4,515

Beta = 4,000 + (30% × 3,200) + (25% × 3,500)
Beta = $5,835

Gamma = 2,000 + (25% × 3,200) + (30% × 3,500)
Gamma = $3,850

Test your understanding 3

(a) Using a single blanket OAR based on labour hours:

The cost of the batch of Pixie Gnomes is **$14,806**

(b) It has been suggested that appropriate cost centre OARs may be more realistic. The OAR in:

(i) the moulding cost centre is **$15**

(ii) the painting cost centre is **$10**

(c) Using cost centre OARs:

The cost of the batch of Pixie Gnomes is **$15,156**

Workings

$$\text{Blanket OAR} = \frac{\$280{,}000}{14{,}000} = \$20 \text{ per labour hour}$$

(a) Cost of batch of Pixie Gnomes

	$
Direct materials	890
Direct labour	3,216
Overheads (535 hours @ $20 per hour)	10,700
TOTAL COST	14,806

(b)

	(i) Moulding	(ii) Painting
Budgeted overheads	$180,000	$100,000
Budgeted hours	12,000 machine hours	10,000 labour hours
OAR	$15 per machine hour	$10 per labour hour

(c) Cost of a batch of Pixie Gnomes using separate cost centre OARs

	$
Direct materials	890
Direct labour	3,216
Moulding overheads (460 × $15)	6,900
Painting overheads (415 × $10)	4,150
TOTAL COST	15,156

Test your understanding 4

Overheads were under absorbed by **$7,460**

OAR =	$\frac{\$148,750}{8,500}$	= $17.50 per machine hour
Overhead absorbed		= 7,928 × $17.50 = $138,740
Actual overhead		= $146,200
Under-absorbed overhead		= $7,460

Test your understanding 5

C

35,000 machine hours were worked in the month.

Workings

OAR =	$\frac{\$45,000}{30,000}$	= $1.50 per hour
Actual overhead	$49,000	
Over-absorbed overhead	$3,500	
Absorbed overhead	$52,500	

$$\text{Machine hours worked} = \frac{\text{Overheads absorbed}}{\text{Overhead absorption rate}}$$

$$= \frac{\$52,500}{\$1.50}$$

$$= 35,000 \text{ hours}$$

Test your understanding 6

Transaction	Debit which account?	Credit which account?
Indirect materials issued from stores	Production overheads account	Material inventory account
Indirect wages analysed in the labour account	Production overheads account	Labour account
Indirect expenses purchased (cash)	Production overheads account	Bank
Production overheads absorbed into the cost of production	WIP account	Production overheads account
Direct materials issued from stores	WIP account	Material inventory account

Chapter

6

Absorption and marginal costing

Chapter learning objectives

Upon completion of this chapter you will be able to:

- explain the importance of, and apply, the concept of contribution
- demonstrate and discuss the effect of absorption and marginal costing on inventory valuation and profit determination
- calculate profit or loss under absorption and marginal costing
- reconcile the profits or losses calculated under absorption and marginal costing
- describe the advantages and disadvantages of absorption and marginal costing.

PER

One of the PER performance objectives (PO12) is to apply different management accounting techniques is different business contexts to effectively manage and use resources. Working through this chapter should help you understand how to demonstrate that objective.

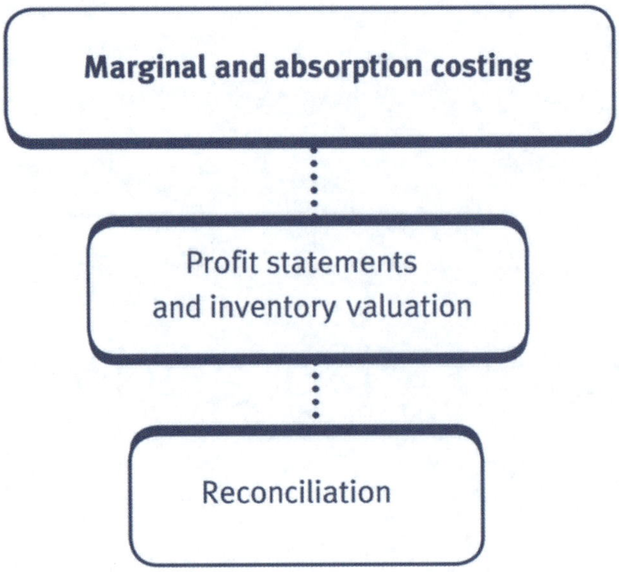

1 The treatment of fixed production overheads

Marginal and absorption costing are two different ways of valuing the cost of units sold and finished units in inventory. The basic unit cost consists of the direct costs; the difference arises due to the treatment of the production overheads:

- absorption costing assigns both the fixed and variable production overheads to each unit. See Chapter 5 for the allocation, apportionment, reapportionment and absorption techniques.
- marginal costing only assigns variable productions overheads to each unit. Fixed production overheads are treated as period costs.

2 Marginal costing

The marginal production cost is the cost of one unit of product or service which would be avoided if that unit were not produced, or which would increase if one extra unit were produced.

The **marginal** cost of a unit of inventory is the total of the **variable** costs required to produce the unit (the marginal cost). This includes direct materials, direct labour, direct expenses and variable production overheads.

No fixed overheads are included in the inventory valuation; they are treated as a period cost and deducted in full against the profits for the period.

Marginal costing is the principal costing technique used in decision making. The key reason for this is that the marginal costing approach allows management's attention to be focused on the changes which result from the decision under consideration.

The contribution concept

The contribution concept lies at the heart of marginal costing. Contribution can be calculated as follows:

Contribution = Sales price – All variable costs

e.g.

Illustration 1 – The concept of contribution

The following information relates to a company that makes a single product – a desk lamp.

	Per lamp		Sales of 1,000 lamps		Sales of 1,500 lamps
	$	$	$	$	$
Sales revenue	600		600,000		900,000
Direct materials	200	200,000		300,000	
Direct labour	150	150,000		225,000	
Variable production overheads	50	50,000		75,000	
Marginal cost of production			**(400,000)**		**(600,000)**
Contribution			**200,000**		**300,000**
Fixed production overheads			(120,000)		(120,000)
Total profit			80,000		180,000
Contribution per lamp			**200**		**200**
Profit per lamp			80		**120**

Fixed costs have been estimated to be $120,000 based on a production level of 1,000 lamps and it expected to remain at this level.

- Profit per lamp has increased from $80 when 1,000 lamps are sold to $120 when 1,500 lamps are sold.
- Contribution per lamp has remained constant at both levels of sales.

Using profit per unit is not particularly useful when making short term decisions as profit per unit depends on how many units are sold. For this reason, the contribution concept is frequently employed by management accountants.

- Contribution gives an idea of how much 'money' there is available to 'contribute' towards paying for the fixed costs of the organisation.
- At varying levels of output and sales, contribution per unit is constant.
- Contribution per unit = Sales price per unit – total variable cost per unit.
- Total contribution = Contribution per unit × Sales volume.
- Profit = Total contribution – Fixed overheads.

Marginal costing statement of profit or loss

In order to be able to prepare a statement of profit or loss under marginal costing, you need to be able to complete the following proforma:

Marginal costing statement of profit or loss

	$	$
Sales		X
Less Cost of sales:		
Opening inventory	X	
Variable cost of production	X	
Less closing inventory	(X)	
		(X)
		X
Less Other variable costs		(X)
Contribution		X
Less fixed costs		(X)
Profit/loss		X

- **Valuation of inventory** – opening and closing inventory are valued at marginal (variable) cost under marginal costing.
- The fixed costs **incurred** are deducted from contribution earned in order to determine the profit for the period, they are a period cost.
- Marginal costing statements are split into all the variable costs before contribution and all the fixed costs after contribution.
- **Note:** only the production variable costs are included in the cost of sales and valuation of inventory. If there are variable non-production costs (i.e. selling costs) these would be deducted before contribution but not included in the cost of sales.

Marginal costing profit statement

In simple terms a marginal costing profit statement is based on cost behaviour.

	$
Sales revenue	1,000
Less: **Variable** costs	600
Contribution	400
Less: **Fixed** costs	150
Profit	250

Test your understanding 1

Buhner Ltd makes only one product, the cost card of which is:

	$
Direct materials	3
Direct labour	6
Variable production overhead	2
Fixed production overhead	4
Variable selling cost	5

The selling price of one unit is $25.

Budgeted fixed overheads are based on budgeted production of 5,000 units.

Sales during the period were 3,000 units and actual fixed production overheads incurred were $25,000.

(a) Calculate the total contribution earned during the period.

(b) Calculate the total profit or loss for the period.

Advantages and disadvantages of marginal costing

- Contribution per unit is constant unlike profit per unit that varies with changes in sales volumes.
- There is no under or over absorption of overheads (and hence no adjustment is required in the statement of profit or loss).
- Fixed costs are a period cost and are charged in full to the period under consideration.
- Marginal costing is useful in the decision-making process.
- It is simple to operate.
- The main disadvantages of marginal costing are that closing inventory is not valued in accordance with IAS 2 principles and that fixed production overheads are not 'shared' out between units of production, but written off in full instead.

3 Absorption costing

Absorption costing is a method of building up a full product cost which adds direct costs and a proportion of production overhead costs by means of one or a number of overhead absorption rates.

Absorption costing values each unit of inventory at the cost incurred to **produce** the unit. This includes an amount added to the cost of each unit to represent the **production** overheads incurred by that product. The amount added to each unit is based on estimates made at the start of the period.

To calculate a production cost per unit the budgeted production costs are divided by the budgeted activity. The calculation of the cost per unit (overhead absorption rate) was looked at in more detail in Chapter 5 – Accounting for overheads.

Absorption costing statement of profit or loss

In order to be able to prepare a statement of profit or loss under absorption costing, you need to be able to complete the following proforma:

Absorption costing statement of profit or loss

	$	$
Sales		X
Less: Cost of sales:		
Opening inventory	X	
Variable cost of production	X	
Fixed overhead absorbed	X	
Less closing inventory	(X)	
		(X)
		X
(under)/over-absorption		(X)/X
Gross profit		X
Less Non-production costs		(X)
Profit/loss		X

- **Valuation of inventory** – opening and closing inventory are valued at full production cost under absorption costing.
- **Under/over-absorbed overhead** – an adjustment for under or over absorption of overheads is necessary in absorption costing statements.
- Absorption costing statements are split into **production** costs in the cost of sales and **non-production** costs after gross profit.

Absorption costing profit statement

In simple terms an absorption costing profit statement is based on function.

	$
Sales revenue	1,000
Less: **Production** costs	600
Contribution	400
Less: **Non-production** costs	150
Profit	250

Test your understanding 2

Duo Ltd makes and sells one product, the Alpha. The following information is available for period 3:

Production (units)	2,500
Sales (units)	2,300
Opening inventory (units)	0

Financial data:	**Alpha**
	$
Unit selling price	90
Unit cost:	
direct materials	15
direct labour	18
variable production overheads	12
fixed production overheads	30
variable selling overheads	1

Fixed production overheads for the period were $52,500 and fixed administration overheads were $13,500.

Required:

(a) Prepare a statement of profit or loss for period 3 based on marginal costing principles.

(b) Prepare a statement of profit or loss for period 3 based on absorption costing principles.

Advantages and disadvantages of absorption costing

- Absorption costing includes an element of fixed production overheads in inventory values (in accordance with IAS 2).
- Analysing under/over absorption of overheads is a useful exercise in controlling costs of an organisation.

- In small organisations, absorbing overheads into the costs of products is the best way of estimating job costs and profits on jobs.
- The main disadvantages of absorption costing are that it is more complex to operate than marginal costing and it does not provide as much useful information for short term decision making.

4 Inventory valuation and profit determination

Absorption versus marginal costing

Marginal costing values inventory at the variable production cost of a unit of product.

Absorption costing values inventory at the full production cost of a unit of product.

- Inventory values will therefore be different at the beginning and end of a period under marginal and absorption costing.
- If inventory values are different, this will have an effect on profits reported in the statement of profit or loss in a period.
- Profits determined using marginal costing principles will therefore be different to those using absorption costing principles.

e.g

Illustration 2 – Impact of inventory on profit

A company commenced business on 1 March making one product only, the cost card of which is as follows:

	$
Direct labour	5
Direct material	8
Variable production overhead	2
Fixed production overhead	5
Standard production cost	20

The fixed production overhead figure has been calculated based on a budgeted normal output of 36,000 units per annum. The fixed production overhead actually incurred in March was $15,000.

Selling, distribution and administration expenses are:

Fixed	$10,000 per month
Variable	15% of the sales value

The selling price per unit is $50 and the number of units produced and sold were:

Production	2,000
Sales	1,500

Prepare the absorption costing and marginal costing statements of profit or loss for March.

Absorption costing statement of profit or loss – March

	$	$
Sales		75,000
Less Cost of sales: (full production cost)		
Opening inventory	–	
Variable cost of production (2,000 × $15)	30,000	
Fixed production overhead absorbed (2,000 × $5)	10,000	
Less Closing inventory **(W1)** (500 × $20)	(10,000)	
		(30,000)
(Under)/over-absorption **(W2)**		(5,000)
Gross profit		40,000
Less Non-production costs **(W3)**		(21,250)
Profit/loss		18,750

Workings

(W1) Closing inventory = opening inventory + production – sales units
= 0 + 2,000 – 1,500 = 500 units

(W2)

	$
Overheads absorbed (2,000 × $5)	10,000
Overheads incurred	15,000
Under-absorption on overheads	5,000

(W3)

Fixed = 10,000

Variable = 15% × $75,000 = $11,250

Total = $(10,000 + 11,250) = $21,250

Marginal costing statement of profit or loss – March

	$	$
Sales		75,000
Less Cost of sales: (marginal production costs)		
Opening inventory	–	
Variable cost of production (2,000 × $15)	30,000	
Less Closing inventory (500 × $15)	(7,500)	
		(22,500)
		52,500
Less Other variable costs (15% × $75,000)		(11,250)
Contribution		41,250
Less Total fixed costs (actually incurred) $(15,000 + 10,000)		(25,000)
Profit/loss		16,250

Reconciling profits reported under the different methods

When inventory levels increase or decrease during a period then profits differ under absorption and marginal costing.

- If inventory levels increase, absorption costing gives the higher profit.
- If inventory levels decrease, marginal costing gives the higher profit.
- If inventory levels are constant, both methods give the same profit.
- NOTE: a useful acronym SIAM – **S**tock (inventory) **I**ncreasing **A**bsorption **M**ore

e.g

Illustration 3 – Reconciling profits

A company commenced business on 1 March making one product only, the cost card of which is as follows (details as per illustration 2).

	$
Direct labour	5
Direct material	8
Variable production overhead	2
Fixed production overhead	5
Full production cost	20

- Marginal cost of production = 5 + 8 + 2 = $15
- Absorption cost of production = 5 + 8 + 2 + 5 = $20
- Difference in cost of production = $5 which is the fixed production overhead element of the absorption cost of production.
- This means that each unit of opening and closing inventory will be valued at $5 more under absorption costing.

The number of units produced and sold was as follows.

	March (units)
Production	2,000
Sales	1,500

Closing inventory is 500 units (as calculated in illustration 2)

- Profit for March under absorption costing = $18,750 (as calculated in illustration 2).
- Profit for March under marginal costing = $16,250 (as calculated in illustration 2).
- Difference in profits = $18,750 – $16,250 = $2,500.

This difference can be analysed as follows

Absorption costing:

- There are zero opening inventories so no fixed production costs have been brought forward.
- $10,000 of fixed production costs have been charged to production (2,000 units × $5).
- $2,500 of this has then been deducted from the cost of sales as part of the closing inventory value (500 × $5).
- An adjustment for the under-absorption of $5,000 has been charged.
- Therefore **$12,500** of fixed costs has been charged in this month's statement of profit or loss ($10,000 – $2,500 + $5,000).

Marginal costing:

- The statement of profit or loss is charged with the full **$15,000** of fixed production overhead costs as none are included in the cost of sales.

Reconciliation:

- Inventory levels are increasing by 500 units (zero opening inventory and 500 units of closing inventory)
- $2,500 ($15,000 – $12,500) less cost is charged in the period using absorption costing principles when compared to marginal costing principles therefore the profit will be $2,500 higher under absorption costing principles.

In an exam question you may be told the profit under either marginal or absorption costing and be asked to calculate the alternative profit for the information provided.

There is a short cut to reconciling the profits:

Absorption costing profit		18,750
(Opening inventory – Closing inventory) × OAR	(0 – 500) × 5	–2,500
Marginal costing profit		16,250

Test your understanding 3

(a) In a period where opening inventory was 5,000 units and closing inventory was 3,000 units, a company had a profit of $92,000 using absorption costing. If the fixed overhead absorption rate was $9 per unit, calculate the profit using marginal costing.

(b) When opening inventory was 8,500 litres and closing inventory was 6,750 litres, a company had a profit of $62,100 using marginal costing. The fixed overhead absorption rate was $3 per litre. Calculate the profit using absorption costing.

5 Chapter summary

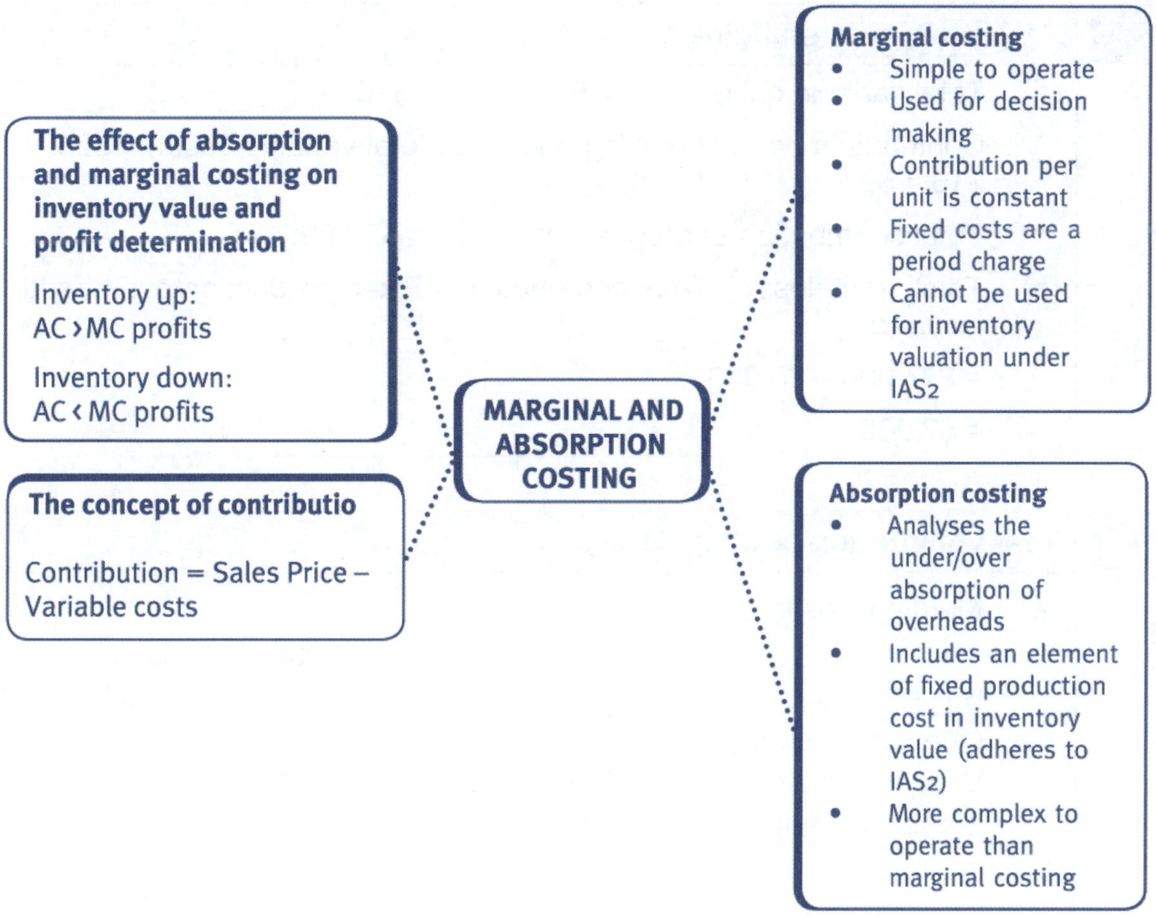

Test your understanding answers

Test your understanding 1

(a) Total variable costs = $(3 + 6 + 2 + 5) = $16

Contribution per unit (selling price less total variable costs) = $25 – $16 = $9

Total contribution earned = 3,000 × $9 = $27,000

(b) Total profit/(loss) = Total contribution – Fixed production overheads incurred

= $27,000 – 25,000

= $2,000

Test your understanding 2

(a) Marginal costing

	$000	$000
Sales		207
Opening inventory	–	
Variable production cost (2,500 × 45)	112.5	
Closing inventory (200 × 45)	(9)	
		(103.5)
		103.5
Variable selling costs (2,300 × $1)		(2.3)
Contribution		101.2
Fixed production costs		(52.5)
Fixed administration costs		(13.5)
Profit		35.2

(b) Absorption costing

	$000	$000
Sales		207
Opening inventory	–	
Full production cost (2,500 × 75)	187.5	
Closing inventory (200 × 75)	(15)	
		(172.5)
		34.5
Over-absorbed overhead (working)		22.5
Gross profit		57
Less: non-production overheads		
variable selling overheads		(2.3)
fixed administration overheads		(13.5)
Profit		41.2

Working

	$
Overhead absorbed = (2,500 × $30)	75,000
Overheads incurred =	52,500
Over-absorbed overhead	22,500

Test your understanding 3

(a)

Absorption costing profit	$92,000
Difference in profit = change in inventory × fixed cost per unit = (5,000 – 3,000) × $9	$18,000
Marginal costing profit	$110,000

Since inventory levels have fallen in the period, marginal costing shows the higher profit figure, therefore marginal costing profit will be $18,000 higher than the absorption costing profit, i.e. $110,000.

(b)

Marginal costing profit	$62,100
Difference in profit = change in inventory × fixed cost per unit = (8,500 – 6,750) × $3	$(5,250)
Absorption costing profit	$56,850

Inventory levels have fallen in the period and therefore marginal costing profits will be higher than absorption costing profits. Absorption costing profit is therefore $5,250 less than the marginal costing profit.

The answer could also be calculated working back up from the marginal costing profit:

Absorption costing profit	$56,850
Difference in profit = change in inventory × fixed cost per unit = (8,500 – 6,750) × $3	$5,250
Marginal costing profit	$62,100

Chapter

7

Job, batch and process costing

Chapter learning objectives

Upon completion of this chapter you will be able to:

- Job and batch costing:
  - describe the characteristics of job and batch costing
  - describe the situation where the use of job or batch costing would be appropriate
  - prepare cost records and accounts in job and batch costing situations
  - establish job and batch costs from given information
- Process costing:
  - describe the characteristics of process costing
  - describe situations where the use of process costing would be appropriate
  - explain the concepts of normal and abnormal losses and abnormal gains
  - distinguish between by-products and joint products
  - value by-products and joint products at the point of separation
  - evaluate the benefit of further processing.

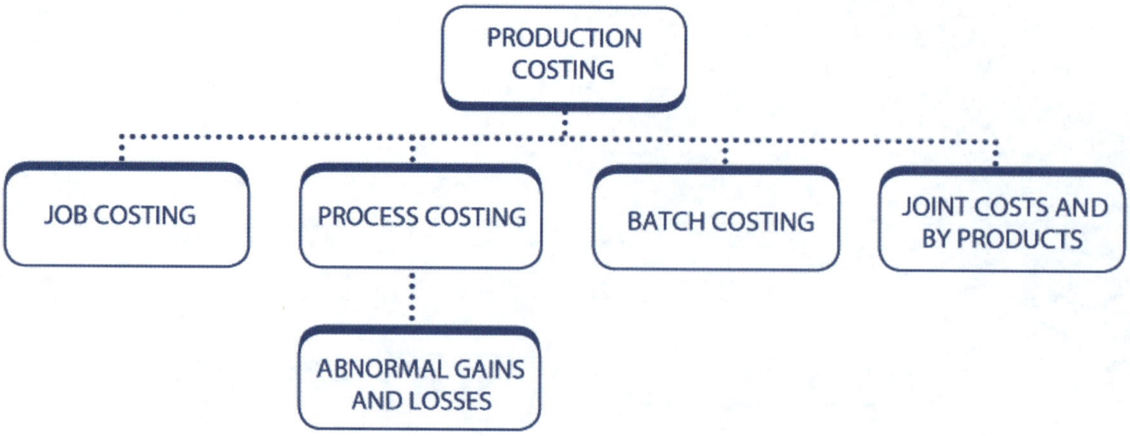

1 Different types of production

Costing systems

- **Specific order costing** is the costing system used when the work done by an organisation consists of **separately identifiable jobs** or **batches**.
- **Continuous operation costing** is the costing method used when goods or services are produced as a direct result of a **sequence of continuous operations or processes**, for example process and service costing.

2 Job and Batch costing

Job costing

Job costing is a form of specific order costing and it is used when a customer orders a specific job to be done. Each job is priced separately and each job is unique.

- The main aim of job costing is to identify the costs associated with completing the order and to record them carefully.
- Individual jobs are given a unique job number and the costs involved in completing the job are recorded on a job cost sheet or job card.
- The selling prices of jobs are calculated by adding a certain amount of profit to the cost of the job.
- Job costing could be used by landscape gardeners where the job would be to landscape a garden; or decorators where the job would be to decorate a room.

Illustration 1 – Job costing

Individual job costs are recorded on a job card similar to the one shown below.

JOB CARD

Customer	Green & Co Ltd		Job No: 342
Description	Transfer machine	Promised delivery date	3.11.X1
Date commenced	25.9.X1	Actual delivery date	13.11.X1
Price quoted	$2,400		
Despatch note no:	7147		

	Materials estimate $1,250		**Labour estimate $100**		**Overhead estimate $176** Hourly rate $11		**Other charges estimate $25**	
Date Reference	**Cost** $	**Total** $	**Hrs**	**Total** $	**Cost** $	**Total** $	**Cost** $	**Total** $
b/f balances		1,200	17	110		187		13
6 Nov Material Requisition 1714	182	1,382						
7 Nov Consultant's test fee							10	23
8 Nov Material Requisition 1937	19	1,401						
9 Nov Material Returns Note	(26)	1,375						
10 Nov Labour analysis			5	138	55	242		

Summary

	$
Materials	1,375
Labour	138
Overhead	242
Other charges	23
	1,778
Invoice price (invoice number 7147 dated 12.12.X1)	2,400
Profit	622

The flow of information in a job costing system is shown as follows:

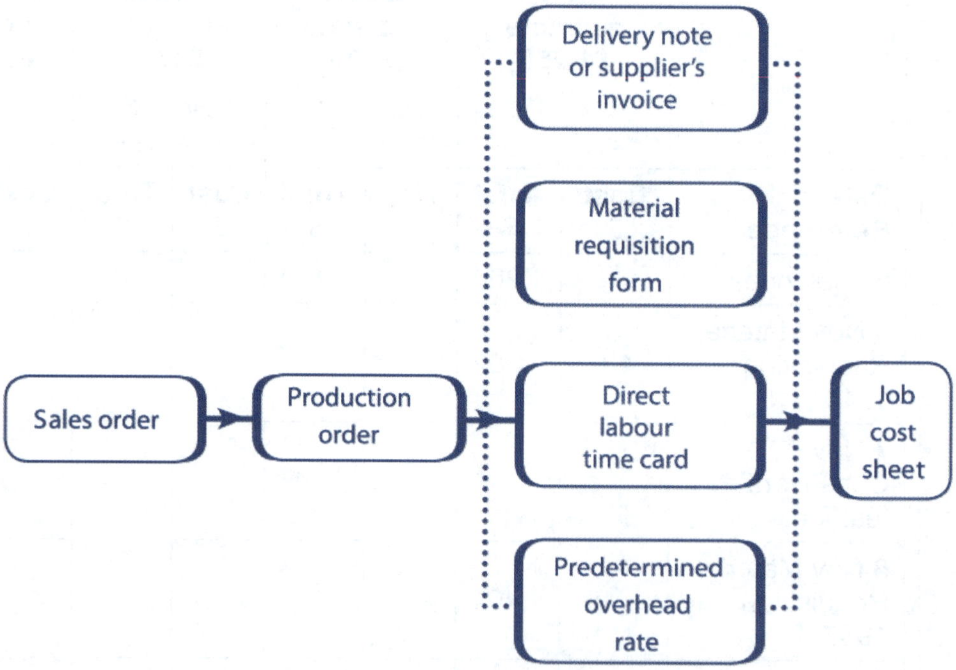

Batch costing

Batch costing is also a form of specific order costing. It is very similar to job costing.

- Within each batch are a number of identical units but each batch will be different.
- Each batch is a separately identifiable cost unit which is given a batch number in the same way that each job is given a job number.
- Costs can then be collected for each batch number. For example materials requisitions will be coded to a batch number to ensure that the cost of materials used is charged to the correct batch.

- When the batch is completed the unit cost of individual items in the batch is found by dividing the total batch cost by the number of items in the batch.

$$\textbf{Cost per unit in batch} = \frac{\textbf{Total production cost of batch}}{\textbf{Number of units in batch}}$$

- Batch costing is very common in the engineering component industry, footwear and clothing manufacturing industries where identical items are produced; for example a batch could contain 100 pairs of size 6 (UK) trainers for a retailer outlet.
- The selling prices of batches are calculated in the same ways as the selling prices of jobs, i.e. by adding a profit to the cost of the batch.

Test your understanding 1

Which of the following are characteristics of job costing?

(i) Homogenous products.

(ii) Customer-driven production.

(iii) Production can be completed within a single accounting period.

A (i) only

B (i) and (ii) only

C (ii) and (iii) only

D (i) and (iii) only

Illustration 2 – Costing for job and batch costing

Jetprint Ltd specialises in printing advertising leaflets and is in the process of preparing its price list. The most popular requirement is for a folded leaflet made from a single sheet of A4 paper. From past records and budgeted figures, the following data has been estimated for a typical batch of 10,000 leaflets:

Artwork	$65
Machine set up	4 hours @ $22 per hour
Paper	$12.50 per 1,000 sheets
Ink and consumables	$40
Printer's wages 4 hours at	$8 per hour

Note: Printer's wages vary with volume.

General fixed overheads are $15,000 per period during which a total of 600 labour hours are expected to be worked.

Required:

Calculate cost for 10,000 and 20,000 leaflets.

Solution

	Producing 10,000 leaflets	**Producing 20,000 leaflets**
	$	$
Artwork	65	65
Machine set up (4 hours @ $22)	88	88
Paper (variable)	125	250
Ink and consumables (variable)	40	80
Printer's wages ($8 per hour)	32	64
General fixed overheads (W1)	100	200
Total cost	450	747

Workings

Artwork and machine set up are only required once at the start of the production run and are not batch size dependant therefore they are fixed costs.

(W1) Overhead absorption rate = $15,000 ÷ 600 = $25 per hour

For 10,000 leaflets, general fixed overheads = 4 hours × $25 = $100

For 20,000 leaflets, general fixed overheads = 8 hours × $25 = $200

Test your understanding 2

A business has a job costing system and prices jobs using total absorption costing. The cost estimates for Job 264 are as follows:

Direct materials 50 kg @ $4 per kg

Direct labour 30 hours @ $9 per hour

Variable production overhead $6 per direct labour hour

Fixed production overheads are budgeted as $80,000 and are absorbed on the basis of direct labour hours. The total budgeted direct labour hours for the period are 20,000.

Other overheads are recovered at the rate of $40 per job.

Calculate the total job cost for Job 264.

3 Process costing

Process costing is the costing method applicable when goods or services result from a sequence of continuous or repetitive operations or processes. Process costing is used when a company is mass producing the same item and the item goes through a number of different stages.

- Process costing is an example of continuous operation costing.
- Examples include the chemical, cement, oil refinery, paint and textile industries.
- One of the features of process costing is that in most process costing environments the products are identical and indistinguishable from each other.
- Another feature of process costing is that the output of one process forms the **material** input of the next process.

e.g

Illustration 3 – Process costing

The following details relate to process 2.

Material transferred from process 1	1,000 units
Material transferred to process 3	1,000 units

- Balance the units

  Input units = Output units

  1,000 = 1,000

Losses and gains in a process

Sometimes in a process, the total of the input units may differ from the total of the output units.

- Losses may occur due to the evaporation or wastage of materials and this may be an expected part of the process.
- Losses may sometimes be sold and generate a revenue which is generally referred to as scrap proceeds or scrap value.

Normal loss

Normal loss is the loss that is **expected** in a process and it is often expressed as a percentage of the materials input to the process.

Illustration 4 – Normal losses

The following data relates to Process 1.

Materials input 1,000 units

Normal loss is 4% of input

Required:

Calculate the normal loss in Process 1

Solution

Normal loss units = 4% × 1,000 = **40** units

Abnormal loss and abnormal gain

Normal loss is the expected loss in a process. If the loss in a process is different to what we are expecting then we have an abnormal loss or an abnormal gain in the process.

Abnormal loss is more loss than expected

Abnormal gain is less loss than expected

Illustration 5 – Abnormal loss

The following data relates to Process 1

Materials input is 1,000 units

Normal loss is 4% of input

Actual output is 944 units

Required:

Calculate the abnormal loss.

Solution

Calculate the normal loss units = 4% × 1,000 = 40 units

Balance the units (identify if there has been extra or less loss)

Input units =	Output units	+	Normal loss	+	Abnormal loss
1,000 =	944	+	40	+	**16**

Illustration 6 – Abnormal gain

The following data relates to Process 1

Materials input is 1,000 units

Normal loss is 4% of input

Actual output is 980 units

Required:

Calculate the abnormal gain.

Solution

Calculate the normal loss units = 4% × 1,000 units = 40 units

Balance the units (identify if there has been extra or less loss)

Input units	+ Abnormal gain	=	Output units	+	Normal loss
1,000	+ **20**	=	980	+	40

Test your understanding 3

The following data relates to Process 1

Normal loss is 8% of input

Actual output is 920 units

Required:

Calculate the material input.

Test your understanding 4

The following data relates to Process 1

Normal loss is 10% of input and Abnormal loss was 2%

Actual output is 572 units

Required:

Calculate the material input and the abnormal loss units.

4 Joint and by-products

Some products may be produced at the same time in the same process before being separated for sale or further individual processing. These products are known as joint products and the separation point is known as the split off point.

For example, different types of carbonated drinks might use a common starting process where syrup, sweeteners and malt are added before they are split up and individual flavourings added.

Joint costs are the total of the raw material, labour, and overhead costs incurred up to the initial split off point.

In some cases by-products are also produced alongside the main joint products.

Joint products

Joint products are two or more products separated in the course of processing, each having a sufficiently **high saleable value** to merit recognition as a main product.

- Joint products include products produced as a result of the oil-refining process, for example, petrol and paraffin.
- Petrol and paraffin have similar sales values and are therefore equally important (joint) products.

By-products

By-products are outputs of **some value** produced incidentally in manufacturing something else (main products).

- By-products, such as sawdust and bark, are secondary products from the timber industry (where timber is the main or principal product from the process).
- Sawdust and bark have a relatively low sales value compared to the timber which is produced and are therefore classified as by-products.

Accounting treatment of joint products

The distinction between joint and by-products is important because the accounting treatment of joint products and by-products differs.

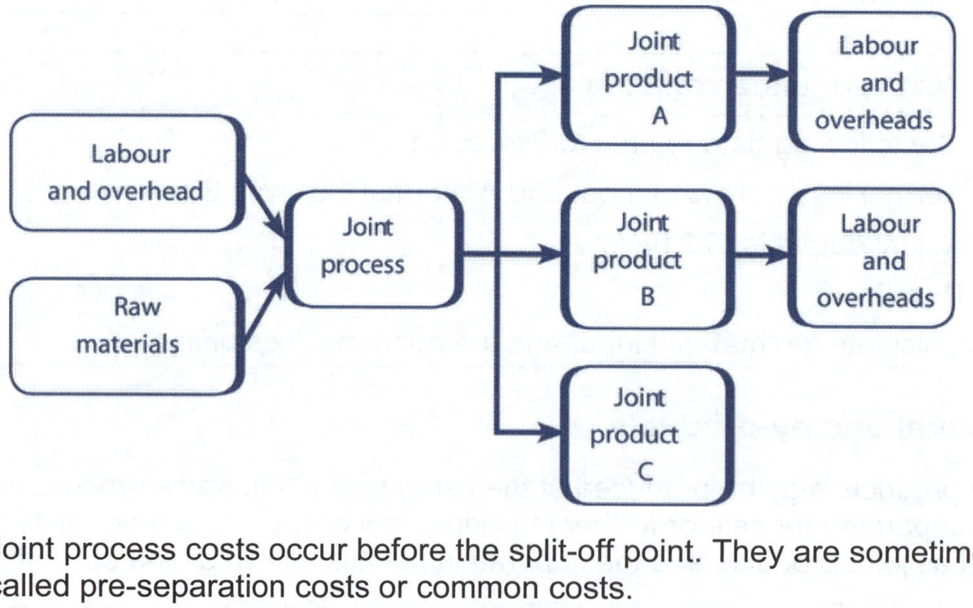

- Joint process costs occur before the split-off point. They are sometimes called pre-separation costs or common costs.
- The joint costs need to be apportioned between the joint products at the split-off point to obtain the cost of each of the products in order to value closing inventory and cost of sales.

- The basis of apportionment of joint costs to products is usually one of the following:
  - sales value of production (also known as market value)
  - production units
  - net realisable value.

e.g

Illustration 7 – Apportioning joint costs

Allison plc produces two products, X and Y, in a single joint process. Last month the joint costs were $75,000 when 10,000 units of Product X and 15,000 units of Product Y were produced. Additional processing costs were $15,000 for Product X and $10,000 for Product Y. Product X sells for $10, and Product Y sells for $5.

The joint cost allocations to Products X and Y using the **net realisable value** method would be:

Calculate the total net realisable value:

X: (10,000 units × $10) – $15,000 = $85,000

Y: (15,000 units × $5) – $10,000 = $65,000

Total net realisable value = $150,000

Calculate the joint cost allocation:

X: $75,000 ÷ $150,000 × $85,000 = $42,500

Y:$75,000 ÷ $150,000 × $65,000 = $32,500

The joint cost allocations to Products X and Y using the **physical units** method would be:

X: $75,000 ÷ 25,000 units × 10,000 units = $30,000

Y: $75,000 ÷ 25,000 units × 15,000 units = $45,000

The joint cost allocations to Products X and Y using the **Market value** method would be:

Calculate the total market value:

X: 10,000 × $10 = $100,000

Y: 15,000 × $5 = $75,000

Total market value = $175,000

Calculate the joint cost allocation:

X: $75,000 ÷ 175,000 × $100,000 = $42,857

Y: $75,000 ÷ 175,000 × $75,000 = $32,143

Accounting treatment of by-products

By-products are of less significance than the main products and may not require precise cost allocation. Factors that can influence the valuation and accounting treatment of by-products:

- Is the value of the by-product known at the time of production?
- Could the by-product be used in other production?
- Is the by-product an alternative to the main products?
- Is there a need for separate profit calculations for sales incentives or for control?

By-products can be accounted for using the following:

Non-cost methods

Non-cost methods make no attempt to allocate joint cost to the by-product but instead the proceeds either increase income or to reduce the cost of the main product.

- **Other income** – The net sales of by-products for the current period is recognised as other income and is reported in the income statement. This method is used where there is little value to the by-product, where any other method would be more expensive than the benefits received, or carrying by-products with the main products would not really affect the cost of the main product.
- **By-product revenue deducted from the main product(s) cost** – The net sales value of the by-products will be treated as a deduction from the cost of the main product(s). This is similar to the accounting treatment of normal loss. This is the most common method of accounting for by-product income.

Cost methods

Cost methods attempt to allocate some joint costs to by-products and to carry inventories at the allocated cost levels.

- **Replacement cost method** – values the by-product inventory at its opportunity cost of purchasing or replacing the by-products.
- **Total costs less by-products valued at standard price method** – By-products are valued at a standard price to avoid fluctuations in by-product value. This means that the main product cost will not be affected by any fluctuations in the by-product price. The standard price may be set arbitrarily, or it may reflect an average price over time. A variance account is used to account for the difference between actual and standard prices.
- **Joint cost pro-rata method** – allocates some of the joint cost to the by-product using any one of the joint cost allocation methods. This method is rarely used in practice.

Illustration 8 – Treatment of joint cost

Process M produces two joint products (A and B) and one by-product (C). Joint costs are apportioned on the basis of sales units.

The following information is relevant.

	Product A	Product B	Total
Sales units	2,000	8,000	10,000
Apportioned joint cost	$3,600	$14,400	$18,000

It is possible to sell by-product C after further processing for $0.50 per unit. The further processing costs are $0.20 per unit. 2,000 units of by-product C are produced.

Required:

If the by-product revenue is deducted from the main products cost how are the joint costs of $18,000 apportioned?

Solution

Income from by-product = $(0.5 – 0.2) × 2,000 = $600

Joint costs are now $18,000 – $600 = $17,400

Total output units = 2,000 + 8,000 = 10,000 units

Joint cost allocated to Product A = $17,400 ÷ 10,000 units × 2,000 units = $3,480

Joint cost allocated to Product B = $17,400 ÷ 10,000 units × 8,000 units = $13,920

Test your understanding 5

A company operates a manufacturing process which produces joint products A and B, and by-product C.

Manufacturing costs for a period total $272,926, incurred in the manufacture of:

Product A 16,000 kg (selling price $6.10 per kg)

Product B 53,200 kg (selling price $7.50 per kg)

Product C 2,770 kg (selling price $1.20 per kg)

Product B requires further processing after separation from the other two products. This costs a total of $201,930.

Product C also requires further processing to make it saleable and this costs $0.40 per kg.

Required:

Calculate the total profit earned by Products A and B in the period, using the net realisable values (net income) to apportion joint costs. Assume that the by-product costs are deducted from the manufacturing costs.

Test your understanding 6

A company produces two products along with a single by-product. The joint process costs total $200,000. Product A can be sold for $450,000 after additional processing of $250,000; Product B can be sold for $600,000 after additional processing of $200,000. The by-product BP incurs additional packaging costs of $5,000 then it can be sold for $25,000. The by-product is accounted for using the by-product revenue deducted from the main product cost approach.

Required:

What would be the joint cost allocation using the net realisable value method?

	A	B
A	$60,000	$120,000
B	$66,667	$133,333
C	$77,143	$102,857
D	$85,714	$114,286

Test your understanding 7

Stone Mayson Inc is a manufacturer of granite slabs. Stone Mayson digs blocks of granite out of its quarry. All the granite extracted goes through the processes of quarrying and cutting. Two joint products (monuments and granite slabs) are produced along with a by-product called grit.

Monuments are cut, polished, and engraved in a variety of standard shapes, sizes, and patterns before being sold. The granite slabs are special-ordered by contractors for kitchen worktops. These slabs are cut and polished to exacting specifications. The small pieces of granite resulting from the cutting process are crushed and sold to farm-suppliers as poultry grit.

Stone Mayson has the following costs and output information:

Process	Cost	Tonnes of output
Quarry	$350,000	
Cutting	$250,000	
Monuments	$300,000	30,000
Granite slabs	$400,000	60,000
Grit	$10,000	5,000

A local farm-supplier purchases all of the grit that is produced at $40 per tonne. Assume that Stone Maysons uses the physical units method to allocate joint costs.

Required:

1 What would be the cost per tonne of monuments and granite slabs, assuming that the grit is accounted for as "Other Income"?

2 What would be the cost per tonne of monuments and granite slabs, assuming that the grit is accounted for as by-product revenue deducted from the main product cost?

Evaluating the benefit of further processing

The main decisions involving joint products are:

- If a joint product appears to be making a loss, management cannot decide to stop making the product. In order to carry on making the other joint products that are making a 'profit', the 'loss-making' joint product will have to be made as well.
- Basis for apportioning the joint costs. The apportionment basis should be 'fair', but entirely different costs and profits can be calculated for joint products, depending on which method of apportionment is used.

It is assumed that further processing of products after the point of separation is independent i.e. a decision to process one joint product in no way affects the decision to process further the other joint products.

The pre-split off costs of the common processing of the joint products are irrelevant to the further processing decision. The joint costs are not affected by whether individual products are further processed, and are therefore not relevant to the decision under consideration.

To evaluate processing of the individual products it is necessary to identify the incremental costs and incremental revenues relating to that further processing, i.e. the additional costs and revenue brought about directly as a result of that further processing.

e.g

Illustration 9 – Further processing of joint products

The following data relates to products A and B produced from a joint process:

	Quantity produced	Sales price at split-off point	Further processing costs	Sales price after further processing
	kg	$ per kg		$ per kg
Product A	100	5	$280 plus $2.00 per kg	8.40
Product B	200	2	$160 plus $1.40 per kg	4.50

Common costs prior to the split-off point are $750.

Should each product be sold at the split-off point, or processed further before sale?

Solution

Evaluation of further processing

	Product A		**Product B**	
	$	$	$	$
Sales value after further processing		840		900
Sales value at split off point		(500)		(400)
Incremental sales revenue from further processing		340		500
Further processing costs				
Fixed	280		160	
Variable	200		280	
		(480)		(440)
Gain/(loss) from further processing		(140)		60

On the basis of these figures the recommendation would be:

Product A Sell at split-off point for $5.

Product B Sell for $4.50 after further processing.

Before a final decision is made on whether to further process a joint product the following should be considered:

- The products in their final state may be in some way 'complementary' i.e. it may only be possible to sell B if A is also available in a further processed state.
- The decision to stop further processing of a product could result in having to reduce the workforce employed and the potential knock-on effects of this, for example the remaining workforce could go out on strike.
- The products all contribute towards the fixed costs of the business. The individual values apportioned to the products may still be incurred even if further processing is stopped.
- The volume of units being produced may affect the decision to proceed with the further processing.

e.g

Illustration 10 – Further processing of joint products

Looking in more detail at the further processing of A it is possible to see that further processing of 1 kg of A results in an incremental contribution of:

	$
Incremental revenue (8.40 – 5.00)	3.40
Incremental variable cost	(2.00)
Incremental contribution	1.40

It is therefore possible to identify the level of activity at which further processing of A becomes worthwhile i.e. the 'break-even volume'.

$$\text{Break-even volume} = \frac{\text{Incremental fixed costs}}{\text{Incremental contribution per kg}}$$

$$= \frac{280}{1.40}$$

$$= 200 \text{ kg}$$

If the volume of A in the future is greater than 200 kg, further processing becomes economically worthwhile.

Test your understanding 8

When deciding, purely on financial grounds, whether or not to process a joint product after the separation point, the information required is:

(i) the value of the common process costs.

(ii) the method of apportioning the common costs between the joint products.

(iii) the sales value of the joint product at the separation point.

(iv) the final sales value of the joint product.

(v) the further processing cost of the joint product.

Which of the statements are correct?

A (i), (ii) and (iii) only

B (iii), (iv) and (v) only

C (iv) and (v) only

D (i), (ii), (iv) and (v) only

5 Chapter summary

Different types of production

Joint and by-products

- Joint products are two or more products separated in processing, each having sufficiently high saleable value
- By-products are outputs of some value produced at the same time as joint products

Job costing

Form of specific order costing used when customer orders a specific job to be done. Each job is priced separately and is unique.

Batch costing

Form of specific order costing which is very similar to job costing. Each batch is a separately identifiable cost unit which is given a batch number.

Process costing

Costing method used when mass production of many identical products takes place, e.g. manufacture of bars of chocolate or cans of soup. All products manufactured are indistinguishable from each other

Process costing with gains and losses

- Normal loss = expected loss.
- Abnormal loss is extra unexpected loss.
- Abnormal gain occurs when actual loss is less than expected.
- Abnormal loss and gain are valued at same value as good output.

Test your understanding answers

Test your understanding 1

C

Job costing is customer-driven with customers ordering a specific job to be done. It is also possible for production to be completed within a single accounting period.

Test your understanding 2

	$
Direct materials 50 kg × $4	200
Direct labour 30 hours × $9	270
Variable production overhead 30 × $6	180
Fixed overheads $80,000/20,000 × 30	120
Other overheads	40
Total cost	810

Test your understanding 3

Input = NL + Output

100% = 8% + 92%

Therefore 920 ÷ 92 × 100 = **1,000 units**

Test your understanding 4

Input = NL + Output + AL

Therefore

Input = 572 ÷ 88 × 100 = 650 units

AL = 572 ÷ 88 × 2 = 13 units

Test your understanding 5

Net revenue from product C = \$(1.2 – 0.4) = \$0.80

Costs to apportion = Joint process costs – net revenue from product C
= \$272,926 – (2,770 kg × \$0.80)
= \$270,710

Net realisable value (16,000 kg × \$6.10) + [(53,200 kg × \$7.50) – \$201,930] = \$97,600 + \$197,070 = \$294,670

Joint cost apportioned to A = \$270,710 ÷ \$294,670 × \$97,600 = \$89,664

Joint cost apportioned to B = \$270,710 ÷ \$294,670 × \$197,070 = \$181,046

Profit from A = \$97,600 – \$89,664 = \$7,936

Profit from B = \$197,070 – \$181,046 = \$16,024

Total profit = **\$23,960**

Test your understanding 6

A

Adjusted joint cost after reduction of net sale of by-product = \$200,000 – (\$25,000 – \$5,000) = \$180,000

Joint cost allocation ratios are computed using the net realisable value method as follows:

A: \$450,000 – \$250,000 = \$200,000

B: \$600,000 – \$200,000 = \$400,000

Total net realisable value = \$600,000

Joint cost allocation is computed as follows:

A: \$180,000 ÷ \$600,000 × \$200,000 = \$60,000

B: \$180,000 ÷ \$600,000 × \$400,000 = \$120,000

Test your understanding 7

1 Grit accounted for as "Other Income":

Joint cost to be allocated = \$350,000 Quarry + \$250,000 Cutting = \$600,000

Total units = 30,000 tons + 60,000 tons = 90,000 tonnes

Joint cost allocated to Monument = \$600,000 ÷ 90,000 tonnes × 30,000 tonnes = \$200,000

Joint cost allocated to Slabs = \$600,000 ÷ 90,000 tonnes × 60,000 tonnes = \$400,000

Total cost for Monument = \$200,000 + \$300,000 = \$500,000

Cost per tonne for Monument = \$500,000 ÷ 30,000 tonnes = **\$16.67 per tonne**

Total cost for Slabs = \$400,000 + \$400,000 = \$800,000

Cost per tonne for Slabs = \$800,000 ÷ 60,000 tonnes = **\$13.33 per tonne**

2 Grit accounted for as by-product revenue deducted from main product cost:

Sales of grit (5,000 tonnes × \$40) = \$200,000

Less: Separable costs of processing = \$10,000

Net realisable value = \$190,000

Joint cost to be allocated = \$350,000 Quarry + \$250,000 Cutting – \$190,000 By-product net sales = \$410,000

Total units = 30,000 tons + 60,000 tons = 90,000 tonnes

Joint cost allocated to Monument = \$410,000 ÷ 90,000 tonnes × 30,000 tonnes = \$136,667

Joint cost allocated to Slabs = \$410,000 ÷ 90,000 tonnes × 60,000 tonnes = \$273,333

Total cost for Monument = \$136,667 + \$300,000 = \$436,667

Cost per tonne for Monument = \$436,667 ÷ 30,000 tonnes = **\$14.56 per tonne**

Total cost for Slabs = \$273,333 + \$400,000 = \$673,333

Cost per tonne for Slabs = \$673,333 ÷ 60,000 tonnes = **\$11.22 per tonne**

Test your understanding 8

B

The value of the common process costs (i) is not relevant because this would not be affected by the decision to process a joint product further. The method of apportioning common costs (ii) is not relevant because this would not affect the total cost incurred. The sales values of the joint product, both at the separation point and after further processing, (iii) and (iv), are relevant because the difference between the two represents the gain in value achieved through further processing. This would then be compared with the further processing cost (v) to ascertain whether the gain in sales value exceeds the cost incurred through further processing. Therefore (iii), (iv) and (v) are relevant.

Chapter

8

Service and operation costing

Chapter learning objectives

Upon completion of this chapter you will be able to:

- define the characteristics of service organisations
- identify situations where the use of service/operation costing is appropriate
- illustrate suitable unit cost measures that may be used in different service/operation situations
- carry out service cost analysis in simple service industry situations.

PER

One of the PER performance objectives (PO12) is to apply different management accounting techniques is different business contexts to effectively manage and use resources. Working through this chapter should help you understand how to demonstrate that objective.

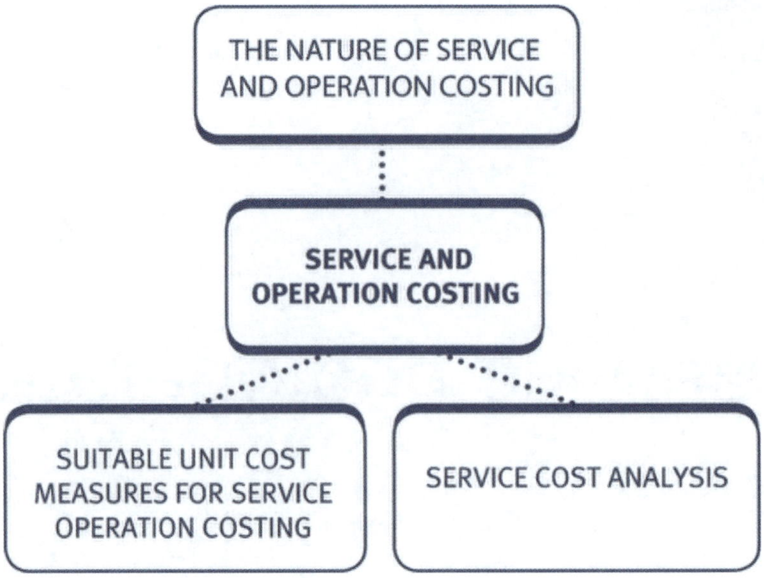

1 Service and operation costing

Service costing

Service costing is used when an organisation or department provides a service, such as an accountancy firm preparing the accounts for a company.

There are four main differences between the 'output' of service industries and the products of manufacturing industries.

- **Intangibility** – output is in the form of 'performance' rather than tangible ('touchable') goods.
- **Heterogeneity** – the nature and standard of the service will be variable due to the high human input.
- **Simultaneous production and consumption** – the service that you require cannot be inspected in advance of receiving it.
- **Perishability** – the services that you require cannot be stored.

e.g

Illustration 1 – The characteristics of service and operation costing

Examples of service industries include the following:

- hotel
- college
- hairdressers
- restaurant.

We can ask the following questions about, e.g. the hotel industry:

1 Is output in the form of performance? Yes – the hotel provides a bed and possibly breakfast. You will judge the service of the hotel on how comfortable the bed was and how tasty the breakfast was. You cannot really 'touch' the performance of the hotel.

2 Is the standard of the service variable? Yes – your stay at the hotel may vary each time you stay there. You may not have such a comfortable bed and your breakfast may not be very tasty each time you visit. The standard of service is therefore variable because lots of different staff work at the hotel – the standard of the service you receive may depend on which staff are on duty.

3 Can you inspect the services in advance of receiving them? In general, you cannot sleep in a hotel bed or eat breakfast at the hotel until you have booked in and made a contract to buy the services of the hotel.

4 Can the hotel services be stored? No – you cannot take your bed away with you, nor can you keep your breakfast – it must be eaten during the morning of your stay.

2 Cost units for service/operation costing

Unit cost measures for service costing

One of the main difficulties in service costing is the establishment of a suitable cost unit.

- Service organisations may use several different cost units to measure the different kinds of service that they are providing.
- Examples for a hotel might include:
  - Meals served for the restaurant
  - Rooms occupied for the cleaning staff
  - Hours worked for the reception staff.
- A **composite cost unit** is more appropriate if a service is a function of two variables.
- Examples of composite cost units are as follows:
  - How much is carried over what distance (tonne-miles) for haulage companies
  - How many patients are treated for how many days (patient-days) for hospitals
  - How many passengers travel how many miles (passenger-miles) for public transport companies.

Cost per service unit

The total cost of providing a service will include labour, materials, expenses and overheads (the same as the costs associated with the products produced in manufacturing industry).

	$
Direct materials	X
Direct labour	X
Direct expenses	X
Overheads absorbed	X
TOTAL COST	XX

- In service costing, it is common for labour to be the only direct cost involved in providing a service and for overheads to make up most of the remaining total costs.
- In service costing costs can be classified as being fixed, variable or semi-variable. If costs are semi-variable, it is necessary to separate them into their fixed and variable constituents using the high/low method.
- The cost per service unit is calculated by establishing the total costs involved in providing the service and dividing this by the number of service units used in providing the service.
- The calculation of a cost per service unit is as follows.

$$\textbf{Cost per service unit} = \frac{\textbf{Total costs for providing the service}}{\textbf{Number of service units used to provide the service}}$$

e.g

Illustration 2 – Suitable unit cost measures for service/operation

The canteen of a company records the following income and expenditure for a month.

	$	$
Income		59,010
Food	17,000	
Drink	6,000	
Bottled water	750	
Fuel costs (gas for cooking)	800	
Maintenance of machinery	850	
Repairs	250	
Wages	15,500	
Depreciation	1,000	

During the month the canteen served 56,200 meals. The canteen's cost unit is one meal.

Required:

Calculate the average cost per meal served and the average income per meal served.

Solution

Total canteen expenditure in month = $42,150

Total meals served in the month = 56,200

$$\text{Average cost per meal served} = \frac{\$42,150}{56,200} = \$0.75 \text{ per meal}$$

$$\text{Average income per meal} = \frac{\$59,010}{56,200} = \$1.05 \text{ per meal}$$

Test your understanding 1

Which of the following are characteristics of service costing?

(i) High levels of direct labour costs as a proportion of total cost.

(ii) Use of composite cost units.

(iii) Use of equivalent units.

A (i) only

B (i) and (ii) only

C (ii) only

D (ii) and (iii) only

3 Service cost analysis

If organisations in the same service industry use the same service cost units then comparisons between the companies can be made easily.

e.g

Illustration 3 – Service cost analysis

The following figures were taken from the annual accounts of two electricity supply boards working on uniform costing methods.

Meter reading, billing and collection costs:

	Board A	Board B
	$000	$000
Salaries and wages of:		
Meter readers	150	240
Billing and collection staff	300	480
Transport and travelling	30	40
Collection agency charges	–	20
Bad debts	10	10
General charges	100	200
Miscellaneous	10	10
	600	1,000
Units sold (millions)	2,880	9,600
Number of consumers (thousands)	800	1,600
Sales of electricity (millions)	$18	$50
Size of area (square miles)	4,000	4,000

Comparative costs for Boards A and B may be collected as follows and are useful in showing how well (or otherwise) individual services are performing.

Comparative costs – year ending 31.12.X5

	Board A	% of total	Board B	% of total
	$000		$000	
Meter reading staff	150	25.0	240	24.0
Billing/collection staff	300	50.0	480	48.0
Transport/travelling	30	5.0	40	4.0
Collection agency	–	–	20	2.0
Bad debts	10	1.7	10	1.0
General charges	100	16.6	200	20.0
Miscellaneous	10	1.7	10	1.0
	600	100.0	1,000	100.0

The information contained in the following table is much more useful for comparison purposes than the meter reading and billing costs information given above.

	Board A	Board B
	$	$
Cost per:		
Million units sold	208	104
Thousand consumers	750	625
$m of sales	33,333	20,000
Square mile area	150	250

Test your understanding 2

Happy Returns Ltd operates a haulage business with three vehicles. The following estimated cost and performance data is available:

Petrol	$0.50 per kilometre on average
Repairs	$0.30 per kilometre
Depreciation	$1.00 per kilometre, plus $50 per week per vehicle
Drivers' wages	$300.00 per week per vehicle
Supervision and general expenses	$550 per week
Loading costs	$6.00 per tonne

During week number 26 it is expected that all three vehicles will be used, 280 tonnes will be loaded and a total of 3,950 kilometres travelled (including return journeys when empty) as shown in the following table:

Working

Journey	Tonnes carried (one way)	Kilometres (one way)
1	34	180
2	28	265
3	40	390
4	32	115
5	26	220
6	40	480
7	29	90
8	26	100
9	25	135
	280	1,975

Calculate the average cost per tonne-kilometre in week 26.

4 Chapter summary

The nature of service and operation costing

- Intangibility
- Heterogeneity
- Simultaneous production and consumption
- Perishability

Examples of service industries

- Hotels
- Airlines
- Public transport
- College/university
- Accountancy/audit firms
- Utility companies
- Distribution/haulage companies

Service and operation costing

Used when an organisation or department provides a service'

Suitable unit cost measures for service and operation costing

Composite cost unit used if service is function of two variables, for example:

- Patient-day
- Passenger-mile
- Guest-day
- Tonne-mile (or km)

Service cost analysis

If organisations in the same industry use the same service cost units then comparisons between companies can be made easily

Test your understanding answers

Test your understanding 1

B

Direct labour costs may be a high proportion on the total cost of providing a service and composite cost units are characteristic features of service costing. (i) and (ii) are therefore applicable and the correct answer is B.

Test your understanding 2

Total costs in Week 26

Petrol	$0.50 × 3,950	$1,975
Repairs	$0.30 × 3,950	$1,185
Depreciation	$1.00 × 3,950	$3,950
Depreciation	$50 × 3	$150
Wages	$300 × 3	$900
Supervision and general expenses	$550 × 1	$550
Loading costs	$6.00 × 280	$1,680
		$10,390

Tonne-km in week 26

Journey	Tonnes carried (one way)	Kilometres (one way)	Tonne-km
1	34	180	6,120
2	28	265	7,420
3	40	390	15,600
4	32	115	3,680
5	26	220	5,720
6	40	480	19,200
7	29	90	2,610
8	26	100	2,600
9	25	135	3,375
	280	1,975	66,325

(Costs averaged over the outward journeys, not the return, as these are necessary, but carry no tonnes.)

$$\text{Average cost per tonne-km} = \frac{\text{Total cost}}{\text{Total tonne-km}}$$

$$= \frac{\$10{,}390}{66{,}325}$$

= $0.157 per tonne-km

Chapter

9

Alternative costing principles

Chapter learning objectives

Upon completion of this chapter you will be able to:

- explain alternative cost management techniques (activity-based costing (ABC), target costing and life cycle costing)
- differentiate alternative cost management techniques from traditional costing techniques (note: calculations are not required).

PER

One of the PER performance objectives (PO12) is to apply different management accounting techniques is different business contexts to effectively manage and use resources. Working through this chapter should help you understand how to demonstrate that objective.

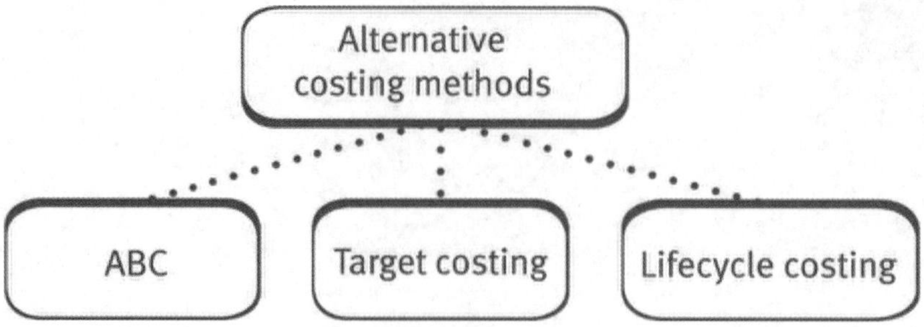

1 Modern production environments

Modern manufacturing is different from traditional manufacturing techniques:

- much more machinery and computerised manufacturing systems are used
- smaller batch sizes are manufactured at the request of customers
- less use of 'direct' labour due to the higher use of computers and machinery.

This has had an impact on production costs:

- more indirect costs (overheads)
- less direct labour costs.

This means that the traditional methods of costing using Absorption costing and Marginal costing are less useful.

- **Absorption costing** charges overheads to products in an arbitrary way – usually based on the volume of production in units or hours.
- **Marginal costing** values products based on the variable cost to produce them and fixed costs are treated as a period charge. In modern environments the variable costs might be small in comparison to the fixed costs and the fixed cost may not be truly fixed if considering all aspects of the production process.

2 Activity based costing (ABC)

Activity based costing (ABC) is an alternative approach to product costing. It is a form of absorption costing, but, rather than absorbing overheads on a production volume basis it firstly allocates them to **cost pools** before absorbing them into units using **cost drivers**.

- A **cost pool** is an **activity** that consumes resources and for which overhead costs are identified and allocated. For each cost pool there should be a cost driver.
- A **cost driver** is a **unit** of activity that consumes resources. An alternative definition of a cost driver is the factor influencing the level of cost.

ABC versus Absorption costing

Imagine the machining department of a business that makes clothing. In a traditional absorption costing system the overhead absorption rate would be based on machine hours because many of the overheads in the machining department would relate to the machines, for example power, maintenance, machine depreciation etc. Using only machine hours as the basis would seem fair, however not only does the machine department have machine related costs, but also in an absorption costing system it would have had a share of rent and rates, heating, lighting apportioned to it. These costs would also be absorbed based on machine hours and this is inappropriate as the machine hours are not directly responsible for the rent or rates.

ABC overcomes this problem by not using departments as gathering points for costs, but instead it uses activities to group the costs (cost pools) which are caused (driven) by an activity. There would be an activity that related to each of the following: power usage, machine depreciation and machine maintenance. Machining would not pick up a share of personnel costs or rent and rates as these would be charged to another activity. For example:

- the cost of setting up machinery for a production run might be driven by the number of set-ups (jobs or batches produced)
- the cost of running machines might be driven by the number of machine hours for which the machines are running
- the cost of order processing might be related to the number of orders dispatched or to the weight of items dispatched
- the cost of purchasing might be related to the number of purchase orders made.

ABCs flexibility reduces the need for arbitrary apportionments.

Using ABC should lead to more accurate product and/or service costs being calculated.

e.g

Illustration 1 – Absorption costing versus ABC

Note: No calculations will be required in the exam. This illustration is provided to aid understanding of the technique.

Mayes plc has a single production centre and has provided the following budgeted information for the next period.

	Product A	Product B	Product C	Total
Production and sales units	40,000	25,000	10,000	75,000
Direct material cost per unit	$25	$20	$18	$1,680,000
Direct labour hours per unit	3	4	2	240,000
Machine hours per unit	2	4	3	210,000
Number of production runs	5	10	25	40
Number of component receipts	15	25	120	160
Number of production orders	15	10	25	50

Direct labour is paid $8 per hour.

Overhead costs in the period are expected to be as follows:

	$
Set-up	140,000
Machine	900,000
Goods inwards	280,000
Packing	200,000
Engineering	180,000
	1,700,000

What are the unit costs of each product using:

(a) the traditional approach based on labour hours?

(b) the ABC method?

Solution

(a) A traditional costing approach would cost each product as follows:

	Product A	Product B	Product C
	$	$	$
Direct materials	25.00	20.00	18.00
Direct labour @$8 per hour	24.00	32.00	16.00
Overheads @$7.08 per hour (W1)	21.24	28.32	14.16
Total cost per unit	**$70.24**	**$80.32**	**$48.16**

(W1) Overhead recovery rate = $1,700,000/240,000 hours = $7.08 per direct labour hour.

(b) An ABC system needs to identify the cost drivers for the overheads not driven by production volume. Assume that these are as follows:

Cost	**Cost driver**
Set-up	Number of production runs
Machine	Machine hours
Goods inwards	Number of receipts
Packing	Number of production orders
Engineering	Number of production orders

The cost per activity is as follows:

- Machine = $900,000/210,000 hours = $4.29 per machine hour (after rounding)
- Set-up cost = $140,000/40 = $3,500 per production run
- Goods inwards = $280,000/160 = $1,750 per component receipt
- Packing = $200,000/50 = $4,000 per production order
- Engineering = $180,000/50 = $3,600 per production order

An ABC approach would allocate overheads to each of the product groups as follows:

	Product A	**Product B**	**Product C**
	$	$	$
Set-up costs			
5 × $3,500	17,500		
10 × $3,500		35,000	
25 × $3,500			87,500
Machine costs			
(2 × 40,000) × $4.29	343,200		
(4 × 25,000) × $4.29		429,000	
(3 × 10,000) × $4.29			128,700
Goods inwards costs			
15 × $1,750	26,250		
25 × $1,750		43,750	
120 × $1,750			210,000
Packing costs			
15 × $4,000	60,000		
10 × $4,000		40,000	
25 × $4,000			100,000
Engineering costs			
15 × $3,600	54,000		
10 × $3,600		36,000	
25 × $3,600			90,000

	Product A	Product B	Product C
	$	$	$
Total overhead cost	500,950	583,750	616,200
Average overhead per unit	**$12.52**	**$23.35**	**$61.62**
Direct material	25.00	20.00	18.00
Direct labour	24.00	32.00	16.00
Total unit cost	**$61.52**	**$75.35**	**$95.62**

When compared to the traditional overhead absorption rate it can be seen that product C is significantly under-costed using the traditional system, while products A and B are over-costed. This situation arises because the large proportion of costs driven by product C are not picked up under the traditional costing system. Since it is the cost-drivers identified in the ABC system which generate the costs in the first place, the ABC system will produce a more accurate final analysis.

Advantages and disadvantages of ABC

ABC has a number of advantages:

- It provides a more accurate cost per unit. As a result, pricing, sales strategy, performance management and decision making should be improved.
- It provides much better insight into what causes overhead costs.
- ABC recognises that overhead costs are not all related to production and sales volume.
- In many businesses, overhead costs are a significant proportion of total costs, and management needs to understand the drivers of overhead costs in order to manage the business properly. Overhead costs can be controlled by managing cost drivers.
- It can be applied to calculate realistic costs in a complex business environment.
- ABC can be applied to all overhead costs, not just production overheads.
- ABC can be used just as easily in service costing as in product costing.

Disadvantages of ABC:

- ABC will be of limited benefit if the overhead costs are primarily volume related or if the overhead is a small proportion of the overall cost.
- It is impossible to allocate all overhead costs to specific activities.
- The choice of both activities and cost drivers might be inappropriate.
- ABC can be more complex to explain to the stakeholders of the costing exercise.
- The benefits obtained from ABC might not justify the costs.

Test your understanding 1

Which THREE of the following explains why an activity based costing system may produce more accurate product costs than a traditional absorption costing system?

(i) Better cost control is possible

(ii) Arbitrary allocation/apportionment of costs are avoided

(iii) Better product pricing is possible

(iv) The choice of cost drivers is easy

(v) Can be applied to service companies

Options:

A (i), (ii), (iii) only

B (i) (iii), (v) only

C (ii), (iii), (iv) only

D (i), (iv), (v) only

Test your understanding 2

Which of the following statements are correct?

(i) A cost driver is any factor that causes a change in the cost of an activity.

(ii) For long-term variable overhead costs, the cost driver will be the volume of activity.

(iii) Traditional absorption costing tends to under-allocate overhead costs to low-volume products.

Options:

A (i) only

B (i) and (iii) only

C (ii) and (iii) only

D (i), (ii) and (iii)

3 Target costing

A target cost is a product cost estimated by subtracting a desired profit margin from a competitive market price. This may be less than the planned initial product cost, but will be expected to be achieved by the time the product reaches the mature production stage.

The conventional approach to product costing is an internal approach. The organisation builds up the cost of the product incurred in its production and will often determine its selling price by adding on an amount to the cost of production. This approach ignores the external environment within which the organisation operates – the market demand conditions and the prices set by competitors may not be fully reflected in the organisation's pricing policy.

Target costing is designed primarily to avoid this problem.

The starting point for target costing is an estimate of a selling price for a new product that will enable a firm to capture a required share of the market. The next step is to reduce this figure by the firm's required level of profit. This will take into account the return required on any new investment and on working capital requirements. This will produce a target cost figure for the organisation. All departments responsible for getting the product to market will estimate costs and must jointly find ways to achieve the target. Value analysis and/or value engineering can be used to reduce costs (discussed in a later chapter).

In essence, conventional costing and pricing methods can be described as bottom up in their approach, they start with internal costs and build up to a selling price.

Target costing is a top down approach – it starts with a target price and derives a cost from that price.

4 Life cycle costing

Life cycle costing tracks and accumulates the actual costs and revenues attributable to each product from inception to abandonment.

This is a technique which compares the revenues from a product with all the costs incurred over the entire product life cycle.

The product life cycle

The product life cycle suggests that all products pass through a number of stages from development to decline and is the basis for life cycle costing.

A diagram depicting the standard life cycle model for a product is shown below:

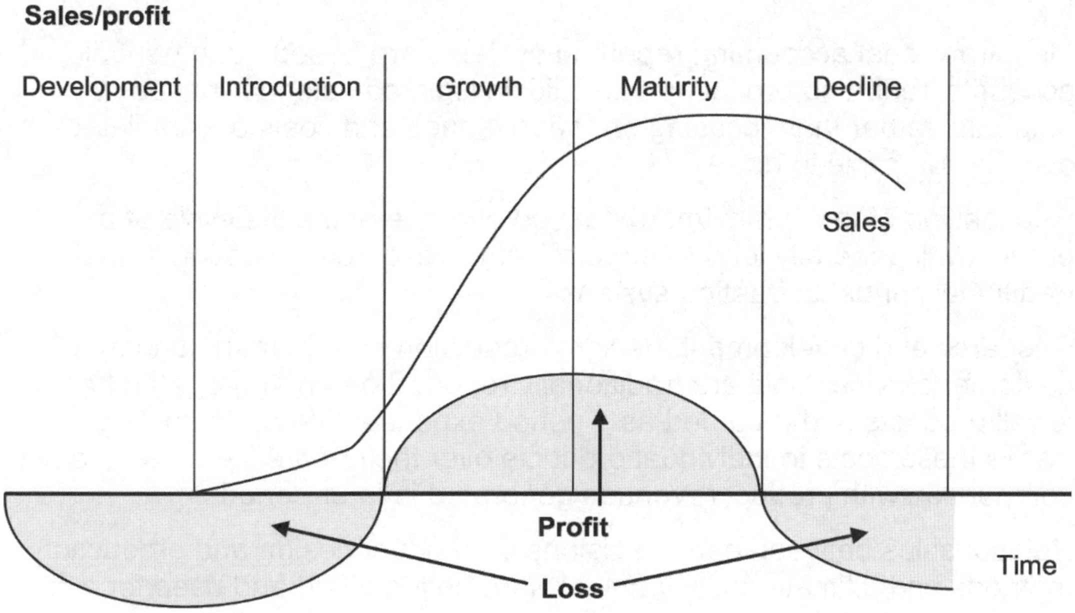

The interpretation of this model is as follows:

- At the **development** stage the product is not yet being sold. Sales are nil and development costs are creating a loss.
- At the **introduction** the product is launched on to the market. Sales volume is likely to be at a low level during this stage whilst the product establishes itself in the market place. In addition, potential customers may not be fully aware of the existence of the product or may be reluctant to try a new product, preferring to remain loyal to the products already established in the market place.
- During the **growth** stage it is hoped that sales volume will increase rapidly as consumers become more familiar with the product and it begins to take over from existing products in the market.
- At some point the growth in sales will slow and probably stop. The product has now reached the **maturity** stage in its life cycle. Sales are still at a high level. At this stage some form of modification may be required to prevent the product from going into the final stage.
- During the **decline** stage, sales will fall, perhaps slowly at first, but the pace of decline is likely to increase. The product may have become outdated or unfashionable, or new products may have entered the market and attracted customers away.

The advantages of life cycle costing are:

- the forecast profitability of a given product over its **entire life** is determined before production begins
- accumulated costs at any stage can be compared with life cycle budgeted costs, product by product, for the purposes of planning and control.

We can compare this approach with more **traditional** management accounting practices.

- Most traditional accounting reporting systems are based upon periodic accounts, reporting product profitability in isolated calendar-based amounts, rather than focusing on the revenues and costs accumulated over the life cycle to date.
- Recognition of the commitment needed over the entire life cycle of a product will generally lead to more effective resource allocation than the traditional annual budgeting system.
- Research and development, design, production set-up, marketing and customer service costs are traditionally reported on an aggregated basis for all products and recorded as a period expense. Life cycle costing traces these costs to individual products over their entire life cycles, to aid comparison with product revenues generated in later periods.
- Relationships between early decisions on product design and production methods and ultimate costs can therefore be identified and used for subsequent planning.

With decreasing product lives, it is important to recognise and monitor the relatively high pre-production and early stage costs product by product.

There are a number of factors that need to be managed in order to maximise a product's return over its lifecycle:

Design costs out of the product:

Around 70% of a product's costs are often incurred at the design and development stages of its life. Decisions made then commit the organisation to incurring the costs at a later date, because the design of the product determines the number of components, the production method, etc. It is absolutely vital therefore that design teams do not work in isolation but as part of a cross-functional team in order to minimise costs over the whole life cycle. Value engineering helps here.

Minimise the time to market:

In a world where competitors watch each other keenly to see what new products will be launched, any new product must get into the market place as quickly as possible. The competitors will monitor each other closely so that they can launch rival products as soon as possible in order to maintain profitability. It is vital, therefore, for the first organisation to launch its product as quickly as possible after the concept has been developed, so that it has as long as possible to establish the product in the market and to make a profit before competition increases. Often it is not so much costs that reduce profits as time wasted.

Maximise the length of the life cycle itself:

Generally, the longer the life cycle, the greater the profit that will be generated, assuming that production ceases once the product goes into decline and becomes unprofitable. One way to maximise the life cycle is to get the product to market as quickly as possible because this should maximise the time in which the product generates a profit.

Another way of extending a product's life is to find other uses, or markets, for the product. Other product uses may not be obvious when the product is still in its planning stage and need to be planned and managed later on. On the other hand, it may be possible to plan for a staggered entry into different markets at the planning stage.

Many organisations stagger the launch of their products in different world markets in order to reduce costs, increase revenue and prolong the overall life of the product. A current example is the way in which some new films are released in the USA months before the UK launch. This is done to build up the enthusiasm for the film and to increase revenues overall. Other companies may not have the funds to launch worldwide at the same moment and may be forced to stagger it.

The implications of life-cycle costing

Pricing

- Pricing decisions can be based on total life-cycle costs rather than simply the costs for the current period.

Decision making

- In deciding to produce a product, a timetable of life-cycle costs helps show what costs need to be allocated to a product so that an organisation can recover its costs. If all costs cannot be recovered, it would not be wise to produce the product or service.
- Life-cycle costing allows an analysis of links between business functions, e.g. a decision taken now to reduce research and development costs may lead to a fall in sales in the future.

Performance management

- Improved control – many companies find that 90% of the product's life-cycle costs are determined by decisions made in the development and launch stages. Focusing on costs after the product has entered production results in only a small proportion of life-cycle costs being manageable. Life-cycle costing thus reinforces the importance of tight control over locked-in costs, such as research and development in the development stage.
- Improved reporting – costs such as research and development and marketing are traditionally reported on an aggregated basis for all products and recorded as a period expense. Life-cycle costing traces these costs to individual products over their entire life cycles, to aid comparison with product revenues generated in later periods.

5 Chapter summary

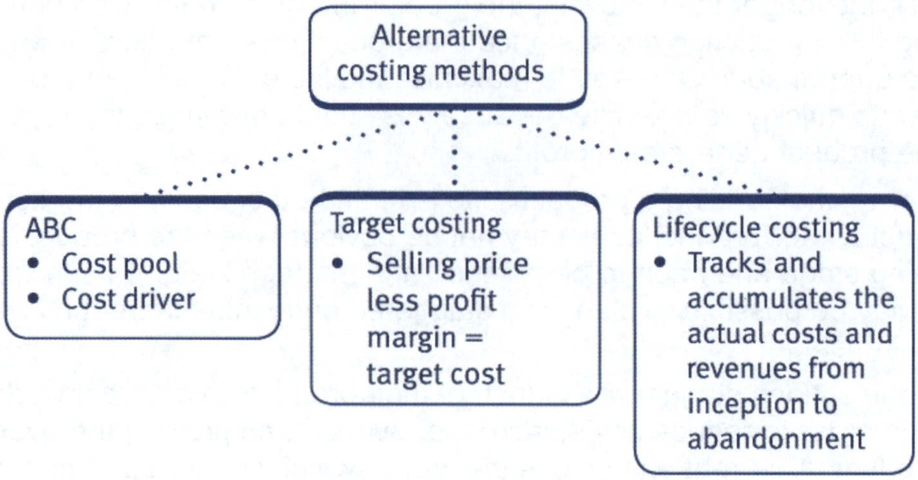

Test your understanding answers

Test your understanding 1

B

ABC provides better information on costs and how they are driven. It should therefore facilitate better cost control although it can be difficult to attach cost drivers to activities and this can make the system expensive to set up initially. It will also still involve some arbitrary cost allocation/ apportionment. For example, in a service industry it may be difficult to determine what drives the chief executive's salary and to determine how this should be allocated/apportioned to services.

Despite these faults, ABC should still provide a **better** allocation/ apportionment of costs to products when compared to traditional costing methods and this should then result in better pricing decisions. The success of ABC in manufacturing industries has led to the adoption of the technique in service industries – and exam questions are just as likely to involve service industries as they are to involve a manufacturing company.

Test your understanding 2

D

Statement (i) provides a definition of a cost driver. Cost drivers for long-term variable overhead costs will be the volume of a particular activity to which the cost driver relates, so Statement (ii) is correct. Statement (iii) is also correct. In traditional absorption costing, standard high-volume products receive a higher amount of overhead costs than with ABC. ABC allows for the unusually high costs of support activities for low-volume products (such as relatively higher set-up costs, order processing costs and so on).

Chapter

10

Sources of data

Chapter learning objectives

Upon completion of this chapter you will be able to:

- describe the three main data sources: machine/sensor, transactional and human/social
- describe the two types of data: categorical (nominal and ordinal) and numerical (continuous and discrete)
- explain the terms descriptive analysis and inferential analysis
- describe and identify sources and categories of information including internal, external, primary and secondary
- explain the uses and limitations of published information/data (including information from the internet)
- identify the data capture costs of management accounting information
- describe the five characteristics of big data (volume, variety, velocity, value and veracity)
- explain the three types of big data: structured, semi-structured and unstructured
- describe the main uses of big data and data analytics for organisations
- explain sampling techniques (random, systematic, stratified, multistage, cluster and quota)
- choose an appropriate sampling method in a specific situation.

  (Note: Derivation of random samples will not be examined.)

PER

One of the PER performance objectives (PO1) is to take into account all relevant information and use professional judgement, your personal values and scepticism to evaluate data and make decisions. You should identify right from wrong and escalate anything of concern. You also need to make sure that your skills, knowledge and behaviour are up-to-date and allow you to be effective in your role. Working through this chapter should help you understand how to demonstrate that objective.

PER

One of the PER performance objectives (PO12) is to apply different management accounting techniques is different business contexts to effectively manage and use resources. Working through this chapter should help you understand how to demonstrate that objective.

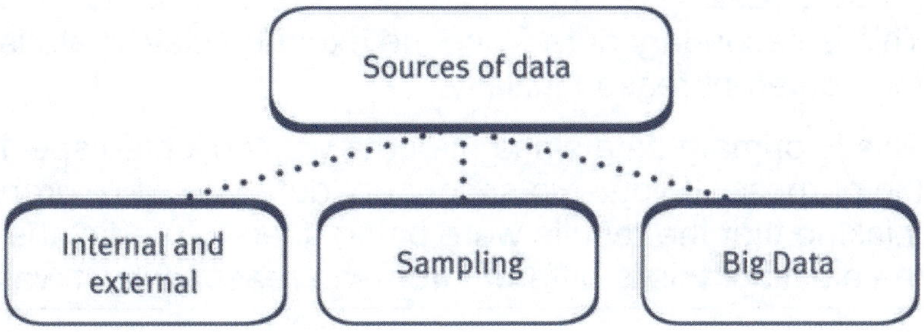

1 Types of data

Primary and secondary data

Primary data is obtained directly from first-hand sources by means of surveys, observation or experimentation. It is data that has not been previously published and is derived from a new or original research study and collected at the source such as in marketing. Primary data is any data which is used solely for the purpose for which it was originally collected.

Secondary data is data that has been previously collected or researched. Sources of secondary data include the internet, libraries, company reports, newspaper, governments and banks. The data collected is useful as it allows the researcher to see the other opinions on their area of study but care must be taken that the data is reliable and accurate. Secondary data is data that has already been collected for some other purpose but can also be used for the purpose in hand.

An important distinction is made here since information collected for one purpose by a business and then, at a later date, used again for another purpose would no longer be primary data.

Illustration 1 – Primary and secondary information

Decide which of the following are primary data and which are secondary data.

(a) Information from clock cards when used for making up wages.

(b) Data from a government publication on the toy industry used by a new toy shop to determine which items to stock.

(c) Expense claim forms submitted by sales representatives used to estimate the car mileage they have travelled.

(d) Results of an election opinion poll published in a newspaper.

Solution

(a) This is primary data, since the data is collected to make up the wages.

(b) This is secondary data; government statisticians collate data from various sources and the data is used in a variety of ways.

(c) This is secondary data since the expense claim data is collected for a different reason initially.

(d) This is primary data since the data was collected specifically for the purpose. If you said secondary data you were probably thinking that the results were being used to predict the result of the election; this is different from the reason why it was collected.

The problem with using secondary data

Primary data is preferable to secondary data since data collected for a specific purpose is likely to be better than data acquired for some other purpose. Some of the problems with secondary data are:

- The data has been collected by someone else. There is no control over how it was collected. If a survey was used, was a suitable questionnaire used? Was a large enough sample taken (was enough data collected)? Was it a reputable organisation that carried out the data collection?
- Is the data up to date? Data quickly becomes out of date, for example, people's consumer tastes change and prices may fluctuate.
- The data may be incomplete. Certain groups of people are sometimes omitted from the published data. For example, do you know which groups are included in the unemployment figures?
- What is the data? Is it actual, seasonally adjusted, estimated or a projection?
- The reason for collecting the data may be unknown. Statistics published on motor cars may include or exclude three wheeled cars, vans and motor caravans. Readers need to know which categories are included in the data.

If secondary data is to be used, these questions need to be answered. Sometimes the answers will be published with the data itself or sometimes it may be possible to contact the people who collected the data. If not, users must be aware of the limitations of making decisions based on information produced from secondary data. Sources of secondary data are numerous and can be broadly categorised as of two forms – those produced by individual organisations and those produced by the government.

Discrete and Continuous data (numerical data)

Discrete data is non-continuous data. Discrete data can only take certain values for example the number of students taking a course (there cannot be half a student). Discrete data is counted.

Continuous data is unbroken data that has no gaps. Continuous data can take on any value (within a range) for example time or distance. Continuous data is measured.

Test your understanding 1

Categorise each of the following variables as either discrete or continuous:

	Discrete	Continuous
Age of 5 years	❑	❑
Time of 2.5 hours	❑	❑
Output of 12,000 kg	❑	❑
Output of 5,000 units	❑	❑

Nominal and Ordinal data (categorical data)

Nominal data is data that is used for naming or labelling variables, without any quantitative value. There is usually no intrinsic ordering to nominal data. Examples include blood type, gender, eye colour and race.

Ordinal data is a data type with a set order or scale to it. However, this order does not have a standard scale on which the difference in variables in each scale is measured. Examples include customer satisfaction survey results, happiness levels, the Likert scale and age groups.

Nominal level data can only be classified, while ordinal data can be classified and ordered.

Descriptive analysis and inferential analysis

A descriptive analysis gives you an idea of the distribution of the data, helps you detect anomalies and enables you identify relationships between variables. Examples include histograms, frequency tables, bar charts, and the calculation of mean, mode, median and standard deviation.

Inferential analysis uses a random sample of data taken from a population to describe and make inferences about the population.

Descriptive analysis summarises the characteristics of a data set. Inferential analysis allows you to test a hypothesis.

2 Sources of data

Information may be **quantitative** or **qualitative** and financial or non-financial. It is mainly needed:

- to assist management in **planning** the most effective use of resources, such as labour and materials
- to assist management in **decision-making** (i.e. choosing between alternative courses of action), for example whether to make a product or purchase it from an outside supplier
- to aid management in **controlling** day-to-day operations, for example by comparing actual results with those planned.

When preparing for a budgeting exercise, management accountants must identify appropriate sources of information.

Machine/sensor data

Sensor data is the output from a device that detects and responds to some type of input from the physical environment.

This kind of data is collected in real-time and the number and timing of observations can be adapted to suit the requirements. Machine/sensor data can be collected automatically or manually. The quality is dependent on the level of sophistication of the sensor to take accurate measurements.

Sensor data can range from measurements taken from robots on production lines, to location data from a mobile phone, to smart meters recording electrical or gas usage in homes.

Transactional data

Transactional data relates to the transactions that take place as an organisation conducts its business.

Large retailers generate large volumes of data on a regular basis, particularly transactional data. Each transaction consists of one or more items of data, for example product IDs, prices, payment information. The quality of data produced from business transactions is related to the ability to gather representative observations and to process them in an appropriate manner.

Examples of transactional data include purchases by a customer, invoices raised, payments made, stock market prices.

Human/social data

Social data is information that social media users share publicly.

Social media, such as Facebook, Instagram and Twitter, can be used by companies to gain information on users' behaviour. Social media networks analyse the data to learn more about the users and connect them with appropriate content and advertising relevant to their interests.

Examples include posts on Facebook, tweets from Twitter and photos on Instagram.

Internal sources of information

Internal information may come from various sources.

Accounting system

The accounting system will collect data from source documents such as invoices, timesheets and journal entries. The data will be sorted and analysed by a coding system by type of expense, department, manager and job. Reports of direct and indirect costs compared to budgets may be produced at regular intervals to help managers plan and control costs. Ad hoc reports may be produced to help managers make specific decisions.

Consider the examples listed below:

- Sales analysed by product will help management to assess the patterns of demand for each product.
- This same information will help plan production and inventory levels.
- In turn, production information will enable the organisation to plan its requirements for raw materials, labour and machine hours.
- Information on material, labour and other costs will allow the organisation to set estimated costs for its products. This will be the basis for a budgetary control and standard costing system.
- In the context of long-term, strategic decision making, the sales analysis given above may help management to assess future product strategies – expand output of those for which demand is increasing, reduce output of those for which demand is falling.
- An aged receivables report would provide the basis for debt collection decisions taken by a credit control manager.
- Figures for wastage rates or product reject rates may allow management to reach decisions on the product quality aspect of the organisation's operations.

Payroll system

The payroll system may provide information concerning detailed labour costs. Hours paid may be analysed into productive and non-productive time such as training, sick leave, holiday and idle time. Labour turnover by department or manager may be analysed and may help management to assess the employment and motivation policies.

Strategic planning system

The strategic planning system may provide information relating to the organisation's objectives and targets. Assumptions relating to the external environment may be detailed. Details of the organisation's capital investment programme and product launch programme may also be recorded here. Some of this information will be commercially sensitive and only accessed by senior managers in the organisation.

Benefits and limitations of internal sources

Benefits

- Readily available data
- Data can easily be sorted and analysed
- Reports can easily be produced when required
- Data relates to the organisation concerned

Limitations

- Data may need to be further analysed to be of use to management accountants

External sources of information

Businesses are finding it increasingly difficult to succeed if they ignore the external environment which will influence their activities. The process known as environmental scanning or environmental monitoring is becoming an increasingly important part of the role of the management accountant. These terms are used to describe the process whereby data is collected from outside, as well as from inside the organisation and used in the decision-making process.

The main sources of external information which we shall consider here are:

- government sources
- business contacts – customers and suppliers
- trade associations and trade journals
- the financial and business press and other media
- the internet.

Government sources

There is a wealth of published statistical data covering many aspects of the nation's economy: population, manpower, trade, agriculture, price levels, capital issues and similar matters. Most of this is produced by national governments.

The primary purpose of this data is to provide information for economic planning at the national level – macroeconomics. The data serves a secondary purpose of providing industry with useful back ground information for deciding on future policies such as raising finance. The data is published in general terms for a type of industry or geographical area but is not company specific.

Macroeconomics is a branch of economics dealing with the performance, structure, behaviour, and decision-making of an economy as a whole, rather than individual markets. In contrast, microeconomics is primarily focused on the actions of individual agents, such as firms and consumers, and how their behaviour determines prices and quantities in specific markets.

Government produced information will be broadly based and general, dealing with the economy as a whole or particular sectors or industries.

Business contacts

An organisation may be looking for information more focused on its own position. Its day-to-day business contacts, customers and suppliers, can be a useful source of this information – and often it is freely available.

Customers can provide information on such matters as:

- the product specification which they require
- their quality requirements
- requirements for delivery periods
- preference for packaging and distribution methods
- feedback on the above and on general aspects of customer service.

Suppliers may be able to provide information on:

- quantity discounts and volume rebates which may help the organisation to decide on order size
- availability of products and services
- alternative products or services which may be available or may become available
- technical specifications of their product.

Trade associations and trade journals

Most major industries have their own trade association. The role of these organisations includes:

- representing their member firms in legal and other disputes
- providing quality assurance schemes for customers of member organisations
- laying down codes of practice to be followed by their member organisations
- publishing trade journals and other information useful for the management and development of their businesses.

Many trade organisations publish their own industry or trade journals which will contain useful news and other information for organisations operating in that industry. Trade journals are also published by many publishing organisations. In the UK one of the best known of these journals is The Grocer aimed at the food and drink retail sector.

The financial press, business press and other media

In the UK, The Financial Times, the Guardian, The Times and the Daily Telegraph together with some regional newspapers provide statistics and financial reviews as well as business and economic news and commentary. These include:

- the FTSE 100 Index – the stock market index of the leading 100 leading companies based on tradeable share value
- the FT All-share Index – an index of all share prices quoted on the stock exchange.

Such information is now also widely available via electronic media. Digital television services available on satellite or cable systems carry specialist business and financial channels and programmes (such as Bloomberg TV) which give both national and world-wide coverage.

The internet

The internet, or the World Wide Web, is a global computer network providing a variety of information and communication tools. Internet service providers, for example Virgin, Sky, BT or Vodafone, allow users to access websites. Many businesses trade through their websites known as e-commerce. The internet can also be searched for all sorts of information using search engines, such as Google or Yahoo!. Business details, product details or general information can be searched for and information is returned.

Weaknesses of the internet

There is no overall authority or control for what is included on the internet, this means that anyone can produce websites, opinion can pose as fact, and information can be misleading. Basically evaluation of a site's authority and accuracy is difficult.

Any data accessed from the internet could have been altered so there is a possibility for inaccurate data to be used.

Much of what is available on the web is of little or no value, except perhaps to the individual who produced it, and the sheer quantity of sites makes the search for quality that much more difficult.

Web sites can change location and leave no "forwarding address," or disappear altogether. Anyone who relies on certain sites for data could find their source has gone.

Most of the information on the web can be accessed for free but costs of building and maintaining and upgrading the systems are significant and likely to increase as more networked information becomes available.

Strengths of the internet

One of the web's strongest assets is its ability to provide current, timely and localised information.

The web's interactive capabilities provide functions not possible through standard print sources. Businesses often provide instant messaging or 'chat now' panels which enable customers to query products before ordering online.

The system of links on a website can bring related materials and information together far more seamlessly and effectively than is possible in print. You can often find 'related links' on a website that will take you to another site to be able access more information.

The web offers flexibility regarding where and when its information can be accessed.

The biggest advantage of the internet is the wealth of information you can access at the click of a button.

Benefits and limitations of external sources

Internal information is produced by the company itself so the users are aware of any limitations in its quality or reliability. External information is not under the control of the organisation – the users may not be aware of any limitations in its quality.

Benefits

- Wide expanse of external sources of information
- Easily accessible especially using the internet
- More general information available
- Can source specific information needs

Limitations

- Data may not be accurate
- Finding relevant information can be time consuming

3 Data capture costs

Direct data is another term that can be used to refer to data that is obtained directly from a source (primary data).

For example, data collected from customers first hand via surveys or interviews, completion of timesheets by employees, scanning of a bar code at a check out.

Indirect data is another term that can be used to refer to data that is derived from other sources (secondary data).

For example, using a market research company to collect data from customers to then draw conclusions about future sales figures.

Cost of information

Capturing, processing, analysing, using and storing data are costs for a business.

For example, the self-service checkouts that record the sales in a store, the maintenance of the checkouts and the cost of storage space in The Cloud that holds the inventory records.

Direct and indirect data capture costs

Direct data capture costs are the costs incurred when inputting data into a system:

- using scanners to read bar codes and/or QR codes
- entry of data, such as an employee inputting time taken to complete a job into timesheet
- machines or measuring devices within manufacturing processes to record the usage of materials
- use of Artificial Intelligence to gather evidence from finger prints or visual features.

Indirect data capture costs include:

- purchasing cost, for example newspaper subscriptions or buying data from a research company
- verification of data reliability, for example cross referencing with other data
- processing data into a useable format.

4 Sampling

The purpose of sampling is to gain as much information as possible about the population by observing only a small proportion of that population i.e. by observing a sample.

The term population is used to mean all the items under consideration in a particular enquiry.

A sample is a group of items drawn from that population. The population may consist of items such as metal bars, invoices, packets of tea, etc; it need not be people.

For example:

- in order to ascertain which television programmes are most popular, a sample of the total viewing public is interviewed and, based on their replies, the programmes can be listed in order of popularity with all viewers.
- during the quality control procedures in a manufacturing business, a sample of the product is taken for testing.

There are three main reasons why sampling is necessary:

1 The whole population may not be known.

2 Even if the population is known the process of testing every item can be extremely costly in time and money, for example, gaining information about the popularity of TV programs by interviewing every viewer.

3 The items being tested may be completely destroyed in the process, for example in order to check the lifetime of an electric light bulb it is necessary to leave the bulb burning until it breaks and is of no further use.

The characteristics of a population can be ascertained by investigating only a sample of that population provided that the following two rules are observed:

1 The sample must be of a certain size. In general terms the larger the sample the more reliable the results will be.

2 The sample must be chosen in such a way that it is representative of the population.

There are several methods of obtaining a sample and these are considered in turn.

Random sampling

A simple random sample is defined as a sample taken in such a way that every member of the population has an equal chance of being selected.

If a 10% sample of a population of 200 items is the required, then the sample size needs to be 20 items. Numbers from a table of random numbers can be taken and the corresponding items are extracted from the population to form the sample e.g. in selecting a sample of invoices for an audit. Since the invoices are already numbered, this method can be applied with the minimum of difficulty.

This method has obvious limitations when either the population is extremely large or, in fact, not known. The following methods are more applicable in these cases.

Systematic sampling

Systematic sampling is a technique for creating a random sample in which each piece of data is chosen at a fixed interval for inclusion in the sample.

If the population is known to contain 50,000 items and a sample of size 500 is required, then 1 in every 100 items is selected. The first item is determined by choosing randomly a number between 1 and 100 e.g. 67, then the second item will be the 167th, the third will be the 267th... up to the 49,967th item.

Strictly speaking, systematic sampling (also called quasi-random) is not truly random as only the first item is selected randomly. However, it gives a very close approximation to random sampling and it is very widely used.

There is danger of bias if the population has a repetitive structure. For example, if a street has five types of house arranged in the order, A B C D E A B C D E... etc, an interviewer visiting every fifth home would only visit one type of house.

Stratified sampling

A stratified sample is made up of different 'layers' or 'groups' of the population. The sample size for each layer is proportional to the size of the 'layer' and is known as sampling with probability proportional to size (pps).

Illustration 2 – Stratified sampling

A sample of 200 people is required to investigate leisure habits in relation to age.

- 20% of the population are over 60 years of age
- 65% between 18 and 60
- 15% are under 18

The sample of 200 people should therefore contain:

- (200 × 20%) 40 who are over 60 years old
- (200 × 65%) 130 people between 18 and 60
- (200 × 15%) 30 under 18 years of age

This method ensures that a representative cross-section of the strata in the population is obtained, which may not be the case with a simple random sample of the whole population.

This method is often used by auditors to choose a sample to confirm receivables' balances. In this case a greater proportion of larger balances will be selected.

Multistage sampling

This method is often applied if the population is particularly large, for example in selecting a sample for a national opinion poll of the type carried out prior to a general election. The process involved here would be as follows:

Step 1 The country is divided into areas (counties) and a random sample of areas is taken.

Step 2 Each area chosen in Step 1 is then subdivided into towns and cities or boroughs and a random sample of these is taken.

Step 3 Each town or city chosen in Step 2 is further divided into roads and a random sample of roads is then taken.

Step 4 From each road chosen in Step 3 a random sample of houses is taken and the occupiers interviewed.

Cluster sampling

This method is similar to the multistage sampling but the final step is to sample all the items as a 'cluster'. In many ways this is a simpler and less costly procedure as no time is wasted finding particular houses and the amount of travelling by interviewers is much reduced.

Quota sampling

With quota sampling the interviewer will be given a list comprising the different types of people to be questioned and the number or quota of each type e.g.:

- 20 males, aged 20 to 30 years, manual workers
- 15 females, 25 to 35, not working
- 10 males, 55 to 60, professional men, etc.

The interviewer can use any method to obtain such people until the various quotas are filled. This is very similar to stratified sampling, but no attempt is made to select respondents by a proper random method, consequently the sample may be very biased.

Sampling methods compared

The objective of a sample is to collect data upon which an opinion can be formed, and a conclusion drawn in respect of the population of which the sample is representative.

Ideally the sample would be chosen at random, and would be large enough so as to be representative of the population. Unfortunately both of these aspects introduce costs which are often unacceptably high.

Alternatives to the truly random sampling method have been outlined. They are all concerned with minimising costs whilst maintaining the representative nature of the sample compared to the population.

In order to use these alternatives, it is often necessary to have some knowledge of the population. Systematic sampling should not be used if the population follows a repetitive pattern. Quota sampling must be used with caution. The data collector may introduce bias because of how they choose how to fill the quota.

Test your understanding 2

The essence of systematic sampling is that:

A each element of the population has an equal chance of being chosen

B members of various strata are selected by the interviewers up to predetermined limits

C every nth member of the population is selected

D every element of one definable subsection of the population is selected

Test your understanding 3

A sample is taken by dividing the population into different age bands and then sampling randomly from the bands, in proportion to their size. What is such a sample called?

A Simple random

B Stratified random

C Quota

D Cluster

Test your understanding 4

A large company wants to survey the opinions of employees using cluster sampling. Which of the following methods should be used?

A Staff are randomly selected from each department in proportion to departmental size

B Staff are selected from the list of employees, taking every nth name

C A sample, which is as representative as possible of the composition of the staff in terms of gender, age and department, is taken by stopping appropriate staff in the corridors and canteen

D One department is selected and all the staff in that department are surveyed

Test your understanding 5

Associate with each of the following sampling methods A – F the most appropriate example from the list 1– 6, given below.

A Simple random sample

B Stratified random sample

C Cluster sample

D Systematic sample

E Quota sample

F Multistage sample

Examples

1 One city is chosen at random from all cities in the United Kingdom, then the electoral register is used to select a 1-per-1,000 sample.

2 Names picked from a hat.

3 Every 10th person is chosen randomly from each ward in a hospital.

4 One secondary school in a town is selected at random, then every pupil in that school is surveyed.

5 One person in ten is chosen from an alphabetical list of employees.

6 People are stopped in the street according to instructions such as 'stop equal numbers of men and women'.

5 Big Data

What is Big Data?

There are several definitions of Big Data. The most common refer to:

- extremely large collections of data that may be analysed to reveal patterns, trends and associations
- data collections so large that conventional methods of storing and processing that data will not work

Big Data is a big buzzword at the moment and some say that it will be even bigger than the Internet. The ability to harness these vast amounts of data will transform our ability to understand the world and will lead to huge advances, for example, in understanding customer behaviour, foiling terrorist attacks, preventing diseases and pinpointing marketing efforts.

Illustration 3 – The use of Big Data by supermarkets

A supermarket is able to take data from a your past buying patterns, its own inventory information, your mobile phone location, social media and weather information to send you, for example, a voucher for barbeque food. It will have used that data to determine if you have bought such items before which would indicate that you own a barbeque, if the weather is nice, if you are within 3 miles of one of their stores and that they have the barbeque food in stock.

The 5Vs

Big Data is **characterised** by the 5Vs:

- **Volume:** organisations now hold huge volumes of data. For example:
  - A **supermarket** will have a data store of all purchases made, when and where they were made, how they were paid for and the use of coupons via loyalty cards swiped at the checkout.
  - An **online retailer** will have a data store of every product looked at and bought and every page visited.
  - **Mobile phone providers** will have a data store of texts, voice mails, calls made, browsing habits and location.
  - **Social media companies**, such as Facebook, will have a data store of all the postings an individual makes (and where they were made), photos posted and contacts.
- **Variety:** Big Data can include much more than simply financial information and can include other organisational data which is operational in nature as well as other internal and external information. This data can be both structured, semi-structured and unstructured in nature:
  - **Structured data** – data that is the easiest to search and organise, because it is usually contained in rows and columns and its elements can be mapped into fixed pre-defined fields. For example, financial data in an excel spreadsheet.
  - **Unstructured data** – data that cannot be contained in a row-column database and does not have an associated data model. For example, the text of an email message. The lack of structure makes unstructured data more difficult to search, manage and analyse, which is why companies have widely discarded unstructured data, until the recent proliferation of artificial intelligence and machine learning algorithms made it easier to process. It can now make up 80% of business data but is more difficult to store and analyse.
  - **Semi-structured data** – is a mix between both of structured and unstructured data. The type of data defined as semi-structured data has some defining or consistent characteristics but doesn't conform to a structure as rigid as is expected within a database.

- **Velocity:** The data must be turned into useful information quickly enough to be of use in decision making and performance management (in real time if possible). The sheer volume and variety of data makes this task difficult and sophisticated methods are required to process the huge volumes of non-uniform data quickly.
- **Value:** will the data have a positive impact a company's business? How much value can it add?
- **Veracity:** is the data accurate enough to be relied upon?

Processing Big Data

The ability to manage Big Data successfully will drive innovation (and potentially competitive advantage) to reduce the time taken to answer key business questions and hence make decisions.

The processing of Big Data is known as **Big Data analytics**. For example, Google Analytics tracks many features of website traffic.

Hadoop software allows the processing of large data sets by utilising multiple servers simultaneously.

Big Data and management accountancy

Big Data is relevant to management accountancy in a number of ways, such as:

- It can help the organisation to **understand its customers' needs and preferences** which can then be used to improve marketing and sales.
- It can **improve forecasting**, for example of future customer spending or of machine replacement cycles, so that more appropriate decisions can be made.
- It can help the organisation to **automate business processes** resulting in improved efficiency.
- It can help to provide more **detailed, relevant and up to date performance measurement**.

Examples of how Big Data is used

- **Consumer facing organisations** monitor social media activity to gain insight into customer behaviour and preferences. This source can also be used to identify and engage brand advocates and detractors, and assess responsiveness to advertising campaigns and promotions.
- **Manufacturing companies** can monitor data from their equipment to determine usage and wear. This allows them to predict the optimal replacement cycle.
- **Financial Services organisations** can use data on customer activity to carefully segment their customer base and therefore accurately target individuals with relevant offers.

- **Politicians** are using social media analytics to establish where they have to campaign the hardest to win the next election.
- **Humanitarian agencies**, such as the United Nations, use phone data to understand population movements during relief operations and outbreaks of disease, meaning they can allocate resources more efficiently and identify areas at risk of new disease outbreaks.

More examples of Big Data in the real world

UPS's delivery vehicles are equipped with sensors which monitor data on speed, direction, braking performance and other mechanical aspects of the vehicle. This information is then used to optimise maintenance schedules and improve efficiency of delivery routes saving time, money and reducing wastage.

Data from the vehicles is combined with customer data, GPS information and data concerning the normal behaviour of delivery drivers. Using this data to optimise vehicle performance and routes has resulted in several significant improvements:

- Over 15 million minutes of idling time were eliminated in one year. This saved 103,000 gallons of fuel.
- During the same year 1.7 million miles of driving was eliminated, saving 183,000 gallons of fuel.

Tesco has sophisticated sensors installed on all refrigeration units to monitor the temperature at regular intervals and to send the information over the internet to a central data warehouse. The data collected is used to identify units that are operating at temperatures that are too low (resulting in energy wastage) or too high (resulting in potential stock obsolescence and a safety risk). Engineers can monitor the data remotely and can then visit the store to rectify any problem that is identified. Previously, store managers may have overlooked a problem or only identified a problem once it had escalated into something more serious.

Netflix has over 100 million users worldwide. The company uses information gathered from analysis of viewing habits to inform decisions on which shows to invest in. Analysing past viewing figures and understanding viewer populations and the shows they are likely to watch allows the analysts to predict likely viewing figures before a show has even aired. This can help to determine if the show is a viable investment.

Test your understanding 6

MC is a mobile phone network provider, offering mobile phones and services on a range of different tariffs to customers across Europe. The company enjoyed financial success until three years ago but increasing competitive pressure has led to a recent decline in sales. There has also been an increase in the level of complaints regarding the customer service provided, and the company's churn rate (number of customers leaving the company within a given time frame) is at an all-time high.

Required:

Discuss how Big Data could help drive the strategic direction of MC company.

Risks associated with Big Data

- The **availability of skills** to use Big Data systems, which is compounded by the fact that many of the systems are rapidly developing and support is not always easily and readily available. There is also an increasing need to combine data analysis skills with a deep understanding of the industry being analysed and this need is not always recognised.
- The **security of data** is a major concern in the majority of organisations and if the organisation lacks the resources to manage data then there is likely to be a greater risk of leaks and losses. There can be a risk to the data protection of organisations as they collect a greater range of data from increasingly personal sources (for example, Facebook).
- It is important to recognise that just because something CAN be measured, this does not necessarily mean it should be. There is a risk that **valuable time is spent measuring relationships that have no organisational value**.
- **Incorrect data** (poor veracity) may result in incorrect conclusions being made.
- There may be **technical difficulties** associated with integrating existing data warehousing and, for example, Hadoop systems.
- The **cost** of establishing the hardware and analytical software needed.

Student accountant article: visit the ACCA website, www.accaglobal.com, to review the articles on 'Big Data and performance management' and 'Big Data'.

6 Chapter summary

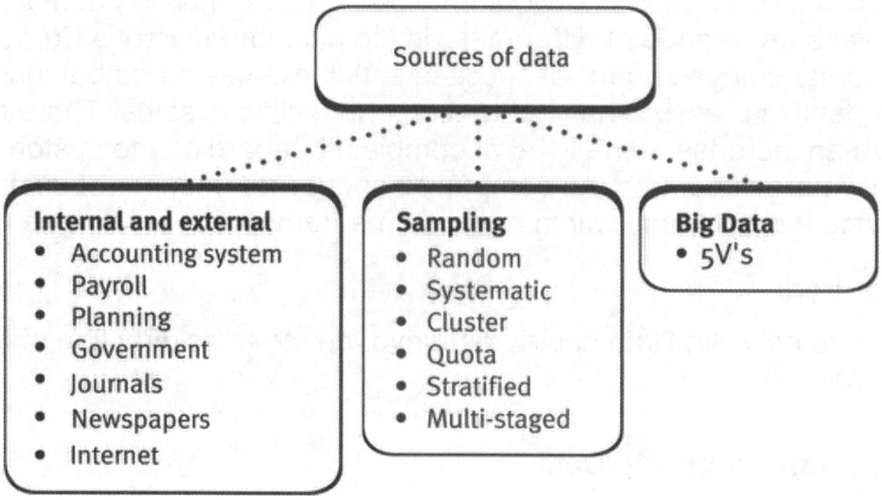

Test your understanding answers

Test your understanding 1

Age of 5 years	Continuous
Time of 2.5 hours	Continuous
Output of 12,000 kg	Continuous
Output of 5,000 units	Discrete

Test your understanding 2

C

In systematic sampling, population members are listed and members selected at regular intervals along the list.

Test your understanding 3

B

In simple random sampling, there is no division of the population into groups. In cluster sampling, only one group is selected and all its members are surveyed. Quota sampling and stratified random sampling are both as described in the question but quota sampling is not random.

Test your understanding 4

D

A is a stratified random sample, B is systematic and C is a quota sample.

Test your understanding 5

A	2
B	3
C	4
D	5
E	6
F	1

Test your understanding 6

Big Data management involves using sophisticated systems to gather, store and analyse large volumes of data in a variety of structured and unstructured formats. Companies are collecting increasing volumes of data through everyday transactions and marketing activity. If managed effectively this can lead to many business benefits although there are risks involved.

A company like MC will already collect a relatively large amount of data regarding its customers, their transactions and call history. It is likely that a significant proportion of their customers are also fairly digitally engaged and therefore data can be gathered regarding preferences and complaints from social media networks. This will be particularly useful to MC as they have seen an increase in complaints and have a high churn rate so engaging with customers will be highly beneficial.

Recent competitive pressure has led to a decline in sales and so MC need to consider the strategic direction which is most appropriate for them to improve performance.

Analysing the large amounts of data available to them will inform decisions on areas such as:

- The type of handsets currently most in demand and therefore the prices required when bundling with tariffs; Main areas of complaint and therefore the areas of weakness which need to be resolved
- Which types of communication are most popular (e.g. data, call minutes, text messages) to ensure the tariffs have the right combinations
- Usage statistics for 'pay as you go' customers, to drive the most appropriate offers and marketing activity
- Most popular competitor offerings with reasons.

Chapter

11

Analysing data

Chapter learning objectives

Upon completion of this chapter you will be able to:

- calculate the mean, mode, and median for ungrouped and the mean for grouped data
- calculate measures of dispersion including the variance, standard deviation and coefficient of variation both grouped and ungrouped data
- calculate expected values for use in decision-making
- explain the properties of a normal distribution
- interpret normal distribution graphs and tables.

PER

One of the PER performance objectives (PO1) is to take into account all relevant information and use professional judgement, your personal values and scepticism to evaluate data and make decisions. You should identify right from wrong and escalate anything of concern. You also need to make sure that your skills, knowledge and behaviour are up-to-date and allow you to be effective in your role. Working through this chapter should help you understand how to demonstrate that objective.

PER

One of the PER performance objectives (PO12) is to apply different management accounting techniques is different business contexts to effectively manage and use resources. Working through this chapter should help you understand how to demonstrate that objective.

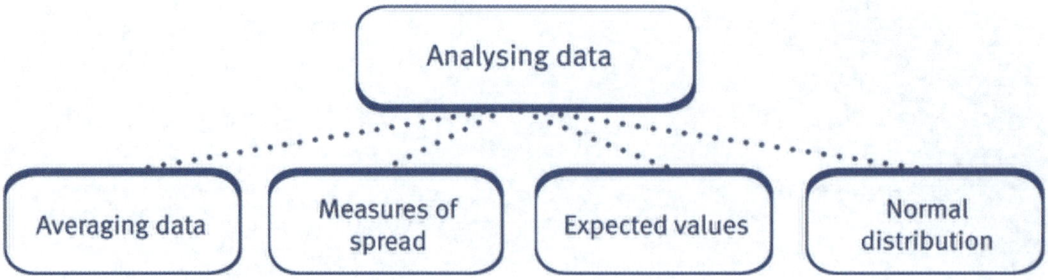

1 Averaging data

We will now look at some common mathematical concepts which help us to analyse and understand our data.

In mathematics there are different measures of average. We are going to look at three: mean, median and mode.

The arithmetic mean

The arithmetic mean, also known as the 'average', is calculated by dividing the sum of the values in question by the number of values.

Using the following set of numbers:

12, 14, 17, 19, 15

The simple average would be (12 + 14 + 17 + 19 + 15) ÷ 5 = **15.4**

This measure is the **arithmetic mean**, or, where there is no possibility of confusion, simply the mean.

Illustration 1 – Calculating the mean

A shopkeeper is about to put his/her shop up for sale. As part of the details of the business, he/she wishes to quote the average weekly takings. The takings in each of the last 6 weeks are:

\$1,120	\$990	\$1,040	\$1,030	\$1,105	\$1,015

Determine the mean weekly takings that the shopkeeper could quote.

Solution

If the weekly takings are denoted by the variable x, then the mean value of x, pronounced 'x-bar' and written as $\overline{x}$, is given by:

$$\overline{x} = \frac{\text{Sum of the values of x}}{\text{Number of values of x}}$$

$$\text{or } \overline{x} = \frac{\Sigma x}{n}$$

where Σ, a Greek capital letter 'sigma', is the mathematical symbol for 'add up', and n is the number of values of x.

In this example:

$$\bar{x} = \frac{1,120 + 990 + 1,040 + 1,030 + 1,105 + 1,015}{6} = \frac{6,300}{6} = \$1,050$$

The shopkeeper could therefore quote a sample mean weekly takings figure of $1,050.

As we can see, this formula is very easy to apply it will, however, need some modification before it can be used to determine the mean from groups of data or a **frequency distribution**.

e.g

Illustration 2 – The mean from a frequency distribution

A company is implementing an efficiency drive and, as part of a leaflet it is to distribute to its employees, it wishes to point out the average daily absenteeism rate. The following data is collated from the records of a sample of 200 working days.

Compute the sample mean number of absentees per day.

Number of absentees per day (x)	Number of days (f)
0	9
1	28
2	51
3	43
4	29
5	18
6	10
7	7
8	5

It should be noted that the 'number of days' column simply gives the frequency of the corresponding x values, and so we shall denote this quantity by *f*. Now, to find the sample mean, the following formula can be applied in a straightforward manner.

$$\bar{x} = \frac{\Sigma fx}{\Sigma f}$$

Solution

x	f	fx
0	9	0
1	28	28
2	51	102
3	43	129
4	29	116
5	18	90
6	10	60
7	7	49
8	5	40
	$\sum f = 200$	$\sum fx = 614$

$$= \frac{614}{200} = 3.07$$

The mean number of absentees in the sample is 3.07 per day.

Test your understanding 1

The following distribution shows the number of employees absent per day for a company over a 22 day period.

No of employees absent	No. of days (frequency)
2	2
3	4
4	3
5	4
6	3
7	3
8	3

Find the arithmetic mean for the above distribution.

The following illustration demonstrates how to calculate the mean in the slightly more complex case where we have grouped data.

e.g

Illustration 3 – Calculating the mean from grouped data

As part of its preparation for a wage negotiation, the HR manager of a company has collated the following data from a sample of payslips. He/she wishes to be able to use the average weekly wage figure in the negotiations.

Evaluate the mean of the sample.

Weekly wage ($)	**Number of employees (f)**
180 – under 185	41
185 – under 190	57
190 – under 195	27
195 – under 200	23
200 – under 205	15
205 – under 210	7

Solution

The extra difficulty in this problem is clear. As the data has been collated into classes, a certain amount of detail has been lost and hence the values of the variable x to be used in the calculation of the mean are not clearly specified. Short of actually having the raw data, the actual wages of the employees in the sample, we can only approximate the value of the mean. To do this, we adopt the approach of taking x to be a representative value of each class, the most plausible being the mid-point. Doing this, we have

x	f	fx
182.50	41	7,482.50
187.50	57	10,687.50
192.50	27	5,197.50
197.50	23	4,542.50
202.50	15	3,037.50
207.50	7	1,452.50
	$\sum f = 170$	$\sum fx = 32{,}400.00$

It is advisable to set out such statistical calculations in the way shown as often figures have to be summed, and so they are best arranged in columns. Now we have:

$$\bar{x} = \frac{\Sigma fx}{\Sigma f} = \frac{32,400}{170} = 190.59$$

Hence, the manager can use an average weekly wage of $190.59 in the negotiations.

Test your understanding 2

The output levels of product Q have been given in the following distribution:

Output of Q (kg)	No. of days (frequency)
350 – under 360	4
360 – under 370	6
370 – under 380	5
380 – under 390	4
390 – under 400	3

Find the arithmetic mean for the above distribution (to two d.p.).

The median

The median is defined as the middle of a set of values, when arranged in ascending (or descending) order.

The median can be used to overcome any issues of skewed data i.e. the distribution is not symmetrical, since the median has half the distribution above it, and half below.

Similarly the median is unaffected by any particularly large or unusual individual measurements whereas the mean would be.

Illustration 4 – Calculating the median

In Illustration 4 we saw that a shop's weekly takings were given by the following sample over six weeks. The sample has an arithmetic mean of $1,050.

$1,120 $990 $1,040 $1,030 $1,105 $1,015

A prospective purchaser of the business notices that the mean is higher than the takings in four of the 6 weeks.

Calculate the median for the purchaser.

Solution

First of all, we arrange the takings figures in ascending order:

$990	$1,015	$1,030	$1,040	$1,105	$1,120

The question now is: what is the middle number of a list of six? With a little thought, you can see that there are two 'middle' values, the third and fourth. The median is thus taken to be the mean of these two values.

$$\text{Median} = \frac{(1{,}030 + 1{,}040)}{2} = 1{,}035$$

Hence, the median weekly takings figure that the prospective purchaser could quote is $1,035.

In the case of an odd number of values, the determination of the median is even easier, as there is a clear single middle item in an odd number of values. In general, if there are n observations, the position of the median is given by (n + 1)/2. With six observations, this gives 7/2 = 3.5, which is the position halfway between the third and fourth observations.

Test your understanding 3

Calculate the median of the following data:

25	52	18	43	27

The mode

The mode or modal value of a data set is that value that occurs most often.

The determination of this value, when you have raw data to deal with, consists simply of a counting process to find the most frequently occurring value.

Illustration 5 – Calculating the mode

Find the mode for the following distribution:

Complaints per week	No of weeks
0	5
1	12
2	7
3	2
4	1

Solution

The mode is the value with the highest frequency, so here the mode is one complaint per week.

Test your understanding 4

Calculate the mode of the following data

2	4	3	4	3
3	3	2	4	3

Expected values (EV)

Probabilities

A probability expresses the likelihood of an event occurring.

Note the terminology here. The 'event' referred to is simply what we want to calculate the probability for, such as 'winning the tender' or 'rolling a six'.

Basic ideas

- If an event is certain to occur, then it has a probability of one.
- If an event is impossible, then it has a probability of zero.
- For any event, the probability of it occurring must lie between zero and one. If you calculate a probability bigger than one, then you have made a mistake.
- The higher the probability is, then the more likely it is that the event will happen.
- In any given scenario, the probabilities associated with all possible outcomes must add up to one.

For example, if trying to win a particular tender for new work, then there are only two possible outcomes. You either win or you don't. If the probability of winning the tender is 0.4 (40%), then the probability of not winning must be 0.6 (60%) as the two probabilities must add up to one.

Illustration 6 – Simple probabilities

An ordinary six-sided die is rolled.

What is the probability that it will show a number less than three?

Solution

It is possible to list all the possible equally likely outcomes, namely the whole numbers from one to six inclusive: 1, 2, 3, 4, 5, 6

The outcomes that constitute the 'event' under consideration, that is, 'a number less than three' are: 1, 2

Hence the proportion of outcomes that constitute the event is 2/6 or 1/3, which is therefore the desired probability.

We could write this as P(Getting a number < 3) = 1/3

Test your understanding 5

Four people are asked to select a card at random from a standard pack of playing cards. A standard pack of playing cards has 52 cards.

These are split into four 'suits':

- 'hearts'
- 'clubs'
- 'diamonds'
- 'spades'

Each 'suit' has 13 cards – the Ace, 2, 3, 4, 5, 6, 7, 8, 9, 10, Jack, Queen and King.

Hearts and diamonds are red cards whereas clubs and spades are black.

The card is replaced before the following selection so each selection is from the full pack. You are told that

(a) A picked a king

(b) B picked a red card

(c) C picked a club

(d) D picked the Ace of Spades

Determine the probability for each selection.

(a) The probability that A picked a king is _________.

(b) The probability that B picked a red card is _________.

(c) The probability that C picked a club is _________.

(d) The probability that D picked the Ace of spades is _________.

Expected values

Many business situations require a choice between numerous courses of action. Given that these choices relate to future outcomes, the results will be uncertain. Clearly, the decision-maker's experience and judgement are important in making 'good' choices in such instances. It is important to make these choices as good as possible as they can affect the future of the organisation, so decision makers will use various techniques to help in making these choices. No technique can totally replace human judgement in business decisions but some can help make the choices clearer and therefore make it easier to decide between them.

One technique which can help judge the financial outcomes of various options is **expected value** (EV).

An expected value is a long run average. It is the weighted average of a probability distribution.

While techniques such as EV can help assess the financial aspect of a decision, there are many other non-financial considerations which must be taken account of in any business decision.

Expected value is calculated as follows:

EV = ∑PX

Where X is the outcome and P is the probability of the outcome.

e.g

Illustration 7 – Expected values

A company has recorded the following daily sales over the last 200 days:

Daily sales (units)	Number of days
100	40
200	60
300	80
400	20

What will be the expected sales level in the future?

Solution

Firstly we will assume that the past is a good indicator of the future.

Next we can convert the above results into a probability distribution (i.e. show the range of possible outcomes and their associated probabilities):

Daily sales (units) (X)		Probability (P)
100	40/200 =	0.2
200	60/200 =	0.3
300	80/200 =	0.4
400	20/200 =	0.1
		1.0

Note: Always check that the probabilities add up to one.

The expected value (EV) of the future sales is then given by:

EV = ∑PX

EV = (0.2 × 100) + (0.3 × 200) + (0.4 × 300) + (0.1 × 400) = **240 units**

So what does this mean?

- On average we will sell 240 units a day.
- On a particular day we will sell 100 or 200 or 300 or 400, so the average cannot actually happen.
- While this worries some, most managers are happy to make decisions based on expected values.

Test your understanding 6

An entity must make a decision between three options, A, B and C. The possible profits and losses are:

- Option A: a profit of $2,000 with probability 0.5 or otherwise a loss of $500
- Option B: a profit of $800 with probability 0.3 or otherwise a profit of $500
- Option C: a profit of $1,000 with probability 0.7, or $500 with probability 0.1 or otherwise a loss of $400

Using EV, which option should be chosen?

Test your understanding 7

A decision-maker is faced with the following options, which can result in the profits shown:

	High sales	**Medium sales**	**Low sales**
	P = 0.5	P = 0.4	P = 0.1
Option 1	$50,000	$10,000	($60,000)
Option 2	$40,000	$10,000	($20,000)
Option 3	$30,000	$15,000	$0

Required:

(a) If the intention is to maximise expected profit, which option should be taken?

(b) Comment on the riskiness of the choice facing the decision-maker.

Limitations of expected values

We are not advocating that the expected value approach is ideal. It is merely an aid to decision-making. At the end of the day, decisions are made by managers using their knowledge, experience and judgement.

Techniques such as expected value can provide information to aid that decision but can never replace the human decision-maker.

A limitation of expected value, which is shared with most other attempts to model reality, is that the outcomes and probabilities need to be estimated. The subsequent analysis can never be more reliable than the estimations upon which it is based.

There is also often a considerable degree of simplification with very limited discrete probability distributions being used when more complex ones or perhaps continuous distributions might be more appropriate.

When the probabilities are empirical, arising from past experience, then they have some degree of reliability unless demand patterns change dramatically. In other cases only subjective estimates of probabilities may be available, and their reliability may be open to question. There is therefore a doubt over this approach when subjective probabilities are used.

If the scenario is a repeated decision, made every day, then the expected values can have a commercial meaning: they are long-term averages. In many cases, however, individuals or companies use this technique in one-off decisions. The result in these cases is of little or no use as the activity will only be carried out once and not repeated many times.

Finally, expected values take no account of the decision-makers' attitude to risk. Avoiding significant downside exposure may be more important than possible gains, although expected values consider each equally. Particularly with one-off decisions, it can only give a guide to decision-makers.

2 Measures of spread

Now we have looked at averages we will look at measures of spread.

Having obtained an average value to represent a set of data, it is natural to question the extent to which the single value is representative of the whole set. Through a simple example we shall see that part of the answer to this lies in how 'spread out' the individual values are around the average. In particular, we shall study the following measures of spread:

- the standard deviation and variance
- the coefficient of variation.

The standard deviation and variance

The standard deviation (σ) is a way of measuring how far away on average the data points are from the mean. In other words, they measure average variability about the mean. As such standard deviation is often used with the mean when describing a data set.

For example, suppose a data set has just two observations: 10 and 30. The mean here is 20 and the standard deviation will be 10 as both observations are 10 units away from the mean.

For more complex examples, calculating the standard deviation involves the following steps:

1 Look at the difference between each data value and the mean

2 To get rid of the problem of negative differences cancelling out positive ones, square the results

3 Work out the average squared difference (this gives the variance)

4 Square root to get the standard deviation

The basic formula for calculating standard deviation is thus

$$\sigma = \sqrt{\frac{\sum(x - \bar{x})^2}{n}}$$

Note: The variance is simply the standard deviation squared. For most calculations and discussions the standard deviation is perfectly adequate but the variance is used in more advanced statistics and probability theory.

In practice, this formula can turn out to be very tedious to apply. It can be shown that the following, more easily applicable, formula is the same:

$$\sigma = \sqrt{\frac{\sum fx^2}{\sum f} - \left(\frac{\sum fx}{\sum f}\right)^2}$$

Illustration 8 – The standard deviation

An analyst is considering two categories of company, A1 and A2, for possible investment. One of his/her assistants has compiled the following information on the price-earnings ratios of the shares of companies in the two categories over the past year.

Price-earnings ratios	**Number of category** A1 companies	**Number of category** A2 companies
4.95 – under 8.95	3	4
8.95 – under 12.95	5	8
12.95 – under 16.95	7	8
16.95 – under 20.95	6	3
20.95 – under 24.95	3	3
24.95 – under 28.95	1	4

Compute the standard deviations of these two distributions and comment. (You are given the means of the two distributions as 15.59 and 15.62, respectively.)

Solution

Concentrating first of all on category A1, we see that we face the same problem as when we calculated the mean of such a distribution, namely that we have classified data, instead of individual values of *x*. Adopting a similar approach as before, we take the mid-point of each class:

x (mid-point)	x^2	f	fx	fx^2
6.95	48.3025	3	20.85	144.9075
10.95	119.9025	5	54.75	599.5125
14.95	223.5025	7	104.65	1,564.5175
18.95	359.1025	6	113.70	2,154.6150
22.95	526.7025	3	68.85	1,580.1075
26.95	726.3025	1	26.95	726.3025
		25	389.75	6,769.9625

Thus the standard deviation is:

$$S = \sqrt{\frac{\Sigma fx^2}{\Sigma f} - \left(\frac{\Sigma fx}{\Sigma f}\right)^2}$$

$$S = \sqrt{\frac{6,769.9625}{25} - \left(\frac{389.75}{25}\right)^2}$$

$$= \sqrt{270.7985 - 243.0481} = \sqrt{27.7504} = 5.27$$

The standard deviation of the price-earnings ratios for category A1 is therefore 5.27.

Adopting a similar approach for A2:

x (mid-point)	x^2	f	fx	fx^2
6.95	48.3025	4	27.80	193.21
10.95	119.9025	8	87.60	959.22
14.95	223.5025	8	119.60	1,788.02
18.95	359.1025	3	56.85	1,077.3075
22.95	526.7025	3	68.85	1,580.1075
26.95	726.3025	4	107.80	2,905.21
		30	468.50	8,503.075

Thus the standard deviation is:

$$S = \sqrt{(283.4358 - 243.8803)} = 6.289$$

The standard deviation in the case of category A2 is 6.29.

These statistics again emphasise the wider spread in the category A2 data than in the category A1 data. Note how a full degree of accuracy (four decimal places) is retained throughout the calculation in order to ensure an accurate final result.

Test your understanding 8

Using the following data relating to absences from work in a company over a period of 22 working days, calculate the standard deviation (to two d.p.).

No. of employees absent (x)	No. of days (frequency) (f)
2	2
3	4
4	3
5	4
6	3
7	3
8	3

Test your understanding 9

Using the data relating to output of product Q, find the standard deviation.

Output of Q (kg)	No. of days (frequency)
350 – under 360	4
360 – under 370	6
370 – under 380	5
380 – under 390	4
390 – under 400	3

The coefficient of variation

The coefficient of variation is a statistical measure of the dispersion of data points in a data series around the mean.

It is calculated as follows:

$$\textbf{Coefficient of variation} = \frac{\textbf{Standard deviation}}{\textbf{Mean}}$$

The coefficient of variation is the ratio of the standard deviation to the mean, and is useful when comparing the degree of variation from one data series to another, even if the means are quite different from each other. Dividing by the mean gives a sense of scale to the standard deviation, so the coefficient of variation is often given as a percentage to aid comparison.

In a financial setting, the coefficient of variation allows you to determine how much risk you are assuming in comparison to the amount of return you can expect from an investment. The lower the ratio of standard deviation to mean return, the better the risk-return trade-off will be.

Note that if the mean in the denominator of the calculation is negative or zero, the ratio will not make sense.

If the means of two sets of data are similar, then it is relatively easy to compare the spreads by looking at the standard deviation figures alone. Another example will show that it is not always so straightforward.

Illustration 9 – The coefficient of variation

Government statistics on the basic weekly wages of workers in two countries show the following.

Country V:	mean = \$120	standard deviation = \$55
Country W:	mean = \$90	standard deviation = \$50

Can we conclude that country V has a wider spread of basic weekly wages?

By simply looking at the two standard deviation figures, we might be tempted to answer 'yes'. In doing so, however, we would be ignoring the fact that the two mean values indicate that wages in country V are inherently higher, and so the deviations from the mean and thus the standard deviation will tend to be higher. To make a comparison of like with like we must use the coefficient of variation:

$$\text{Coefficient of variation} = \frac{\text{Standard deviation}}{\text{Mean}}$$

Thus

$$\text{Coefficient of variation of wages in country V} = \frac{55}{120} = 45.8\%$$

$$\text{Coefficient of variation of wages in country W} = \frac{50}{90} = 55.6\%$$

Hence we see that, in fact, it is country W that has the higher variability in basic weekly wages.

Test your understanding 10

In country P, the coefficient of variation for the salaries of trainee accountants is 40%, while in country Q it is 60%.

Which of the following statements can be made on the basis of this information? Select all that apply.

A In P, 40% of trainee accountants have a below-average salary.

B In Q, the lowest salary of trainee accountants is 60% of the average.

C Salaries of trainee accountants are more variable in Q than in P.

D Salaries of trainee accountants are higher on average in Q than in P.

3 Normal distribution

We will now combine what we have learned about probability with what we learned about mean and standard deviation and look at normal distributions. Distribution refers to the way data is spread out.

In the following section we will be using the notation μ for mean and σ for standard deviation.

Consider the following histograms:

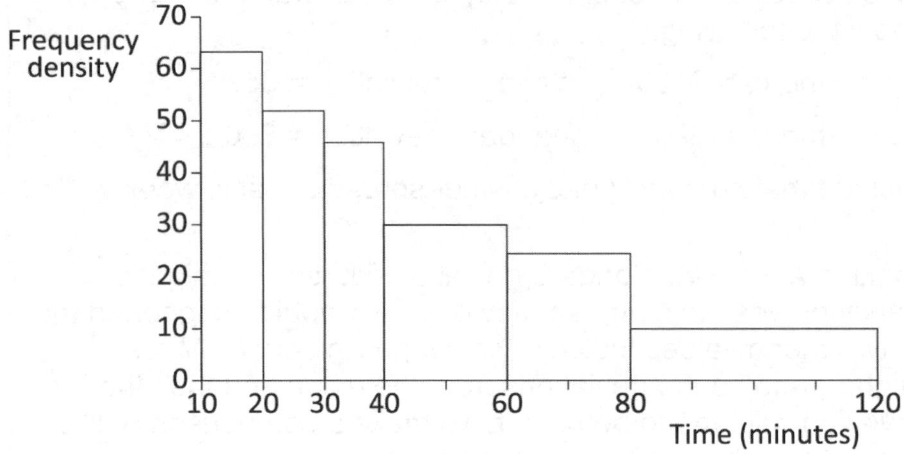

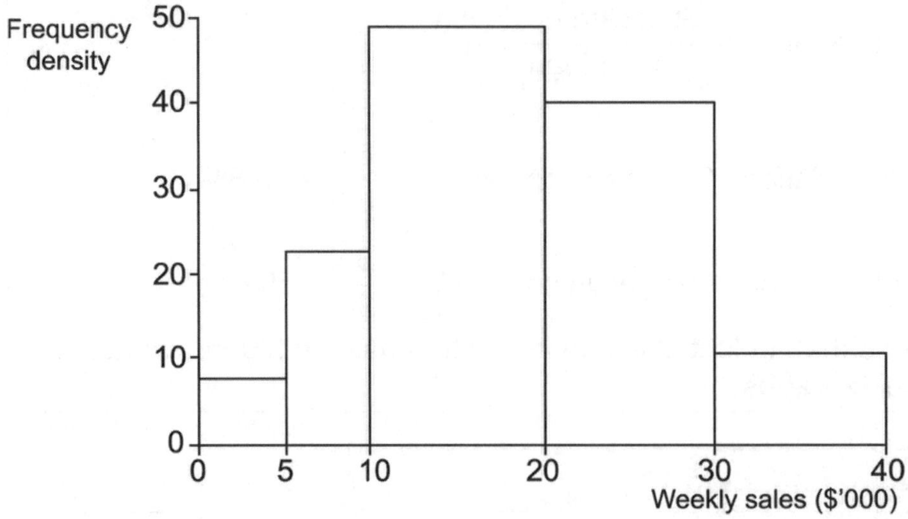

We can see that the 'distribution' or spreading out of the data is different in each of these examples.

Now consider the following histogram:

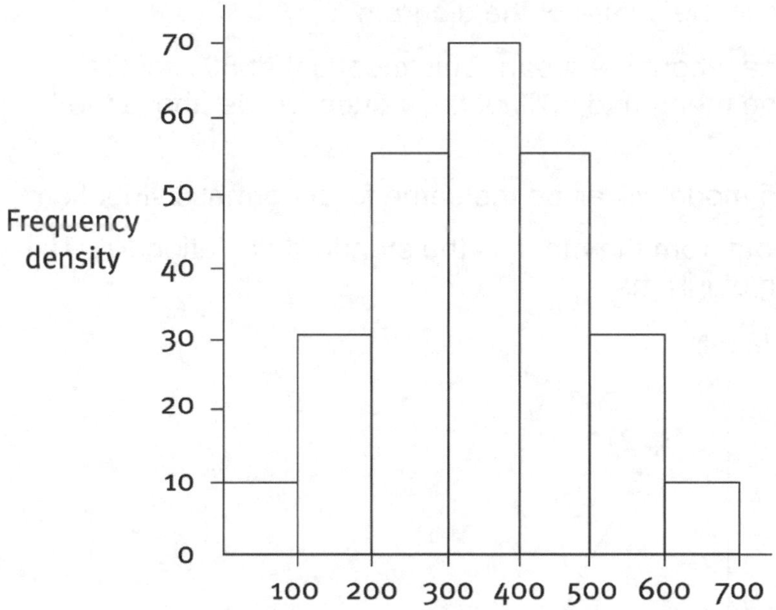

In this case the data is symmetrical and peaks in the centre. This is called a **normal distribution**. We can draw a line around this distribution to show the shape more clearly. This is called a **bell curve**.

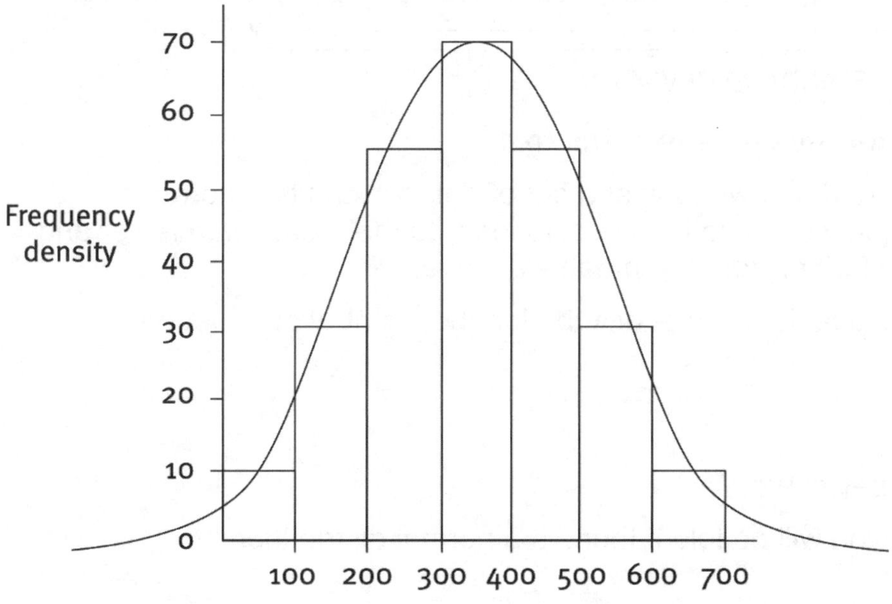

We will use this bell curve throughout this section to show a normal distribution.

Normal distributions can be found when we measure things such as:

- Exam results
- Staff performance gradings
- The heights of a group of people etc.

A normal distribution has the following characteristics:

- the mean (μ) is shown in the centre of the diagram.
- the curve is symmetrical about the mean. This means that 50% of the values will be below the mean and 50% of the values will be above the mean.
- the mean, median and mode will all be the same for a normal distribution.

How far the values spread out from the mean is the standard deviation (σ). This can be seen in the following diagram:

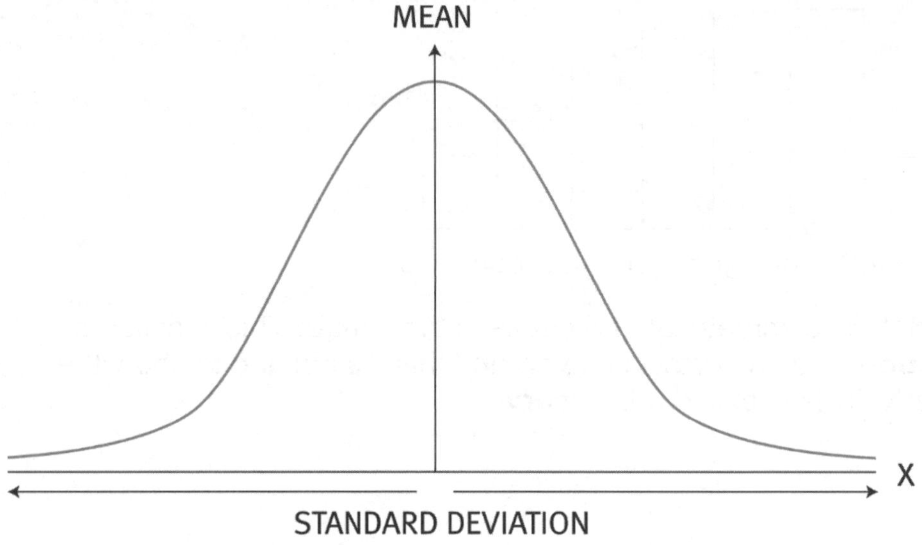

The total area under the curve is equal to 1.

From this we can see that if we look at a set of data which fits a normal distribution the majority of values will occur closer to the mean, with fewer and fewer occurring the further from the mean we move.

Note: To be able to use the normal distribution the distribution must be:

- Continuous
- Symmetrical
- Shaped as a bell curve.

In an assessment, you will be told if there is a normal distribution.

So how can we use this in decision making?

If we can think of a standard normal distribution curve with three standard deviations as follows:

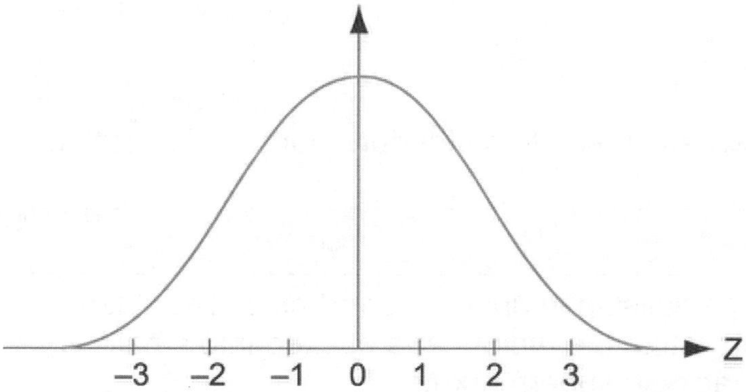

In general 68% of values are within one standard deviation (between –1 and 1), 95% of values are within two standard deviations (between –2 and 2) and 99.7% of values are within three standard deviations (between –3 and 3).

From this we can see that if we look at a set of data which fits a normal distribution the majority of values will occur closer to the mean, with fewer and fewer occurring the further from the mean we move.

If we know the mean and the standard deviation for a distribution we can work out the percentage chance (probability) of a certain value occurring. For example a light bulb manufacturer may want to know how many bulbs will fail after a certain amount of time, or a chocolate bar manufacturer may want to know how many chocolate bars will weigh less than the minimum weight shown on the packaging.

As the curve is symmetrical, the values on the positive side will be exactly the same as the values on the negative side. In this way we can calculate either and assume it will be the same for the other side, for example if the chocolate bar manufacturer found that 0.05% of bars were lower that the acceptable weight, then 0.05% bars will also be higher than the acceptable weight.

The percentage figures can be obtained using normal distribution tables, which are given in your exam. **Note:** The tables only show the positive values.

To use the tables we must first convert our normal distribution to a **standard normal distribution**.

A standard normal distribution has:

a mean of 0

a standard deviation of 1.

This special distribution is denoted by z and can be calculated as:

$$\mathbf{z = \frac{x - \mu}{\sigma}}$$

Where:

z is the z score

x is the value being considered

μ is the mean

σ is the standard deviation

This calculation is used to convert any value to a standard normal distribution.

e.g

Illustration 10 – z score

RST is a food producer, specialising in dried fruit and nuts. The dried fruit and nuts are prepared within the factory and packed into small bags which are sold as snacks in supermarkets.

The weights of the snack bags are normally distributed with a mean weight of 70g and a standard deviation of 5g.

RST can use normal distribution to calculate the probabilities that a bag selected at random would be of an acceptable weight.

The food producer would like to know the probability that the bag selected at random weighs less than 60g.

Required:

Calculate the z score.

$$z = \frac{x - \mu}{\sigma}$$

Z = (60 – 70) ÷ 5 = –2

Looking up the normal distribution tables

Once we have calculated our 'z score' we can look this up on the normal distribution table to find the area under the curve, which equates to the percentage chance (probability) of that value occurring.

So if we have calculated a z score of 1.00. From the table the value is 0.3413.

	0·00	0·01	0·02	0·03
0·8	0·2881	0·2910	0·2939	0·2967
0·9	0·3159	0·3186	0·3212	0·3238
1·0	0·3413	0·3438	0·3461	0·3485
1·1	0·3643	0·3665	0·3686	0·3708

This means that (0.3413 ÷ 1.0) or 34.13% is the area shown from 0 – 1 on the diagram.

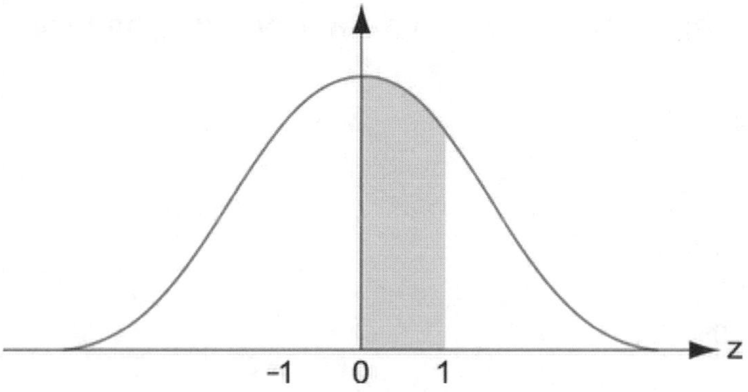

From this we can deduce that 34.13% would be the area shown from 0 to –1 on the diagram. So we can say that 68.26% values will fall within one standard deviation (–1 to 1).

e.g

Illustration 11 – z score

What is the table value for z = 2.63?

With this value you look down the first column to find 2.6, then along the top row till you find 0.03. Where they intersect gives the value for 2.63. The value is 0.4957, or 49.57%.

	0·00	0·01	0·02	0·03
2·3	0·4893	0·4896	0·4898	0·4901
2·4	0·4918	0·4920	0·4922	0·4925
2·5	0·4938	0·4940	0·4941	0·4943
2·6	0·4953	0·4955	0·4956	0·4957
2·7	0·4965	0·4966	0·4967	0·4968

e.g

Illustration 12 – z score

RST is a food producer, specialising in dried fruit and nuts. The dried fruit and nuts are prepared within the factory and packed into small bags which are sold as snacks in supermarkets.

The weights of the snack bags are normally distributed with a mean weight of 70g and a standard deviation of 5g.

RST can use normal distribution to calculate the probabilities that a bag selected at random would be of an acceptable weight.

The food producer would like to know the probability that the bag selected at random weighs less than 60g.

The z score is –2

Required:

Calculate the probability that a bag selected at random weighs less than 60g

Look up the table value for z

	0·00	0·01	0·02	0·03
1·9	0·4713	0·4719	0·4726	0·4732
2·0	0·4772	0·4778	0·4783	0·4788
2·1	0·4821	0·4826	0·4830	0·4834

The table value for 2 is 0.4772, we assume as a normal distribution exists that the value for –2 is the same.

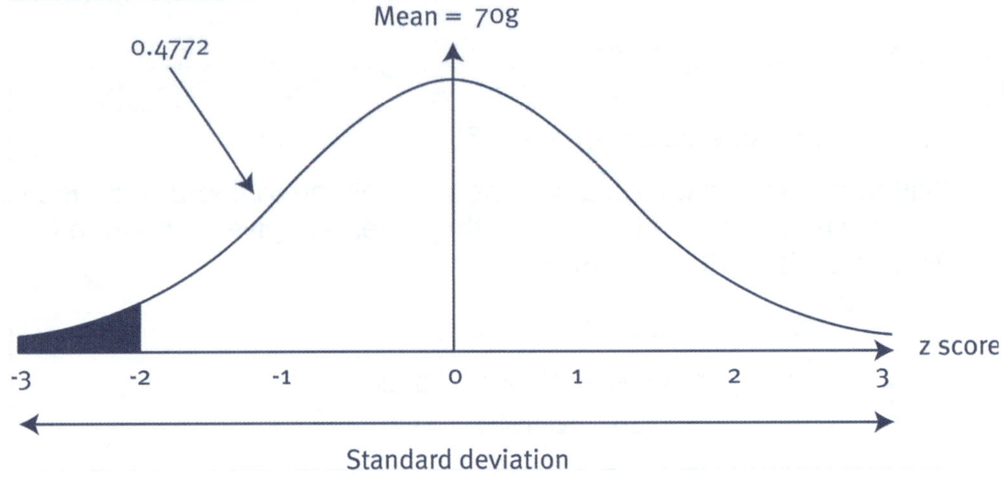

Therefore the probability that a bag selected at random weighs less than 60g = (0.5 – 0.4772) = 0.0228 or 2.3%.

Remember the total area under the curve = 1 therefore if we are considering half of it we have 0.5.

e.g

Illustration 13 – Looking up normal distribution tables

Consider the areas shown under the following graphs, look up the normal distribution tables to find the probability of the shaded areas. (TE is an abbreviation of table entry)

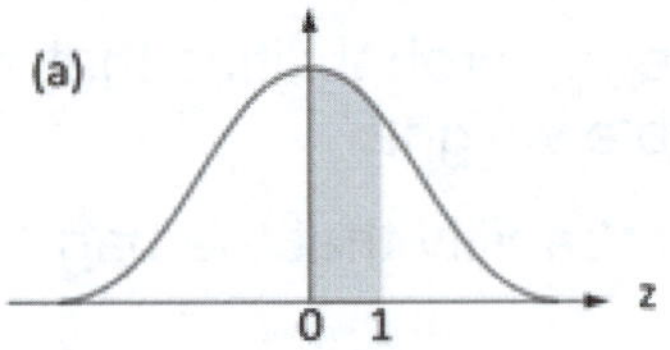

$P(0 < z < 1)$; the probability that our z score falls between 0 and 1

TE(1) = 0.3413 = 34.13%

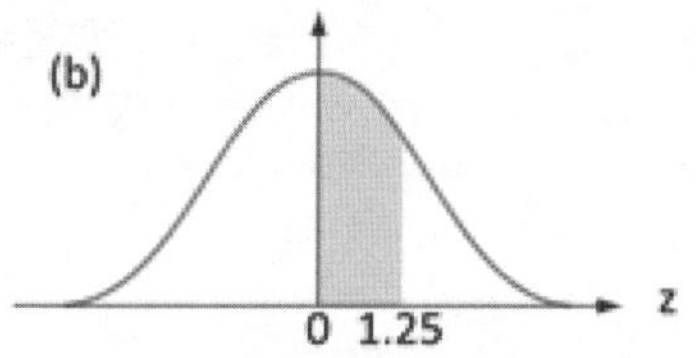

P(0< z < 1.25); the probability that our z score falls between 0 and 1.25

TE(1.25) = 0.3944 = 39.44%.

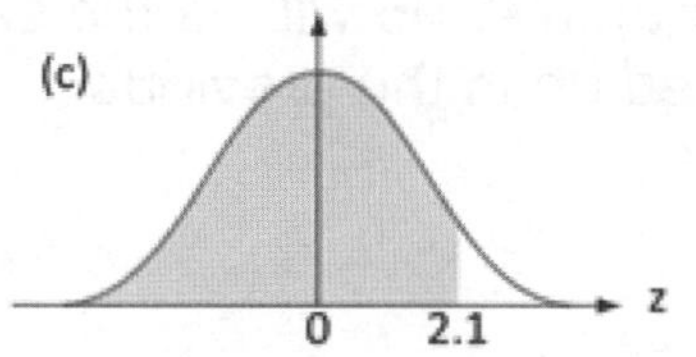

P(z < 2.1); the probability that our z score is negative or is under 2.1

P(z < 2.1) = 0.5 + TE(2.1) = 0.5 + 0.4821 = 0.9821 = 98.21%.

This probability includes all the negative values of z, which have a probability of 0.5, as well as those between 0 and 2.1 which can be found on the table in row 2.1.

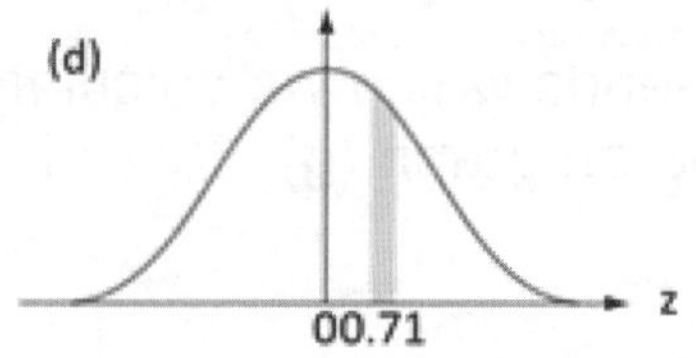

P(0.7 < z < 1); the probability that our z score falls between 0.7 and 1

P(0.7 < z < 1) = TE(1) – TE(0.7) = 0.3413 – 0.2580 = 0.0833 = 8.33%.

This is given by the small area under the curve from 0 to 0.7 subtracted from the larger area from 0 to 1.

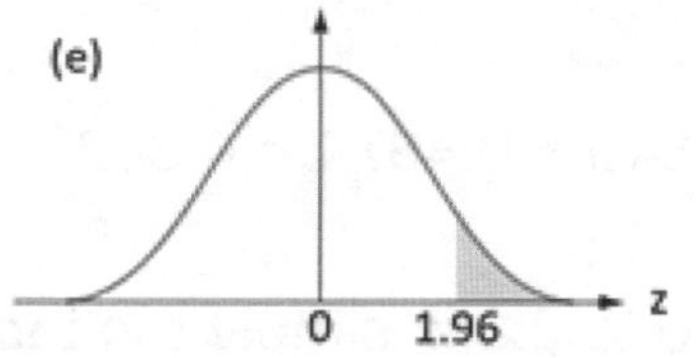

P(z > 1.96); the probability that our z score is higher than 1.96

P(z > 1.96) = 0.5 – TE(1.96) = 0.5 – 0.475 = 0.025 = 2.5%.

This tail-end area is given by the area under half the curve (i.e. 0.5) minus the area from 0 to 1.96.

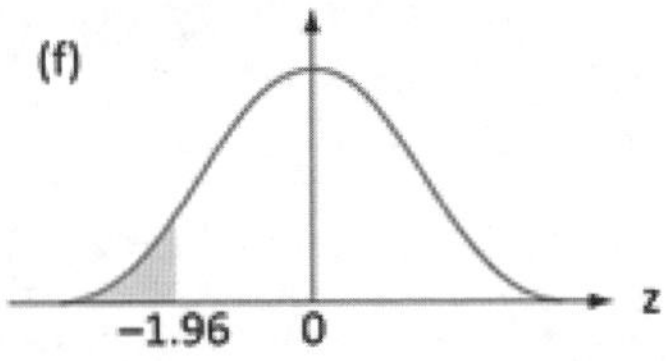

P(z < –1.96); the probability that our z score is lower than –1.96

P(z < – 1.96) = P(z >1.96) = 0.025 = 2.5%.

As the graph is symmetrical, the area lower than -1.96 will be the same as the area higher than 1.96 which we looked up in the previous question.

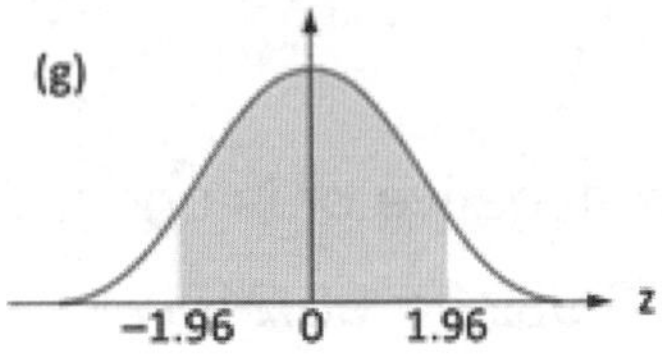

P(–1.96 < z < 1.96); the probability that our z score falls between – 1.96 and 1.96

P(–1.96 < z < 1.96) = 1 – 2 × 0.025 = 0.95 = 95%.

This is the total area of 1 minus the two tail-ends which we calculated in the previous two questions. Look at the area on graph (g). 95% of entries will fall within the shaded area.

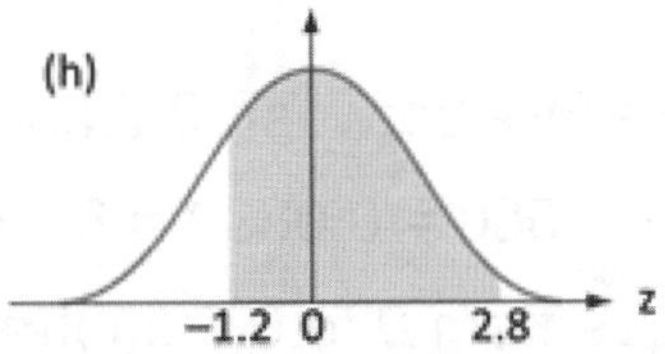

P(–1.2 < z < 2.8); the probability that our z score falls between –1.2 and 2.8

P(–1.2 < z < 2.8) = TE(1.2) + TE(2.8) = 0.3849 + 0.4974 = 0.8823 = 88.23%.

We have split this area into two. That from 0 to 2.8 is simply the table entry and that from –1.2 to 0 equals the area from 0 to +1.2 by symmetry, so it can be looked up in the table.

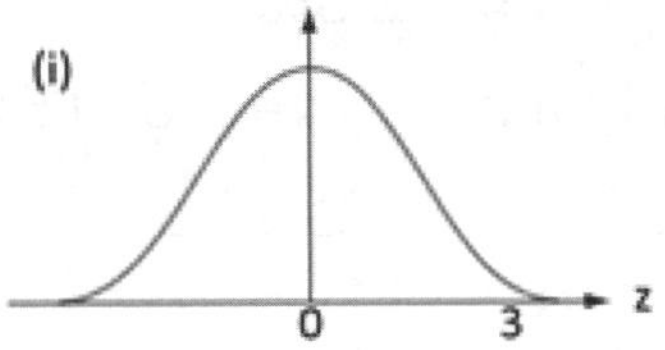

P(z > 3); the probability that our z score is higher than 3

P(z > 3) = 0.5 – 0.49865 = 0.00135 = 0.135%.

The method here is the standard one for tail-end areas but we wanted to make two points. The first is that virtually all normal frequencies lie between three standard deviations either side of the mean. The second is that, for symmetrical data, the standard deviation will be approximately one-sixth of the range.

Test your understanding 11

Evaluate the following probabilities from the standard normal distribution (mean = 0; standard deviation = 1):

A $P(0 < z < 2.03)$

B $P(-1.27 < z < 0)$

C $P(z > 0.55)$

D $P(z < -1.55)$

E $P(z > -1.23)$

F $P(z < 0.88)$

G $P(-0.91 < z < 1.08)$

H $P(0.23 < z < 0.34)$

Illustration 14 – Normal distribution example

RST is a food producer, specialising in dried fruit and nuts. The dried fruit and nuts are prepared within the factory and packed into small bags which are sold as snacks in supermarkets.

The weights of the snack bags are normally distributed with a mean weight of 70g and a standard deviation of 5g.

RST can use normal distribution to calculate the probabilities that a bag selected at random would be of an acceptable weight.

Required:

Calculate the maximum weight that has no more than a 1% chance of being exceeded.

We have been given the probability of 1%. We want to work out what weight that relates to.

Working back, to get a probability of 1%, the table entry must have been:

0.5 – 0.01 = **0.49**

Look up the tables for the entry of 0.49.

	0·00	0·01	0·02	0·03
2·3	0·4893	0·4896	0·4898	0·4901

This equates to a Z value of between 2.32 and 2.33. Because we want a probability of no more than 1% we shall use the 2.33.

Converting this back to pack weights gives a figure of 70g + (5g × 2.33) = 81.65g. This is the mean pack weigh of 70g plus 2.33 lots of the standard deviation of 5g.

Test your understanding 12

A machine produces components with diameter of mean 5 cm and standard deviation 0.1 cm. The production of this component follows a normal distribution.

What proportion of the components produced will have diameters of the following dimensions?

A between 5 and 5.2 cm

B between 4.9 and 5 cm

C over 5.15 cm

D between 4.8 and 5.1 cm

E between 5.1 and 5.2 cm

4 Chapter summary

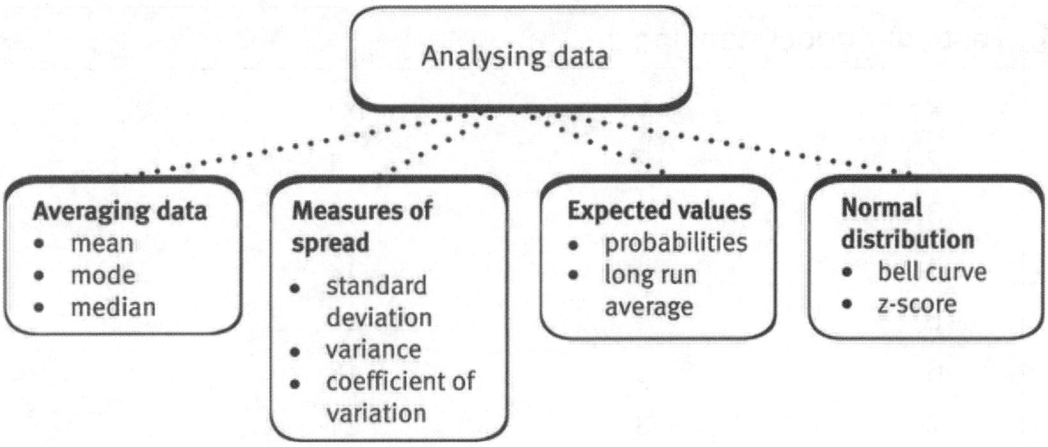

Test your understanding answers

Test your understanding 1

x	f	fx
2	2	4
3	4	12
4	3	12
5	4	20
6	3	18
7	3	21
8	3	24
	$\Sigma f =$ 22	$\Sigma fx =$ 111

Mean, $\bar{x} = \frac{\Sigma fx}{\Sigma f} = \frac{111}{22}$ = 5,045 = 5 employees, to nearest whole number

Test your understanding 2

Mid-point X	Frequency f	fx
355	4	1,420
365	6	2,190
375	5	1,875
385	4	1,540
395	3	1,185
	$\Sigma f =$ 22	$\Sigma fx =$ 8,210

Mean, $\bar{x} = \frac{\Sigma fx}{\Sigma f} = \frac{8,210}{22}$ = 373.18 kg (to two d.p.)

Test your understanding 3

(a) First write the data in ascending order:

18 25 27 43 52

The median is calculated as (n + 1) ÷ 2, so in this example the median is (5 + 1) ÷ 2 = 3. The median is in the third position and is therefore 27.

Test your understanding 4

The mode is the value with the highest frequency, so here the mode is 3

Test your understanding 5

(a) The probability that A picked a king is **1/13**.

(b) The probability that B picked a red card is **1/2**.

(c) The probability that C picked a club is **1/4**.

(d) The probability that D picked the Ace of spades is **1/52**.

Workings

There are 4 kings in a pack of 52 cards, so the probability = 4/52 = **1/13**

There are 26 red cards (hearts + diamonds) in a pack of 52 cards, so the probability = 26/52 = **1/2**

There are 13 clubs in a pack of 52 cards, so the probability = 13/52 = **1/4**

There is only one Ace of Spades in a pack of 52 cards, so the probability = **1/52**

Test your understanding 6

Option A should be chosen.

The expected value of each option is:

EV(A) = \$2,000 × 0.5 + -\$500 × 0.5 = **\$750**

EV(B) = \$800 × 0.3 + \$500 × 0.7 = **\$590**

EV(C) = \$1,000 × 0.7 + \$500 × 0.1 + -\$400 × 0.2 = **\$670**

However, when we look at the workings, we can see that while A gives the highest expected value, there is a 50% chance that there will be a loss of \$500. It may be the case that the organisation could not afford this loss, or would maybe not be prepared to take that risk. Option B gives the lowest expected value but it is a 'safer' option in that both potential outcomes result in a profit. So while expected value can aid decision making, other factors must be considered, such as the decision maker's attitude to risk.

Test your understanding 7

(a) **Option 1 should be taken.**

EV (1) = \$50 × 0.5 + \$10 × 0.4 + -\$60 × 0.1 = \$23

EV (2) = \$40 × 0.5 + \$10 × 0.4 + -\$20 × 0.1 = \$22

EV (3) = \$30 × 0.5 + \$15 × 0.4 + \$0 × 0.1 = \$21

(b) Notice that option 1 is very risky, with a 10% chance of making a loss greater than the maximum possible profit. Many decision-makers would choose option 2 as having a very similar expected profit with considerably lower risk.

Test your understanding 8

x	f	fx	fx^2
2	2	4	8
3	4	12	36
4	3	12	48
5	4	20	100
6	3	18	108
7	3	21	147
8	3	24	192
	22	111	639

$$S = \sqrt{\frac{\sum fx}{\sum f} - \left(\frac{\sum fx}{\sum f}\right)^2} = \sqrt{\frac{639}{22} - \left(\frac{111}{22}\right)^2}$$

$$= \sqrt{(29.0455 - 25.4566)} = \sqrt{3.5889} = 1.89 \text{ (to two d.p.)}$$

Test your understanding 9

Mid-point x	Frequency f	fx	fx^2
355	4	1,420	504,100
365	6	2,190	799,350
375	5	1,875	703,125
385	4	1,540	592,900
395	3	1,185	468,075
	22	8,210	3,067,550

$$S = \sqrt{\frac{\sum fx^2}{\sum f} - \left(\frac{\sum fx}{\sum f}\right)^2} = \sqrt{\frac{3{,}067{,}550}{22} - \left(\frac{8{,}210}{22}\right)^2}$$

$$= \sqrt{(139{,}434.0909 - 139{,}264.6694}$$

$$= \sqrt{169.4215} = 13.02 \text{ (to two d.p.)}$$

Test your understanding 10

Only statement C can be made on the basis of the information given.

Test your understanding 11

A $P(0 < z < 2.03) = TE(2.03) = 0.4788 = 47.88\%$

B $P(-I.27 < z < 0) = TE(1.27) = 0.3980 = 39.8\%$ (by symmetry)

C $P(z > 0.55) = 0.5 - TE(0.55) = 0.5 - 0.2088 = 0.2912 = 29.12\%$

D $P(z < -1.55) = P(z > 1.55) = 0.5 - TE(1.55) = 0.5 - 0.4394 = 0.0606 = 6.06\%$

E $P(z > -1.23) = P(z < 1.23) = 0.5 + TE(1.23) = 0.5 + 0.3907 = 0.8907 = 89.07\%$

F $P(z < 0.88) = 0.5 + TE(0.88) = 0.5 + 0.3106 = 0.8106 = 81.06\%$

G $P(-0.91 < z < 1.08) = TE(0.91) + TE(1.08) = 0.3186 + 0.3599 = 0.6785 = 67.85\%$

H $P(0.23 < z < 0.34) = TE(0.34) - TE(0.23) = 0.1331 - 0.0910 = 0.0421 = 4.21\%$

Test your understanding 12

Although this question concerns proportions, it is essentially a problem on probabilities. We are dealing with a normal distribution with μ = 5 and σ = 0.1. The values in the tables are for a normal distribution with μ = 0 and standard deviation = 1 so we will need to standardise the values in this question using:

$$z = \frac{x - \mu}{\sigma}$$

Where:

z is the z score

x is the value being considered

μ is the mean

σ is the standard deviation

This calculation is used to convert any value to standard normal distribution.

Working for A:

If x = 5: $z = \frac{5-5}{0.1} = 0$

If x = 5.2: $z = \frac{5.2-5}{0.1} = 2$

Then we get the equivalent probability involving z: P(0 < z < 2)

All of the other parts are calculated in the same way, so we end up with:

Question		**Standardised**
A	P(5 < x < 5.2)	P(0 < z < 2)
B	P(4.9 < x < 5)	P(–1 < z < 0)
C	P(x > 5.15)	P(z > 1.5)
D	P(4.8 < x < 5.1)	P(–2 < z < 1)
E	P(5.1 < x < 5.2)	P(1 < z < 2)

We can now look up these Z values on the normal distribution tables.

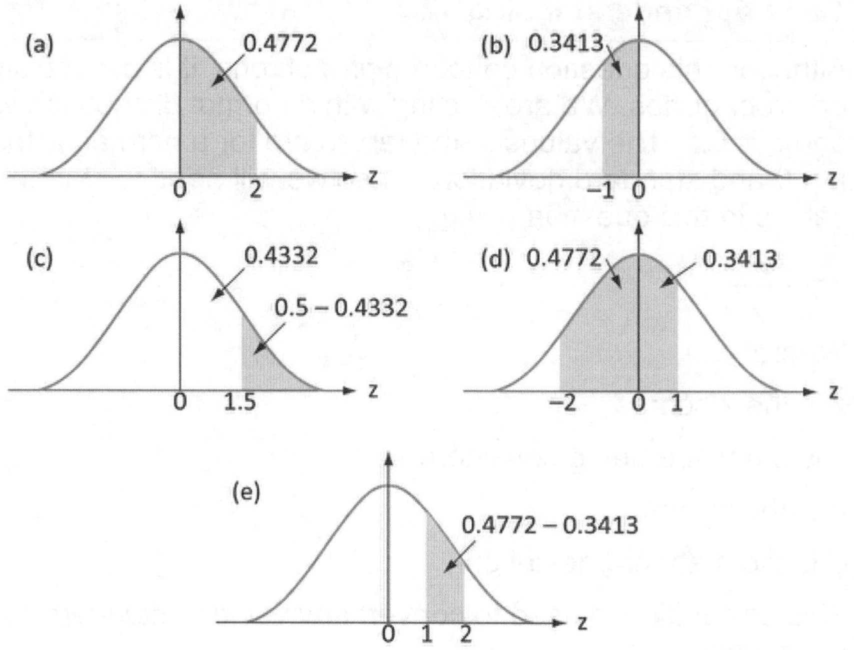

Part A: P(0 < z < 2)

This probability (area) is depicted as the shaded area in graph (a). From the tables we get 0.4772.

Therefore 0.4772 (47.72%) of components produced will have diameters between 5 and 5.2 cm

Part B: P(–1 < z < 0)

This probability (area) is depicted as the shaded area in graph (b). This is the area shown in graph (b). However, we recall that the normal curve is symmetric about its mean; hence the shaded area is the same as the corresponding area to the right of the central dividing line, between the z-values 0 and 1. Tables give this area to be 0.3413.

Therefore, 0.3413 (34.13%) of components produced will have diameters between 4.9 and 5 cm

Part C: P(z > 1.5)

This area, shown in graph (c), cannot be read directly from the table of probabilities. However, the area immediately to its left (between z-values 0 and 1.5) can: it is 0.4332. Now, as the total area under the curve is 1, and the central dividing line splits the area into two symmetrical halves, the area to the right of the dividing line is 0.5. Hence the area required is 0.5 – 0.4332 = 0.0668.

Therefore, 0.0668 (6.68%) of components produced will have diameters over 5.15 cm

Part D: P(–2 < z < 1)

This is the shaded area in graph (d). The central dividing line splits this area into two parts, convenient for direct readings from the table:

z from –2 to 0	=	0.4772	(the symmetry property has been used here, as in part (b) of this example
z from 0 to 1	=	0.3415	
Total	=	0.8185	

Therefore, 0.8185 (81.85%) of components produced will have diameters between 4.8 and 5.1 cm

Part E: P(1 < z < 2)

The tables show that the area between:

z-values 0 and 1 = 0.3413

z-values 0 and 2 = 0.4772

Now, the shaded area in graph (e) can be seen to be the difference between these:

0.4772 – 0.3413 = 0.1359

Therefore 0.1359 (13.59%) of components produced will have diameters between 5.1 and 5.2 cm.

Note: The crucial role of the diagrams above should be noted. Such graphs need not be drawn very accurately, but their use is strongly advised in order to make correct use of the probabilities taken from the table.

Chapter

12

Analytical techniques in budgeting and forecasting

Chapter learning objectives

Upon completion of this chapter you will be able to:

- analysis of cost data
  - explain the concept of correlation coefficient and coefficient of determination
  - calculate and interpret correlation coefficient and coefficient of determination
  - establish a linear function using regression analysis and interpret the results
- use linear regression coefficients to make forecasts of costs and revenues
- adjust historical and forecast data for price movements.
- explain the advantages and disadvantages of linear regression analysis
- describe the product life cycle and explain its importance in forecasting
- explain the principles of time series analysis (cyclical, trend, seasonal variation and random elements)
- calculate moving averages
- calculation of trend, including the use of regression coefficients

- use trend and season variation (additive and multiplicative) to make budget forecasts
- explain the advantages and disadvantages of time series analysis
- explain the purpose of index numbers
- calculate simple and multi-item (weighted) index numbers for one or more variables, including Laspeyre and Paasche indices.

PER

One of the PER performance objectives (PO13) is to plan business activities and control performance, making recommendations for improvement. Working through this chapter should help you understand how to demonstrate that objective.

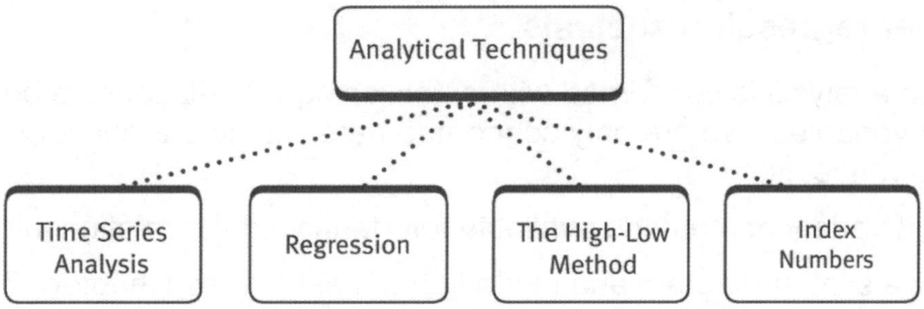

1 The need for forecasting

Budgets are based on forecasts. Forecasts might be prepared for:

- the volume of output and sales
- sales revenue (sales volume and sales prices)
- costs.

The purpose of forecasting in the budgeting process is to establish realistic assumptions for planning. Forecasts might also be prepared on a regular basis for the purpose of feed-forward control reporting.

A forecast might be based on simple assumptions, such as a prediction of a 5% growth in sales volume or sales revenue. Similarly, budgeted expenditure might be forecast using a simple incremental budgeting approach, and adding a percentage amount for inflation on top of the previous year's budget.

On the other hand, forecasts might be prepared using a number of forecasting models, methods or techniques that look to calculate trends and variations over previous years. The reason for using these models and techniques is that they might provide more reliable forecasts.

Possible forecasting techniques:

- the high-low method (see Chapter 2)
- linear regression analysis
- time series analysis
- index numbers.

You may find that more than one technique will be used to forecast information for example index numbers can be used to adjust prices after regression analysis or the high low method has been applied to a set of data. It is also possible to use regression analysis rather than moving averages in time series analysis. This will be demonstrated later in this chapter.

2 Linear regression analysis

Regression analysis is concerned with establishing the relationship between a number of variables. We are only concerned here with linear relationships between 2 variables.

There are a variety of methods available for identifying the relationship:

1 Draw a scatter diagram and plot a line of best fit (see Chapter 17)

The data is plotted on a graph. The y-axis represents the dependent variable, i.e. the variable that depends on the other. The x-axis shows the independent variable, i.e. the variable which is not affected by the other variable.

From the scatter diagram, the line of best fit can be estimated. The aim is to use our judgement to draw a line through the middle of data with the same slope as the data.

2 The high-low method (see Chapter 2)

3 Least squares regression analysis

Least squares regression analysis

Regression analysis finds the line of best fit computationally rather than by estimating the line on a scatter diagram. It seeks to minimise the distance between each point and the regression line.

The equation of a straight line is:

$$y = a + bx$$

where y = dependent variable

a = intercept (on y-axis)

b = gradient

x = independent variable

and $$b = \frac{n\sum xy - \sum x \sum y}{n\sum x^2 - (\sum x)^2}$$

where n = number of pairs of data

and $a = \bar{y} - b\bar{x}$

Alternative formula for a

$$a = \frac{\sum y}{n} - \frac{b\sum x}{n}$$

Illustration 1 – Regression analysis

Marcus Aurelius Ltd is a small supermarket chain that has 6 shops. Each shop advertises in their local newspapers and the marketing director is interested in the relationship between the amount that they spend on advertising and the sales revenue that they achieve. He/she has collated the following information for the 6 shops for a previous week:

Shop	Advertising expenditure	Sales revenue
1	80	730
2	60	610
3	120	880
4	90	750
5	70	650
6	30	430

He/she has further performed some calculations for a linear regression calculation as follows:

- the sum of the advertising expenditure (x) column is 450
- the sum of the sales revenue (y) column is 4,050
- when the two columns are multiplied together and summed (xy) the total is 326,500
- when the advertising expenditure is squared (x^2) and summed, the total is 38,300

Required:

Calculate the line of best fit using regression analysis.

Solution

$$b = \frac{n\sum xy - \sum x \sum y}{n\sum x^2 - (\sum x)^2}$$

$$= \frac{6 \times 326{,}500 - 450 \times 4{,}050}{6 \times 38{,}300 - 450^2}$$

$$= \frac{136{,}500}{27{,}300} = 5$$

$$a = \bar{y} - b\bar{x}$$

$$= \frac{4{,}050}{6} - 5 \times \frac{450}{6} = 300$$

The regression equation is y = 300 + 5x

Interpretation of the line

Mathematical interpretation

If x = 0, then y = 300 and then each time x increases by 1, y increases by 5

Business interpretation

If no money is spent on advertising then sales would still be $300, then for every additional $1 increase in advertising, sales revenue would increase by $5.

Linear regression in budgeting

Linear regression analysis can be used to make forecasts or estimates whenever a linear relationship is assumed between two variables, and historical data is available for analysis.

The regression equation can be used for predicting values of y from a given x value.

1 If the value of x is within the range of our original data, the prediction is known as interpolation.

2 If the value of x is outside the range of our original data, the prediction is known as extrapolation.

In general, interpolation is much safer than extrapolation.

Linear regression can also be used:

- to establish a trend line from a time series. Time series is explained later in this chapter.
  - The independent variable (x) in a time series is time.
  - The dependent variable (y) is sales, production volume or cost etc.
- as an alternative to using the high-low method in cost behaviour analysis. It should be more accurate than the high-low method, because it is based on more items of historical data, not just a 'high' and a 'low' value.
  - The independent variable (x) in total cost analysis is the volume of activity.
  - The dependent variable (y) is total cost.
  - The value of a is the amount of fixed costs.
  - The value of b is the variable cost per unit of activity.

When a linear relationship is identified and quantified using linear regression analysis, values for a and b are obtained, and these can be used to make a forecast for the budget. For example:

- a sales budget or forecast can be prepared
- costs can be estimated, for a budgeted level of activity.

Test your understanding 1

A company is investigating its current cost structure. An analysis of production levels and costs over the first six months of the year has revealed the following:

Month	Production level (units)	Production costs ($)
January	90	2,400
February	100	2,780
March	97	2,560
April	105	2,580
May	110	2,900
June	115	3,000

Further analysis has produced the following data:

$\sum x = 617$; $\sum y = 16{,}220$; $\sum xy = 1{,}677{,}220$; $\sum x^2 = 63{,}859$

Required:

(a) Use regression analysis to identify:

(i) variable cost per unit

(ii) monthly fixed costs.

(b) It is expected that in July, production will be 120 units. Estimate the cost of July's production and comment on the accuracy of your estimate.

Benefits of simple linear regression

1 Simple and easy to use.

2 Looks at the basic relationship between two sets of data.

3 Can be used to forecast and to produce budgets.

4 Information required to complete the linear regression calculations should be readily available.

5 Computer spreadsheet programmes often have a function that will calculate the relationship between two sets of data.

6 Simplifies the budgeting process.

Limitations of simple linear regression

1. Assumes a linear relationship between the variables.
2. Only measures the relationship between two variables. In reality the dependent variable is affected by many independent variables.
3. Only interpolated forecasts tend to be reliable. The equation should not be used for extrapolation.
4. Regression assumes that the historical behaviour of the data continues into the foreseeable future.
5. Interpolated predictions are only reliable if there is a significant correlation between the data (see next section).

3 Correlation

Regression analysis attempts to find the straight line relationship between two variables. Correlation is concerned with establishing how strong the straight line relationship is.

Positive and negative correlation

Correlation can be positive or negative.

Positive correlation means that high values of one variable are associated with high values of the other and that low values of one are associated with low values of the other.

Negative correlation means that low values of one variable are associated with high values of the other and vice versa.

Degrees of correlation

Two variables might be:

(a) perfectly correlated

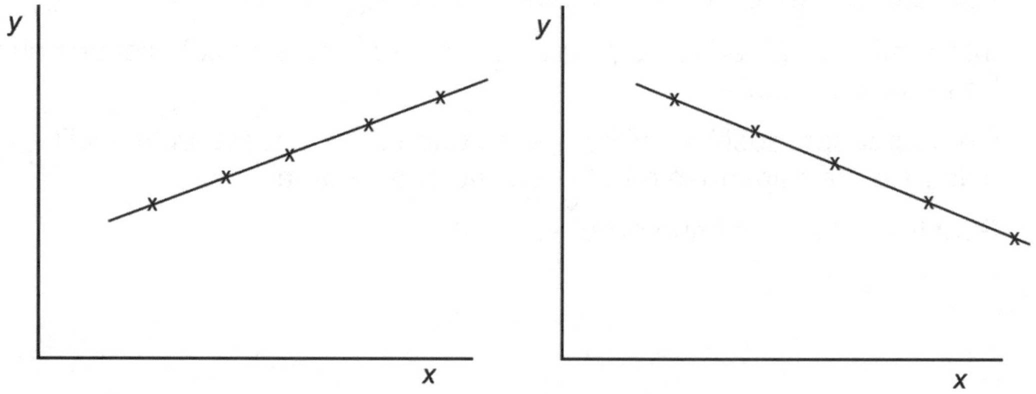

The graph on the left shows perfect positive correlation and the graph on the right show perfect negative correlation. All the pairs of values lie on a straight line. There is an exact linear relationship between the two variables.

(b) partly correlated

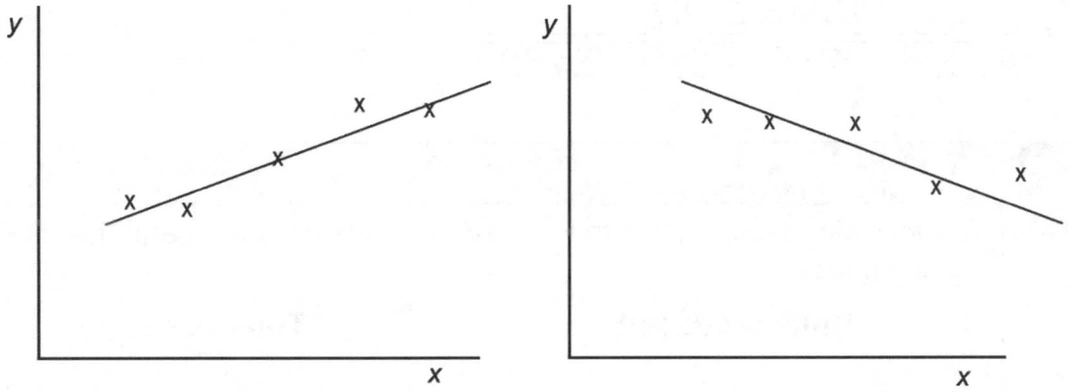

In the first diagram there is not an exact relationship, but low values of x tend to be associated with low values of y, and high values of x tend to be associated with high values of y.

In the second diagram again there is not an exact relationship, but low values of x tend to be associated with high values of y and vice versa.

(c) uncorrelated

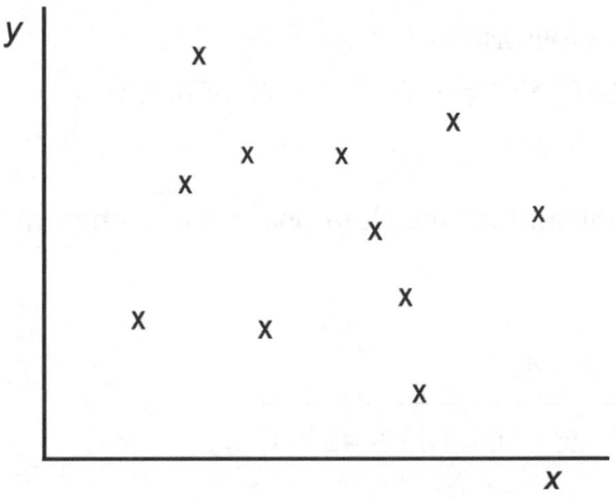

The values of the two variables seem to be completely unconnected.

The correlation coefficient

The degree of correlation can be measured by the Pearsonian correlation coefficient, r (also known as the product moment correlation coefficient).

r must always be between –1 and +1.

If r = +1, there is perfect positive correlation

If r = 0, there is no correlation

If r = –1, there is perfect negative correlation

For other values of r, the meaning is not so clear. It is generally taken that if r > 0.8, then there is strong positive correlation and if r < – 0.8, there is strong negative correlation.

r is calculated as follows:

$$r = \frac{n\sum xy - \sum x \sum y}{\sqrt{[(n\sum x^2 - (\sum x)^2)(n\sum y^2 - (\sum y)^2)]}}$$

Illustration 2 – Correlation

The following table shows the number of units produced and the total costs incurred.

Units produced	Total costs
	$
100	40,000
200	45,000
300	50,000
400	65,000
500	70,000
600	70,000
700	80,000

The table above produces the following data:

$\sum x = 28$; $\sum y = 420$; $\sum xy = 1,870$; $\sum x^2 = 140$; $\sum y^2 = 26,550$; $n = 7$

Required:

Calculate the correlation coefficient for the data given and comment on the result obtained.

Solution

$$r = \frac{(7 \times 1,870) - (28 \times 420)}{\sqrt{[((7 \times 140) - (28 \times 28))((7 \times 26,550) - (420 \times 420))]}}$$

$$= \frac{(13,090 - 11,760)}{\sqrt{[(980 - 784)\ (185,850 - 176,400)]}}$$

$$= \frac{1,330}{\sqrt{(196 \times 9,450)}}$$

$$= +0.98$$

A correlation coefficient of + 0.98 indicates a high degree of positive correlation between the variables. In general, the closer that r is to +1 (or – 1) the higher the degree of correlation.

Test your understanding 2

Which of the following is NOT a feasible value for the correlation coefficient?

A +1.2

B +0.6

C 0

D –0.9

Test your understanding 3

If $\sum x = 440$, $\sum y = 330$, $\sum x^2 = 17{,}986$, $\sum y^2 = 10{,}366$, $\sum xy = 13{,}467$ and $n = 11$, then the value of r, the coefficient of correlation, to two decimal places, is:

A 0.98

B 0.63

C 0.96

D 0.59

Test your understanding 4

Marcus Aurelius Ltd is a small supermarket chain that has 6 shops. Each shop advertises in their local newspapers and the marketing director (MD) is interested in the relationship between the amount that they spend on advertising and the sales revenue that they achieve. The MD has collated the following information for the 6 shops for a previous month:

Shop	Advertising expenditure	Sales revenue
1	80	730
2	60	610
3	120	880
4	90	750
5	70	650
6	30	430

The MD has further performed some calculations for a linear regression calculation as follows:

- the sum of the advertising expenditure (x) column is 450
- the sum of the sales revenue (y) column is 4,050
- when the two columns are multiplied together and summed (xy) the total is 326,500
- when the advertising expenditure is squared (x^2) and summed, the total is 38,300
- when the sales revenue is squared (y^2) and summed, the total is 2,849,300.

Calculate the correlation coefficient.

The coefficient of determination, r^2

The coefficient of determination, r^2 measures the proportion of changes in y that can be explained by changes in x when a straight line relationship has been established.

Test your understanding 5

Calculate the coefficient of determination for the small supermarket chain in TYU 4 and comment.

4 Time series analysis

A time series is a series of figures recorded over time, e.g. unemployment over the last 5 years, output over the last 12 months.

Time series analysis is a technique used to:

- identify whether there is any underlying historical trend
- use this analysis of the historical trend to forecast the trend into the future
- identify whether there are any seasonal variations around the trend
- apply estimated seasonal variations to a trend line forecast in order to prepare a forecast season by season.

A time series has 4 components:

- Trend
- Seasonal variations
- Cyclical variations
- Residual or random variations.

The trend

Most time series follow some sort of long term movement. In time series analysis the trend is measured by:

1 **Inspection**. A graph of the data is produced and the trend line is drawn by eye with the aim of plotting the line so that it lies in the middle of the data points.

2 **Least squares regression analysis**. x represents time (each month would be given a number e.g. January =1, February =2 etc) and y is the data.

3 **Moving averages**. This method attempts to remove seasonal or cyclical variations by a process of averaging.

Moving averages

A moving average is a series of averages calculated from historical time series data.

By using moving averages, the variations in a time series can be eliminated leaving a 'smoothed' set of figures which is taken as the trend.

It is important that the correct cycle is chosen for the moving average; otherwise the result will not be as good as it should be. For instance, if there are seasonal variations present in a time series and the pattern is repeated every third period (quarterly), the moving average should be calculated based on three periods at a time to get the best results. It is possible to calculate a moving average based on any length of cycle.

e.g

Illustration 3 – Moving averages

A business is forecasting the value of their sales for the first quarter of the coming year. Current year values to date are as follows:

Month	Sales value
June	851
July	771
August	916
September	935
October	855
November	1,000
December	1,019

Required:

Using moving averages calculate the forecast sales values for January to March.

Solution

Calculate the 3 month moving average total

Month	**Sales value** $	**Moving average total** $
June	851	
July	771	2,538
August	916	2,622
September	935	2,706
October	855	2,790
November	1,000	2,874
December	1,019	

Calculate the trend by dividing the 3 month moving average total by 3 to get the average for the 3 months.

Month	**Sales value** $	**Moving average total** $	**Trend** $
June	851		
July	771	2,538	846
August	916	2,622	874
September	935	2,706	902
October	855	2,790	930
November	1,000	2,874	958
December	1,019		

Extrapolate the trend. In this example, the trend is increasing by a constant $28 each month.

Month	**Trend** $
June	
July	846
August	874
September	902
October	930
November	958
December	986
January	1,014
February	1,042
March	1,070

If the trend was not constant then the following technique can be used to calculate an average:

= (Last known trend – first known trend) ÷ (number of sets of data –1)

= (958 – 846) ÷ (5 – 1) = $28

Seasonal variations

Once the trend has been found, the seasonal variation can be determined. Seasonal variations are **short-term fluctuations** in value due to different circumstances which occur at different times of the year, on different days of the week, different times of day, for example traffic is greatest in the morning and evening rush hours.

If there is a straight-line trend in the time series, seasonal variations must cancel each other out. The total of the seasonal variations over each cycle should be zero. Seasonal variations can be measured:

- in units or in monetary values
- as a percentage value or index value in relation to the underlying trend.

Seasonal variations are used to forecast future figures by amending the trend.

There are two main models:

1 **The additive model.** Here the seasonal variation is expressed as an absolute amount to be added on to the trend to find the actual result, e.g. ice cream sales in summer are expected to be $200,000 above the trend.

Forecast = Trend + Seasonal variation

2 **The multiplicative model**. Here the seasonal variation is expressed as a ratio/proportion/percentage to be multiplied by the trend to arrive at the actual figure, e.g. ice cream sales are expected to be 50% more than the trend.

Forecast = Trend × Seasonal variation

e.g

Illustration 4 – Seasonal variations

Consider a business with the following actual results in a year:

Year	Quarter	Units sold
20X1	1	130
20X1	2	160
20X1	3	140
20X1	4	170

The trend is expected to increase by 10 units per quarter and has been calculated as 135 units for the first quarter. This provides the following table:

Year	Quarter	Units sold	Trend
20X1	1	130	135
20X1	2	160	145
20X1	3	140	155
20X1	4	170	165

Required:

How might these figures be used to develop a time series model in order to forecast unit sales in each quarter of year 2, using

(a) an additive approach

(b) a multiplicative approach.

Solution

Compare the trend figures with the actual figures for year 1 in order to determine the seasonal variation from the trend for each quarter. This variation can be expressed as (a) an absolute value for each quarter (the additive model) or (b) a percentage of the trend (the multiplicative, or proportional, model).

Year	Quarter	Units sold	Trend	(a) Variation	(b) Variation %
20X1	1	130	135	–5	–3.70%
20X1	2	160	145	15	+10.34%
20X1	3	140	155	–15	–9.68%
20X1	4	170	165	5	3.03%

Note that the multiplicative model seasonal variations may be expressed in several different ways. For example, the quarter 1 variation may be expressed as 96.3% or 0.963.

These variation figures can then be applied to an extrapolated trend in order to produce a quarterly forecast for unit sales in Year 2. The two modelling approaches produce two alternative forecasts:

Year	Quarter	Trend	Forecast Additive approach	Forecast Multiplicative approach
20X2	1	175	175 – 5 = 170	175 × 0.963 = 168.5
20X2	2	185	185 + 15 = 200	185 × 1.1034 = 204
20X2	3	195	195 – 15 = 180	195 × 0.9032 = 176
20X2	4	205	205 + 5 = 210	205 × 1.0303 = 211

A more detailed approach to moving averages

A small business operating holiday homes in Scotland wishes to forecast next year's sales for the budget, using moving averages to establish a straight-line trend and seasonal variations.

Year	Quarter	Trend	Seasonal variation
1	3	100	–6
	4	102	25
2	1	106	–22
	2	111	–5
	3	114	6
	4	116	25
3	1	118	–24
	2	120	–8
	3	123	7
	4	126	21
4	1	129	–17
	2	134	–16

Step 1

Average trend

= (Last known trend – first known trend) ÷ (number of sets of data – 1)

= (134 – 100) ÷ (12 – 1) = 3.09

Step 2

Since the seasonal variations, in this example, change, an average adjustment is computed, by adding together each quarter's variations and dividing by the number of observations.

	Quarter			
Year	**1**	**2**	**3**	**4**
1	–	–	(6)	25
2	(22)	(5)	6	25
3	(24)	(8)	7	21
4	(17)	(16)	–	–
Sum	(63)	(29)	7	71
Average	(21)	(9.67)	2.33	23.7

Seasonal variations need to add up to zero so a small adjustment is made.

	1	2	3	4	Total
Average	(21)	(9.67)	2.33	23.7	–4.64
Adjustment	1.16	1.16	1.16	1.16	+4.64
Average adjusted	(19.84)	(8.51)	3.49	24.86	0

These figures can then be applied to the extrapolated trend.

Suppose we want to predict **year 5 quarter 3** sales. This would be done as follows:

Step 1 Extrapolate the trend figure

Starting from the last trend figure available, add on the appropriate number of trend increments.

Year 4 Quarter 2 = 134

Year 5 Quarter 3 = 134 + 5 movements

= 134 + (5 × 3.09)

= 149.45

Step 2 Adjust for average seasonal variation for quarter 3

Prediction = 149.45 + 3.49 = 152.94

Cyclical variations

Cyclical variations are **medium-term to long term** influences usually associated with the economy. These cycles are rarely of consistent length and we would need 6 or 7 full cycles of data to be sure that the cycle was there.

Residual or random variations

Residual or random variations are caused by irregular items, which cannot be predicted, such as a fire or flood. Regression analysis can also be used within a time series context. The period numbers are the independent variables and the item being measured over time is the dependent variable.

Forecasting with time series

In the short term, we are only interested in the first two components of time series, the trend and any seasonal variations. When we are looking to forecast for a budget the cyclical variations are too long term and residual variations are too unpredictable.

A trend over time, established from historical data, and adjusted for seasonal variations, can be used to make predictions for the near future.

Illustration 5 – Regression in time series

A company has its own temperature-regulated greenhouses to enable year round growing of herbs and other ingredients. They are preparing the forecast purchases of manure (in tonnes) for next year.

Month (x)	**Tonnes purchased (y)**	**xy**	x^2
1	5,150	5,150	1
2	5,241	10,482	4
3	5,487	16,461	9
4	5,615	22,460	16
5	5,280	26,400	25
6	5,456	32,736	36
7	5,648	39,536	49
8	5,890	47,120	64
9	5,448	49,032	81
10	5,689	56,890	100
11	5,847	64,317	121
12	6,000	72,000	144
$\sum x=78$	$\sum y = 66{,}751$	$\sum xy = 442{,}584$	$\sum x^2=650$

Required:

Estimate the forecast purchases of manure (in tonnes) for month 17.

Solution

By using regression analysis we can produce the equation of a straight line (or trend) and then extrapolate to estimate future values.

n = 12

$$b = \frac{12 \times 442{,}584 - 78 \times 66{,}751}{12 \times 650 - 78^2}$$

b = 60.86

$$a = \frac{66{,}751}{12} - 60.86 \times \frac{78}{12}$$

a = 5,167

y = 5,167 + 60.86x

So month 17 would be:

y = 5,167 + 60.86 × 17

y = 6,202 tonnes

Test your understanding 6

W plc is preparing its budgets for next year.

The following regression equation has been found to be a reliable estimate of W plc's deseasonalised sales in units:

y = 10x + 370

Where y is the total sales units and x refers to the accounting period. Quarterly seasonal variations have been found to be:

Q1	Q2	Q3	Q4
+20%	+15%	–10%	–25%

In accounting period 33 (which is quarter 4) identify the seasonally adjusted sales units:

A 525

B 589

C 750

D 975

Test your understanding 7

A company will forecast its quarterly sales units for a new product by using a formula to predict the base sales units and then adjusting the figure by a seasonal index.

The formula is BU = 4,000 + 80Q

Where BU = Base sales units and Q is the quarterly period number.

The seasonal index values are:

Quarter 1	105%
Quarter 2	80%
Quarter 3	95%
Quarter 4	120%

Identify the forecast increase in sales units from Quarter 3 to Quarter 4:

A 25%

B 80 units

C 100 units

D 1,156 units

Advantages and disadvantages of time series analysis

The advantages of forecasting using time series analysis are that:

- forecasts are based on clearly-understood assumptions
- trend lines can be reviewed after each successive time period, when the most recent historical data is added to the analysis; consequently, the reliability of the forecasts can be assessed
- forecasting accuracy can possibly be improved with experience.

The disadvantages of forecasting with time series analysis are that:

- there is an assumption that what has happened in the past is a reliable guide to the future
- there is an assumption that a straight-line trend exists
- there is an assumption that seasonal variations are constant, either in actual values using the additive model (such as dollars of sales) or as a proportion of the trend line value using the multiplicative model.

None of these assumptions might be valid.

5 Index numbers

Introduction

In a business context there will be many situations where a series of numbers will be produced giving information regarding a number of accounting periods or years. For example, the total revenue produced by a hotel is seen to be increasing year by year which might be interpreted as meaning that the company is generating growth – more rooms, more hotels, more guests.

But there could be another explanation which may be less appealing to management – it may be that the increase in revenue results from an increase in prices charged (room rates) which have been adjusted over time to reflect inflation in the economy. The increase in revenue may not necessarily indicate any increase in volume of activity generated by the company – the company may simply be charging higher prices.

More useful information could be derived in this sort of situation by the use of an index number.

What is an index number?

An index number is a technique for comparing, over time, changes in some feature of a group of items (e.g. price, quantity consumed, etc) by expressing the property each year as a percentage of some earlier year.

The year that is used as the initial year for comparison is known as the **base year**. The base year for an index should be chosen with some care. As far as possible it should be a **'typical year'** therefore being **as free as possible from abnormal occurrences**. The base year should also be fairly recent and revised on a regular basis.

e.g

Illustration 6 – Example of an index calculation

The table below shows the sales performance of the Station Hotel. Revenue from rooms let 20X0–20X4 (all figures in $000s)

	20X0	20X1	20X2	20X3	20X4
Station Hotel	1,150	1,250	1,200	1,250	1,300

If 20X0 is the year used for comparison of subsequent selling prices then this is the base year and the index for the 20X0 price is 100.

Year	Selling prices	Index
	$	
20X0	20	100
20X1	23	
20X2	26	
20X3	25	
20X4	28	

The index for each subsequent year must then be calculated by comparing that year's price to the price in 20X0.

The calculation of the index for each year is as follows:

Current year figure/base year figure × 100

Year	Selling prices		Index
	$		
20X0	20		100
20X1	23	23/20 × 100	115
20X2	26	26/20 × 100	130
20X3	25	25/20 × 100	125
20X4	28	28/20 × 100	140

This now shows that:

- in 20X1 the increase in room rate over the 20X0 price was 15%
- the 20X2 price shows an increase of 30% over the 20X0 price
- the 20X3 price an increase of 25% over 20X0
- the 20X4 price an increase of 40% over 20X0.

This simple calculation immediately provides more information for management. Revenue figures can now be adjusted to reflect these changes in the selling price of products.

The revenue figures may be restated at a common price level to reflect the volume changes underlying sales i.e. strip out the extra revenue that is due to an increase the selling price.

The general adjustment carried out to restate costs or revenues at a common price level is to multiply by:

Where the base year is the year chosen as the common price level.

If revenue were restated at 20X4 prices, the revised revenue figures for Station Hotel would be:

Year	**Revenue** ($000)	**Index adjustment**	**Adjusted revenue**
20X0	1,150	140/100	1,610
20X1	1,250	140/115	1,522
20X2	1,200	140/130	1,292
20X3	1,250	140/125	1,400
20X4	1,300	140/140	1,300

Index number for base year/index number for current year

This shows that volume fell considerably between 20X0 and 20X2 but improved in 20X3 and then fell again in 20X4.

This adjustment is often carried out using the Retail Price Index or a specific industry price index as a measure of price inflation. Organisations can restate their sales or costs at a price level which reflects general price inflation to assess their real performance.

Types of index numbers

Index numbers are used in a variety of situations and to measure changes in all sorts of items. As the uses of index numbers are so diverse a number of different types of indices have been developed.

We shall deal below with the following:

- simple indices
- chain based indices
- multi-item (or weighted) indices.

Simple index numbers

A simple index is one that measures the changes in either price or quantity of a single item.

As was seen in Illustration 6 a simple index measures the percentage change for a single item in comparison to the base year.

There are therefore two types of simple indices:

- a price index
- a quantity index.

These simple indices are also known as relatives so we may refer to a price or quantity relative. If the index is a price index then this will show the percentage increase in price of the item since the base year. If the index is a quantity index then this will show the increase in quantity or volume since the base year.

We can use a formula to calculate a simple index using 0 as the indicator for the base year and 1 as the indicator for the current year.

The formulae for calculating simple indices are:

$$\text{Simple price index} = \frac{p_1}{p_0} \times 100$$

$$\text{Simple quantity index} = \frac{q_1}{q_0} \times 100$$

Where:

P_0 is the price at time 0

P_1 is the price at time 1

q_0 is the quantity at time 0

q_1 is the quantity at time 1

e.g

Illustration 7 – Quantity index

6,500 items were sold in 20X4 compared with 6,000 in 20X3.

Required:

Calculate the simple quantity index for 20X4 using 20X3 as base year.

Solution

$$\text{Simple quantity index} = \frac{q_1}{q_0} \times 100$$

$$= \frac{6{,}500}{6{,}000} \times 100$$

$$= 108.3$$

This means that the quantity sold has increased by 8.3% of its 20X3 figure.

Chain base index numbers

A chain base index number expresses each year's value as a percentage of the value for the **previous** year.

If a series of index numbers are required for different years, showing the rate of change of the variable from one year to the next, the chain base method is used.

This simply means that each index number is calculated using the previous year as base. If the rate of change is **increasing**, then the index numbers will be rising; if it is **constant**, the numbers will remain the same and if it is **decreasing** the numbers will be falling.

e.g

Illustration 8 – Chain base index numbers

A shop keeper received the following amounts from the sale of radios:

	$
20X1	1,000
20X2	1,100
20X3	1,210
20X4	1,331
20X5	1,464

Is it correct to say that the annual rate of increase in revenue from sales of radios is getting larger?

Solution

$$\text{Chain base index} = \frac{\text{This year's value}}{\text{Last year's value}} \times 100$$

Year	**Sales ($)**	**Chain base index**	
20X1	1,000		
20X2	1,100	$\frac{1,100}{1,000} \times 100$	= 110
20X3	1,210	$\frac{1,210}{1,100} \times 100$	= 110
20X4	1,331	$\frac{1,331}{1,210} \times 100$	= 110
20X5	1,464	$\frac{1,464}{1,331} \times 100$	= 110

Although the sales revenue from radios has increased each year, the chain base index numbers have remained static at 110. Therefore, the annual rate of increase of sales revenue from radios is remaining constant rather than increasing.

The chain base is also a suitable index to calculate if the weights ascribed to the various items in the index are changing rapidly. Over a period of years, this index would have modified itself to take account of these changes whereas in a fixed-base method after a number of years the whole index would have to be revised to allow for the changed weighting.

Multi-item (weighted) index numbers

A weighted index measures the change in overall price or overall quantity of a number of different items compared to the base year.

The best known example of this type of index is in the way inflation is measured in the UK (and many other countries). The UK measure of inflation is known as the Consumer Price Index, which is an index, built up from a sample of a number of items making up the regular expenditure of families and individuals – various types of food, clothing, travel, etc. As it includes a number of different items, it falls into the multi-item or weighted index category.

An organisation might produce three different products and an index is to be constructed to measure the selling price changes of all three products (a weighted price index). In order to do this the percentage change in each of the three selling price must first be calculated individually and the results must then be weighted to reflect the relative importance of each of the three products.

For a price index:

Step 1 Calculate the simple price index for each of the items.

Step 2 These price indices must then be weighted in some suitable manner in order to produce an overall price index.

Similarly if a quantity index is to be calculated:

Step 1 Calculate the simple quantity index for each of the items.

Step 2 These quantity indices must then be weighted in some suitable manner in order to produce an overall quantity index.

e.g

Illustration 9 – A weighted index

An organisation produces three products. Information about the selling prices of these three products for the last two years are as follows:

	Selling price 20X2	**Selling price** 20X3
	$	$
Product A	2	3
Product B	9	10
Product C	25	30

In order to produce a weighted index of the overall price increase over the period, weightings are to be assigned to each of the three products based on sales quantities as follows:

	Quantity
Product A	4,000
Product B	3,000
Product C	1,000

Required:

Calculate a weighted price index for 20X3 for these three products (with 20X2 as the base year) using the sales quantities given as weights.

Solution

	Price index	**Quantity weighting**	**Total Price index × Quantity**
A	3/2 × 100 = 150	4,000	600,000
B	10/9 × 100 = 111	3,000	333,000
C	30/25 × 100 = 120	1,000	120,000
		8,000	1,053,000

$$\text{Weighted price index} = \frac{1{,}053{,}000}{8{,}000} = 131.6$$

This shows an increase in prices on average of 31.6% over the year.

Test your understanding 8

A production process uses 10 batches of product A and 30 of product B each year. The costs are as follows:

Item	20X2	20X3
Product A	$6.50	$6.90
Product B	$2.20	$2.50

With 20X2 as the base year construct a weighted price index using:

(a) production quantity as the weighting

(b) production cost as the weighting.

Laspeyre and Paasche index numbers

In the previous illustration the number of units of each product have remained the same in each year. These quantities were used to weight the index calculation and, as the quantities were constant year on year, there was no complication caused.

We are now going to look at the calculation of weighted indices where the figures used to weight change over the time period in question.

There are two approaches, named after the individuals who developed them.

Laspeyre index numbers

Laspeyre index numbers use the **base** year quantity or **base** year price to weight the index.

Price index = $\frac{\Sigma(\text{Current year price} \times \text{Base year quantity})}{\Sigma(\text{Base year price} \times \text{Base year quantity})} \times 100$

OR **Price index** = $\frac{\Sigma P_1Q_0}{\Sigma P_0Q_0} \times 100$

Quantity index = $\frac{\Sigma(\text{Current year quantity} \times \text{Base year price})}{\Sigma(\text{Base year quantity} \times \text{Base year price})} \times 100$

OR **Quantity index** = $\frac{\Sigma Q_1P_0}{\Sigma Q_0P_0}$

e.g **Illustration 10 – Laspeyre index numbers**

Using the following information calculate the Laspeyre price index and the Laspeyre quantity index.

	20X2		20X3	
Product	**Quantity**	**Unit price** $	**Quantity**	**Unit price** $
A	10	6.50	5	6.90
B	30	2.20	40	2.50

The base year is 20X2.

Laspeyre price index

Product	**20X2 Price**	**20X3 Price**	**20X2 Quantity**	P_1Q_0	P_0Q_0
	(P_0)	(P_1)	(Q_0)		
A	6.50	6.90	10	69	65
B	2.20	2.50	30	75	66
			Σ	144	131

Laspeyre price index = $\frac{144}{131} \times 100 = 110$

Laspeyre quantity index

Product	**20X2 Quantity**	**20X3 Quantity**	**20X2 Price**	Q_1P_0	Q_0P_0
	(Q_0)	(Q_1)	(P_0)		
A	10	5	6.50	32.5	65
B	30	40	2.20	88	66
			Σ	120.5	131

Laspeyre quantity index = $\frac{120.5}{131} \times 100 = 92$

Test your understanding 9

The average prices of two products, along with the number of units used annually by a company, are given in the following table:

Product	Year 1 Price per unit	Year 2 Price per unit	Year 1 Units	Year 2 Units
A	10	11	10	15
B	20	24	1	5

What is the Laspeyre price index for year 2 based on year 1?

A 134

B 112

C 120

D 89.5

Advantages of Laspeyre indices

- Cheaper, as the obtaining of new quantities each year, which may be a costly exercise, is avoided.
- Easier to calculate where a series of years are being compared, since the denominator remains the same for all years.

Disadvantages of Laspeyre indices

- An out-of-date consumption pattern may be used, so that trends become unrealistic.
- As prices rise, quantities purchased tend to fall if there are alternative goods available. This decrease is not reflected in the Laspeyre index which tends therefore to overestimate the effect of rising prices.

Paasche index numbers

Paasche index numbers use the **current** year quantity or **current** year price to weight the index.

Price index = $\frac{\sum(\text{Current year price} \times \text{Current year quantity})}{\sum(\text{Base year price} \times \text{Current year quantity})} \times 100$

OR **Price index** = $\frac{\sum P_1Q_1}{\sum P_0Q_1} \times 100$

Quantity index = $\frac{\sum(\text{Current year quantity} \times \text{Current year price})}{\sum(\text{Base year quantity} \times \text{Current year price})} \times 100$

OR **Quantity index** = $\frac{\sum Q_1P_1}{\sum Q_0P_1} \times 100$

e.g

Illustration 11 – Paasche index numbers

Using the following information calculate the Paasche price index and the Paasche quantity index.

	20X2		20X3	
Product	**Quantity**	**Unit price** $	**Quantity**	**Unit price** $
A	10	6.50	5	6.90
B	30	2.20	40	2.50

The base year is 20X2.

Paasche price index

Product	**20X2 Price**	**20X3 Price**	**20X3 Quantity**	**P_1Q_1**	**P_0Q_1**
	(P_0)	(P_1)	(Q_1)		
A	6.50	6.90	5	34.5	32.5
B	2.20	2.50	40	100	88
				134.5	120.5

Paasche price index = $\frac{134.5}{120.5} \times 100 = 112$

Paasche quantity index

Product	**20X2 Quantity**	**20X3 Quantity**	**20X3 Price**	**Q_1P_1**	**Q_0P_1**
	(Q_0)	(Q_1)	(P_1)		
A	10	5	6.90	34.5	69
B	30	40	2.50	100	75
				134.5	144

Paasche quantity index = $\frac{134.5}{144} \times 100 = 93$

Test your understanding 10

The average prices of two products, along with the number of units used annually by a company, are given in the following table:

Product	Year 1 Price per unit	Year 2 Price per unit	Year 1 Units	Year 2 Units
A	10	11	10	15
B	20	24	1	5

What is the Paasche price index for year 2 based on year 1?

A 285

B 250

C 87.7

D 114

Advantage of Paasche indices

- Since current year weights are used, this results in an index based on the current pattern of consumption so that a less frequent revision of base year is needed.

Disadvantages of Paasche indices

- Where a series of years is involved, the amount of calculation is greater as both the numerator and the denominator need to be recalculated each year.
- Can only be constructed if up-to-date quantity information is available.
- Rising prices have the opposite effect on the weights, so a Paasche price index tends to underestimate the effect of inflation.

Advantages and disadvantages of index numbers

Advantages

- They aid management to understanding the information presented to them.
- Indices present changes in data or information over time in percentage terms.
- They make comparison between items of data easier and more meaningful – it is relatively easy to make comparisons and draw conclusions from figures when you are starting from a base of 100.
- The ability to calculate separate price and quantity indices allows management to identify the relative importance of changes in each of two variables.

Disadvantages

- There may be no single correct way of calculating an index, especially the more sophisticated index numbers. The user of the information should bear in mind the basis on which the index is calculated.
- The overall result obtained from multi-item index numbers are averages.
- They should only be applied to the items which are included in the index calculation.
- They are relative values, not absolute figures and may not give the whole picture.

Index numbers and forecasting

The accuracy of forecasting is affected by the need to adjust historical data and future forecasts to allow for price or cost inflation.

- When historical data is used to calculate a trend line or line of best fit, it should ideally be adjusted to the same index level for prices or costs. If the actual cost or revenue data is used, without adjustments for inflation, the resulting line of best fit will include the inflationary differences.
- When a forecast is made from a line of best fit, an adjustment to the forecast should be made for anticipated inflation in the forecast period.

e.g

Illustration 12

A company has its own temperature-regulated greenhouses to enable year round growing of herbs and other ingredients. They are preparing the forecast purchases of manure (in tonnes) for next year.

Regression analysis has been carried out and the following trend equation has been derived:

y = 5,167 + 60.86x

Where y is the forecast tonnes of manure and x is the period number.

The purchase price per tonne in month 7 was $56 when the cost index was 125. The cost index for month 18 is expected to be 142.

Required:

Calculate the purchase cost for month 18.

Solution

y = 5,167 + 60.86 × 18

y = 6,262 tonnes purchased

Purchase cost = 6,262 × $56 × 142/125 = $398,363

Test your understanding 11

Production overhead costs at company BW are assumed to vary with the number of machine hours worked. A line of best fit will be calculated from the following historical data, with costs adjusted to allow for cost inflation over time.

Year	Total production overheads $	Number of machine hours	Cost index
20X8	143,040	3,000	192
20X9	156,000	3,200	200
20Y0	152,320	2,700	224
20Y1	172,000	3,000	235

Required:

(a) Calculate the costs in 20Y1 terms

(b) Using your answers to (a) calculate the line of best fit using the high low method

(c) Calculate the expected total overhead cost in 20Y2 if the machine hours worked is 3,100 and the cost index is 250.

Test your understanding 12

A domestic electrical appliance was introduced on to the market in 2003. At the point of sale customers are offered the chance to purchase an insurance policy to cover repairs and parts for the first five years of operation. These policies cannot be purchased later on, only when the appliance is first bought. The table below shows the total industry sales of this appliance for the years 2003 to 2009 together with the number of insurance policies sold and a general price index for electrical goods.

Year	Sales of appliances $000	Policy sales (number)	Price index for electrical goods (2001 = 100)
2003	3,600	400	120
2004	6,250	300	125
2005	9,170	600	131
2006	14,000	1,200	140
2007	21,600	1,700	144
2008	27,000	2,200	150
2009	41,600	2,000	160

Required:

(a) Deflate the appliance sales figures to 2001 prices. **(2 marks)**

(b) Calculate the coefficient of determination between the deflated appliance sales figures and the insurance policy sales using the following information:

– $\sum x$ = Total sales (measured in $millions) = $84

– $\sum y$ = Total number of policies sold (measured in thousands) = 8.4

– $\sum xy = 136$

– $\sum x^2 = 1{,}408$

– $\sum y^2 = 13.78$ **(2 marks)**

(c) The following statement relates to the coefficient of determination calculated in b.

The coefficient of determination means that **(Gap 1)** of the changes in **(Gap 2)** can be explained by changes in the level of the **(Gap 3)**. The other **(Gap 4)** of changes are caused by other factors.

Select the correct phrase to complete the sentences:

– 16.3%

– 83.7%

– deflated appliance sales

– policy sales.

(2 marks)

(d) Using the data provided in b calculate the least squares regression equation to predict insurance policy sales from deflated appliance sales.

(2 marks)

(e) The total sales of the electrical appliance in 2010 are estimated at $51 million at 2010 prices and the price index for electrical goods in the year 2010 based on 2001 is predicted to be 170.

Use the least squares regression equation to obtain a forecast of insurance policy sales for 2010.

(2 marks)

(Total: 10 marks)

6 The product life cycle and forecasting

The product life cycle (seen in Chapter 9) can also be used during the forecasting procedure.

The forecasting techniques that we have considered so far assume that a straight line relationship exists and will exist into the future. We also assume that the trend identified by the straight line relationship will also be maintained indefinitely. If an organisation knows where a product is in its life cycle, they can use this knowledge to plan the marketing of that product more effectively and, more importantly, the organisation may be able to derive an approximate forecast of its sales from knowledge of the current position of the product in its life cycle. It is too simplistic to assume that sales will continue on a linear upward trend forever, every product eventually reaches maturity and may go on to decline.

The product life cycle model is seen to have a number of uses in management and management accounting. However there are some limitations:

- it is over simplistic to assume that all products comply with the product life cycle curve
- it is difficult for management to establish a precise position of a product in the life cycle curve.

7 Chapter summary

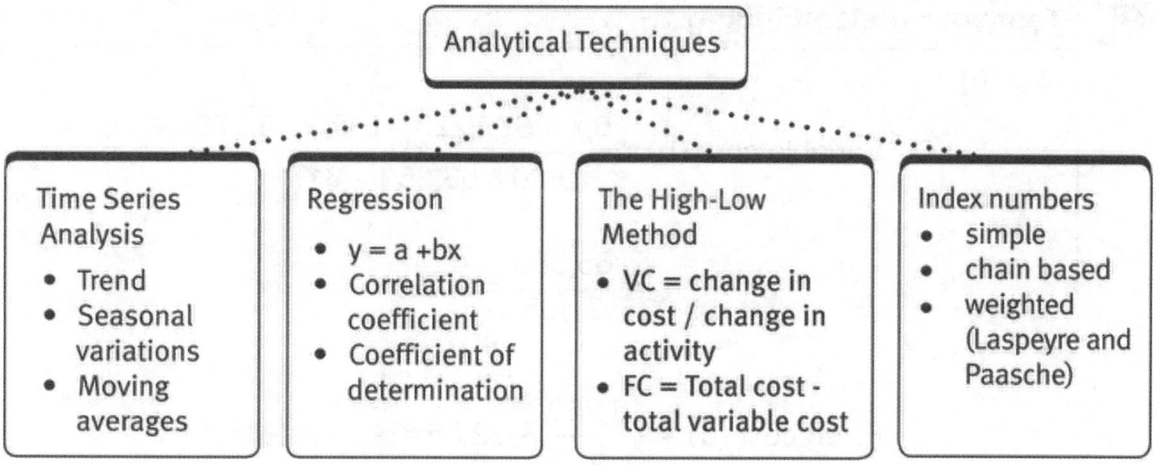

Test your understanding answers

Test your understanding 1

(a) (i)

$$\text{Variable cost (b)} = \frac{6 \times 1,677,220 - 617 \times 16,220}{6 \times 63,859 - 617^2}$$

$$= \frac{55,580}{2,465} = \$22.55$$

(ii)

$$\text{Fixed cost (a)} = \frac{16,220}{6} - 22.55 \times \frac{617}{6}$$

$$= 2,703.33 - 2,318.89$$

$$= \$384.44$$

(b) The estimated cost of 120 units will be given by the linear cost equation:

y = \$384.44 + \$22.55x = 384.44 + (22.55 × 120) = \$3,090.44

It should be noted that since this is outside the range of values for which costs are known it might be inaccurate.

Test your understanding 2

A

Test your understanding 3

B

$$r = \frac{11 \times 13,467 - 440 \times 330}{\sqrt{[(11 \times 17,986 - 440^2)(11 \times 10,366 - 330^2)]}}$$

$$r = \frac{2,937}{\sqrt{(4,246 \times 5,126)}} = 0.63$$

Test your understanding 4

$$r = \frac{n\sum xy - \sum x \sum y}{\sqrt{[(n\sum x^2 - (\sum x)^2)\ (n\sum y^2 - (\sum y)^2)]}}$$

$$r = \frac{6 \times 326{,}500 - 450 \times 4{,}050}{\sqrt{[(6 \times 38{,}300 - 450^2)\ (6 \times 2{,}849{,}300 - 4{,}050^2)]}}$$

$$r = \frac{136.500}{\sqrt{27{,}300 \times 693{,}300}}$$

r = 0.992

Test your understanding 5

The coefficient of determination

$r^2 = 0.992^2 = 0.984$

This means that 98.4% of the changes in sales can be explained by changes in advertising. The other 1.6% of changes are caused by other factors.

Test your understanding 6

A

y = 10x + 370

We are told that x refers to the accountancy period, which is 33, therefore:

y = 370 + 33 × 10 = 700

This is the trend, however and we need to consider the seasonal variation too. Accounting period 33 is quarter 4. Quarter 4 is a bad quarter and the seasonal variation is –25%, therefore the expected results for period 33 are 25% less than the trend.

Expected sales = 700 × 75% = 525 units

Test your understanding 7

D

Sales in quarter 3 (Q = 3)		
Base = 4000 + (80 × 3)	=	4,240
Seasonal adjustment		95%
Actual sales	=	4,028
Sales in quarter 4 (Q = 4)		
Base = 4000 + (80 × 4)	=	4,320
Seasonal adjustment		120%
Actual sales	=	5,184
Overall increase in sales	=	5,184 – 4,028 = 1,156 units

Test your understanding 8

(a) **Quantity weighting**

Calculate the simple price index

Product A = $6.90/$6.50 × 100 = 106.2

Product B = $2.50/$2.20 × 100 = 113.6

Determine the weightings to be used – total production batches

Product A	10
Product B	30
	40

Apply weightings to price indices

	Price index	Quantity weighting	Total price index × Quantity
A	106.2	10	1,062
B	113.6	30	3,408
		40	4,470

$$\text{Weighted price index} = \frac{4,470}{40} = 111.8$$

(b) **Cost weighting**

Use simple price index calculated in (a)

Determine the weighting to be used – total production cost

	Price in 20X2	**Number of units**	**Total value price × number of units**
A	\$6.50	10	65
B	\$2.20	30	66
			131

Apply weightings to price indices

	Price index	**Quantity weighting**	**Total price index × Quantity**
A	106.2	65	6,903
B	113.6	66	7,498
		131	14,401

$$\text{Weighted price index} = \frac{14{,}401}{131} = 109.9$$

Test your understanding 9

B

Product	Year 1 Price	Year 2 Price	Year 1 Quantity	P_1Q_0	P_0Q_0
	P_0	P_1	Q_0		
A	10	11	10	110	100
B	20	24	1	24	20
			Σ	134	120

Laspeyre price index = 134/120 × 100 = **112**

Test your understanding 10

D

Product	Year 1 Price	Year 2 Price	Year 2 Quantity	P_1Q_1	P_0Q_1
	P_0	P_1	Q_1		
A	10	11	15	165	150
B	20	24	5	120	100
			Σ	285	250

Paasche price index = 285/250 × 100 = **114**

Test your understanding 11

(a) As the line of best fit is based on 20Y1 prices, use this as the common price level. Costs should therefore be adjusted by a factor:

$$\frac{\text{Index level to which costs will be adjusted}}{\text{Actual index level of costs}}$$

Year	**Actual overheads**	**Car index**	**Adjustment factor**	**Costs at 20Y1 price level**
	$			$
20X8	143,040	192	× 235/192	175,075
20X9	156,000	200	× 235/200	183,300
20Y0	152,320	224	× 235/224	159,800
20Y1	172,000	235	× 235/235	172,000

(b) VC = (183,300 – 159,800)/(3,200 – 2,700) = $47

FC = 183,300 – (47 × 3,200) = $32,900

(c) [TC = 32,900 + (47 × 3,100)] × (250/235) = $190,000

Test your understanding 12

(a)

Year	Sales of appliances $000		Deflated sales $000
2003	3,600	× 100/120	3,000
2004	6,250	× 100/125	5,000
2005	9,170	× 100/131	7,000
2006	14,000	× 100/140	10,000
2007	21,600	× 100/144	15,000
2008	27,000	× 100/150	18,000
2009	41,600	× 100/160	26,000

(b)

$$r = \frac{n\sum xy - \sum x \sum y}{\sqrt{[(n\sum x^2 - (\sum x)^2)\ (n\sum y^2 - (\sum y)^2)]}}$$

$$r = \frac{7 \times 136 - 84 \times 8.4}{\sqrt{[(7 \times 1{,}408 - 84^2)\ (7 \times 13.78 - 8.4^2)]}}$$

$$r = \frac{246.4}{\sqrt{2{,}800 \times 25.9}}$$

$r = 0.915$

$r^2 = 0.915^2 = 0.837$

(c) The coefficient of determination means that **83.7%** of the changes in **policy sales** can be explained by changes in the level of the **deflated appliance sales**. The other **16.3%** of changes are caused by other factors.

(d)

$$b = \frac{n\sum xy - \sum x \sum y}{n\sum x^2 - (\sum x)^2}$$

$$= \frac{7 \times 136 - 84 \times 8.4}{7 \times 1{,}408 - 84^2}$$

$$= \frac{246.4}{2{,}800} = 0.088$$

$$a = \bar{y} - b\bar{x}$$

$$a = \frac{8.4}{7} - 0.088 \times \frac{84}{7} = 0.144$$

The Regression equation is $y = 0.144 + 0.088x$

Where x is deflated appliance sales ($m)

And y is policy sales (000s)

(e) Deflated appliance sales = $51 million × 100/170 = $30 million

Policy sales = 0.144 + 0.088 × 30

= 2.784 (000s)

= 2,784 policies

Chapter

13

Budgeting

Chapter learning objectives

Upon completion of this chapter you will be able to:

- explain why organisations use budgeting
- describe the planning and control cycle in an organisation
- explain the administrative procedures used in the budgeting process
- describe the stages in the budgeting process (including sources of relevant data, planning and agreeing draft budgets and purpose of forecasts and how they link to budgeting)
- explain the importance of motivation in performance management
- identify factors in a budgetary planning and control system that influence motivation
- explain the impacts of targets upon motivation
- discuss managerial incentive schemes
- discuss the advantages and disadvantages of a participative approach to budgeting
- explain top down, bottom up approaches to budgeting
- explain the importance of principal budget factor in constructing the budget
- prepare sales budgets
- prepare functional budgets (production, raw materials usage and purchases, labour, variable and fixed overheads)
- prepare cash budgets

- prepare master budgets (statement of profit or loss and statement of financial position)
- explain and illustrate 'what if' analysis and scenario planning
- describe the impact of the general economic environment on costs/revenue in budgets
- explain the importance of considering sustainability in budget preparation
- explain the importance of flexible budgets in control
- explain the disadvantages of fixed budgets in control
- identify situations where fixed or flexible budgetary control would be appropriate
- flex a budget to a given level of volume
- calculate simple variances between flexed budget, fixed budget and actual sales, costs and profits
- define the concept of responsibility accounting and its significance in control
- explain the concept of controllable and uncontrollable costs
- prepare control reports suitable for presentation to management (to include recommendation of appropriate control action).

PER

One of the PER performance objectives (PO13) is to plan business activities and control performance, making recommendations for improvement. Working through this chapter should help you understand how to demonstrate that objective.

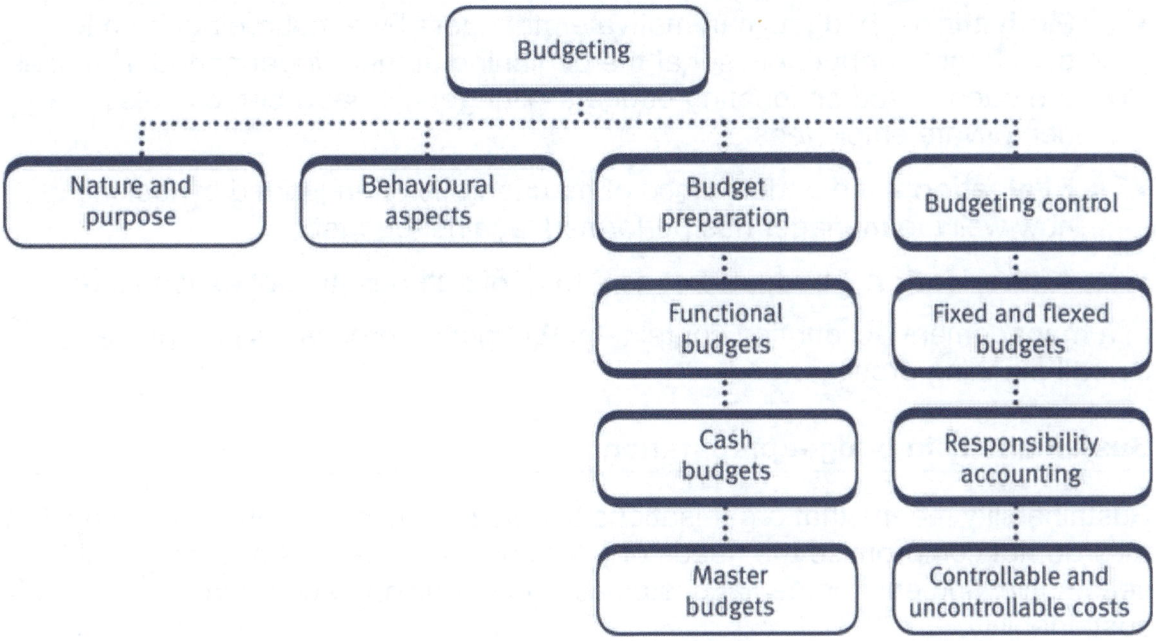

1 The purpose of budgeting

A budget is a quantitative expression of a plan of action prepared in advance of the period to which it relates.

Budgets set out the costs and revenues that are expected to be incurred or earned in future periods.

Most organisations prepare budgets for the business as a whole. The following budgets may also be prepared by organisations:

- Departmental budgets.
- Functional budgets for sales, production, expenditure and so on.
- Statements of profit or loss and Statements of financial position in order to determine the expected future profits.
- Cash budgets in order to determine future cash flows.

Purpose of budgeting

The main aims of budgeting are:

- **Planning for the future** – in line with the objectives of the organisation.
- **Controlling costs** – by comparing the plan or the budget with the actual results and investigating significant differences between the two.
- **Co-ordination** of the different activities of the business by ensuring that managers are working towards the same common goal (as stated in the budget).
- **Communication** – budgets communicate the targets of the organisation to individual managers.

- **Motivation** – budgets can motivate managers by encouraging them to beat targets or budgets set at the beginning of the budget period. Bonuses are often based on 'beating budgets'. Budgets, if badly set, can also demotivate employees.
- **Evaluation** – the performance of managers is often judged by looking at how well the manager has performed 'against budget'.
- **Authorisation** – budgets act as a form of authorisation of expenditure.

In a management accounting context, the budgeting process is part of the overall planning process.

Sustainability in budget preparation

Sustainability means that organisations should use resources in such a way that they do not compromise the needs of future generations. Businesses should seek social and environmental sustainability in addition to economic sustainability.

Rather than taking a reactive, passive approach to sustainability, finance professionals should take the initiative in raising awareness of social responsibility and the need to consider the impact of decisions and actions on sustainability. However, they need to remain objective while doing this.

This will involve promoting sustainable practices through the organisation in relation to the following:

Products and services

- Does making the product use inputs/materials/ingredients from renewable sources only?
- Does the firm source raw materials in ways that support their replenishment, safeguard natural habitats and ensure good animal welfare standards?
- What is the expected life of the product?
- How much of the product (including packaging) can be recycled?
- Is the level of packaging excessive?
- Can the product/service be made more inclusive? E.g. the introduction into the Mattel Barbie range of dolls with different skin tones, hair types and body types and dolls with disabilities.

Customers

- Does the firm have a recycling programme?
- What incentives are given to customers to encourage them to recycle?
- Does the firm encourage/help customers reduce their carbon footprint?

The supply chain

- Does the firm incorporate environmental considerations when selecting suppliers? For example, would it use a supplier with a poor record on pollution?
- Does the firm use suppliers who are geographically close to reduce the impact of transportation in terms of fuel used and exhaust emissions?
- Does the firm pay fair prices to suppliers or does it use its buying powers to drive prices down to very low levels?
- Does the firm encourage/help suppliers reduce their carbon footprint?
- Does the firm help suppliers reduce waste sent to landfill?

The workplace

- Does the firm have measurable targets for energy/water usage?
- Is the building energy efficient?
- Is the workplace a safe, comfortable, pleasant environment to work in?

Employees

- Does the firm look after its employees in terms of working conditions, employment rights, job security, etc. or are staff 'hired and fired' when necessary?
- Does the firm contribute to community projects?
- Does the firm ensure equitable treatment to all employees?

Other business functions and processes

- Does the firm take into account environmental impacts of activities when making decisions?
- Does the firm measure the impact of social initiatives?

Business sustainability is about ensuring that organisations implement strategies that contribute to long–term success.

Organisations that act in a sustainable manner not only help to maintain the well–being of the planet and people, they also create businesses that will survive and thrive in the long run.

In addition, it may be in the firm's **financial** interest to act sustainably.

Directors have a duty to try to increase the wealth of their shareholders and some would see sustainability as conflicting with this objective.

However, many would argue that sustainability should result in better business performance in the long run.

The benefits of acting in a more sustainable fashion are evidenced by the large number of businesses adopting sustainable policies. Stakeholder benefits can be listed as follows:

- Workers/local community: reduced waste and pollution will lead to a more pleasant, healthier environment. Guarantee of an appropriate minimum wage will lead to a better standard of living. Better workplace conditions will attract a higher calibre of workers and reduce accidents/injuries.
- Customers: many customers prefer dealing with businesses that follow sustainable policies such as looking after the environment or providing good working conditions and opportunities for workers, as they are seen as being more ethical.
- Supply chain: integrating sustainability into the supply chain will help suppliers achieve their own sustainability goals.
- Shareholders: Shareholders look for an economically sound investment. Reduction of waste and increased efficiency can improve business profits. This could lead to higher long-term returns for investors.
- Public: Businesses that are economically sound provide a stable job market for workers. Reduced emissions or a lower carbon footprint can lead to fewer environmental problems, such as acid rain and soil erosion.

As well as the ethical arguments above, organisations may want to consider acting sustainably for other reasons such as the positive impact it can have on organisational profits.

e.g

Illustration 1 – How sustainability can boost profits

- Sustainability may help directly increase sales of products and services in the short-term by making products more attractive to buyers.

  For example, some customers may buy your product because a label on it says it has been manufactured using extra-safe working conditions for the labour force, or because it is Fairtrade.
- It may result in **cost savings**.

  For example, lower energy usage may reduce costs and increase profit.
- It may create **positive PR** and thus contribute to the business in the long run.

  While sustainability may not enhance product sales right away, it can enhance the image of a company, which in turn contributes to better business in the long term.
- Avoiding **fines** for pollution.

  The Deepwater Horizon oil spill in 2006 resulted in BP being fined \$4.5 billion by the US Department of Justice. However, it is estimated that the total cost to date is in excess of \$42 billion in terms of criminal and civil settlements and payments to a trust fund.

2 Behavioural aspects of budgeting

If budgets are to be effective, attention must be paid to the behavioural aspects i.e. the effect of the system on people in the organisation and vice versa. Poor managerial performance and poor financial results are often due to the method of implementation and operation of a control system, rather than to the system itself.

Senior management need to be fully committed to the budgeting system and it is equally important that lower levels of management and operational staff in the organisation should be similarly committed and motivated.

Budgets are one important way of influencing the behaviour of managers within an organisation. There are very few, if any, decisions and actions that a manager can take which do not have some financial effect and which will not subsequently be reflected in a comparison between budgeted and actual results. This all-embracing nature of budgets is probably the most important advantage that a budgetary system has over most other systems in a typical organisation. However, if managers and employees have no confidence in the budgetary processes in operation, it is unlikely that they will operate as an effective control. One reason why objectives may not be met is if those operating the budget are not committed to it.

Imposed style/top down approach to budgeting

The top down approach is where budgets are set by higher levels of management and then communicated to the lower levels of management to whose areas of responsibility they relate. This is also known as an imposed budget.

In this approach lower level managers are not allowed to participate in the budget setting process.

The main problem with this approach is that those responsible for operating the budget will see it as something in which they have had no say. They lack ownership of the budget and as such they will be reluctant to take responsibility for it. It is unlikely to motivate the employees to achieve the budgetary targets set for them.

However, it can be argued that this top down approach may be the only approach to budgeting which is feasible if:

- lower level employees have no interest in participating in the process
- they are not technically capable of participating in budget setting
- only top level management have access to information which is necessary for budgeting purposes – perhaps information which is commercially sensitive.

Participative/bottom up approach to budgeting

The bottom up approach to budgeting is where lower level managers are involved in setting budget targets. This is known as a participative budget.

If individual managers are involved in setting budget targets, it is likely that they will accept those targets and strive actively towards the attainment of them.

In this way actual performances should be improved by the motivational impact of budgets.

The main problem is if budgets are used both in a motivational role and for the evaluation of managerial performance, then the problem of budgetary bias may arise.

Budgetary bias is where a manager deliberately sets a lower revenue target or a higher cost target.

The effects of this sort of bias can be minimised by careful control at the budget setting stage and by monitoring the budget from one year to the next.

An extension of the bottom up approach is the concept of budget challenging – employees are given the chance to question a budget presented to them (in a positive way) before it is finalised.

The setting of budgets and targets

The aim of setting budgets is to provide a challenge for employees and managers that is achievable with an appropriate level of effort.

- If a budget target is set that is too easy, then actual performance will appear to be better than the budget but it will not have challenged the employees. Human behaviour will tend to lead to individuals putting in the minimum possible effort to achieve a set target.
- If the budget is too difficult, managers become discouraged at what they regard as unattainable. This may de-motivate and as a result, actual performance falls short of what might reasonably have been expected.

The budget should therefore fall between these two extremes and incorporate just the right degree of difficulty which will lead to the optimal level of performance. At this level the budget should be challenging enough to motivate a manager to optimise his/her performance without being too ambitious.

The right level of difficulty is that which is acceptable to that individual manager. This level of acceptability will differ from manager to manager, as each individual behaves and reacts in a different way in similar circumstances.

Motivation

Motivation is the drive or urge to achieve an end result. An individual is motivated if they are moving forward to achieving goals or objectives.

Motivation may affect many aspects of the life of an individual. You have to be motivated to pass your ACCA examinations and to gain a recognised accounting qualification. At work you are motivated to achieve promotion and to gain a position of greater authority and responsibility within the organisation.

In a business context, if employees and managers are not motivated, they will lack the drive or urge to improve their performance and to help the organisation to achieve its goals and move forward. Motivation is very important in a business.

There is evidence that suggests that management accounting planning and control systems can have a significant effect on manager and employee motivation.

These include:

- the level at which budgets and performance targets are set
- manager and employee reward systems
- the extent to which employees participate in the budget setting process.

Incentive schemes

Budgets by themselves have a limited motivational effect. It is the reward structure that is linked to achieving the budget requirements, or lack of reward for non-achievement, which provides the real underlying motivational potential of budgets.

Managers may receive financial rewards (for example, bonuses) and non-financial rewards (for example, promotion or greater responsibility) based on their ability to meet budget targets. The reward will need to be seen as worthwhile if it is to motivate a manager to achieve the budget.

It is usual to assess the performance of a manager by a comparison of budgeted and actual results for his/her area of responsibility in the organisation. The choice of which particular measures to use is important to ensure that the individual manager sees the attainment of his/her targets as worthwhile for him/herself and at the same time in the best interests of the organisation as a whole.

The characteristics of a good employee reward system as follows:

- **Fairness** – the system should reward effort which helps the organisation achieve its objectives.
- **Motivational** – it should motivate the managers and employees to behave congruently i.e. in a way which assists the organisation to achieve its objectives.

- **Understandability** – the system should be such that it is clear to managers what they need to do to achieve the rewards. Unduly complex reward systems, perhaps based on complex bonus formulae are unlikely to be effective in generating improved performance.
- **Consistently applied** – the system should operate in the same way for all employees or, if not possible, for all employees at a given level in the organisation.
- **Objective** – the system should be based on measurable criteria with a minimum of subjectivity. It should also be such that it is not open to manipulation by managers in their own interests.
- **Universal** – all employees and managers at all levels in the organisation should be subject to an appraisal and reward system.

An incentive scheme ties pay directly to performance and the reward should encourage improvements in performance. It can be tied to the performance of an individual or a team of employees. The scheme should link performance to organisational goals.

There are three main types of incentive schemes

- **Performance related pay** (PRP)
  - Piecework – reward related to the pace of work or effort. The faster the employee works, the higher the output and the greater the reward.
  - Management by objectives (MBO) – key results are identified for which rewards will be paid on top of salary.
  - Points system – this is an extension to MBO reward systems where a range of rewards is available based on a point system derived from the scale of improvement made such as the amount of cost reduction achieved.
  - Commission – paid on the performance of an individual typically paid to salaried staff in sales functions, where the commission earned is a proportion of total sales.
- **Bonus schemes** – usually a one off as oppose to PRP schemes which are usually a continual management policy.
- **Profit sharing**
  - Usually available to a wide group of employees (often companywide) where payments are made in the light of the overall profitability of the company.
  - Share issues may be part of the scheme.

Incentives need to encourage effort or action towards the delivery of organisational objectives there can be potential conflict when contrasting long and short term objectives. (e.g. sales staff offering discounts to customers to win extra orders this year to get a bonus, at the expense of next year's sales)

- Long-term incentive schemes will be those that are designed to continually motivate and deliver organisational objectives.
- Short-term incentive schemes will be those that motivate in the short-term but do not deliver on-going motivation and are often achieved at the detriment of longer term objectives.

Remember that incentives do not have to be financial in order to motivate employees. Ongoing development and training of staff members can also be motivational for them. This is because it can improve their long-term career prospects and enable them to move into more challenging, interesting roles.

3 The budgetary process

The overall planning and control process is summarised in the diagram that follows:

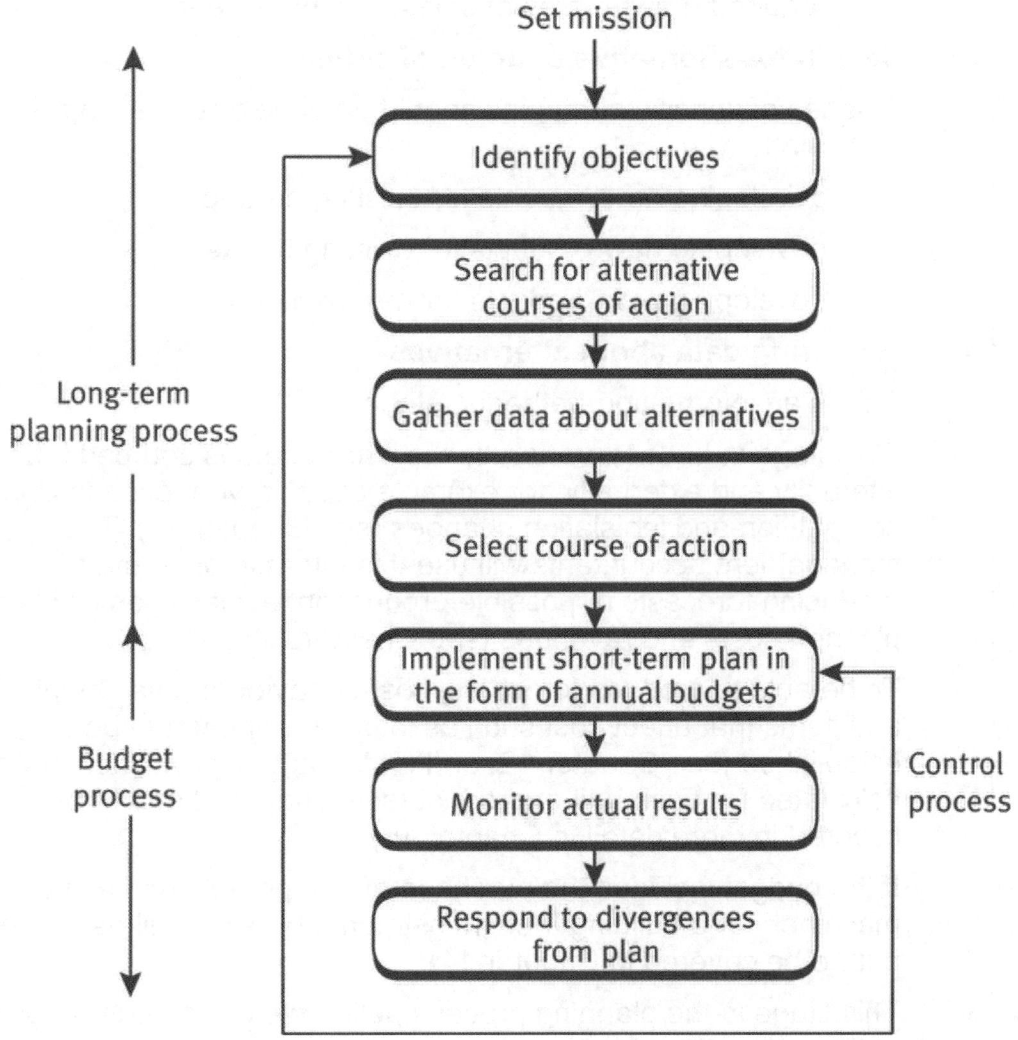

Stages of the planning and control cycle

The eight stages are explained below:

1 **Set mission**

This involves establishing the broad overall aims and goals of the organisation – these may be both economic and social.

2 **Identify objectives**

This requires the company to specify objectives towards which it is working. These objectives may be in terms of:

- economic targets
- type of business
- goods/services to be sold
- markets to be served
- market share
- profit objectives
- required growth rates of sales, profits, assets.

3 **Search for alternative courses of action**

A series of specific strategies should be developed dealing particularly with:

- developing new markets for existing products
- developing new products for existing markets
- developing new products for new markets.

4 **Gathering data about alternatives**

This is an information-gathering stage.

This stage in budget preparation is where data is sourced both internally and externally, for example costs, revenues, possible competition and legislation changes (see Chapter 10). The management accountants will use this information to start producing forecasts of possible production levels, sales levels and planned costs and revenues (see Chapter 12).

To be able to produce forecasts, cost behaviours (see Chapter 2) and items that affect cost such as inflation will need to be established (see Chapter 12) and a standard cost will need to be calculated for each unit of product (see Chapter 2 and to be covered in more detail in Chapter 15).

If the budget includes the purchase of equipment such as new machinery or a building then investment appraisal will be carried out (to be covered in Chapter 14).

This stage in the planning process pulls together a large amount of this syllabus.

5 **Select course of action**

Having made decisions, long-term plans based on those decisions are created.

6 **Implement short-term plan in the form of annual budgets**

This stage signals the move from long-term planning to short-term plans in the form of annual budgeting. The budget provides the link between the strategic plans and their implementation in management decisions. The budget should be seen as an integral part of the long-term planning process.

7 **Monitor actual outcomes**

This is the particular role of the cost accountant, keeping detailed financial and other records of actual performance compared with budget targets (to be covered in Chapter 15).

8 **Respond to divergences from plan**

This is the control process in budgeting, responding to divergences from plan either through budget modifications or through identifying new courses of action.

How are budgets prepared?

Before any budgets can be prepared, the long-term objectives of an organisation must be defined so that the budgets prepared are working towards the goals of the business.

Once this has been done, the budget committee can be formed, the budget manual can be produced and the limiting factor can be identified.

- **Budget committee is formed** – a typical budget committee is made up of the chief executive, budget officer (management accountant) and departmental or functional heads (sales manager, purchasing manager, production manager and so on). The budget committee is responsible for communicating policy guidelines to the people who prepare the budgets and for setting and approving budgets.
- **Budget manual is produced** – an organisation's budget manual sets out instructions relating to the preparation and use of budgets. It also gives details of the responsibilities of those involved in the budgeting process, including an organisation chart and a list of budget holders.
- **Limiting factor is identified** – in budgeting, the limiting factor is known as the principal budget factor. Generally there will be one factor that will limit the activity of an organisation in a given period. It is usually sales that limit an organisation's performance, but it could be anything else, for example, the availability of special labour skills.

If sales are the principal budget factor, then the sales budget must be produced first. If there is something else limiting the business, i.e. a resource such as material or labour hours, then this would become the principal budget factor that other budgets are based on.

The preparation of functional budgets is explained in the next section.

- **Final steps in the budget process** – once the budget relating to the limiting factor has been produced then the managers responsible for the other budgets can produce them. The entire budget preparation process may take several weeks or months to complete. The final stages are as follows.

  1 Initial budgets are prepared.

  2 Initial budgets are reviewed and integrated into the complete budget system.

  3 After any necessary adjustments are made to initial budgets, they are accepted and the master budget is prepared (budgeted statement of profit or loss, statement of financial position and cash flow). This master budget is then shown to higher management for final approval.

  4 Budgets are reviewed regularly. Comparisons between budgets and actual results are carried out and any differences arising are known as variances.

General economic environment

The economic environment will have an impact on the costs and revenues of a business both nationally and internationally. The impact of changing interest rates, exchange rates, inflation and general economic activity will impact on the productivity and profitability of businesses.

Interest rates affect the cost of borrowing money. If interest rates rise this can impact businesses by increasing the cost of overdrafts and loans they use for financing business activities and also impact consumers as general living costs, for example mortgage repayments, will increase.

Inflation refers to a rise in a broad price index representing the overall price level for goods and services in the economy. When the general price level rises, each unit of currency will be able to purchase fewer goods and services. Inflation reflects a reduction in the purchasing power per unit of money. Inflation may discourage investment and savings.

An exchange rate is expressed in terms of the quantity of one currency that can be exchanged for one unit of the other currency. It can be thought of as the price of a currency. Exchange rates between different countries can affect the level of international trade. Receivable or payable balances in foreign currencies are open to risk if exchange rates change; prices may need to be revised in response to an exchange rate movements and investment in overseas subsidiaries may be positively or negatively affected by a change in the value of the money.

The general state of the economy will impact on businesses – is the economy in a boom or bust period? Businesses will need to consider the general economic state and how it is forecast to change when forecasting productivity and pricing strategies.

Gross Domestic Product (GDP)

The Gross Domestic Product (GDP) is a measure of the value of economic activity within a country.

GDP is the sum of the market values, or prices, of all final goods and services produced in an economy during a period.

GDP measures the health of a country. It is a number that expresses the worth of the output of a country in local currency. This economic indicator reflects the monetary value of goods (from food products to vehicles, machinery and textiles) and services (such as health care, education, etc.) produced in the country over a certain period, usually a year or a quarter of a year.

A country with a high GDP is a good economy while a country with a low GDP is poor economy.

The ideal GDP growth rate is between 2% and 3%. The GDP growth rate measures how healthy the economy is. When the number is positive, the economy is growing. When the number is negative, the economy is contracting.

GDP enables businesses, policymakers and central banks to judge whether the economy is contracting or expanding and promptly take necessary action.

4 Budget preparation

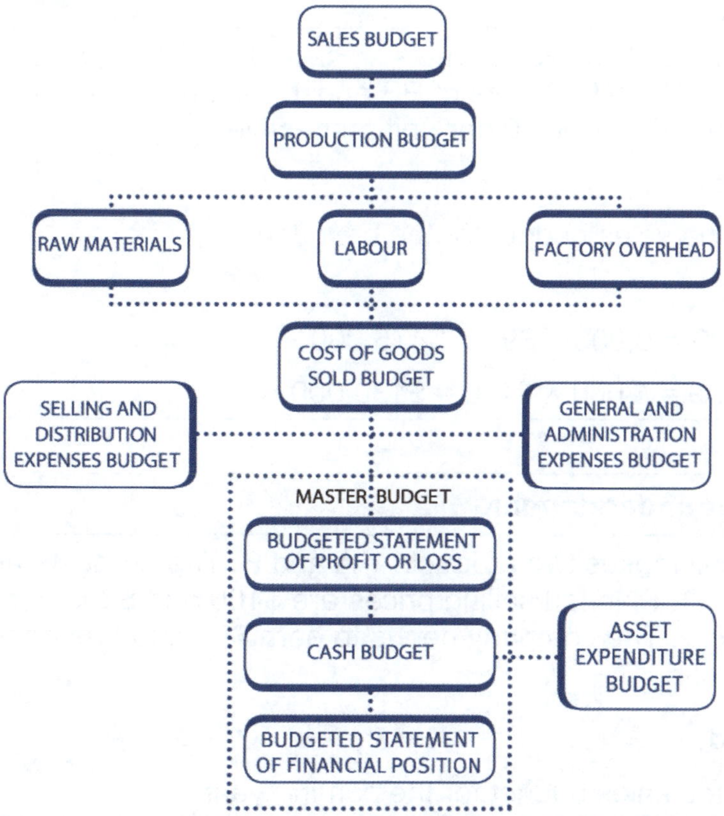

- The diagram is based on sales being the principal budget factor.
- If labour were the principal budget factor, then the labour budget would be produced first and this would determine the production budget.
- Once the production budget has been determined then the remaining functional budgets can be prepared.

5 Functional budgets

A functional budget is a budget of income and/or expenditure which applies to a particular function of the business. The main functional budgets that you need to be able to prepare are:

- sales budget
- production budget
- raw material usage budget
- raw material purchases budget
- labour budget
- overheads budget.

Sales budgets

Sales budgets are fairly straightforward to prepare as the following illustration will demonstrate.

e.g

Illustration 2 – Sales budget

A company makes two products – PS and TG. Sales for next year are budgeted to be 5,000 units of PS and 1,000 units of TG. Planned selling prices are \$95 and \$130 per unit respectively.

Required:

Prepare the sales budget for the next year.

Solution

Sales – PS = 5,000 × \$95 = \$475,000

Sales – TG = 1,000 × \$130 = \$130,000

Test your understanding 1

A company makes two products – A and B. The products are sold in the ratio 1:1. Planned selling prices are \$100 and \$200 per unit respectively. The company needs to earn \$900,000 revenue in the coming year.

Required:

Prepare the sales budget for the coming year.

Production budgets

Budgeted production levels can be calculated as follows:

Forecast sales
(Opening inventory of finished goods)
Closing inventory of finished goods
Budgeted production

Illustration 3 – Production budgets

A company makes two products, PS and TG. Forecast sales for the coming year are 5,000 and 1,000 units respectively.

The company has the following opening and required closing inventory levels.

	PS units	TG units
Opening inventory	100	50
Required closing inventory	1,100	50

Required:

Prepare the production budget for the coming year.

Solution

Production budget	**PS units**	**TG units**
Sales budget	5,000	1,000
– Opening inventory	(100)	(50)
+ Closing inventory	1,100	50
Budgeted production in units	6,000	1,000

Material budgets

There are two types of material budget that you need to be able to calculate, the usage budget and the purchases budget.

- The **material usage budget** is simply the budgeted production for each product multiplied by the quantity (e.g. kg) required to produce one unit of the product.
- The **material purchases budget** is made up of the following elements.

Forecast material usage
(Opening inventory of raw material)
Closing inventory of raw material
Material purchases budget

e.g

Illustration 4 – Material budgets

A company produces Products PS and TG and has budgeted to produce 6,000 units of Product PS and 1,000 units of Product TG in the coming year.

The data about the materials required to produce Products PS and TG is given as follows.

	PS	**TG**
Finished products:	per unit	per unit
Kg of raw material X	12	12
Kg of raw material Y	6	8

Direct materials:

	Raw material	
	X	Y
	kg	kg
Desired closing inventory	6,000	1,000
Opening inventory	5,000	5,000

Standard rates and prices:

Raw material X	$0.72 per kg
Raw material Y	$1.56 per kg

Required:

Prepare the following:

(a) The material usage budget.

(b) The material purchase budget.

Solution

	Material X	**Material Y**
	kg	kg
For production of PS **(W1)**	72,000	36,000
For production of TG **(W2)**	12,000	8,000
Material usage budget	84,000	44,000
– Opening inventory	(5,000)	(5,000)
+ Closing inventory	6,000	1,000
Material purchases budget (units)	85,000	40,000

Material purchases budget	$
X $0.72 per kg × 85,000	61,200
Y $1.56 per kg × 40,000	62,400

Workings

(W1) Budgeted production of Product PS = 6,000 units

Therefore: 6,000 × 12 kg per unit = 72,000 kg of Material X required.

Therefore: 6,000 × 6 kg per unit = 36,000 kg of Material Y required.

(W2) Budgeted production of Product TG = 1,000 units

Therefore: 1,000 × 12 kg per unit = 12,000 kg of Material X required.

Therefore: 1,000 × 8 kg per unit = 8,000 kg of Material Y required.

Test your understanding 2

An ice cream manufacturer is in the process of preparing budgets for the next few months, and the following draft figures are available.

Sales forecast

June	6,000 cases
July	7,500 cases
August	8,500 cases
September	7,000 cases
October	6,500 cases

Each case uses 2.5 kg of ingredients and it is policy to have inventories of ingredients at the end of each month to cover 50% of next month's production.

There are 600 cases of finished ice cream in inventory on 1 June and it is policy to have inventories at the end of each month to cover 10% of the next month's sales.

(a) The production budget (in cases) for June and July will be:

June cases

July cases

(b) The ingredient purchases budget (in kg) for August = kg

Labour budgets

Labour budgets are based on the number of hours multiplied by the labour rate per hour as the following illustration shows.

Illustration 5 – Labour budgets

A company produces Products PS and TG and has budgeted to produce 6,000 units of Product PS and 1,000 units of Product TG in the coming year.

The data about the labour hours required to produce Products PS and TG is given as follows.

Finished products:

	PS per unit	TG per unit
Direct labour hour	8	12

Standard rate for direct labour = $5.20 per hour

Required:

Prepare the labour budget for the coming year.

Solution

	Hours		$
For Product PS 6,000 × 8 hrs	48,000		
For Product TG 1,000 × 12 hrs	12,000		
	60,000	@ $5.20	312,000

Test your understanding 3

A contract cleaning firm estimates that it will take 2,520 actual cleaning hours to clean an office block. Unavoidable interruptions and lost time are estimated to take 10% of the workers' time. If the wage rate is $8.50 per hour, the budgeted labour cost will be:

A $19,278

B $21,420

C $23,562

D $23,800

Overhead budgets

The following illustration demonstrates the calculation of overhead budgets.

Illustration 6 – Overhead budgets

A company produces Products PS and TG and has budgeted to produce 6,000 units of Product PS and 1,000 units of Product TG in the coming year.

The following data about the machine hours required to produce Products PS and TG and the standard production overheads per machine hour is relevant to the coming year.

	PS per unit	**TG per unit**
Machine hour	8	12

Production overheads per machine hour

Variable	$1.54 per machine hour
Fixed	$0.54 per machine hour

Required:

Calculate the overhead budget for the coming year.

Solution

Overhead budget	$
Variable costs 60,000 hours × $1.54	92,400
Fixed costs 60,000 hours × $0.54	32,400
	124,800

Workings

Machine hours – Product PS = 6,000 units × 8 hours = 48,000 machine hours

Machine hours – Product TG = 1,000 units × 12 hours = 12,000 machine hours

Total machine hours = 48,000 + 12,000 = 60,000

Test your understanding 4

Newton Ltd manufactures two products. The expected sales for each product are shown below.

	Product 1	Product 2
Sales in units	3,000	4,500

Opening inventory is expected to be:

Product 1	500 units
Product 2	700 units

Management have stated their desire to reduce inventory levels, and closing inventory is budgeted as:

Product 1	200 units
Product 2	300 units

Two types of material are used in varying amounts in the manufacture of the two products. Material requirements are shown below:

	Product 1	Product 2
Material M1	2 kg	3 kg
Material M2	3 kg	3 kg

The opening inventory of material is expected to be:

Material M1	4,300 kg
Material M2	3,700 kg

Management are keen to reduce inventory levels for materials, and closing inventory levels are to be much lower. Expected levels are shown below:

Material M1 2,200 kg

Material M2 1,300 kg

Material prices are expected to be 10% higher than this year and current prices are $1.10/kg for material M1 and $3.00/kg for material M2.Two types of labour are used in producing the two products. Standard times per unit and expected wage rates for the forthcoming year are shown below:

Hours per unit	Product 1	Product 2
Skilled labour	3	1
Semi-skilled labour	4	4

Skilled labour is to be paid at the rate of $9/hour and semi-skilled labour at the rate of $6/hour.

Production overheads per labour hour are as follows:

Variable $3.50 per labour hour

Fixed $5.50 per labour hour

Calculate the following:

(a) The number of units of product 1 to be produced

(b) The number of units of product 2 to be produced

(c) The quantity of material M1 to be used

(d) The quantity of material M2 to be used

(e) The quantity of material M1 to be purchased and the value of the purchases

(f) The quantity of material M2 to be purchased and the value of the purchases

(g) The number of hours of skilled labour and the cost of this labour

(h) The number of hours of semi-skilled labour and the cost of this labour

(i) The total overhead budget.

6 Cash budgets

A **cash forecast** is an estimate of cash receipts and payments for a future period under existing conditions.

A **cash budget** is a commitment to a plan for cash receipts and payments for a future period after taking any action necessary to bring the forecast into line with the overall business plan.

Cash budgets are used to:

- assess and integrate operating budgets
- plan for cash shortages and surpluses
- compare with actual spending.

Cash forecasts can be prepared based on:

- Receipts and payments forecast. This is a forecast of cash receipts and payments based on predictions of sales and cost of sales and the timings of the cash flows relating to these items.
- Statement of financial position forecast. This is a forecast derived from predictions of future statements of financial position. Predictions are made of all items except cash, which is then derived as a balancing figure.

In the exam it is most likely to be part of a receipts and payments forecast i.e. calculating the receipts from receivables or the payments to payables.

Illustration 7 – Preparing a cash flow forecast

Every type of cash inflow and outflow, along with their timings, must be forecast. Note that cash receipts and payments differ from sales and cost of sales in the statement of profit and loss because:

- not all cash receipts or payments affect the statement of profit and loss, e.g. the issue of new shares or the purchase of a non-current asset
- some statement of profit and loss items are derived from accounting conventions and are not cash flows, e.g. depreciation or the profit/loss on the sale of a non-current asset
- the timing of cash receipts and payments does not coincide with the statement of profit and loss accounting period, e.g. a sale is recognised in the statement of profit or loss when the invoice is raised, yet the cash payment from the receivable may not be received until the following period or later.

A cash flow forecast proforma

Month:	1	2	3	4
	$	$	$	$
Receipts (few lines)				
Sub total				
Payments (Many lines)				
Sub total				
Net cash flow				
Balance brought down				
Balance carried down				

Receipts from receivables

If a business offers credit sales these will be recorded in the statement of profit or loss at the point when the sale is made. This does not reflect the actual cash received by the business.

To calculate the cash receipts from the credit sales there are two things to consider:

- the value of the receipts – how much cash will be received from the credit sales
- the timing of the receipts – when will the cash be received from the credit sales.

e.g

Illustration 8 – Forecast cash receipts

The forecast sales for an organisation are as follows:

	January	February	March	April
	$	$	$	$
Sales	6,000	8,000	4,000	5,000

All sales are on credit and receivables tend to pay in the following pattern:

	%
In month of sale	10
In month after sale	40
Two months after sale	45

The organisation expects the rate of irrecoverable debts to be 5%.

Required:

Calculate the forecast cash receipts from receivables in April.

Solution

Cash from:		$
April sales:	10% × $5,000	500
March sales:	40% × $4,000	1,600
February sales:	45% × $8,000	3,600
		5,700

Payments to payables

If a business makes credit purchases these will be recorded in the statement of profit or loss at the point when the purchase is made. This does not reflect the actual cash paid by the business.

To calculate the cash payments for the credit purchases there are two things to consider:

- the value of the payment – how much cash will be paid to the payable?
- the timing of the payment – when will the cash be paid to the payable?

It may be necessary to calculate the amount due to be paid based on quantities purchased.

e.g

Illustration 9 – Forecast cash payment

A manufacturing business makes and sells widgets. Each widget requires two units of raw materials, which cost $3 each. Production and sales quantities of widgets each month are as follows:

Month	**Sales and production units**
December (actual)	50,000
January (budget)	55,000
February (budget)	60,000
March (budget)	65,000

In the past, the business has maintained its inventories of raw materials at 100,000 units. However, it plans to increase raw material inventories to 110,000 units at the end of January and 120,000 units at the end of February. The business takes one month's credit from its suppliers.

Required:

Calculate the forecast payments to suppliers each month, for raw material purchases.

Solution

When inventories of raw materials are increased, the quantities purchased will exceed the quantities consumed in the period. Figures for December are shown because December purchases will be paid for in January, which is in the budget period.

Quantity of raw material purchased in units:

	December	January	February	March
Production	50,000	55,000	60,000	65,000
Usage (× 2)	100,000	110,000	120,000	130,000
– opening inventory	(100,000)	(100,000)	(110,000)	(120,000)
+ closing inventory	100,000	110,000	120,000	120,000
Purchases (units)	100,000	120,000	130,000	130,000
At $3 per unit	300,000	360,000	390,000	390,000

Having established the purchases each month, we can go on to budget the amount of cash payments to suppliers each month. Here, the business will take one month's credit.

	January	February	March
	$	$	$
Payment to suppliers	300,000	360,000	390,000

At the end of March, there will be payables of $390,000 for raw materials purchased, which will be paid in April.

Test your understanding 5

A small manufacturing company is to commence operations on 1 July. The following estimates have been prepared:

	July	August	September
Production (units)	40	50	50

It is planned to have raw material inventories of $10,000 at the end of July, and to maintain inventories at that level thereafter. There is no opening inventory.

Costs and other information:

	Per unit
	$
Material cost	280
Labour cost	160
Variable overheads	40

Fixed overheads are expected to be $5,000 per month, including $1,000 depreciation.

Labour is paid in the month incurred, and all other expenditures the following month.

Required:

(a) The budgeted cash payments for raw materials are:

July	$
August	$
September	$

(b) The total of the budgeted cash payments for labour and overhead in August is $______________

Test your understanding 6

The following budgeted statement of profit or loss has been prepared for Quest Company for the four months January to April Year 5:

	January	February	March	April
	$000	$000	$000	$000
Sales	60.0	50.0	70.0	60.0
Cost of production	50.0	55.0	32.5	50.0
(Increase)/decrease in inventory	(5.0)	(17.5)	20.0	(5.0)
Cost of sales	45.0	37.5	52.5	45.0
Gross profit	15.0	12.5	17.5	15.0
Administration and selling overhead	(8.0)	(7.5)	(8.5)	(8.0)
Operating profit	7.0	5.0	9.0	7.0

- 40% of the production cost relates to direct materials. Materials are bought in the month prior to the month in which they are used. Purchases are paid for one month after purchase.

- 30% of the production cost relates to direct labour which is paid for when it is used.
- The remainder of the production cost is production overhead.
- $5,000 per month is a fixed cost which includes $3,000 depreciation. Fixed production overhead costs are paid for when incurred.
- The remaining overhead is variable. The variable production overhead is paid 40% in the month of usage and the balance one month later. Unpaid variable production overhead at the beginning of January is $9,000.
- The administration and selling costs are paid quarterly in advance on 1 January, 1 April, 1 July and 1 October. The amount payable is $15,000 per quarter.
- All sales are on credit. 20% of receivables are expected to be paid in the month of sale and 80% in the following month. Unpaid trade receivables at the beginning of January were $44,000.
- The company intends to purchase capital equipment costing $30,000 in February which will be payable in March.
- The bank balance on 1 January Year 5 is expected to be $5,000 overdrawn.

Required:

Complete the cash budget for each of the months January to March Year 5 for Quest Company.

	January	February	March	
	$	$	$	
Receipts				
Sales				2 marks
	_____	_____	_____	
Payments				
Capital expenditure				0.5 marks
Direct materials				2 marks
Direct labour				1 mark
Fixed production overheads				1 mark
Variable production overheads				1 mark
Admin/selling overhead				0.5 marks
	_____	_____	_____	

Total outflow				
	____	____	____	
Net cash flow for month				1 mark
Opening balance				
	____	____	____	
Closing balance				1 mark
	____	____	____	
				(Total: 10 marks)

7 Preparing master budgets

Having prepared budgets for sales and costs, the master budget can be summarised as a statement of profit or loss, a cash budget (as seen in the previous section) and a statement of financial position as at the end of the budget period.

Test your understanding 7

Hash makes one product the Brown. Sales for next year are budgeted at 5,000 units of Brown. Planned selling price is $230.

Hash expects to have the following opening inventory and required closing inventory levels of finished products:

	Units
Opening inventory	100
Required closing inventory	1,100

Budgeted production data for the product is as follows:

Finished products	**Units**
Raw material X: Kg per unit	12
Direct labour hours per unit	8
Raw material inventories	
Opening inventory (kg)	5,000
Planned closing inventory (kg)	6,000
Standard rates and prices:	
Direct labour rate per hour	$7
Material X purchase price per kg	$2
Production overhead absorption rates	
Variable	$1 per direct labour hour
Fixed	$8 per direct labour hour

Budgeted administration and marketing overheads are $225,000.

The opening Statement of financial position is expected to be as follows:

	$	$
Non-current assets		950,000
Inventory	66,000	
Trade receivables	260,000	
Cash	25,000	
	351,000	
Trade payables	86,000	
Other short-term liabilities	24,000	
	110,000	
Net current assets		241,000
Net assets		1,191,000

Non-current assets in the statement of financial position are expected to increase by $40,000, but no change is expected in trade receivables, trade payables and other short-term liabilities.

There are no plans at this stage to raise extra capital by issuing new shares or obtaining new loans. The company currently has an overdraft facility of $300,000 with its bank.

Required:

Complete the following:

The production budget	Units	0.5 marks
The raw material usage budget	kg	0.5 marks
The raw material purchases budget	$	0.5 marks
The direct labour budget	$	0.5 marks
The overhead budget	$	0.5 marks
The cost per unit of Brown	$	0.5 marks

Budgeted Statement of profit or loss

	$	$	
Sales revenue		[ ]	0.5 marks
Cost of sales			
Opening inventory	[ ]		0.5 marks
Production cost	[ ]		0.5 marks
Closing inventory	[ ]		0.5 marks
		[ ]	0.5 marks
Gross profit		[ ]	0.5 marks
Administration and marketing		(225,000)	
Operating profit		[ ]	0.5 marks

Budgeted Statement of financial position

	$	$	
Non-current assets		[ ]	0.5 marks
Inventory	[ ]		1 mark
Trade receivables	260,000		
Cash	[ ]		1 mark
Trade payables	86,000		
Other short term liabilities	24,000		
	110,000		
Net current assets		[ ]	
Net assets		[ ]	1 mark

(Total: 10 marks)

What if analysis

'What-if' analysis is a form of sensitivity analysis, which allows the effects of changes in one or more data value to be quickly recalculated.

Most budgets are produced under conditions of uncertainty as we are unable to perfectly predict the future. The majority of the costs and revenues put in the budget are estimates. These costs and revenues are used to calculate a profit figure for the business. This profit figure may be mathematically accurate, but the level of accuracy may be misleading.

Most budgets are quite complex, involving a large number of inputs. What-if analysis is a technique whereby each of the inputs can be changed both individually and in combination to see the effects on the final results.

An example of basic what-if analysis would be flexing a fixed budget to see how changes in activity levels affect the costs and revenues and therefore the profit of the business. This is discussed in the Budgetary control section of this chapter.

What-if analysis can be very detailed and the 'what-if' function on a spreadsheet package can be a very useful tool to have available.

Scenario planning

Scenario planning is a strategic planning tool used to make flexible long-term plans. It aims to define critical uncertainties and develop possible scenarios in order to identify the impacts and the responses to give for each one uncertainty.

Scenario planning involves the following steps:

1 Identify high impact, high uncertainty factors in the environment.

Once identified, factors need to be ranked according to importance and uncertainty.

2 For each factor, identify different possible futures.

Precision is not possible but developing a view of the future against which to evaluate and evolve strategies is important.

3 Cluster together different factors to identify various consistent future scenarios.

This process usually results in between seven and nine mini scenarios.

4 'Writing the scenario' – for the most important scenarios (usually limited to three), build a detailed analysis to identify and assess future implications.

As part of this, planners typically develop a set of optimistic, pessimistic and most likely assumptions about the impact of key variables on the company's future strategy.

The result of this detailed scenario construction should include:

- financial implications – anticipated net profits, cash flow and net working capital for each of three versions of the future
- strategic implications – possible opportunities and risks
- the probability of occurrence, usually based on past experience.

5 For each scenario, identify and assess possible courses of action for the firm. For each scenario, identify and assess possible courses of action for the firm.

6 Monitor reality to see which scenario is unfolding.

7 Revise scenarios and strategic options as appropriate.

Pros and cons of scenario planning

Pros	Cons
• focuses management attention on the future and possibilities • encourages creative thinking • can be used to justify a decision • encourages communication via the participation process • can identify the sources of uncertainty • encourages companies to consider fundamental changes in the external environment.	• costly and inaccurate – uses up substantial resources and time • tendency for cultural distortion and for people to get carried away • the risk of the self-fulfilling prophecy, i.e. thinking about the scenario may be the cause of it • many scenarios considered will not actually occur.

8 Budgetary control

Feedback and feedforward controls

Feedback is the comparison of budget and actual performance with a view to revising plans, budgets or operations. The control action takes place after the event.

Budgetary control systems are typically feedback systems – an expenditure budget is set then a comparison is made with actual expenditure at the end of the budget period. If this shows that actual expenditure exceeds budget then it is not possible to take control action to prevent this overspending as it has already been incurred. The information can be used to avoid the situation happening again in the future.

Feedback controls are of limited use because they operate too late in the control system. It is important, therefore, that an organisation also has in place 'feedforward control'.

Planning is a form of feedforward control.

An example of a feedforward control is cash budgeting which will warn management if a major cash surplus or deficit is expected to arise at some date in the future so that management can take action now.

Budgetary control cycle

Control can be defined as the process whereby management take decisions in order to attempt to ensure that an organisation achieves its objectives.

The budgetary control cycle can be illustrated as follows.

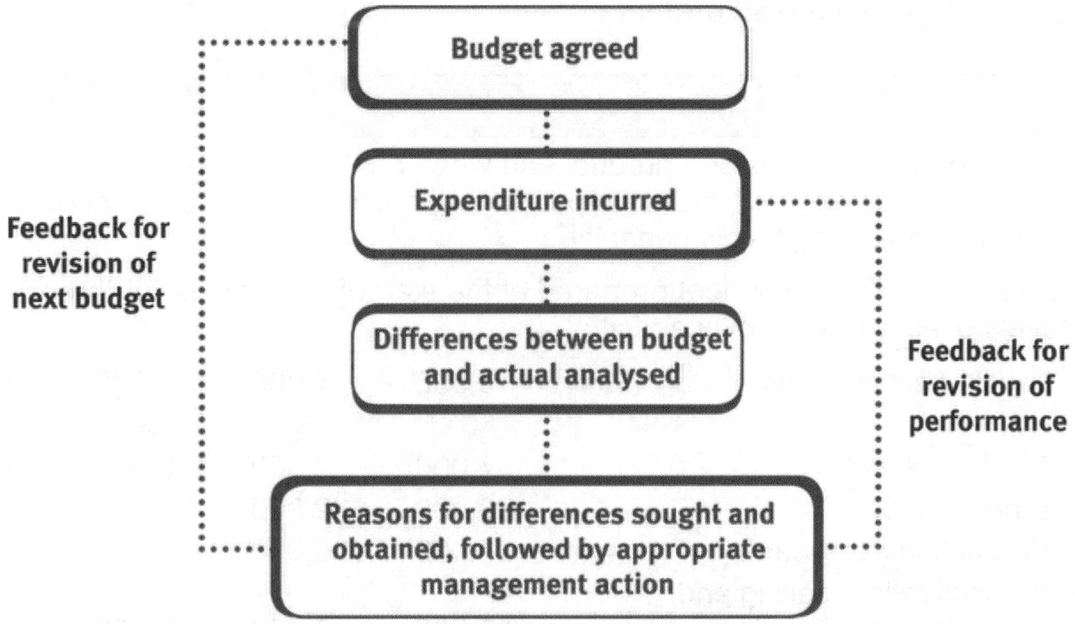

The essential feature of any budgetary control system is the process of comparing budgeted (expected results) with actual results. The difference between these figures is usually referred to as a variance.

Variances may be either adverse or favourable.

- Adverse variances (Adv) or (A) decrease profits.
- Favourable variances (Fav) or (F) increase profits.

9 Fixed and flexible budgets

A fixed budget is a budget produced for a single level of activity. A fixed budget will remain the same no matter the volume of sales or production. A fixed budget is not particularly useful for control; it is predominantly used in the planning stage of budget preparation and is often referred to as the original budget.

A flexible budget is one which, by recognising cost behaviour patterns, is designed to change as volume of activity changes. A flexible budget should represent what the costs and revenues were expected to be at different activity levels. It is particularly useful for control as the original (fixed) budget can be flexed to show the costs and revenues for the actual level of activity.

The key points to note are:

- A fixed budget is set at the beginning of the period, based on estimated production. This is the original budget. At the same time a flexible budget may be produced at a range of activity levels.
- Actual results are compared with the relevant section of the flexible budget, that which corresponds to the actual level of activity. This is referred to as the **flexed budget**.

e.g

Illustration 10 – Preparing a flexed budgets

Wye Ltd manufactures one product and when operating at 100% capacity can produce 5,000 units per period, but for the last few periods has been operating below capacity.

Below is the flexible budget prepared at the start of last period, for three levels of activity at below capacity:

Level of activity (units)	3,500	4,000	4,500
	$	$	$
Direct materials	7,000	8,000	9,000
Direct labour	28,000	32,000	36,000
Production overheads	34,000	36,000	38,000
Administration, selling and distribution overheads	15,000	15,000	15,000
Total cost	84,000	91,000	98,000

In the event, the last period turned out to be even worse than expected, with production of only 2,500 units. The following costs were incurred:

	$
Direct materials	4,500
Direct labour	22,000
Production overheads	28,000
Administration, selling and distribution overheads	16,500
Total cost	71,000

Required:

Use the information given above to prepare the following.

(a) A flexed budget for 2,500 units.

(b) A budgetary control statement.

Solution

(a) **Flexed budget for 2,500 units**

	$
Direct materials (W1) (2,500 × $2)	5,000
Direct labour (W2) (2,500 × $8)	20,000
Production overheads (W3)	30,000
Administration, selling and distribution overheads (W4)	15,000
Total cost	70,000

Workings

(W1) Material is a variable cost – $2 per unit

$$\text{Variable material cost} = \frac{\$7{,}000}{\$3{,}500} = \$2 \text{ per unit}$$

(W2) Labour is a variable cost – $8 per unit.

$$\text{Variable Labour cost} = \frac{\$28{,}000}{\$3{,}500} = \$8 \text{ per unit}$$

(W3) Production overheads are semi-variable. Using the high/low method, the variable cost is $4 per unit; the fixed cost is $20,000. The cost for 2,500 units therefore = $20,000 + (2,500 × $4) = $30,000.

$$\text{Variable cost per unit} = \frac{\$(38{,}000 - 34{,}000)}{\$4{,}500 - 3{,}500} = \$4 \text{ per unit}$$

Total fixed cost by substituting at high activity level:

Total cost = $38,000

Total variable cost = 4,500 × $4 = $18,000

Fixed cost = $38,000 – $18,000 = $20,000

(W4) Other overheads are fixed.

(b) **Budgetary control statement**

	Flexed budget 2,500 units	Actual 2,500 units	Variance
	$	$	$
Direct materials	5,000	4,500	500 (F)
Direct labour	20,000	22,000	2,000 (A)
Production overheads	30,000	28,000	2,000 (F)
Administration, selling and distribution overheads	15,000	16,500	1,500 (A)
Total cost	70,000	71,000	1,000 (A)

A budgetary control statement identifies where the planned level of cost has either been exceeded or kept within the budget. It is then possible to investigate possible causes and recommend appropriate control action.

Note: Chapter 15 has more detail on possible causes and control action that could be taken.

Test your understanding 8

ASD operates a system of flexible budgets. The flexed budgets for expenditure for the first two quarters of year 3 are given below.

Required:

Assuming the cost structures in quarters 1 and 2 continue, complete the statement of the budget cost allowances for quarter 3, when production was 15,000 units.

	Quarter 1	Quarter 2	Quarter 3
Units	10,000	13,000	15,000
	$	$	$
Direct materials	130,000	169,000	
Direct labour	74,000	96,200	
Production overhead	88,000	109,000	
Administration overhead	26,000	26,000	
Total budget cost allowance	347,700	421,700	

Test your understanding 9

Bug Ltd manufactures one uniform product. Activity levels in the assembly department are an average level of activity of 20,000 units production per four-week period. The actual results for four weeks in October are:

	Budget 20,000 units	Actual 17,600 units
	$	$
Direct labour	20,000	19,540
Direct expenses	800	1,000
Direct material	4,200	3,660
Depreciation	10,000	10,000
Semi-variable overheads	5,000	4,760
	40,000	38,960

Assume that at a level of production of 15,000 units, semi-variable overheads are forecast to be $4,500.

Produce a budgetary control statement showing the actual costs, flexed costs and variances produced.

10 Responsibility accounting

Budgetary control and responsibility accounting are seen to be inseparable.

It is important to ensure that each manager has a well-defined area of responsibility and the authority to make decisions within that area, and that no parts of the organisation remain as 'grey' areas where it is uncertain who is responsible for them. If this is put into effect properly, each area of the organisation's activities is the responsibility of a manager. This structure should then be reflected in the organisation chart.

An area of responsibility may be structured as:

- a cost centre – where the manager is responsible for cost control only
- a revenue centre – where the manager is responsible for generation of revenues only
- a profit centre – the manager has control over sales revenues as well as costs
- an investment centre – the manager is empowered to take decisions about capital investment for the department.

Each centre has its own budget, and the manager receives control information relevant to that budget centre. Costs (and revenue, assets and liabilities where applicable) must be traced to the person primarily responsible for taking the related decisions, and identified with the appropriate department.

Identifying costs with responsible managers

It is important to appreciate that in many cases it may not be obvious which centre or manager is responsible for given activities, even if a clearly defined organisation chart is in place and appropriate responsibility accounting units have been set up.

e.g **Illustration 11 – Responsibility accounting**

The marketing department insists on a special rush order being produced which necessitates additional hours being worked in a number of production departments.

Who should be held responsible for the costs incurred in producing the order?

A possible approach might include the following:

- Charge the costs to the marketing department as they initiated the transaction and caused the additional costs to be incurred.
- However, this might involve a complex cost accumulation exercise in several production departments as they attempt to identify the costs, including overheads which relate to that order – is this worthwhile?
- The charging of the costs to the marketing department might encourage managers of production departments to over-allocate costs to the order as a means of improving the performance of their department by moving costs across to the marketing department.

Allocation of non-manufacturing costs

Non-manufacturing costs present their own specific problems of budgetary control. Such costs are unlikely to vary with the level of production activity, but they may represent a significant proportion of total costs. Therefore, specific budgetary control techniques must be developed to deal with such costs.

These costs would include such areas as research and development, administration and finance, marketing and distribution.

Since the costs are not related to production activity, some alternative activity measure must be identified. Possible examples would be marketing costs per sales order and purchasing costs per delivery.

The problem of dual responsibility

A common problem is that the responsibility for a particular cost or item is shared between two (or more) managers. For example:

- the responsibility for payroll costs may be shared between the personnel and production departments
- material costs between purchasing and production departments.

The reporting system should be designed so that the responsibility for performance achievements (i.e. better or worse than budget) is identified as that of a single manager.

The following guidelines may be applied:

- If a manager controls quantity and price – that manager is responsible for all expenditure variances.
- If manager controls quantity but not price – that manager is responsible only for variances due to usage.
- If manager controls price but not quantity – that manager is responsible only for variances due to input prices.
- If manager controls neither quantity nor price – all variances are uncontrollable from the point of view of that manager. We should now be asking the question who in the organisation chart is responsible for control of the expenditure.

Controllable and uncontrollable costs

Controllable costs and revenues are those costs and revenues which result from decisions within the authority of a particular manager or unit within the organisation. These should be used to assess the performance of managers.

Over a long time-span most costs are controllable by someone in the organisation. For example – rent may be fixed for a number of years but there may eventually come an opportunity to move to other premises as such:

- rent is controllable in the long term by a manager fairly high in the organisation structure if the opportunity arises to move premises or negotiate with the land lord
- but in the short term rent is uncontrollable even by senior managers.

There is no clear-cut distinction between controllable and non-controllable costs for a given manager. There may be joint control with another manager. The aim under a responsibility accounting system will be to assign and report on the cost to the person having primary responsibility.

e.g

Illustration 12 – Controllable and uncontrollable costs

An example of the two different approaches to controllable and uncontrollable costs is provided by raw materials. The production manager will have control over usage, but not over price, when buying is done by a separate department. For this reason the price and usage variances are separated and, under the first approach, the production manager would be told only about the usage variance, a separate report being made to the purchasing manager about the price variance. The alternative argument is that if the production manager is also told about the price variance, he/she may attempt to persuade the purchasing manager to try alternative sources of supply.

It is recognised that incorrect allocation of costs to managers could result in a lowering of morale and a reduction of motivation.

To be fully effective, any system of financial control must provide motivation and incentives. If this requirement is not satisfied, managers will approach their responsibilities in a very cautious and conservative manner. It is often found that adverse variances attract investigation therefore failure to distinguish controllable from uncontrollable costs can alienate managers as potentially adverse variances will occur that appear to be under their control but are not.

When adverse variances are reported this implies poor performance by the managers. If they are unable to correct or explain the adverse variances, then they may suffer negative sanctions. They may miss out on a salary increase, or they may be demoted. Positive inducements may be offered to encourage managers to avoid adverse variances. A manager who meets budget may be granted a performance related salary bonus or promotion. If a cost is not controllable by a manager they could be incorrectly penalised or incorrectly rewarded.

It has been seen that an essential element in budgetary control is performance evaluation. Actual results are compared with budget or standard in order to determine whether performance is good or bad. What is being evaluated is not just the business operation but the managers responsible for it. The purpose of budgetary control is to encourage managers to behave in a manner that is to the best advantage of the organisation. Compliance with budget is enforced by a variety of negative and positive sanctions so it is essential that costs allocated to managers are controllable by those managers.

11 Chapter summary

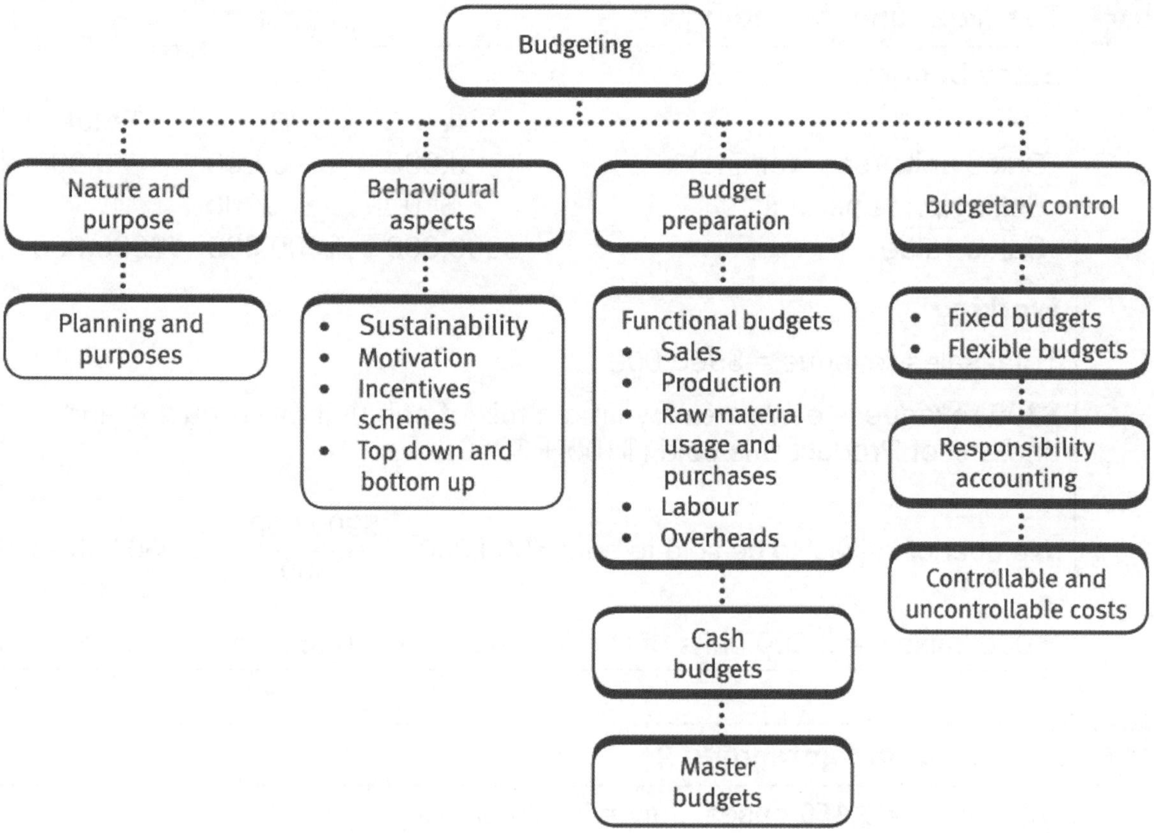

Test your understanding answers

Test your understanding 1

Sales budget

	A	B	Total
Sales units (see working)	3,000	3,000	6,000
Selling price per unit	$100	$200	
Sales value	$300,000	$600,000	$900,000

Working

Total sales revenue = $900,000

$300 revenue is earned every time a mix of one unit of Product A and one unit of Product B is sold ($100 + $200).

Number of 'mixes' to be sold to earn $900,000 $\dfrac{\$900{,}000}{\$300}$ = 3,000 'mixes'

3,000 'mixes' = 3,000 units of Product A and 3,000 units of Product B.

Test your understanding 2

(a) June = **6,150** cases, July = **7,600** cases

	June	July	August	September
Sales	6,000	7,500	8,500	7,000
Closing inventory	750	850	700	650
Opening inventory	(600)	(750)	(850)	(700)
Production budget	**6,150**	**7,600**	8,350*	6,950**

Closing inventory for June is calculated as 10% of July sales = 7,500 × 10% = 750. All other months are calculated in the same way.

(b) August ingredients purchases = **19,125 kg**

		August kg
Production quantity	8,350* × 2.5 kg	20,875
Closing inventory	6,950** × 2.5kg × 50%	8,687.50
Opening inventory	8,350 × 2.5kg × 50%	(10,437.50)
		19,125

Test your understanding 3

D

The budgeted labour cost is $23,800

Actual expected total time = $\frac{2,520}{0.9}$ = 2,800 hours

Budgeted labour cost = 2,800 × $8.50 = $23,800.

Test your understanding 4

Answer a and b

	Product 1	**Product 2**
Sales forecast	3,000	4,500
– Opening inventory	(500)	(700)
+ Closing inventory	200	300
Production budget	**2,700**	**4,100**

Answers c, d, e and f

	Material M1	**Material M2**
Product 1 usage	5,400	8,100
Product 2 usage	12,300	12,300
Materials usage budget	**17,700**	**20,400**

	Material M1	**Material M2**
Material usage	17,700	20,400
– Opening inventory	(4,300)	(3,700)
+ Closing inventory	2,200	1,300
Material purchases budget (units)	**15,600**	**18,000**
Material price per kg	$1.21	$3.30
Material purchases budget (value)	**$18,876**	**$59,400**

Workings

Material prices are as follows:

M1 : $1.10 × 1.1 = $1.21

M2 : $3.00 × 1.1 = $3.30

Material usages are as follows:

Product 1 – Material M1 usage = 2 × 2,700 = 5,400

Product 2 – Material M1 usage = 3 × 4,100 = 12,300

Product 1 – Material M2 usage = 3 × 2,700 = 8,100

Product 2 – Material M2 usage = 3 × 4,100 = 12,300

Answers g and h

	Skilled	**Semi-skilled**
Product 1 hours	8,100	10,800
Product 2 hours	4,100	16,400
Labour budget (hours)	**12,200**	**27,200**
Labour rate per hour	$9	$6
Labour budget ($)	**109,800**	**163,200**

Product 1 – skilled hours = 3 × 2,700 = 8,100

Product 2 – skilled hours = 1 × 4,100 = 4,100

Product 1 – semi-skilled hours = 4 × 2,700 = 10,800

Product 2 – semi-skilled hours = 4 × 4,100 = 16,400

Answer i

Number of hours of skilled labour = 12,200 (see above)

Number of hours of semi-skilled labour = 27,200 (see above)

Total hours worked = 12,200 + 27,200 = 39,400

		$
Variable costs	39,400 hours × $3.50	137,900
Fixed costs	39,400 hours × $5.50	216,700
		354,600

Test your understanding 5

(a)

July	$0
August	$21,200
September	$14,000

Working

	July	**August**	**September**
Opening inventory	0	($10,000)	($10,000)
Purchases	40 × $280 = $11,200	50 × $280 = $14,000	50 × $280 = $14,000
Closing inventory	$10,000	$10,000	$10,000
Total purchases	$21,200	$14,000	$14,000

Cash payments each month are for the previous month's purchases. Therefore, no payments are made in July.

(b)

	$
August labour cost 50 × $160	8,000
July variable overhead cos 40 × $40	1,600
Fixed overhead cash cost ($5,000 – $1,000 depreciation)	4,000
	$13,600

Test your understanding 6

	Jan	Feb	Mar
	$	$	$
Receipts			
Sales (W1)	56,000	58,000	54,000
Payments			
Capital expenditure	–	–	30,000
Direct materials (W2)	20,000	22,000	13,000
Direct labour	15,000	16,500	9,750
Fixed production overheads (W3)	2,000	2,000	2,000
Variable production overheads (W3)	13,000	10,600	8,800
Admin/selling overhead	15,000	–	–
Total outflow	65,000	51,100	63,550
Net cash flow for month	(9,000)	6,900	(9,550)
Opening balance	(5,000)	(14,000)	(7,100)
Closing balance	(14,000)	(7,100)	(16,650)

(W1) Cash from sales

	Total sales	January	February	March
	$	$	$	$
Opening receivables		44,000	–	–
January	60,000	12,000	48,000	–
February	50,000	–	10,000	40,000
March	70,000	–	–	14,000
		56,000	58,000	54,000

(W2) Payments for materials purchases

	December	January	February	March	April
	$	$	$	$	$
Total cost of production	–	50,000	55,000	32,500	50,000
Material cost of production (40%)	–	20,000	22,000	13,000	20,000
Purchases paid in the month prior to usage	20,000	22,000	13,000	20,000	Un-known
Payments are made in the month following purchase.	–	20,000	22,000	13,000	20,000

(W3) Payments for overheads

	January	February	March
	$	$	$
Total cost of production	50,000	55,000	32,500
Overhead cost of production (30%)	15,000	16,500	9,750
Fixed costs	(5,000)	(5,000)	(5,000)
Variable overhead costs	10,000	11,500	4,750

Of the monthly fixed overhead costs of $5,000, $3,000 is depreciation which is not a cash expenditure.

Monthly fixed cost cash expenditure is therefore $2,000.

The opening balance of unpaid variable production overhead cost at the beginning of January is $9,000. This cost should be paid for in January. Variable overheads are paid 40% in the month of expenditure and 60% the following month.

Test your understanding 7

The production budget (1)	6,000 units
The raw material usage budget (2)	72,000 kg
The raw material purchases budget (3)	$146,000
The direct labour budget (4)	$336,000
The overhead budget (5)	$432,000
The cost per unit of Brown (6)	$152

Budgeted Statement of profit or loss

	$	$
Sales revenue 5,000 × $230		1,150,000
Cost of sales		
Opening inventory 100 × $152	15,200	
Production cost 6,000 × $152	912,000	
Closing inventory 1,100 × $152	(167,200)	
		(760,000)
Gross profit		390,000
Administration and marketing		(225,000)
Profit		165,000

Budget statement of financial position

	$	$
Non-current assets $950,000 $40,000		990,000
Inventory (7)	179,200	
Trade receivables	260,000	
Cash (8)	36,800	
	476,000	
Trade payables	86,000	
Other short term liabilities	24,000	
	110,000	
Net current assets		366,000
Net assets $1,191,000 + $165,000		1,356,000

Workings

Production budget

Sales	5,000
Opening inventory	(100)
Closing inventory	1,100
1 *Production units*	6,000

Raw material budget

Production	6,000
kg per unit	× 12
2 *Usage (kg)*	72,000
Opening inventory	(5,000)
Closing inventory	6,000
Purchases (kg)	73,000
Cost per kg	× 2
3 *Purchases ($)*	146,000

Labour budget

Production	6,000
Hours per unit	× 8
Labour hours	48,000
Rate per hour	× 7
4 *Labour cost ($)*	336,000

Overhead budget

Labour hours	48,000
Cost per hour ($1 + $8)	× 9
5 *Overhead cost ($)*	432,000

Cost of one unit of Brown

Direct material (12 kg × $2)	$24
Direct labour (8 hr × $7)	$56
Overheads (8 hr × ($1 + $8))	$72
6 *Cost per unit*	$152

Inventory

Raw materials (6,000 × $2)	$12,000
Finished goods (1,100 × $152)	$167,200
7 *Inventory valuation*	$179,200

Cash

Opening balance	$25,000
Profit for the period	$165,000
Cash spent on NCA	($40,000)
Change in inventory	($113,200)
8 *Closing cash balance*	$36,800

Test your understanding 8

	Quarter 1	Quarter 2	Quarter 3
Units	10,000	13,000	15,000
	$	$	$
Direct materials	130,000	169,000	195,000
Direct labour	74,000	96,200	111,000
Production overhead	88,000	109,000	123,000
Administration overhead	26,000	26,000	26,000
Total budget cost allowance	347,700	421,700	455,000

Cost behaviour patterns need to be identified. Examine the total costs – administration overhead is a fixed cost as the total cost is constant as activity level changes.

Calculate the cost per unit – Direct materials and direct labour are variable costs as the cost per unit is constant.

Production overheads must be a semi-variable cost as the cost per unit and the total cost changes as activity level changes.

Flex the budget based on cost behaviours:

Direct materials = 130,000/10,000 × 15,000 = 195,000

Direct labour = 74,000/10,000 × 15,000 = 111,000

Production overheads – high low method

VC = (109,000 – 88,000)/(13,000 – 10,000) = $7 per unit

Test your understanding 9

1 **Identify the cost behaviours and calculate the cost per unit based on budget**

	Behaviour	**Cost per unit**
Direct labour	variable	20,000/20,000 = $1
Direct expenses	variable	800/20,000 = $0.04
Direct material	variable	4,200/20,000 = $0.21
Depreciation	fixed	n/a
Semi-variable overheads	semi variable	see working

Working for semi-variable overhead (high low method)

Variable cost = change in cost/change in activity

= ($5,000 – $4,500)/(20,000 – 15,000)

= $0.10

Fixed cost = total cost – total variable cost

= $5,000 – ($0.10 × 20,000)

= $3,000

2 **Produce the budget control statement**

	Actual 17,600 units	**Flexed 17,600 units**	**Variance**
	$	$	
Direct labour	19,540	17,600	1,940 A
Direct expenses	1,000	704	296 A
Direct material	3,660	3,696	36 F
Depreciation	10,000	10,000	–
Semi-variable overheads (W)	4,760	4,760	–
	38,960	36,760	2,200 A

Working for semi-variable overheads

Variable element 17,600 × $0.10 = $1,760

Fixed element $3,000

Total cost = $1,760 + $3,000 = $4,760

Chapter

14

Investment appraisal

Chapter learning objectives

Upon completion of this chapter you will be able to:

- discuss the importance of investment planning and control
- define and distinguish between asset and expense items
- outline the issues to consider and the steps involved in the preparation of an asset expenditure budget
- explain and illustrate the difference between simple and compound interest, and between nominal and effective interest rates
- explain and illustrate compounding and discounting
- explain the distinction between cash flow and profit and the relevance of cash flow to investment appraisal
- identify and evaluate relevant cash flows for individual investment decisions
- explain and illustrate the net present value (NPV) and internal rate of return (IRR) methods of discounted cash flow
- calculate present value using annuity and perpetuity formulae
- calculate NPV, IRR and payback (discounted and non-discounted)
- interpret the results of NPV, IRR and payback calculations of investment viability.

PER

One of the PER performance objectives (PO13) is to plan business activities and control performance, making recommendations for improvement. Working through this chapter should help you understand how to demonstrate that objective.

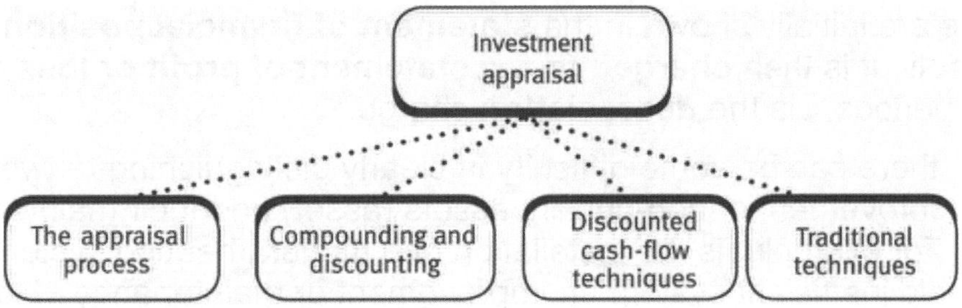

1 Investment appraisal

When a business spends money on new non-current assets it is known as asset expenditure. Spending is normally irregular and for large amounts. It is expected to generate long-term benefits.

Investment decisions normally represent the most important decisions that an organisation makes, since they commit a substantial proportion of a firm's resources to actions that are likely to be irreversible.

Many different investment projects exist including:

- replacement of assets
- cost-reduction schemes
- new product/service developments
- product/service expansions
- statutory, environmental and welfare proposals.

The distinction between asset and expense items is important:

Expense items

Expense items are expenditure incurred in:

(a) the purchase of assets acquired for conversion into cash (e.g. goods for resale)

(b) the manufacturing, selling and distribution of goods and the day-to-day administration of the business

(c) the maintenance of the revenue-earning capacity of the non-current assets (i.e. repairs, etc).

Expense items are generally charged to the **statement of profit or loss** for the period in which the expenditure was incurred.

Asset items

Asset items is expenditure incurred in:

(a) the acquisition of non-current assets required for use in the business and not for resale

(b) the alteration or significant improvement of non-current assets for the purpose of increasing their revenue-earning capacity.

Asset items are initially shown in the **statement of financial position** as non-current assets. It is then **charged to the statement of profit or loss** over a number of periods, via the **depreciation** charge.

In practice, there can be some difficulty in clearly distinguishing between alteration/improvement of non-current assets (asset) and their maintenance (expense). For example, is the installation of a modern heating system to replace an old inefficient system an improvement or maintenance? However, you should not need to make such decisions in your exam.

Appraisal methods

There are three widely used appraisal methods:

1 The payback period (using both discounted and non-discounted cash flows).

2 Net present value (NPV).

3 Internal rate of return (IRR).

All three methods consider the time value of money, assuming the discounted payback method is used. They are known as **discounted cash flow (DCF) techniques**.

Asset expenditure budgeting process

An asset expenditure budget:

- is a programme of asset expenditure covering several years
- includes authorised future projects and projects currently under consideration.

One stage in the asset expenditure budgeting process is **investment appraisal**. This appraisal has the following features:

- estimates of future costs and benefits over the project's life
- assessment of the level of expected returns earned.

The asset expenditure budgeting process consists of a number of stages:

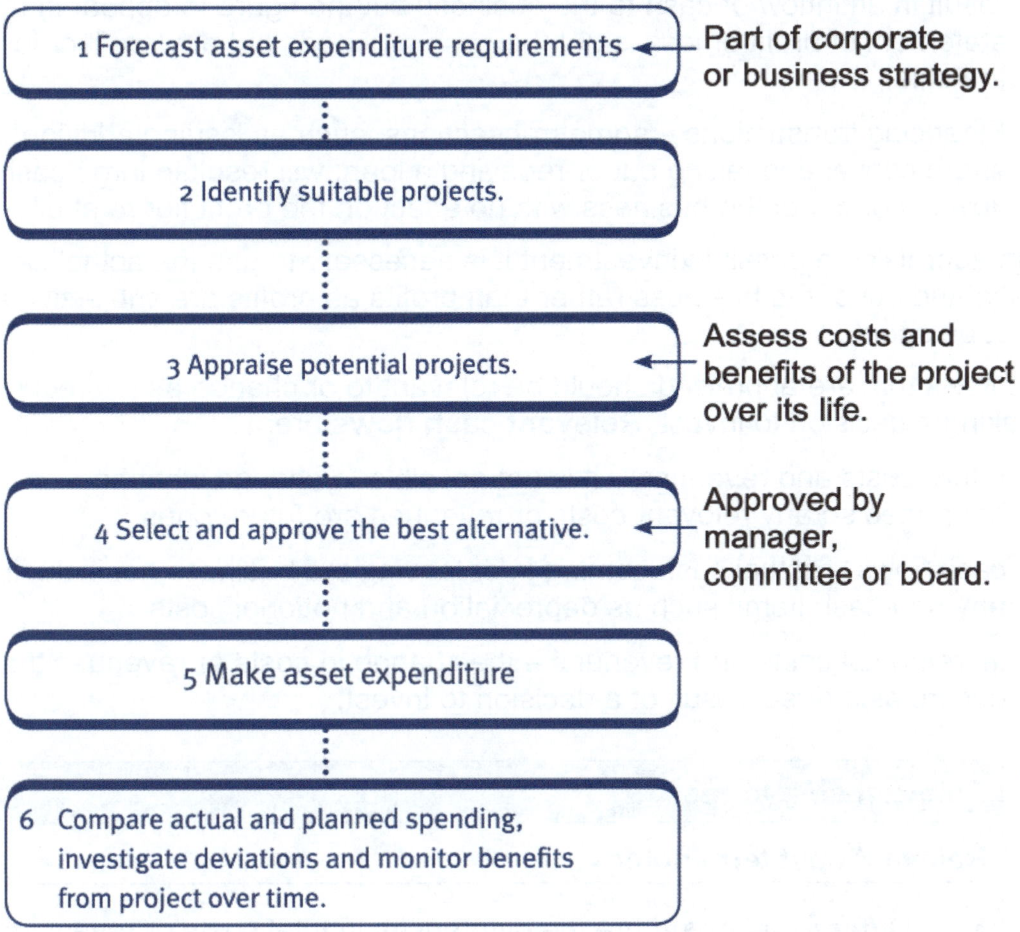

2 Cash flows used for investment appraisal

In investment appraisal it is more appropriate to evaluate future **cash flows rather than accounting profits**. Cash and profit are very different. Profit is calculated on the statement of profit or loss and cash is a current asset on the statement of financial position. The differences arise because:

- Revenue is recognised in the statement of profit or loss when it is earned but this is not necessarily when the cash is received.
- Costs are recognised in the statement of profit or loss when they are incurred but this is not necessarily when the cash is paid.
- Non-cash expenses – the statement of profit or loss of a business is charged with a number of non-cash expenses such as depreciation and provisions for doubtful debts. Although these are correctly charged as expenses in the statement of profit or loss, they are not cash flows and will not reduce the cash balance of the business.
- Purchase of non-current assets – these are often large cash outflows of a business but the only amount that is charged to the statement of profit or loss is the annual depreciation charge not the entire cost of the non-current asset.

- Sale of non-current assets – when a non-current asset is sold this will result in an inflow of cash to the business but the figure to appear in the statement of profit or loss is not the cash proceeds but any profit or loss on the sale.
- Financing transactions – some transactions, such as issuing additional share capital and taking out or repaying a loan, will result in large cash flows in or out of the business with no effect on the profit figure at all.

When appraising a possible investment it is necessary to use the actual cash flows in and out of the business rather than profits as profits are subjective and cannot be spent.

Cash flows that are appraised should be relevant to or change as a direct result of making a decision to invest. **Relevant cash flows** are:

- future costs and revenues – it is not possible to change what has happened so any relevant costs or revenues are future ones
- cash flows – actual cash coming in or leaving the business not including any non-cash items such as depreciation and notional costs
- incremental costs and revenues – the change in costs or revenues that occurs as a direct result of a decision to invest.

Relevant cost terms

Relevant cost terminology

- **Differential costs** are the differences in total costs or revenues between two alternatives.
- **Opportunity cost** is an important concept in decision making. It represents the best alternative that is foregone in taking the decision. The opportunity cost emphasises that decision making is concerned with alternatives and that the cost of taking one decision is the profit or contribution foregone by not taking the next best alternative.
- **Avoidable costs** are the specific costs associated with an activity that would be avoided if that activity did not exist.

Non-relevant cost terminology

- **Sunk costs** are past or historical costs which are not directly relevant in decision making, for example, development costs or market research costs.
- **Committed costs** are future costs that cannot be avoided, whatever decision is taken.

- **Non-cash flow costs** are costs which do not involve the flow of cash, for example, depreciation and notional costs. A notional cost is a cost that will not result in an outflow of cash either now or in the future, for example, sometimes the head office of an organisation may charge a 'notional' rent to its branches. This cost will appear in the accounts of the organisation but will not result in a 'real' cash expenditure.
- **General fixed overheads** are usually not relevant to a decision. However, some fixed overheads may be relevant to a decision; for example, stepped fixed costs may be relevant if fixed costs increase as a direct result of a decision being taken.
- **Carry amount of non-current assets** are not relevant costs because like depreciation, they are determined by accounting conventions rather than by future cash flows.

e.g

Illustration 1 – Relevant costs

A company is evaluating a proposed expenditure on an item of equipment that would cost $160,000.

A technical feasibility study has been carried out by consultants, at a cost of $15,000, into benefits from investing in the equipment.

It has been estimated that the equipment would have a life of four years, and annual profits would be $8,000, after deducting annual depreciation of $40,000 and an annual charge of $25,000 for a share of the existing fixed cost of the company.

Required:

What are the relevant cash flows for this investment?

Solution

The $160,000 to be spent on the new item of equipment is relevant as it is a future cash flow incurred as a direct result of making the decision.

The $15,000 already spent on the feasibility study is a sunk cost – it has already been spent – therefore it is not relevant.

Depreciation and apportioned fixed overheads are not relevant. Depreciation is not a cash flow and apportioned fixed overheads represent costs that will be incurred anyway.

It is possible to estimate annual cash flows by adjusting profits for non-cash items.

	$
Estimated profit	8,000
Add back depreciation	40,000
Add back apportioned fixed costs	25,000
Annual cash flows	73,000

The $73,000 annual cash flows will also be relevant for the life of the investment.

Test your understanding 1

A manufacturing company is considering the production of a new type of widget. Each widget will take two hours to make.

Fixed overheads are apportioned on the basis of $1 per labour hour.

If the new widgets are produced, the company will have to employ an additional supervisor at a salary of $15,000 per annum. The company will produce 10,000 widgets per annum.

Required:

What are the relevant cash flows?

3 The time value of money

One characteristic of all asset expenditure projects is that the cash flows arise over the long term (a period usually greater than 12 months). Under this situation it becomes necessary to carefully consider the time value of money.

Money received today is worth more than the same sum received in the future, i.e. it has a **time value**.

For an investor, the effective time value of money is due to:

1. Cost of finance – if the funds were available now the cash could be used to repay or reduce a loan, in turn reducing interest charges on the loan
2. Investment opportunities – the funds could be invested to earn a return, often expressed as a percentage return
3. Inflation – erodes the purchasing power of the funds as prices of commodities increase
4. Risk – funds received sooner are more certain.

Cost of finance and investment opportunities are often discussed in terms of "interest rates" – the interest being saved by reducing the loan amount outstanding and the interest received from an investment.

All four of the factors above combine to express the time value of money as an interest rate.

The time value of money

Potential for earning interest

If an investment is to be justified, it needs to earn at least a minimum amount of profit, so that the return compensates the investor for both the amount invested and also for the length of time before the profits are made. For example, if a company could invest $80,000 now to earn revenue of $82,000 in one week's time, a profit of $2,000 in seven days would be a very good return. However, if it takes four years to earn the money, the return would be very low.

Therefore money has a time value. It can be invested to earn interest or profits, so it is better to have $1 now than in one year's time. This is because $1 now can be invested for the next year to earn a return, whereas $1 in one year's time cannot. Another way of looking at the time value of money is to say that $1 in six years' time is worth less than $1 now.

There are different forms of interest which are discussed in the next section:

- Simple
- Compound
- Nominal
- Effective.

Impact of inflation

In most countries, in most years prices rise as a result of inflation. Therefore funds received today will buy more than the same amount a year later, as prices will have risen in the meantime. The funds are subject to a loss of purchasing power over time.

Risk

The earlier cash flows are due to be received, the more certain they are – there is less chance that events will prevent cash flows occurring. Earlier cash flows are therefore considered to be more valuable.

Simple interest

Simple interest is calculated based on the original sum invested. Any interest earned in earlier periods is not included. Simple interest is often used for a single investment period that is less than a year.

To calculate the future value of an amount invested under these terms you could use the following formula:

$$V = X + (X \times r \times n)$$

Where V = Future value

X = Initial investment (present value)

r = Interest rate (expressed as a decimal)

n = Number of time periods

e.g

Illustration 2 – Simple interest

$100 is invested in an account for six months. The interest rate is 10% per annum.

Required:

Calculate the value of the account after six months.

Solution

$V = X + (X \times r \times n)$

$V = 100 + (100 \times 0.1 \times (6/12)) = \$105$

Nominal interest rate

The nominal interest rate is the stated interest rate for a time period – for example a month or a year.

Effective annual interest rate

The effective annual interest rate is the interest rate that includes the effects of compounding a nominal interest rate for one year.

FORMULA FOR EFFECTIVE ANNUAL INTEREST RATE

$$r = (1 + i/n)^n - 1$$

Where r = Effective annual interest rate

i = Nominal interest rate

n = Number of time periods

e.g

Illustration 3 – Nominal and effective interest rate

The nominal interest rate is 10% per year compounded on a monthly basis.

Required:

A company is going to invest for 12 months what is the effective interest rate?

Solution

$r = (1 + i/n)^n - 1$

$r = (1 + 0.1/12)^{12} - 1$

$r = 0.1047$

The effective interest rate of receiving 10% interest per annum compounded on a monthly basis for 12 months is the same as receiving 10.47% interest per annum with no compounding.

Compound interest

Compounding calculates the future (or terminal) value of a given sum invested today for a number of years.

To compound a sum, the figure is increased by the amount of interest it would earn over the period. Interest is earned on interest gained in earlier periods.

e.g

Illustration 4 – Compounding

$100 is invested in an account for five years. The interest rate is 10% per annum.

Required:

Calculate the value of the account after five years.

Solution

To compound a sum of money, the value is increased by the amount of interest it will earn over the period it is invested.

Therefore the $100 invested for 5 years will earn:

In year 1 $100 + ($100 × 10%) = $110

In year 2 $110 + ($110 × 10%) = $121

In year 3 $121 + ($121 × 10%) = $133.10

In year 4 $133.10 + ($133.10 × 10%) = $146.41

In year 5 $146.41 + ($146.41 × 10%) = $161.05

This can also be calculated using a formula:

FORMULA FOR COMPOUNDING

$V = X(1 + r)^n$

Where V = Future value

X = Initial investment (present value)

r = Interest rate (expressed as a decimal)

n = Number of time periods

Illustration 5 – Compounding

$100 is invested in an account for five years. The interest rate is 10% per annum.

Required:

Calculate the value of the account after five years using the formula.

Solution

$V = X(1+r)^n$

$V = 100\ (1.10)^5 = \$161.05$

Test your understanding 2

$450 is invested in an account earning 6.25% interest p.a.

Required:

Calculate the fund value after 12 years.

Test your understanding 3

$5,000 is required in 10 years. $x is invested in an account earning 5% interest p.a.

Required:

Calculate the value of $x.

Test your understanding 4

A company has $1,000,000 to invest for 12 months.

The choices available are:

- a deposit account offering nominal interest at 10% per year, with interest calculated quarterly
- a deposit account offering nominal interest at 10.25% per year, with interest calculated annually.

Required:

Which deposit account gives the higher effective interest rate?

Discounting

Discounting performs the opposite function to compounding. Compounding finds the future value of a sum invested now, whereas discounting considers a sum receivable in the future and establishes its equivalent value today. This value in today's terms is known as the **Present Value (PV)**.

In potential investment projects, cash flows will arise at many different points in time. Calculating the present value of future cash flows is a key technique in investment appraisal decisions.

Assumptions used in discounting

Unless told otherwise you should assume:

- **All cash flows occur at the start or end of a year.**

  Although in practice many cash flows accrue throughout the year, for discounting purposes they are all treated as occurring at the start or end of a year. Note that if today (T_0) is 01/01/20X1, the dates 31/12/20X1 and 01/01/20X2, although technically separate days, can be treated for discounting as occurring at the same point in time, i.e. at T_1.

- **Initial investments occur at once (T_0), other cash flows start in one year's time (T_1).**

  In project appraisal, the investment needs to be made before the cash flows can accrue. Therefore, unless the examiner specifies otherwise, it is assumed that investments occur in advance. The first cash flows associated with running the project are therefore assumed to occur one year after the project begins, i.e. at T_1.

FORMULAE FOR DISCOUNTING

Present value = Future value × discount factor — LEARN

Where: Discount factor = $\frac{1}{(1+r)^n}$ or $(1+r)^{-n}$ — GIVEN

where: r is the interest rate expressed as decimal

n is the number of time periods

The discount factors for whole interest rates from 1 % to 20% can be looked up on the discount tables found at the front of this text. These will be provided in the exam. You would need to use the formula if a decimal interest rate (for example 3.6%) was given.

Test your understanding 5

Calculate how much should be invested now in order to have $250 in eight years' time? The account pays 12% interest per annum.

Test your understanding 6

Calculate the present value of $25,000 receivable in six years' time, if the interest rate is 10% p.a.

The cost of capital

In the above discussions we referred to the rate of interest. There are a number of alternative terms used to refer to the rate a firm should use to take account of the time value of money:

- cost of capital
- discount rate
- required return.

Whatever term is used, the rate of interest used for discounting should aim to reflect the cost of the finance that will be tied up in the investment.

4 The payback period

The payback period is the time a project will take to pay back the money spent on it. It is based on expected cash flows and provides a measure of liquidity.

It is the time which elapses until the initial investment is recovered. It considers cash flows only. It can be assumed that, with this technique, the cash flows can occur evenly during the year.

Decision criteria

- Compare the payback period to the company's maximum return time allowed and if the payback is quicker the project should be accepted.
- Faced with mutually-exclusive projects choose the project with the shortest payback.

Calculation – Constant annual flows

$$\text{Payback period} = \frac{\text{Initial investment}}{\text{Annual cash inflow}}$$

A payback period may not be for an exact number of years. To calculate the payback in years and months you should multiply the decimal fraction of a year by 12 to get the number of months.

Test your understanding 7

An expenditure of $2 million is expected to generate net cash inflows of $500,000 each year for the next seven years.

Required:

Calculate the payback period for the project?

Test your understanding 8

A project will involve spending $1.8 million now. Annual cash flows from the project would be $350,000.

Required:

Calculate the payback period for the project.

Calculations – Uneven annual flows

If cash flows are uneven (a more likely state of affairs), the payback has to be calculated by working out the cumulative cash flow over the life of a project.

Illustration 6 – Payback period

Mickey Ltd is considering two mutually-exclusive projects with the following details:

Project A

Initial investment	$450,000					
Scrap value in year 5	$20,000					
Year:		1	2	3	4	5
Annual cash flows ($000)		200	150	100	100	100

Project B

Initial investment	$100,000					
Scrap value in year 5	$10,000					
Year:		1	2	3	4	5
Annual cash flows ($000)		50	40	30	20	20

Assume that the initial investment is at the start of the project and the annual cash flows accrue evenly over the year.

Required:

Calculate which project the company should select if the objective is to minimise the payback period?

Solution

Project A

	Cash flow $000	Cumulative cash flow $000
Year 0	(450)	(450)
Year 1	200	(250)
Year 2	150	(100)
Year 3	100	0

Payback period = 3 years

Project B

	Cash flow $000	Cumulative cash flow $000
Year 0	(100)	(100)
Year 1	50	(50)
Year 2	40	(10)
Year 3	30	20

Project B requires $10,000 during year 3 to payback. Over the 3rd year $30,000 cash is being received. Assuming that cash accrues evenly over the year it will take 1/3 of a year to recoup the remaining cash to pay back. 1/3 × 12 months = 4 months.

Payback period = 2 years 4 months

Project B should be accepted

Non-cash flows

Payback uses cash flows not profits in the calculation – if you are provided with profits then non-cash flows, such as depreciation, need to be added back on the profit to calculate cash.

Discounted payback

One of the major criticisms of using the payback period is that it does not take into account the time value of money. The discounted payback technique attempts to overcome this criticism. The technique is identical – but the present value of the cash flow is calculated before calculating the cumulative cash flow.

e.g

Illustration 7 – Discounted payback period

Mickey Ltd is considering two mutually-exclusive projects with the following details:

Project A

Initial investment	$450,000				
Scrap value in year 5	$20,000				
Year:	1	2	3	4	5
Annual cash flows ($000)	200	150	100	100	100

Project B

Initial investment	$100,000				
Scrap value in year 5	$10,000				
Year:	1	2	3	4	5
Annual cash flows ($000)	50	40	30	20	20

Assume that the initial investment is at the start of the project and the annual cash flows accrue evenly over the year.

Required:

Calculate the discounted payback period for both projects if the relevant cost of capital is 10%.

Solution

		Project A			Project B		
Year	**Discount factor** 10%	**Cash flow** $000	**Present value** $000	**Cumulative cash flow** $000	**Cash flow** $000	**Present value** $000	**Cumulative cash flow** $000
0	1.000	(450)	(450)	(450)	(100)	(100)	(100)
1	0.909	200	181.8	(268.2)	50	45.45	(54.55)
2	0.826	150	123.9	(144.3)	40	33.04	(21.51)
3	0.751	100	75.1	(69.2)	30	22.53	1.02
4	0.683	100	68.3	(0.9)			
5	0.621	120	74.52	73.62			

Project A now pays back in just over 4 years and Project B in just under 3 years. Project B is still preferable to Project A but the payback period has increased as time value of money is applied to the cash flows.

Advantages	Disadvantages
• Simple to understand • Payback is a simple measure of risk. Firms selecting projects on the basis of payback periods may avoid liquidity problems • Uses cash flows, not subjective accounting profits • Emphasises the cash flows in the earlier years	• Is not a measure of absolute profitability • Ignores the time value of money. **Note:** A discounted payback period may be calculated to overcome this problem • Does not take into account cash flows beyond the payback period

Advantages and disadvantages of Payback

Payback has a number of advantages

- As a concept payback is easily understood and is easily calculated.
- Rapidly changing technology. If new plant is likely to be scrapped in a short period because of obsolescence, a quick payback is essential.
- Improving investment conditions. When investment conditions are expected to improve in the near future, attention is directed to those projects that will release funds soonest, to take advantage of the improving climate.
- Payback favours projects with a quick return. It is often argued that these are to be preferred for three reasons.
  - Rapid project payback leads to rapid company growth – but in fact such a policy will lead to many profitable investment opportunities being overlooked because their payback period does not happen to be particularly swift.
  - Rapid payback minimises risk – the logic being that the shorter the payback period, the less there is that can go wrong. Not all risks are related to time, but payback is able to provide a useful means of assessing time risk. It is likely that earlier cash flows can be estimated with greater certainty.
  - Rapid payback maximises liquidity – but liquidity problems are best dealt with separately, through cash forecasting.
- Payback uses cash flows, rather than profits, and so is less likely to produce an unduly optimistic figure distorted by assorted accounting conventions which might permit certain costs to be carried forward and not affect profit initially.

The disadvantages of payback are:

- Project returns may be ignored. In particular, cash flows arising after the payback period are totally ignored.
- Timing of cash flows are ignored. Cash flows are effectively categorised as pre-payback or post-payback, but no more accurate measure is made.
- The time value of money is ignored (unless discounted payback is used).
- There is no objective measure as to what length of time should be set as the minimum or maximum payback period. Investment decisions are therefore subjective.
- Payback takes no account of the effects on business profits and periodic performance of the project, as evidenced in the financial statements. This is critical if the business is to be reasonably viewed by users of the accounts.

5 Net present value (NPV)

The NPV of an investment represents the net benefit or loss of benefit in present value terms for an investment opportunity.

A positive NPV represents the surplus funds earned on a project. This means that it tells us the impact on shareholder wealth.

Decision criteria

- Any project with a positive NPV is viable.
- Projects with a negative NPV are not viable.
- Faced with mutually-exclusive projects, choose the project with the highest NPV.

What does the NPV actually mean

Suppose, in an investment problem, we calculate the NPV of certain cash flows at 12% to be – $97, and at 10% to be zero, and yet at 8% the NPV of the same cash flows is + $108. Another way of expressing this is as follows.

- If the funds were borrowed at 12% the investor would be $97 out of pocket – i.e. the investment earns a yield below the cost of capital.
- If funds were borrowed at 10% the investor would break even – i.e. the investment yields a return equal to the cost of capital.

- If funds were borrowed at 8% the investor would be $108 in pocket – i.e. the investment earns a return in excess of the cost of capital.

In other words, a positive NPV is an indication of the surplus funds available to the investor now as a result of accepting the project.

e.g

Illustration 8 – Net present value (NPV)

Mickey Ltd is considering two mutually-exclusive projects with the following details:

Project A

Initial investment	$450,000				
Scrap value in year 5	$20,000				
Year:	1	2	3	4	5
Annual cash flows ($000)	200	150	100	100	100

Project B

Initial investment	$100,000				
Scrap value in year 5	$10,000				
Year:	1	2	3	4	5
Annual cash flows ($000)	50	40	30	20	20

Assume that the initial investment is at the start of the project and the annual cash flows accrue evenly over the year.

Required:

Calculate the Net Present Value to the nearest $000 for Projects A and B if the relevant cost of capital is 10%.

Solution

		Project A		Project B	
Year	**Discount factor**	**Cash flow** $000	**Present value** $000	**Cash flow** $000	**Present value** $000
0		(450)	(450)	(100)	(100)
1	0.909	200	182	50	45
2	0.826	150	124	40	33
3	0.751	100	75	30	23
4	0.683	100	68	20	14
5	0.621	120	75	30	19
		NPV =	74	NPV =	34

Test your understanding 9

An organisation is considering an investment in new equipment. The estimated cash flows are as follows.

Year	Cash flow $
0	(240,000)
1	80,000
2	120,000
3	70,000
4	40,000
5	20,000

The company's cost of capital is 9%.

Required:

Calculate the NPV of the project to assess whether it should be undertaken.

Advantages	Disadvantages
• Does consider the time value of money • It is a measure of absolute profitability • Considers cash flows • It considers the whole life of the project • A company selecting projects on the basis of NPV maximisation should maximise shareholders wealth	• Fairly complex • Not well understood by non-financial managers • It may be difficult to determine the cost of capital

Advantages and disadvantages of NPV

When appraising projects or investments, NPV is considered to be superior to other methods. This is because it:

- considers the time value of money – discounting cash flows to their present value takes account of the impact of interest, inflation and risk over time.
- is an absolute measure of return – the NPV of an investment represents the potential surplus raised by the project. This allows a business to plan more effectively.

- is based on cash flows not profits – the subjectivity of profits makes them less reliable than cash flows and therefore less appropriate for decision making.
- considers the whole life of the project – NPV takes account of all relevant flows associated with the project. Discounting the flows takes account of the fact that later flows are less reliable.
- should lead to maximisation of shareholder wealth. If the cost of capital reflects the investors' (i.e. shareholders') required return, then the NPV reflects the theoretical increase in their wealth. For a company, this is considered to be the primary objective of the business.

However, there are some potential drawbacks:

- It is difficult to explain to managers. To understand the meaning of the NPV calculated requires an understanding of discounting. The method is not as intuitive as techniques such as payback.
- It requires knowledge of the cost of capital. The calculation of the cost of capital is, in practice, more complex than identifying interest rates. It involves gathering data and making a number of calculations based on that data and some estimates. The process may be deemed too protracted for the appraisal to be carried out.
- It is relatively complex. For the reasons explained above, NPV may be rejected in favour of simpler techniques.

6 Internal rate of return (IRR)

This is the rate of return, or discount rate, at which a project has a NPV of zero.

Graph showing the NPV of one project appraised at different discount rates

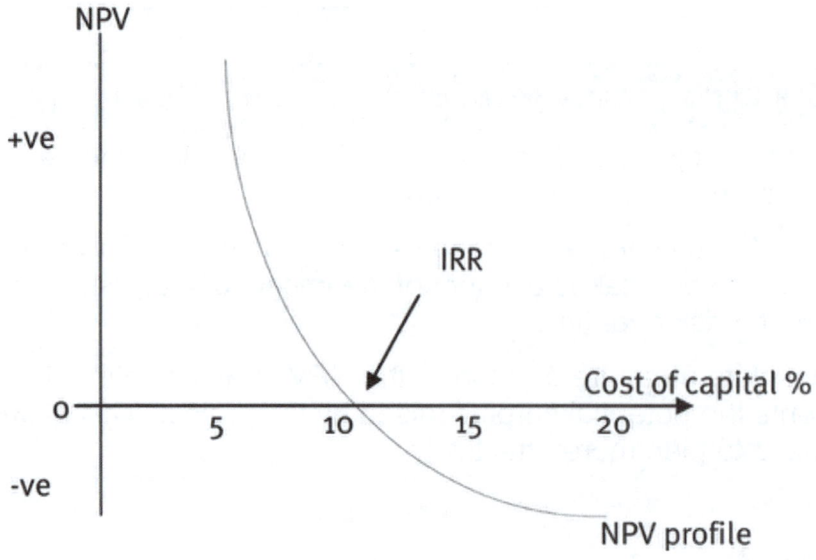

Decision criteria

- If the IRR is greater than the company's cost of capital the project should be accepted.
- Faced with mutually-exclusive projects choose the project with the higher IRR.

Calculating the IRR (using linear interpolation)

The steps in linear interpolation are:

(a) Calculate two NPVs for the project at two different costs of capital

(b) Use the following formula to find the IRR:

FORMULA FOR IRR

$$IRR = L + \frac{N_L}{N_L - N_H} \times (H - L)$$

LEARN

where:

L = Lower rate of interest

H = Higher rate of interest

N_L = NPV at lower rate of interest

N_H = NPV at higher rate of interest.

e.g

Illustration 9 – Internal rate of return (IRR)

Net cash flows from Project A are:

Year	Net cash flow $000
0	(450)
1	200
2	150
3	100
4	100
5	120

The NPV of Project A at a discount rate of 10% is $73,620.

Required:

Calculate the internal rate of return of Project A.

Solution

		Project A	
Year	**Discount factors at 20%**	**Net cash flow** $000	**PV** $000
0	1.000	(450)	(450)
1	0.833	200	167
2	0.694	150	104
3	0.579	100	58
4	0.482	100	48
5	0.402	120	48
		NPV @ 20% =	(25)

$$IRR = L + \frac{N_L}{N_L - N_H} \times (H - L)$$

$$IRR = 10 + \frac{74}{74 - -25} \times (20 - 10)$$

$$IRR = 10 + \frac{74}{99} \times (10)$$

IRR = 10 + (0.747 × 10)

IRR = 17.5%

Further explanation of IRR

Using the NPV method, PVs are calculated by discounting cash flows at a given cost of capital, and the difference between the PV of costs and the PV of benefits is the NPV. In contrast, the IRR method of DCF analysis is to calculate the exact DCF rate of return that the project is expected to achieve.

If an investment has a positive NPV, it means it is earning more than the cost of capital. If the NPV is negative, it is earning less than the cost of capital. This means that if the NPV is zero, it will be earning exactly the cost of capital.

Conversely, the percentage return on the investment must be the rate of discount or cost of capital at which the NPV equals zero. This rate of return is called the IRR or the DCF yield and if it is higher than the target rate of return then the project is financially worth undertaking.

Estimating the IRR

An investment has a NPV with a discount rate of 10% of $4,400 and a NPV at a discount rate of 20% of –$31,000.

The IRR will be closer to 10% then 20% as $4,400 is closer to zero than – $31,000.

We can estimate the IRR:

- There is a difference of 10% between the 10% and 20% used for the NPV calculations
- There is a difference in NPV value of $31,000 + $4,400 = $35,400
- Each percentage change is approximately (31,000 + 4,400)/10 = $3,540
- For the project to break even $4,400 is required, this is represented by $4,400/$3,540 = 1.24%
- The IRR can be estimated as 10% + 1.24% = 11.24%.

For examination purposes, the choice of rates to estimate the IRR is less important than your ability to perform the calculation to estimate it.

Test your understanding 10

You are given the following:

At 20% the NPV is $8,510

At 30% the NPV is – $9,150

Required:

Calculate the internal rate of return.

Test your understanding 11

A potential project's predicted cash flows gives a NPV of $50,000 at a discount rate of 10% and –$10,000 at a rate of 15%.

Required:

Calculate the IRR.

Test your understanding 12

Identify the correct explanation of the internal rate of return – it is the interest rate that equates the present value of expected future net cash flows to:

A the initial cost of the investment outlay

B the depreciation value of the investment

C the terminal (compounded) value of future cash receipts

D the firm's cost of capital

Advantages	Disadvantages
• Does consider the time value of money • It is a percentage so should be easily understood by nonfinancial managers • Considers cash flows • It considers the whole life of the project • It can be calculated without reference to the cost of capital • A company selecting projects where the IRR exceeds the cost of capital should increase shareholders' wealth	• It is not a measure of absolute profitability • Interpolation only provides an estimate of the true IRR • Fairly complicated to calculate – although spreadsheets now have built-in programs • The IRR of projects may conflict with the NPV. If this occurs the NPV must take precedence • It is possible for non-conventional cash flows to give rise to no IRR or multiple IRRs

Advantages and disadvantages of IRR

Using IRR as an appraisal technique has many advantages:

- IRR considers the time value of money. The current value earned from an investment project is therefore more accurately measured.
- IRR is a percentage and therefore easily understood. Although managers may not completely understand the detail of the IRR, the concept of a return earned is familiar and the IRR can be simply compared with the required return of the organisation.
- IRR uses cash flows not profits. These are less subjective as discussed previously.
- IRR considers the whole life of the project rather than ignoring later flows.

- A firm selecting projects where the IRR exceeds the cost of capital should increase shareholders' wealth. This holds true provided the project cash flows follow the standard pattern of an outflow followed by a series of inflows.

However there are a number of difficulties with the IRR approach:

- It is not a measure of absolute profitability. A project of $1,000 invested now and paying back $1,100 in a year's time has an IRR of 10%. If a company's required return is 6%, then the project is viable according to the IRR rule but most businesses would consider the absolute return too small to be worth the investment.
- Interpolation only provides an estimate (and an accurate estimate requires the use of a spreadsheet programme).
- The cost of capital calculation itself is also only an estimate and if the margin between required return and the IRR is small, this lack of accuracy could actually mean the wrong decision is taken.
- Non-conventional cash flows may give rise to no IRR or multiple IRRs. For example, a project with an outflow at T0 and T2 but income at T1 could, depending on the size of the cash flows, have a number of different profiles.

7 Annuities and perpetuities

Annuities

An annuity is a constant annual cash flow for a number of years.

Calculating the NPV of a project with even cash flows

When a project has equal annual cash flows the annuity factor may be used to calculate the NPV.

The **annuity factor** (AF) is the name given to the sum of the individual discount factors (also referred to as the cumulative discount factor).

The present value of an annuity can therefore be quickly found using the formula:

$$PV = \text{Annual cash flow} \times AF$$

Like with calculating a discount factor, the AF can be found using an annuity formula or annuity tables.

The formula is:

$$AF = \frac{1-(1+r)^{-n}}{r}$$

For example, for a six-year annuity at 10%:

The AF

Formula or **Tables** (given in examination)

Formula

$$\frac{1-(1+r)^{-n}}{r}$$

$$= \frac{1-(1.1)^{-6}}{0.1}$$

$$= 4.355$$

Tables

(given in examination)

You can simply find the AF from the annuity table by locating the DF at the 10% column and the six-year row, i.e. 4.355

Calculating the IRR of a project with even cash flows

There is a simpler technique available, using annuity tables, if the project cash flows are annuities.

1 Calculate the cumulative discount factor = Initial investment ÷ Annual inflow.

2 Find the life of the project, n.

3 Look along the n year row of the cumulative DF until the closest value is found.

4 The column in which this figure is found is the IRR.

e.g

Illustration 10 – Calculating IRR using annuities

Find the IRR of a project with an initial investment of $1.5 million and three years of inflows of $700,000 starting in one year.

Solution

NPV Calculation:

		Cash flow	DF (c) %	PV
		$000		$000
Time				
0	Investment	(1,500)	1	(1,500)
1 – 3	Inflow	700	(b)	(a)
NPV				Nil

- The aim is to find the discount rate (c) that produces an NPV of nil.
- Therefore the PV of inflows (a) must equal the PV of outflows, $1,500,000.

- If the PV of inflows (a) is to be $1,500,000 and the size of each inflow is $700,000, the DF required (b) must be 1,500,000 ÷ 700,000 = 2.143.
- The discount rate (c) for this is the 3-year factor which can be found by looking along the 3-year row of the cumulative DF shown in the annuity table.

Periods (n)	Discount rate (r) 11%	12%	13%	14%	15%	16%	17%	18%	19%	20%
1	0.901	0.893	0.885	0.877	0.870	0.862	0.855	0.847	0.840	0.833
2	1.713	1.690	1.668	1.647	1.626	1.605	1.585	1.566	1.547	1.528
3	2.444	2.402	2.361	2.322	2.283	2.246	2.210	2.174	2.140	2.106
4	3.102	3.037	2.974	2.914	2.855	2.798	2.743	2.690	2.639	2.589
5	3.696	3.605	3.517	3.433	3.352	3.274	3.199	3.127	3.058	2.991

- The figure of 2.140 appears under the 19% column suggesting an IRR of 19% is the closest.

Test your understanding 13

(a) Pluto Ltd has been offered a project costing $50,000. The returns are expected to be $10,000 each year for seven years. Cost of capital is 10%. Calculate whether the project can be accepted.

(b) Calculate the IRR of the project?

Perpetuities

A **perpetuity** is an annual cash flow that occurs forever.

It is often described by examiners as a cash flow continuing 'for the foreseeable future'.

Calculating the NPV of a project with a perpetuity

The PV of a perpetuity is found using the formula:

$$PV = \frac{\text{Cashflow}}{r}$$

or

$$PV = \text{Cash flow} \times \frac{1}{r}$$

$\frac{1}{r}$ is known as the perpetuity factor.

Calculating the IRR of a project with a perpetuity

$$\text{IRR of a perpetuity} = \frac{\text{Annual inflow}}{\text{Initial investment}} \times 100$$

Test your understanding 14

An investment of $50,000 is expected to yield $5,670 per annum in perpetuity.

Required:

Calculate the net present value of the investment opportunity if the cost of capital is 9%.

Test your understanding 15

$100,000 is deposited in a bank account paying 8% interest each year.

Required:

Calculate the maximum sum that can be withdrawn from the account at the end of each year in perpetuity.

Test your understanding 16

In order to earn a perpetuity of $2,000 per annum calculate how much would need to be invested today. The account will pay 10% interest.

Test your understanding 17

What is the IRR of an investment that costs $20,000 and generates $1,600 for an indefinitely long period.

Test your understanding 18

A company is considering a project with a three-year life producing the following costs and revenues:

	$
Cost of machine	100,000
Depreciation of machine (for three years)	20,000 p.a.
Residual value of machine	40,000
Annual cost of direct labour	20,000
Annual charge for foreman (10% apportionment)	5,000
Annual cost of components required	18,000
Annual net revenues from machine	80,000
Cost of capital	20%

Identify which of the following is closest to the net present value of the machine:

A ($13,000)

B ($11,380)

C $11,610

D $22,370

Test your understanding 19

A project has a normal pattern of cash flows (i.e. an initial outflow followed by several years of inflows). Identify what would be the effects of an increase in the company's cost of capital on the internal rate of return (IRR) of the project and its discounted payback period (DPP)?

	IRR	DPP
A	Decrease	Decrease
B	Decrease	Increase
C	No change	Increase
D	No change	Decrease

Test your understanding 20

Blue Inc produces paint and is considering investing in a new mixing machine. The expected costs and benefits of the new mixing machine are as follows:

- The machine will cost $30,000 to purchase
- Depreciation will be charged at 20% on a straight line basis
- Sales are predicted to increase by 10% on the current predicted sales for the next 5 years. The current predictions are as follows: Year 1 $20,000; Year 2 $22,000; Year 3 $23,000; Year 4 $25,000; Year 5 $28,000
- Staff training costs are currently $1,200 per annum, this will increase to $1,400 in the first year but will then drop to $1,000 in subsequent years
- Operating costs will be reduced from current levels of $15,000 per annum to $10,000 per annum.

The following information is relevant to this decision:

- The payback period will be 4 years and 1 month. The company's policy is for projects to pay back within 5 years.
- The net present value is $5,774 negative.
- The internal rate of return is 7%. The company's cost of capital is 16%.

Required:

Calculate and state the relevant value of the cash flow for each of the following. A zero should be used to indicate no relevant value. Use brackets to indicate an outflow of cash.

	Year 0	Year 1	Year 2	Year 3	Year 4	Year 5	
Purchase cost							0.5 marks
Depreciation							0.5 marks
Sales revenue							2 marks
Training costs							2 marks
Operating cost							1 mark

Complete the phrases below, deleting words/phases where appropriate (marked with *)

The payback period of 4 years and 1 month is *within/outside** the company's policy of 5 years, and on this criterion the investment *should go/should not go** ahead. **1 mark**

The NPV is *positive/negative** and on this criterion the investment *should go /should not go** ahead. **1 mark**

The IRR, at 7%, is *above/below** the company's 16% cost of capital and on this criterion the investment *should go/should not go** ahead. **1 mark**

Overall the investment *should/should not** proceed because the *Payback/NPV/IRR** is the dominant criterion. **1 mark**

(Total: 10 marks)

Annuities/perpetuities in advance

The use of annuity factors and perpetuity factors both assume that the first cash flow will be occurring in one year's time. If this is not the case, you will need to adjust your calculation.

Advanced annuities and perpetuities

Some regular cash flows may start now (at T_0) rather than in one years' time (T_1).

Calculate the PV by ignoring the payment at T0 when considering the number of cash flows and then adding one to the annuity or perpetuity factor.

Illustration – Advanced annuities and perpetuities

A 5-year $600 annuity is starting today. Interest rates are 10%. Find the PV of the annuity.

Solution

This is essentially a standard 4-year annuity with an additional payment at T_0. The PV could be calculated as follows:

	T_0		T_1	T_2	T_3	T_4
CF	600		600	600	600	600
	↓		↘	↓	↓	↙
PV	600	+	600 × 4-year 10% AF			

PV = 600 + 600 × 3.17 = 600 + 1902 = $2,502.

The same answer can be found more quickly by adding 1 to the AF:

PV = 600 × (1 + 3.17) = 600 × 4.17 = $2,502.

Illustration – Advanced perpetuities

A perpetuity of $2,000 is due to commence immediately. The interest rate is 9%. What is the PV?

Solution

This is essentially a standard perpetuity with an additional payment at T0. The PV could be calculated as follows:

T_0	T_1	T_2	T_3	T_4....
2,000	2,000 → ∞			

PV (2000) + (2000 × 9% perpetuity formula)

Again, the same answer can be found more quickly by adding 1 to the perpetuity factor.

$$2000 \times \left(1 + \frac{1}{0.09}\right) = 2{,}000 \times 12.11 = \$24{,}222$$

Annuities/perpetuities in arrears

Delayed annuities and perpetuities

Some regular cash flows may start later than T_1.

These are dealt with by:

(a) applying the appropriate factor to the cash flow as normal

(b) discounting your answer back to T_0.

Illustration – Delayed annuities and perpetuities

What is the PV of $200 incurred each year for four years, starting in three years' time, if the discount rate is 5%?

Solution

Method: A four-year annuity starting at T_3

(1-4)

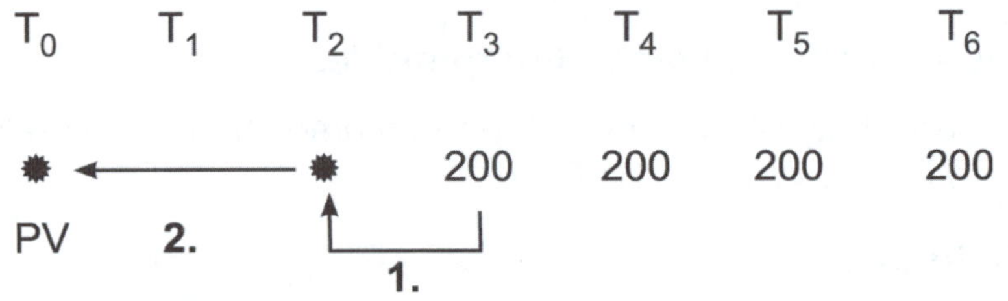

Step 1 Discount the annuity as usual

200 × 4 yr 5% AF = 200 × 3.546 = 709.2

Note that this gives the value of the annuity at T_2

Step 2 Discount the answer back to T_0

709.2 × 2 yr 5% DF = 709.2 × 0.907 = $643

Annuity or perpetuity factors will discount the cash flows back to give the value one year before the first cash flow arose. For standard annuities and perpetuities this gives the present (T_0) value since the first cash flow started at T_1.

However for delayed cash flows, applying the factor will find the value of the cash flows one year before they began, which in this example is T_2. To find the PV, an additional calculation is required – the value must be discounted back to T_0.

Care must be taken to discount back the appropriate number of years. The figure here was discounted back two years because the first step gave the value at T_2. It can help to draw a timeline as above and mark on the effect of the first step (as shown with a 1. here) to help you remember.

8 Chapter summary

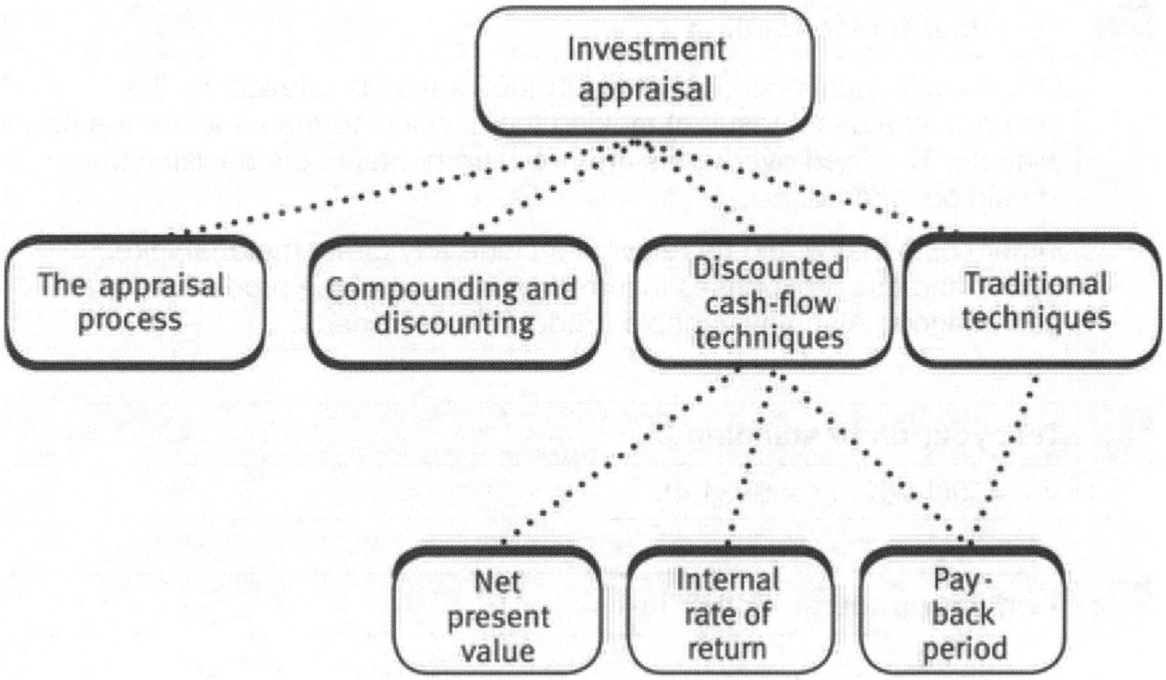

Test your understanding answers

Test your understanding 1

Of the costs mentioned, only the $15,000 salary is relevant as it is incurred as a direct result of making the decision to manufacture the new widgets. The fixed overheads are not incremental to the decision and should be ignored.

Other costs that would be relevant include any direct material, direct labour and direct expenses incurred as a result of the production of the new widgets. Also any variable production overheads.

Test your understanding 2

$V = 450(1.0625)^{12} = \$931.45$

Test your understanding 3

$$X = \frac{5,000}{1.05^{10}} = \$3,070$$

Test your understanding 4

It might seem that the better investment is the deposit account offering 10.25% per year, but this is not the case.

When interest is quoted at 10% per year, payable quarterly, this means the effective annual interest rate is:

$r = (1 + 0.1/4)^4 - 1$

$r = 10.38\%$ per year

This is a higher rate.

Test your understanding 5

$X = 250 \times 0.404 = \$101$

Test your understanding 6

$PV = 25,000 \times 0.564 = \$14,100$

Test your understanding 7

$$\text{Payback Period} = \frac{\$2m}{\$500,000}$$

Payback Period = 4 years

Test your understanding 8

$$\text{Payback} = \frac{\$1,800,000}{\$350,000} = 5.1429 \text{ years}$$

0.1429 of a year × 12 months = 1.7 months (rounded = 2 months)

The answer can therefore be stated as either:

- 5.1 years
- 5 years 2 months

assuming cash flows occur evenly throughout the year.

Test your understanding 9

Year	Cash flow $	DF at 9%	PV $
0	(240,000)	1.000	(240,000)
1	80,000	0.917	73,360
2	120,000	0.842	101,040
3	70,000	0.772	54,040
4	40,000	0.708	28,320
5	20,000	0.650	13,000
NPV			+ 29,760

The PV of cash inflows exceeds the PV of cash outflows by $29,760, which means that the project will earn a DCF return in excess of 9%, i.e. it will earn a surplus of $29,760 after paying the cost of financing. It should therefore be undertaken.

Test your understanding 10

At 20% the NPV is $8,510

At 30% the NPV is – $9,150

$$IRR = 20 + \frac{8,510}{8,510 - -9,150} \times (30 - 20)$$

$$IRR = 20 + \frac{8,510}{17,660} \times 10$$

IRR = 20 + (0.482 × 10)

IRR = 24.8%

Test your understanding 11

$$IRR = 10\% + \frac{50,000}{50,000 - -10,000} \times (15\% - 10\%) = 14.17$$

Test your understanding 12

A

At the IRR, PV of future net cash flows = initial outlay.

Test your understanding 13

(a)

Year	Cash flow	Discount factor	Present value
	$		$
0	(50,000)	1.000	(50,000)
1 – 7	10,000	4.868	48,680
			(1,320)

(b) $10,000 × annuity factor = $50,000

Annuity factor = 5

Using the tables and a life of seven years, the closest annuity factor to 5 is 5.033. This means the IRR is approximately 9%

Test your understanding 14

NPV = ($50,000) + $5,670 ÷ 0.09 = $13,000

Test your understanding 15

Maximum withdrawal = $100,000 × 0.08 = $8,000 per annum in perpetuity.

Test your understanding 16

Initial investment required = $2,000 ÷ 0.10 = $20,000.

Test your understanding 17

$$IRR = \frac{\text{Annual inflow}}{\text{Initial investment}} \times 100 = \frac{\$1,600}{\$20,000} \times 100 = 8\%$$

Test your understanding 18

C

Revenue – components – labour = $80,000 – $18,000 – $20,000 = $42,000

Year	**Cash flow** $000		**Discount factor**	**Present value** $000
0	Initial cost	(100)		(100)
1 – 3	Annual cash	42	2.106	88.452
3	Residual	40	0.579	23.16
				11.612

Net present value = $11,612

Test your understanding 19

C

The IRR will be unaffected by the cost of capital. As the discount rate increases future cash flow reduce in present value terms, therefore the discounted payback period will increase.

Test your understanding 20

	Year 0	Year 1	Year 2	Year 3	Year 4	Year 5	
Purchase cost	(30,000)	0	0	0	0	0	0.5 marks
Depreciation	0	0	0	0	0	0	0.5 marks
Sales revenue	0	2,000	2,200	2,300	2,500	2,800	2 marks
Training costs	0	(200)	200	200	200	200	2 marks
Operating cost	0	5,000	5,000	5,000	5,000	5,000	1 mark

Notes

The business is already operating therefore the investment appraisal process will look at the **incremental** costs/revenues that the new machine will produce.

- **Depreciation** is not an actual cash flow so it is not included in the appraisal calculation.
- **Sales revenue** should only include the increase (or extra revenue) of 10% on current predictions.
- **Training costs** should only include the extra cost (year 1) or the saving (years 2 to 5) when compared to current predicted costs.
- **Operating costs** are actually classed as an inflow as there is a saving in cost when compared to the current predicted cost.

Completed sentences

The payback period of 4 years and 1 month is **within** the company's policy of 5 years, and on this criterion the investment **should go** ahead.

The NPV is **negative** and on this criterion the investment **should not go** ahead.

The IRR, at 7%, is **below** the company's 16% cost of capital and on this criterion the investment **should not go** ahead.

Overall the investment **should not** proceed because the **NPV** is the dominant criterion.

Chapter

15

Standard costing

Chapter learning objectives

Upon completion of this chapter you will be able to:

- explain the purpose and principles of standard costing
- explain and illustrate the difference between standard, marginal and absorption costing
- establish the standard cost per unit under marginal costing and absorption costing
- calculate sales price and volume variance
- calculate materials total, price and usage variance
- calculate labour total, rate and efficiency variances
- calculate variable overhead total, expenditure and efficiency variance
- calculate fixed overhead total, expenditure and, where appropriate, volume, capacity and efficiency variance
- interpret the variances
- discuss the relative significance of variances
- explain potential action to eliminate variances
- explain factors to consider before investigating variances, explain possible causes of the variances and recommend control action
- explain the interrelationships between the variances
- calculate actual or standard figures where the variances are given

- reconcile budgeted profit with actual profit under standard absorption costing
- reconcile budgeted profit or contribution with actual profit or contribution under standard marginal costing.

PER

One of the PER performance objectives (PO13) is to plan business activities and control performance, making recommendations for improvement. Working through this chapter should help you understand how to demonstrate that objective.

PER

One of the PER performance objectives (PO14) is to measure and assess departmental and business performance. Working through this chapter should help you understand how to demonstrate that objective.

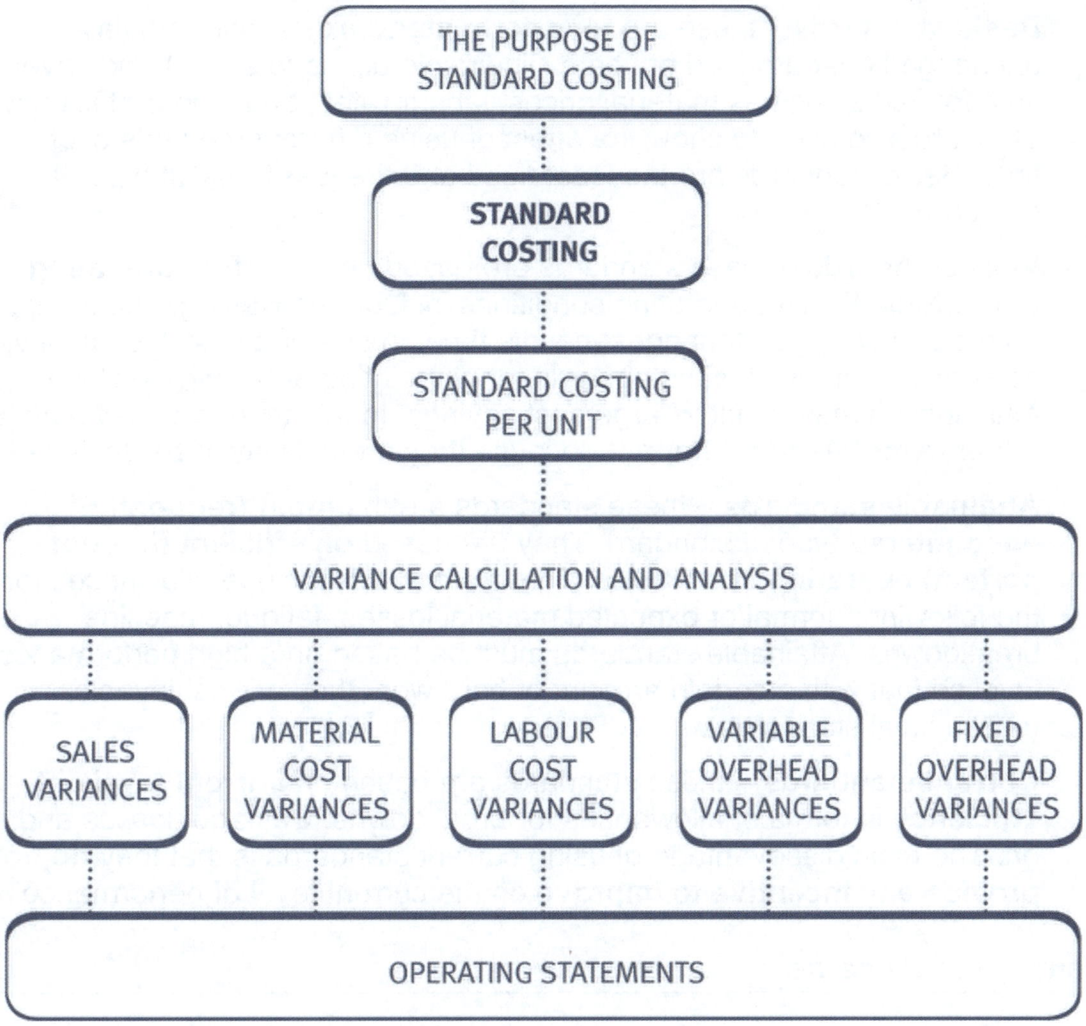

1 Standard costing

A **standard cost** is the planned unit cost of a product or service. It is an indication of what a unit of product or service **should** cost.

Standard costs represent 'target' costs and they are therefore useful for planning, control and motivation. They are also commonly used to simplify inventory valuation.

Types of cost standards

There are four main types of cost standards.

- Basic standards.
- Ideal standards.
- Attainable standards.
- Current standards.

- **Basic standards** – these are **long-term standards** which remain unchanged over a period of years. Their sole use is to show trends over time for items such as material prices, labour rates, and labour efficiency. They are also used to show the effect of using different methods over time. Basic standards are the least used and the **least useful** type of standard.
- **Ideal standards** – these standards are based upon **perfect operating conditions**. Perfect operating conditions include: no wastage; no scrap; no breakdowns; no stoppages; no idle time. In search for perfect quality, companies can use ideal standards for pinpointing areas where close examination may result in large cost savings. Ideal standards may have an **adverse motivational impact** because they are unlikely to be achieved.
- **Attainable standards** – these standards are the **most frequently encountered** type of standard. They are based **on efficient (but not perfect) operating conditions.** These standards include allowances for the following: normal or expected material losses; fatigue; machine breakdowns. Attainable standards must be based on a high performance level so that with a certain amount of hard work they are achievable (unlike ideal standards).
- **Current standards** – these standards are based on **current levels of efficiency** in terms of allowances for breakdowns, wastage, losses and so on. The main disadvantage of using current standards is that they **do not provide any incentive to improve** on the current level of performance.

Standard costs cards

In order to prepare budgets we need to know what an individual unit of a product or service is expected to cost.

- A standard cost may be based on either marginal costing or absorption costing.
- Standard costs also provide an easier method of accounting since it enables simplified records to be kept.
- Once estimated, standard costs are usually collected on a standard cost card.

e.g

Illustration 1 – Standard costs per unit

K Ltd manufactures Product 20K. Information relating to this product is given below.

Budgeted output for the year: 900 units

Standard details for one unit:

Direct materials:	40 square metres at $5.30 per square metre
Direct wages:	Bonding department 24 hours at $5.00 per hour
	Finishing department 15 hours at $4.80 per hour

Budgeted costs and hours per annum are as follows:

	$	**Hours**
Variable overhead		
Bonding department	45,000	30,000
Finishing department	25,000	25,000
Fixed overhead apportioned to this product:		
Production	$36,000	
Selling, distribution and administration	$27,000	

Note: Variable overheads are recovered (absorbed) using hours; fixed overheads are recovered on a per unit basis.

Required:

Prepare a standard cost card in order to establish the standard cost of one unit of Product 20K and enter the following subtotals on the card:

1 prime cost

2 marginal cost

3 total absorption cost

4 total standard cost.

Solution

Standard cost card – Product 20K		$ per unit
Direct materials (40 × $5.30)		212
Direct labour:		
Bonding (24 hours at $5.00)		120
Finishing (15 hours at $4.80)		72
1	**Prime cost**	404
	Variable overhead:	
	Bonding ($45,000/30,000 × 24 hours)	36
	Finishing ($25,000/25,000 × 15 hours)	15
2	**Marginal cost**	455
	Production overheads ($36,000/900)	40
3	**Total absorption cost**	495
	Non-production overheads ($27,000/900)	30
4	**Total standard cost**	525

Test your understanding 1

The following statement shows budgeted and actual costs for the month of October for Department X.

Month ended 31 October	**Original budget**	**Actual result**
	$	$
Sales	600,000	550,000
Direct materials	150,000	130,000
Direct labour	200,000	189,000
Production overhead		
Variable with direct labour	50,000	46,000
Fixed	25,000	29,000
Total costs	425,000	394,000
Profit	175,000	156,000
Direct labour hours	50,000	47,500
Sales and production units	5,000	4,500

Note: There is no opening and closing inventory.

(a) Calculate the standard cost per unit under absorption costing.

(b) Calculate standard cost per unit under marginal costing.

2 Variance analysis

As well as being the basis for preparing budgets, standard costs are also used for calculating and analysing variances.

Basic variance analysis has been seen in the Budgeting chapter when comparing the flexed budget with the actual results.

The following variance analysis produces more detailed results as to the causes of the differences between what the costs and revenues should have been and what they actually were.

The variances that will be looked at are:

- Sales variances
- Raw material variances
- Labour variances
- Variable overhead variances
- Fixed overhead variances.

Two of the variances discussed in the following sections are calculated differently depending on the costing system a business uses:

- The sales volume variance will be calculated using standard contribution under marginal costing systems and using standard profit under absorption costing systems.
- The fixed overhead variance under marginal costing only consists of the fixed overhead expenditure variance, whereas under absorption costing the total fixed overhead variance is split into expenditure and volume (the volume can be further split into capacity and efficiency).

3 Sales variances

There are two causes of sales variances

- a difference in selling price
- a difference in sales volume

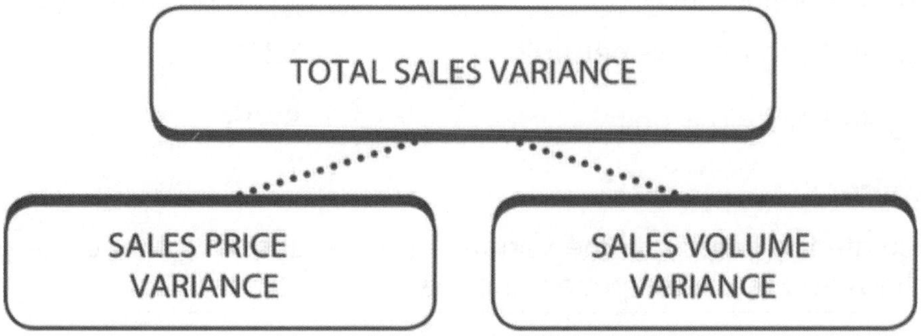

Sales volume variance

The sales volume variance calculates the effect on profit of the actual sales volume being different from that budgeted. The effect on profit will differ depending upon whether a marginal or absorption costing system is being used.

- Under absorption costing any difference in units is valued at the standard profit per unit.
- Under marginal costing any difference in units is valued at the standard contribution per unit.

Sales volume variance

(Actual quantity sold – Budget quantity sold) × **Standard margin**.

The **Standard margin** is the standard contribution per unit (marginal costing), or the standard profit per unit (absorption costing).

If the actual quantity sold is greater than the budget this will produce a favourable variance as it increases profit.

Sales price variance

The sales price variance shows the effect on profit of selling at a different price from that expected.

Sales price variance

(Actual price – Budget price) × Actual quantity sold

If the actual price is greater than the budget this will produce a favourable variance as it increases profit.

e.g **Illustration 2 – Sales variances**

The following data relates to 20X8.

Actual sales:	1,000 units @ $650 each
Budgeted output and sales for the year:	900 units
Standard selling price:	$700 per unit
Budgeted contribution per unit:	$245
Budgeted profit per unit:	$205

Required:

Calculate the sales volume variance (under absorption and marginal costing) and the sales price variance.

Solution

Sales volume variance – absorption costing

(1,000 units – 900 units) × $205 = $20,500 Fav

Sales volume variance – marginal costing

(1,000 units – 900 units) × $245 = $24,500 Fav

Sales price variance

($650 – $700) × 1,000 = $50,000 Adv

Test your understanding 2

Radek Ltd has budgeted sales of 400 units at $2.50 each. The variable costs are expected to be $1.80 per unit, and fixed costs are to be absorbed at $0.20 per unit.

The actual sales were 500 units at $2 each and variable costs were $1.50 and fixed costs were as expected.

Calculate the sales price and sales volume variances (using marginal and absorption costing).

Test your understanding 3

W Ltd budgeted sales of 6,500 units but actually sold only 6,000 units. Its standard cost card is as follows:

	$
Direct materials	25
Direct wages	8
Variable overheads	4
Fixed overheads	18
Total standard cost	55
Standard gross profit	5
Standard selling price	60

The actual selling price for the period was $61.

Calculate the sales price and sales volume variances for the period (using absorption costing).

4 Materials cost variances

There are two causes of material cost variances

- a difference in purchase price
- a difference in quantity used.

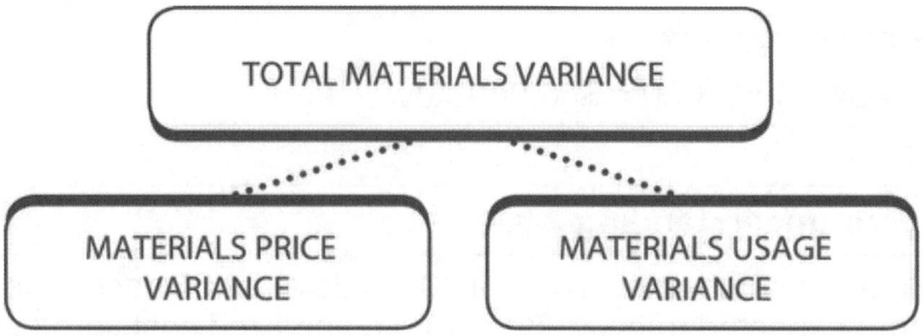

Materials total variance

The materials total variance is the difference between:

(a) the actual cost of direct material and

(b) the standard material cost of the actual production (flexed budget).

The total variance can be analysed into two sub-variances:

- A materials price variance analyses whether the company paid more or less than expected for the materials purchased.
- The purpose of the materials usage variance is to quantify the effect on profit of using a different quantity of raw material from that expected for the actual production achieved.

Material variances

Material price variance = (actual quantity bought × actual price) – (actual quantity bought × standard price).

Material usage variance = (actual quantity used × standard price) – (standard quantity used for actual production × standard price).

OR

1 Actual quantity × Actual price

Price variance (the difference between row 1 and row 2)

2 Actual quantity × Standard price

Usage variance (the difference between row 2 and row 3)

3 **Standard quantity* × Standard price**		
	Total variance	(the total of the price and the usage variances)

* the standard quantity is the amount of material that should have been used to produce the actual output.

Illustration 3 – Material cost variances

The following information relates to the production of Product X.

Extract from the standard cost card of Product X.

Direct materials (40 square metres × $5.30 per square metre) $212.

Actual results for direct materials in the period: 1,000 units were produced and 39,000 square metres of material costing $210,600 in total were purchased and used.

Required:

Calculate the materials total, price and usage variances for Product X in the period.

Solution

Actual quantity × Actual price		$210,600	
	Price variance		**$3,900 (A)**
Actual quantity × Standard price		$206,700	
39,000 × $5.30	**Usage variance**		**$5,300 (F)**
Standard quantity × Standard price		$212,000	
1,000 × 40 × $5.30	**Total variance**		**$1,400 (F)**

Test your understanding 4

James Marshall Ltd makes a single product with the following budgeted material costs per unit:

2 kg of material A at $10/kg

Actual details:

Output 1,000 units

Material purchased and used 2,200 kg

Material cost $20,900

Required:

Calculate materials price and usage variances.

Material inventory and variances

We need to consider cases where all the material purchased is not used and inventory therefore remains at the end of the period.

The most important thing to understand is that the materials price variance is calculated based on the total of all the materials purchased in the period, whether they are used or not.

This means that any inventory carried to the next period is carried at its standard cost.

Note that the materials usage variance is based on the quantity of materials used as before.

e.g

Illustration 4 – Closing inventory

X Ltd purchases 4,000 kg of material at a cost of $8,400. It uses 3,300 kg to produce 600 units of product A. Product A's standard cost card for material is as follows:

	Standard cost per unit
	$
Material 5 kg @ $2 per kg	10.00

Required:

Calculate the price variance, the usage variance and the value of closing inventory.

Solution

Price variance – is calculated on all the materials purchased whether they are used in production or not.

Usage variance – is calculated based on the amount of material used.

The value of the closing inventory is the difference between purchased and used, valued at standard price.

		$	
Actual quantity purchased × Actual price		= 8,400	
	Price variance		**400 A**
Actual quantity purchased × Standard price 4,000 × $2		= 8,000	
	Value of closing inventory 700 × $2		**1,400 A**
Actual quantity used × Standard price 3,300 × $2		= 6,600	
	Usage variance		**600 A**
Standard quantity × Standard price 600 × 5 kg × $2		= 6,000	

Test your understanding 5

Blossom Ltd manufactures and sells garden statues.

The budget and actual results for materials in November are as follows:

Budget production of 7,500 units using 22,500 kg costing $90,000.

Actual production 6,500 units, 20,800 kg of material purchased costing $91,520.

There was no opening inventory of raw materials at the start of November but there were 500 kg of closing inventory at the end of November.

Required:

Calculate the material price variance, the material usage variance and the valuation of the closing inventory at standard cost.

5 Labour cost variances

There are two causes of labour cost variances

- a difference in rate paid
- a difference in hours worked.

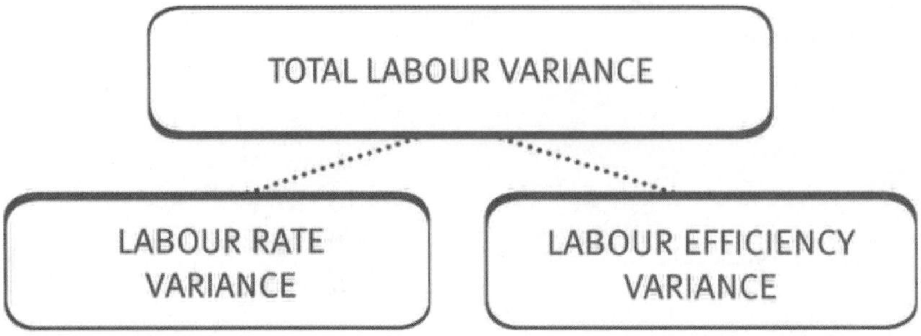

Labour total variance

The labour total variance is the difference between:

(a) the actual cost of direct labour and

(b) the standard direct labour cost of the actual production (flexed budget).

The total variance can be analysed into two sub-variances:

- A labour rate variance analyses whether the company paid more or less than expected for labour.
- A labour efficiency variance analyses whether the company used more or less labour hours than expected.

1 Actual hours × Actual rate		
	Rate variance	(the difference between row 1 and row 2)
2 Actual hours × Standard rate		
	Efficiency variance	(the difference between row 2 and row 3)
3 Standard hours* × Standard rate		
	Total variance	(the total of the rate and the efficiency variances)

* the standard hours are the number of hours that should have been worked to produce the actual output.

Illustration 5 – Labour cost variances

The following information relates to the production of Product X.

Extract from the standard cost card of Product X

	$
Direct labour:	
Bonding (24 hrs @ $5 per hour)	120

Actual results for wages:

Production	1,000 units produced
Bonding	23,900 hours costing $131,450 in total

Required:

Calculate the labour total, rate and efficiency variances in the Bonding department for Product X in the period.

Solution

Actual hours × Actual rate		**$131,450**	
	Rate variance		**$11,950 (A)**
Actual hours × Standard rate **23,900 × $5.00**		**$119,500**	
	Efficiency variance		**$500 (F)**
Standard hours × Standard rate **1,000 × 24 hours × $5.00**		**$120,000**	

The labour total variance in the Bonding department is the sum of the rate and efficiency variances, i.e.

$11,950 (A) + $500 (F) = $11,450 (A)

Test your understanding 6

Roseberry Ltd makes a single product and has the following budgeted information:

Budgeted production	1,000 units
Budgeted labour hours	3,000 hours
Budgeted labour cost	$15,000
Actual results:	
Output	1,100 units
Hours paid for	3,400 hours
Labour cost	$17,680

Required:

Calculate the labour total, rate and efficiency variances for Roseberry Ltd.

6 Variable overhead variances

Variable overhead variances are very similar to those for materials and labour because, like these direct costs, the variable overhead cost also changes when activity levels change.

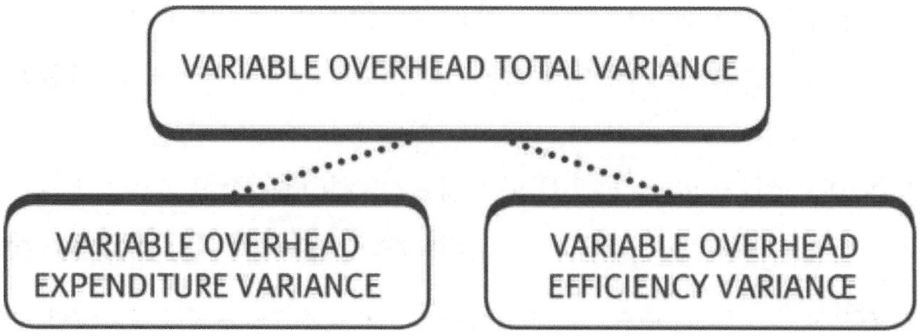

Variable overhead total variance

It is normally assumed that variable overheads vary with direct labour hours and the variable overhead total variance will therefore be due to one of the following:

- the variable overhead cost per hour was different to that expected (an expenditure variance)
- working more or less hours than expected for the actual production (an efficiency variance).

1 **Actual hours × Actual rate**		
	Expenditure variance	(the difference between row 1 and row 2)
2 **Actual hours × Standard rate**		
	Efficiency variance	(the difference between row 2 and row 3)
3 **Standard hours* × Standard rate**		
	Total variance	(the total of the rate and the efficiency variances)

* the standard hours are the number of hours that should have been worked to produce the actual output.

Variable overhead variances

- if variable overheads vary with production volume rather than direct labour hours it is not possible to calculate the sub-variances of expenditure and efficiency
- in such situations, only the variable overhead total variance can be calculated using the standard variable overhead cost per unit.

Illustration 6 – Variable overhead variances

The following information relates to the production of Product X.

Extract from the standard cost card of Product X

	$
Direct labour:	
Bonding (24 hrs @ $5 per hour)	120
Variable overhead:	
Bonding (24 hrs @ $1.50 per hour)	36

Actual results for production and labour hours worked:

Production	1,000 units produced
Bonding	23,900 hours

Actual results for variable overheads:

Bonding Total cost $38,240

Required:

Calculate the variable overhead total, expenditure and efficiency variances in the Bonding department for Product X for the period.

Solution

Variable overhead variances in Bonding department

Actual hours × Actual rate	$38,240		
		Expenditure variance	**$2,390 (A)**
Actual hours × Standard rate			
23,900 hours × $1.50	$35,850		
		Efficiency variance	**$150 (F)**
Standard hours × Standard rate			
1,000 × 24 hours × $1.50	$36,000		
		Total variance	**$2,240 (A)**

Test your understanding 7

The budgeted output for Carr Ltd for May was 1,000 units of product A. Each unit requires two direct labour hours. Variable overheads are budgeted at $3/labour hour.

Actual results:

Output	900 units
Labour hours worked	1,980 hours
Variable overheads	$5,544

Required:

Calculate variable overhead total, expenditure and efficiency variances.

Diagrammatic view of cost variances

Consider the cost of materials for producing 1,000 units of product X.

The standard cost of one unit is calculated as 2 kg of material at $2 per kg = $4 per unit.

To produce 1,000 units in period 1, the process actually uses 2,200 kg which cost $2.30 per kg.

The actual and standard costs for materials can be calculated as follows:

Standard cost of 1,000 units = 2,000 kg × $2 = $4,000

Actual cost of 1,000 units = 2,200 kg × $2.30 = $5,060

Total cost variance $1,060 (adverse)

This can be shown in a diagram as follows:

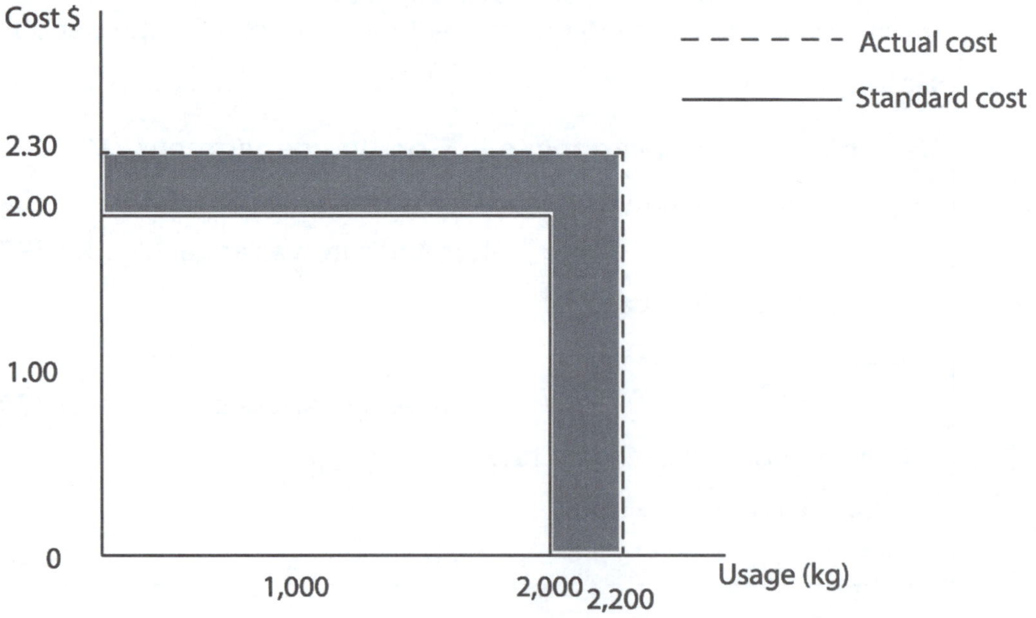

The shaded area shows the excess of the total actual cost over the total standard cost.

We need to analyse this into two parts:

(a) the price variance, i.e. the amount of the excess cost caused by actually paying $2.30 rather than standard $2.00 per unit

(b) the usage variance, i.e. the amount of the excess cost caused by actually using 2,200 kg rather than the standard 2,000 kg.

This is shown in the diagram by dividing the shaded area of total excess cost into two parts as shown below:

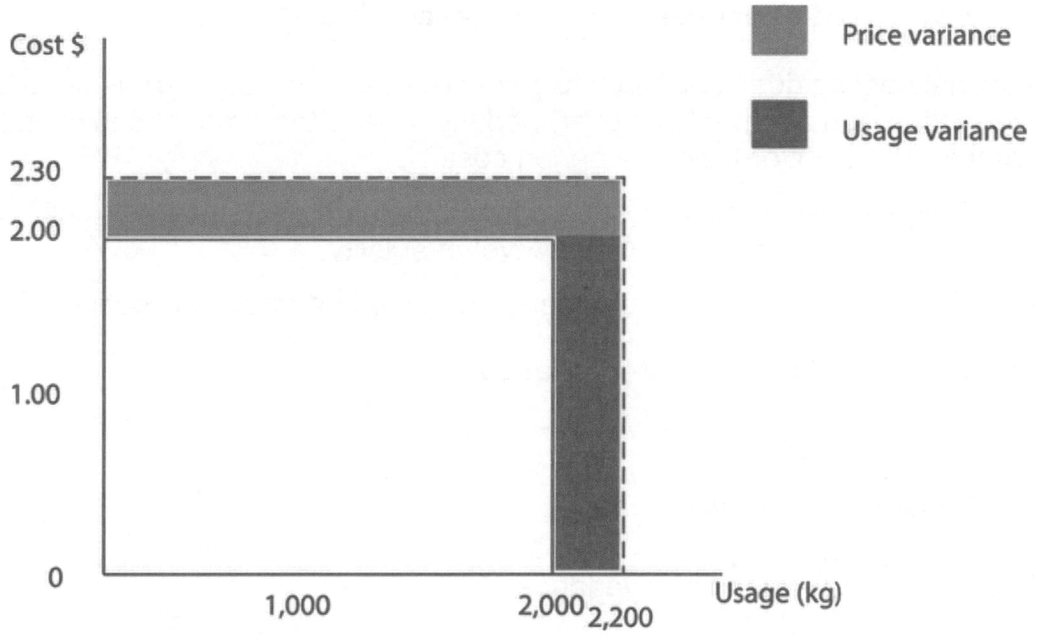

(a) The price variance is calculated as:

Quantity actually purchased × Actual price

2,200 kg × $2.30 = $5,060

Compared to:

Quantity actually purchased × Standard price

2,200 kg × $2.00 = $4,400

This is an adverse variance of $660 as we actually paid more than we should have paid.

(b) The usage variance is calculated as:

Quantity actually purchased × Standard price

2,200 kg × $2.00 = $4,400

Compared to:

Quantity that should have been used × Standard price

1,000 units × 2 kg × $2.00 = $4,000

This is an adverse variance of $400 as we actually used more than we should have used.

7 Fixed overhead variances

Fixed overhead variances show the effect on profit of differences between actual and expected fixed overheads.

- By definition, actual and expected fixed overheads should not change when there is a change in the level of activity, consequently many of the variances calculated are based upon budgets.
- However, the effect on profit depends upon whether a marginal or absorption costing system is being used.

Fixed overhead variances in a marginal costing system

Marginal costing does not relate fixed overheads to units. There is no under- or over-absorption and the fixed overhead incurred is the amount shown in the statement of profit or loss as a period cost.

- Since fixed overhead costs are fixed, they are not expected to change when there is a change in the level of activity.
- There is only one fixed overhead variance in a marginal costing system.

Fixed overhead expenditure variance

	$
Actual expenditure	X
Less: Budget expenditure	(X)
Fixed overhead expenditure variance	X

If actual expenditure is greater than budgeted expenditure there is an adverse variance.

Fixed overhead variances in an absorption costing system

- In absorption costing, fixed overheads are related to cost units by using absorption rates.
- This means that the calculation for fixed overhead variances in an absorption costing system can relate to both a change in expenditure and a change in production levels or volume.

The fixed overhead variances in an absorption costing system are as follows:

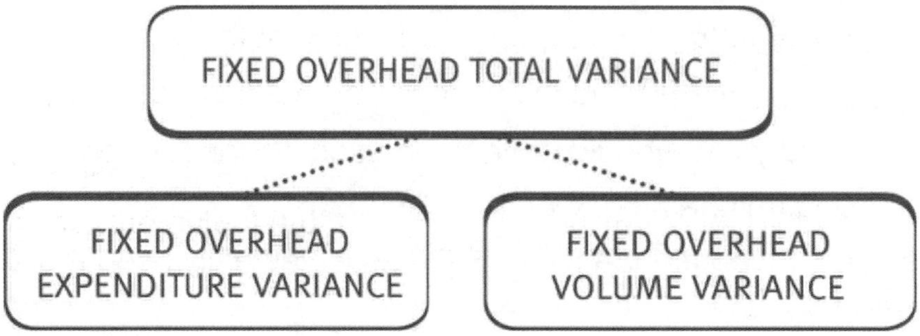

Fixed overhead total variance

In an absorption costing system, the fixed overhead total variance measures the effect on profit of there being a difference between the actual cost incurred and the amount absorbed based on budgeted costs and activity. This means that the fixed overhead total variance is equivalent to the under- or over-absorption of overhead in a period.

Under absorption costing, the total variance can be further subdivided into an expenditure and volume variance.

Fixed overhead expenditure variance

The fixed overhead expenditure variance shows the effect on profit of the actual fixed overhead expenditure differing from the budgeted value. It is calculated in exactly the same way for both marginal and absorption costing.

	$
Actual expenditure	X
Less: Budget expenditure	(X)
	—
Fixed overhead expenditure variance	X
	—

If actual expenditure is greater than budgeted expenditure there is an adverse variance.

Fixed overhead volume variance

The fixed overhead volume variance is the difference between the budgeted overhead expenditure and the amount of overhead that was absorbed by actual production.

The calculation for this differs depending on whether the fixed overhead absorption rate (FOAR) at the start of the period was based on **units** produced or **hours** worked to produce the units.

Units produced	$
Actual units × Fixed overhead absorption rate per unit	X
Less: Budgeted expenditure	(X)
	—
Fixed overhead volume variance	X

OR:

Hours worked	$
Standard hours for actual production × FOAR per standard hour	X
Less: Budgeted expenditure	(X)
	—
Fixed overhead volume variance	X

Illustration 7 – Fixed overhead variances

The following information is available for a company for Period 4.

Budget

Output	$22,960
Unit	6,560

Actual

Fixed production overheads	$24,200
Unit	6,460

Required:

Calculate the following:

(a) fixed overhead absorption rate per unit

(b) fixed overhead expenditure variance for marginal costing

(c) fixed overhead expenditure variance for absorption costing

(d) fixed overhead volume variance for marginal costing

(e) fixed overhead volume variance for absorption costing

(f) fixed overhead total variance for marginal costing

(g) fixed overhead total variance for absorption costing.

Solution

(a) FOAR = $22,960/6,560 = $3.50 per unit

(b) Fixed overhead expenditure variance for marginal costing.

Actual expenditure	$24,200
Less Budgeted expenditure	$22,960
Fixed overhead expenditure variance	$1,240 (A)

(c) The fixed overhead expenditure variance for absorption costing is calculated in exactly the same way as that for marginal costing.

(d) There is no fixed overhead volume variance for marginal costing. This is because under marginal costing, fixed overheads are not expected to change when there is a change in volume of activity.

(e) Fixed overhead volume variance for absorption costing

Actual units × FOAR per unit 6,460 × $3.50	$22,610
Less Budgeted expenditure	$22,960
Fixed overhead volume variance	$350 (A)

The variance is adverse because fewer units were produced than expected.

(f) The fixed overhead total variance for marginal costing is the same as the expenditure variance for marginal costing, i.e. $1,240 (A).

(g) The fixed overhead total variance for absorption costing is the total of the expenditure and volume variances for absorption costing, i.e. $1,240 (A) + $350 (A) = $1,590 (A).

Fixed overhead capacity and efficiency variances

In absorption costing systems, if the fixed overhead is absorbed based on **hours**, then the fixed overhead **volume** variance can be subdivided into capacity and efficiency variances.

- The capacity variance measures whether the workforce worked more or less hours than **budgeted** for the period:

	$
Actual hours × FOAR per hour	X
Less: Budget expenditure	(X)
Fixed overhead capacity variance	X

If actual capacity is greater than budgeted capacity there is a favourable variance as more hours have been worked therefore a greater capacity has been achieved.

- The efficiency variance measures whether the workforce took more or less time than **standard** in producing their output for the period:

	$
Standard hours for actual production × FOAR per hour	X
Less: Actual hours × FOAR per hour	(X)
Fixed overhead efficiency variance	X

If the standard hours are greater than the actual hours there is a favourable variance as the workforce have been more efficient and needed less hours to complete the task that was planned.

Together, these two sub-variances explain why the level of activity was different from that budgeted, i.e. they combine to give the fixed overhead volume variance.

Illustration 8 – Fixed overheads variances

The following information is available for a company for Period 4.

Fixed production overheads	$22,960
Units	6,560

The standard time to produce each unit is 2 hours

Actual

Fixed production overheads	$24,200
Units	6,460
Labour hours	12,600 hrs

Required:

Calculate the following:

(a) fixed overhead absorption rate per hour

(b) fixed overhead capacity variance

(c) fixed overhead efficiency variance

(d) fixed overhead volume variance.

Solution

(a) FOAR = $22,960/(6,560 units × 2 hours) — $1.75 per hour

(b)

Actual hours × FOAR per hour	$22,050
12,600 × $1.75	
Less Budgeted expenditure	($22,960)
Capacity variance	$910 (A)

(c)

Standard hours × FOAR per hour	$22,610
6,460 × 2 × $1.75	
Less Actual hours × FOAR per hour	
12,600 × $1.75	($22,050)
Efficiency variance	$560 (F)

(d) The fixed overhead volume variance is the sum of the capacity and efficiency variances, i.e.

$910 (A) + $560 (F) = 350 (A).

This can be proved as follows:

Standard hours × FOAR per hour	$22,610
(6,460 × 2 hours × $1.75)	
Less: Budgeted expenditure	($22,960)
Total variance	$350 (A)

Test your understanding 8

Last month, 40,000 production hours were budgeted in CTD, and the budgeted fixed production overhead cost was $250,000. Actual results show that 38,000 hours were worked and paid, and the standard hours for actual production were 35,000. CTD operates a standard absorption costing system.

What was the fixed production overhead capacity variance for last month?

A $12,500 Adverse

B $12,500 Favourable

C $31,250 Adverse

D $31,250 Favourable

Fixed overheads and under/over absorption

The fixed overhead **total** variance in an absorption costing system is the same as any **under/over-absorption** of overhead.

Illustration 9 – Under/over adsorption

Gatting Ltd produces a single product. Fixed overheads are budgeted at $12,000 and budgeted output is 1,000 units.

Actual results:

Output	1,100 units
Overheads incurred	$13,000

Calculate the following:

(a) fixed overhead expenditure variance

(b) fixed overhead volume variance

(c) fixed overhead total variance

(d) under/over absorption

Solution

(a) Fixed overhead expenditure variance

Actual expenditure	$13,000
Less Budgeted expenditure	$12,000
Expenditure variance	$1,000 (A)

(b) Fixed overhead volume variance

Actual units × FOAR (1,100 × $12,000/1,000 units)	$13,200
Less Budgeted expenditure	$12,000
Volume variance	$1,200 (F)

(c) Fixed overhead total variance

Fixed overhead expenditure variance	$1,000 (A)
Fixed overhead volume variance	$1,200 (F)
Total variance	$200 (F)

(d) FOAR per unit = $12,000/1,000 = $12 per unit

Overhead absorbed = 1,100 × $12	$13,200
Overhead incurred	$13,000
Over-absorption	$200

Diagrammatic view of fixed overhead variances

A total adverse variance represents an under absorption of overhead. In the diagram below the under absorption is $30.

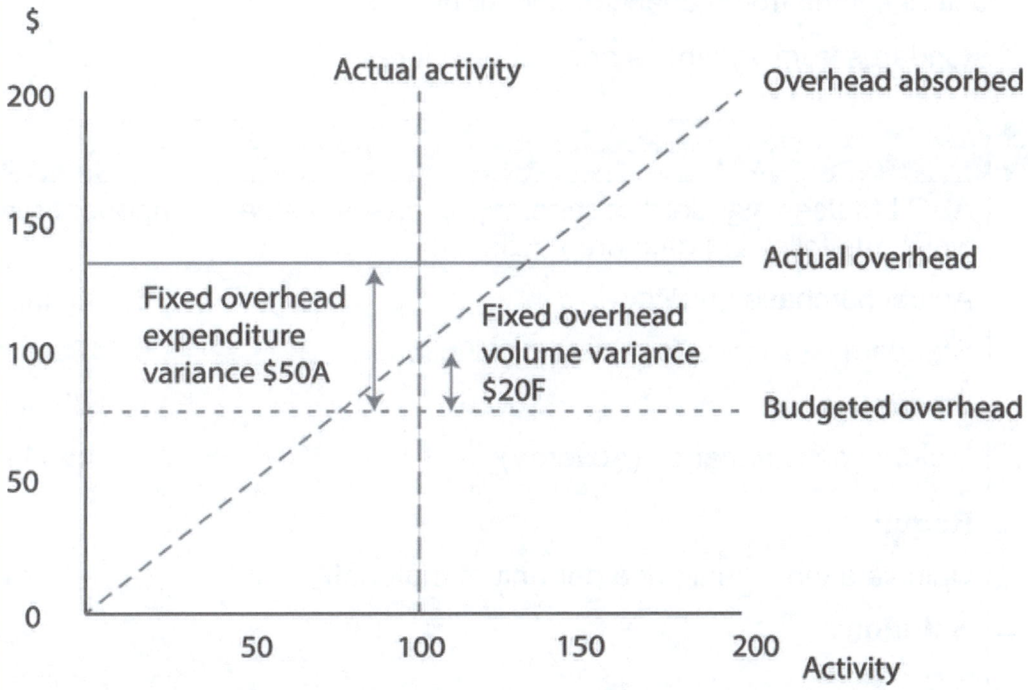

A total favourable variance represents an over absorption of overheads. In the diagram below the over absorption is $10.

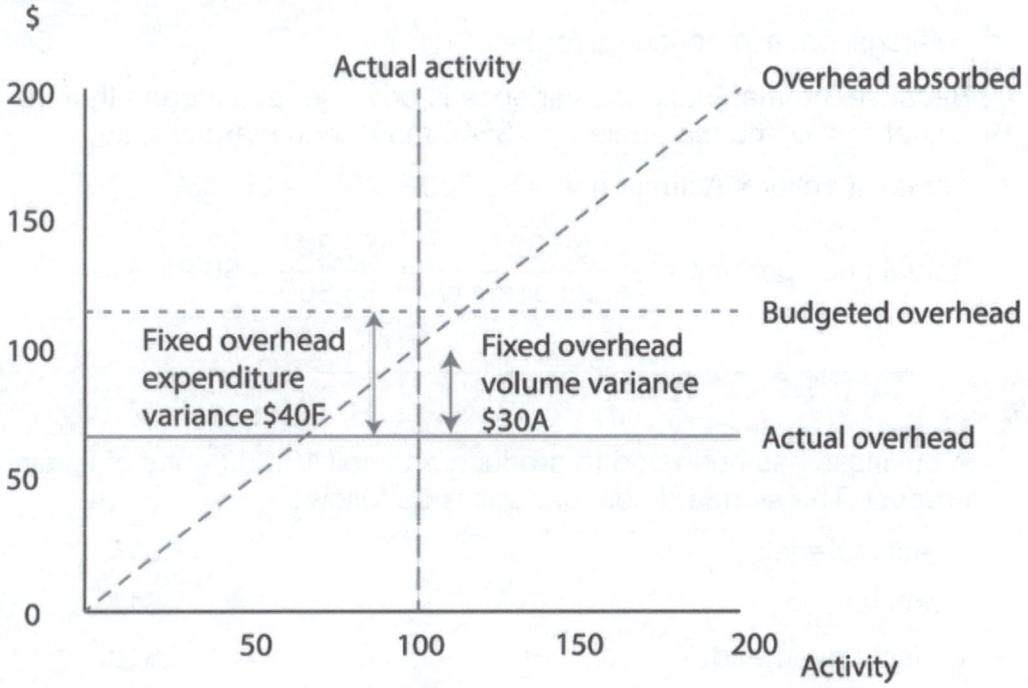

8 Calculating actual or standard from variance data

To test your understanding of variances you may have to calculate the following variance calculations:

- actual figures from variances and standards
- standards from variances and actual figures.

Illustration 10 – Materials

ABC Ltd uses standard costing. It purchases a small component for which the following data are available:

Actual purchase quantity	6,800 units
Standard allowance for actual production	5,440 units
Standard price	$0.85/unit
Material price variance (Adverse)	($544)

Required:

Calculate the actual price per unit of material.

Solution

	$
Actual quantity × Actual price = 6,800 × Ap =	?
Actual quantity × Standard price = 6,800 × $0.85 =	5,780
Material price variance (given) =	544 (A)

Because the material price variance is adverse, this means that the actual cost of the materials was $544 more than standard, i.e.

Actual quantity × Actual price = $5,780 + $544 = $6,324

$$\text{Actual price per unit} = \frac{\$6,324}{\text{Actual quantity}} = \frac{\$6,324}{\$6,800} = \$0.93$$

Illustration 11 – Fixed overheads

A business has budgeted to produce and sell 10,000 units of its single product. The standard cost per unit is as follows:

Direct materials	$15
Direct labour	$12
Variable overhead	$10
Fixed production overhead	$8

During the period the following variances occurred:

fixed overhead expenditure variance	$4,000 adverse
fixed overhead volume variance	$12,000 favourable

Required:

Calculate the following.

(a) Actual fixed overheads in the period.

(b) Actual production volume in the period.

Solution

(a) The actual fixed overheads are calculated as follows.

Actual fixed overheads	?
Budgeted fixed overheads ($8 × 10,000)	$80,000
Fixed overhead expenditure variance	$4,000 (A)

Because the fixed overhead expenditure variance is adverse, this means that the actual fixed overheads were $4,000 more than budgeted.

Budgeted fixed overheads	+	Fixed overhead expenditure variance	=	Actual fixed overheads
$80,000	+	$4,000	=	$84,000

(b) The actual production volume is calculated as follows.

Actual units × standard fixed overhead rate per unit × $8	?
Budgeted expenditure	$80,000
Fixed overhead volume variance	$12,000 (F)

Actual units × standard fixed overhead rate per unit = $80,000 + $12,000 = $92,000

$$\text{Actual units} = \frac{\$92{,}000}{\$8} = 11{,}500 \text{ units}$$

Test your understanding 9

In a period, 11,280 kilograms of material were used at a total standard cost of $46,248. The material usage variance was $492 adverse.

Required:

Calculate the standard allowed weight of material for the period.

Test your understanding 10

In a period 6,500 units were made and there was an adverse labour efficiency variance of $26,000. Workers were paid $8 per hour, total wages were $182,000 and there was a nil rate variance.

Required:

Calculate how many standard labour hours there were per unit.

Test your understanding 11

A company uses standard marginal costing. Last month the standard contribution on actual sales was $44,000 and the following variances arose:

Total variable costs variance	$6,500 Adverse
Sales price variance	$2,000 Favourable
Sales volume contribution variance	$4,500 Adverse

Required:

What was the actual contribution for last month?

A $33,000

B $35,000

C $37,500

D $39,500

Test your understanding 12

Brake Ltd manufactures and distributes brake discs to the automotive sector. The company operates an integrated standard cost system in which:

- Purchases of materials are recorded at standard cost
- Direct material costs and direct labour costs are variable
- Production overheads are fixed and absorbed using direct labour hours.

Actual and budgeted data for May are shown below:

- Budgeted direct materials per unit – 2 kg at $5 per kg
- Direct labour – 0.5 hours per unit
- Budgeted production for the month was 10,000 units
- 22,500 Kgs of material were purchased
- The total standard cost of the materials was $115,000

- 6,000 direct labour hours were worked at a cost of $6 per hour
- Budgeted Fixed production overheads in the period were $240,000
- Actual fixed production overheads in the period were $260,000.

Variances calculated for May are as follows:

- Material price variance $11,250 A
- Labour efficiency variance $1,750 A.

Required:

1 Calculate the actual number of brake discs manufactured

2 Calculate the actual price paid per kg of material

3 Calculate the material usage variance

4 Calculate the standard rate per labour hour

5 Calculate the labour rate variance

6 Calculate the fixed overhead expenditure variance

7 Calculate the overhead absorption rate per labour hour

8 Calculate the fixed overhead capacity variance

9 Calculate the fixed overhead efficiency variance

10 Calculate the fixed overhead volume variance.

10 marks

9 Operating statements

Variances are often summarised in an operating statement. The statement allows for budgeted values to be reconciled with actual values.

If the statement starts with budgeted profit (absorption costing) or budgeted contribution (marginal costing) then:

- Add the favourable variances as these increase profit/contribution
- Subtract the adverse variance as these decrease profit/contribution.

The main differences between absorption and marginal costing operating statements are as follows:

- The marginal costing operating statement has a sales volume variance that is calculated using the standard contribution per unit rather than a standard profit per unit as in absorption costing.
- There is no fixed overhead volume variance in the marginal costing operating statement.

Illustration 12 – Operating statements

TG manufactures Product Z. Its standard selling price is $55. The production and sales budget for the quarter ended 31 March 20X3 was 7,500 units.

The standard specification per unit of Product Z comprises:

Direct labour 4 standard hours at $6/hour

Direct material 1.2 kg at $10/kg

Standard variable overhead 4 standard hours at $1/hour

Budgeted fixed overhead $75,000

At the end of the quarter the management accounts showed the following:

Production and sales of Product Z in units	7,700
Actual sales revenue	$424,270
Actual direct material (8,855 kg)	$89,436
Actual direct labour (31,570 hours)	$192,577
Actual variable overhead	$30,750
Actual fixed overhead	$72,400

(a) Prepare a statement reconciling budgeted and actual profit in the quarter, using absorption costing.

(b) Prepare a statement reconciling budgeted and actual profit in the quarter, using marginal costing.

Note: The variance calculations can be found in the following supplementary reading.

Absorption costing: profit reconciliation statement

			$
Budgeted profit (7,500 units × $5)			37,500
Sales variances:	(F)	(A)	
	$	$	
Sales price variance	770		
Sales profit volume variance	1,000		
			1,770 (F)
Actual sales minus the standard full cost of sales [$424,270 – (7,700 × $50)]			39,270

Cost variances	(F)	(A)	
	$	$	
Direct material price		886	
Direct material usage	3,850		
Direct labour rate		3,157	
Direct labour efficiency		4,620	
Variable overhead expenditure	820		
Variable overhead efficiency		770	
Fixed overhead expenditure	2,600		
Fixed overhead volume	2,000		
	9,270	9,433	163 (A)
Actual profit			39,107

Marginal costing: profit reconciliation statement

			$
Budgeted profit (7,500 units × $5)			37,500
Add: Budgeted fixed costs			75,000
Budgeted contribution			112,500
Sales variances:	(F)	(A)	
	$	$	
Sales price variance	770		
Sales contribution volume variance	3,000		
			3,770 (F)
Actual sales minus the standard marginal cost of sales [$424,270 – (7,700 × 40)]			116,270

[$424,270 – (7,700 × 40)]

Cost variances	(F)	(A)	
	$	$	
Direct material price		886	
Direct material usage	3,850		
Direct labour rate		3,157	
Direct labour efficiency		4,620	
Variable overhead expenditure	820		
Variable overhead efficiency		770	
	4,670	9,433	4,763 (A)
Actual contribution			111,507
Budgeted fixed overhead		75,000	
Fixed overhead expenditure variance		2,600 (F)	
Actual fixed costs			72,400
Actual profit			39,107

Variance calculations for the operating statement

The fixed overhead cost per unit in absorption costing is $75,000/7,500 units = $10.

This gives a standard cost of 4 hours/unit at a rate of $2.50/hour.

	$	$
Standard sales price per unit		55
Direct materials (1.2 kg × $10)	12	
Direct labour (4 hours × $6)	24	
Variable overhead (4 hours × $1)	4	
Standard marginal cost		(40)
Standard contribution per unit		**15**
Standard fixed overhead		(10)
Standard profit per unit		**5**

Sales volume variances

Absorption costing

(Actual quantity – Budget quantity) × Std profit

(7,700 – 7,500) × 5 = $1,000 (F)

Marginal costing

(Actual quantity – Budget quantity) × Std contribution

(7,700 – 7,500) × $15 = $3,000 (F)

Sales price variance

(Actual price – Budget price) × Actual quantity

($424,270/7,700 – $55) × 7,700 = $770 (F)

Direct materials variances

	$
Actual quantity 8,855 kg × Actual price	89,436
Direct materials price variance	**886 (A)**
Actual quantity 8,855 kg × Standard price $10	88,550
Direct material usage variance	**3,850 (F)**
Standard quantity 7,700 units × 1.2 kg × Standard price	92,400

Direct labour variances

	$
Actual hours 31,570 hours × Actual rate	192,577
Direct labour rate variance	**3,157 (A)**
Actual hours 31,570 hours × Standard rate $6	189,420
Direct labour efficiency variance	**4,620 (A)**
Standard hours 7,700 units × 4 hours × Standard rate $6	184,800

Variable overhead variances

	$
Actual hours 31,570 hours × Actual rate	30,750
Variable overhead expenditure variance	820 (F)
Actual hours 31,570 hours × Standard rate $1	31,570
Variable overhead efficiency variance	770 (A)
Standard hours 7,700 hours × 4 hours × Standard rate $1	30,800

Fixed overhead variances

	$
Actual fixed overhead cost	72,400
Budgeted fixed overhead cost	75,000
Fixed overhead expenditure variance	**2,600 (F)**
Actual units 7,700 × FOAR $10 per unit	**77,000**
Budgeted units 7,500 units × FOAR $10 per unit	**75,000**
Fixed overhead volume variance	**2,000 (F)**

Actual profit/contribution

	$	$
Sales		424,270
Direct materials	89,436	
Direct labour	192,577	
Variable overhead	30,750	
Total variable costs		(312,763)
Contribution		111,507
Fixed overheads		(72,400)
Profit		39,107

Test your understanding 13

Below is a statement of variances for A Ltd:

Sales price variance	$2,100 (F)
Sales volume variance	$1,800 (F)
Materials price variance	$6,000 (A)
Materials usage Variance	$2,000 (A)
Labour rate variance	$1,000 (A)
Labour efficiency Variance	$1,500 (F)
Fixed overhead expenditure variance	$2,800 (A)
Fixed overhead volume variance	$2,100 (A)

The budgeted profit for the period was $300,000

Required:

Calculate the actual profit.

Test your understanding 14

The budgeted contribution for R Limited last month was $32,000. The following variances were reported.

Variance	$
Sales volume contribution	800 adverse
Material price	880 adverse
Material usage	822 favourable
Labour efficiency	129 favourable
Variable overhead efficiency	89 favourable

No other variances were reported for the month.

The actual contribution earned by R Limited last month was

A $1,440

B $32,960

C $31,360

D $32,560

Test your understanding 15

Chapel Ltd manufactures a chemical protective called Rustnot. The following standard costs apply for the production of 100 cylinders:

		$
Materials	500 kg @ $0.80 per kg	400
Labour	20 hours @ $1.50 per hour	30
Fixed overheads	20 hours @ $1.00 per hour	20
		450

Chapel Ltd uses absorption costing.

The monthly production/sales budget is 10,000 cylinders sold at $6 per cylinder.

For the month of November the following actual production and sales information is available:

Produced/sold		10,600 cylinders
Sales value		$63,000
Material purchased and used	53,200 kg	$42,500
Labour	2,040 hours	$3,100
Fixed overheads		$2,200

(a) Calculate the following variances were calculated for November:

Sales volume variance		1 mark
Sales price variance		1 mark
Materials price variance		0.5 marks
Materials usage variance		0.5 marks
Labour rate variance		0.5 marks
Labour efficiency variance		0.5 marks
Fixed overhead expenditure variance		1 mark
Fixed overhead volume variance		1 mark

6 marks

(b) Prepare the operating statement for November using the variances you have calculated.

			$
Budgeted profit			
Sales volume variance			
Sales price variance			
Cost variances:	F $	A $	
Material price			
Material usage			
Labour rate			
Labour efficiency			
Fixed overhead expenditure			
Fixed overhead volume			
Total			
Actual profit			

4 marks

10 Reporting of variances

Causes of variances

The causes of variances can be classified under four headings:

- **Planning errors**

  Planning errors lead to the setting of inappropriate standards or budgets. This may be due to carelessness on the part of the standard setter (not taking account of known changes in the production process or expected price rises, for example) or due to unexpected external changes (a market shortage of a resource leading to increased price). These need to be isolated and a revision of the standard considered for future budgets.

- **Measurement errors**

  Measurement errors include errors caused by inaccurate completion of timesheets or job cards and inaccurate measurement of quantities issued from stores.

- **Random factors**

  Random factors are by definition uncontrollable, although they need careful monitoring to ensure that they are not, in fact, one of the other types of variance.

- **Operational factors**

  Operational factors occur during the production of the product or the provision of the service. Factors could include less efficient staff being employed and material spillages.

Examples of causes of variances

Sales variances

Causes of sales variances include the following:

- unplanned price increases (sales price variance)
- unplanned price reduction, for example, when trying to attract additional business (sales price variance)
- unexpected fall in demand due to recession (sales volume variance)
- additional demand attracted by reduced price (sales volume variance)
- failure to satisfy demand due to production difficulties (sales volume variance).

Materials variances

Materials price variances may be caused by:

- supplies from different sources
- unexpected general price increases
- changes in quantity discounts
- substitution of one grade of material for another
- material price standards are usually set at a mid-year price so, if prices are rising, you would expect a favourable price variance early in a period and an adverse variance later on in a budget period.

Materials usage variances may be caused by:

- a higher or lower incidence of scrap
- an alteration to product design
- substitution of one grade of material for another. A lower grade of material may be more difficult to work with, so there may be a higher wastage rate and, in turn, an adverse usage variance may arise.

Labour variances

Labour price variances may be caused by:

- an unexpected national wage award
- overtime or bonus payments which are different from planned/budgeted
- substitution of one grade of labour for another higher or lower grade.

Labour efficiency variances may be caused by:

- changes in working conditions or working methods, for example, better supervision
- consequences of the learning effect (the more a task is completed the quicker it is done)
- introduction of incentive schemes or staff training
- substitution of one grade of labour for another higher or lower grade.

Variable overhead variances

Variable overhead expenditure variances may be caused by:

- incorrect budgets being set at the beginning of a period.
- overheads consisting of a number of items, such as: indirect materials, indirect labour, maintenance costs, power, etc. Consequently, any meaningful interpretation of the expenditure variance must focus on individual cost items.

Variable overhead efficiency variances may be caused by:

- changes in working methods and condition, for example, better supervision
- consequences of the learning effect
- introduction of incentive schemes or staff training
- substitution of one grade of labour for another higher or lower grade.

Note that the possible causes of variable overhead efficiency variances are the same as those for the labour efficiency variance as it is assumed that variable overheads vary with direct labour hours.

Fixed overhead variances

Fixed overhead expenditure variances may be caused by:

- changes in prices relating to fixed overhead expenditure, for example, increase in factory rent
- seasonal differences, e.g. heat and light costs in winter. When the annual budget is divided into four equal quarters, no allowances are given for seasonal factors and the fact that heat and light costs in winter are generally much higher than in the summer months. (Of course, over the year, the seasonal effect is cancelled out.)

Fixed overhead volume variances may be caused by:

- changes in the production volume due to changes in demand or alterations to stockholding policies
- changes in the productivity of labour or machinery
- **lost production through strikes.**

Interrelationships between variances

The cause of a particular variance may affect another variance in a corresponding or opposite way. This is known as interrelationships between variances. Here are some examples:

- if supplies of a specified material are not available, this may lead to a favourable price variance (use of cheaper material), an adverse usage variance (more wastage caused by cheaper material), an adverse fixed overhead volume variance (production delayed while material was unavailable) and an adverse sales volume variance (inability to meet demand due to production difficulties)
- a new improved machine becomes available which causes an adverse fixed overhead expenditure variance (because this machine is more expensive and depreciation is higher) offset by favourable wages efficiency and fixed overhead volume variances (higher productivity)
- workers trying to improve productivity (favourable labour efficiency variance) might become careless and waste more material (adverse materials usage variance).

In each of these cases, if one variance has given rise to the other, there is an argument in favour of combining the two variances and ascribing them to the common cause. In view of these possible interrelationships, care has to be taken when implementing a bonus scheme. If the chief buyer is rewarded for producing a favourable price variance, this may cause trouble later as lower quality materials give rise to adverse usage variances.

One of the most common interrelationships that is seen is the link between sales price and sales volume. It is often found that a decrease in price will lead to an increase in volume sold and vice versa. If businesses offer bulk discounts to customers the more volume that is bought the lower the sales price of each item becomes. This will keep the customer happy but the business will need to check the overall impact of the discount on the sales revenue.

Possible solutions for variances

Each variance should be considered in turn and any interdependence should be considered before solutions can be arrived at. Following are a number of possible solutions for variances that arise:

- Reduce the sales price to be more competitive to increase volume of sales.
- Offer deals (buy one get one free) to increase volume of sales.
- Increase advertising to improve volume of sales without impacting on price.
- Tighter control on costs to improve the contribution/profit made on sales.
- A change of supplier may be an option for improving prices for materials.
- Negotiation of bulk or trade discounts for materials purchased.

- Investigate whether it is possible to have a discount for early payment of bills.
- Updating machinery/changing manufacturing techniques may make the usage of materials better and may also improve the efficiency of the labour force.
- Better quality control over the materials that are used in production may reduce wastage.
- Better supervision of staff may reduce idle time and errors in production.
- Increased training may reduce errors and make the staff more efficient.
- Offering performance related bonuses may increase efficiency.
- Closer monitoring of budgets may make the budgets more accurate.

This list is not exhaustive and it would be necessary to take each variance in turn and investigate the best way to improve the situation.

Reporting of variances

In reporting variances, the concept of responsibility accounting should be followed so that a variance report to an individual manager should only include figures relating to his/her own area of responsibility i.e. within his/her area of control. If more figures are given, then they are usually reported in the form of 'for information only' as a help to a manager in seeing the total picture or context in which his/her figures arise.

Several questions may be asked before deciding whether or not to investigate a variance. These include:

- Is the variance controllable?
- Is the expected benefit from control action likely to exceed the expected cost?
- What is the likelihood of successfully being able to correct a variance?
- Is the variance significant?
- Is the variance steadily getting worse?

Significance of variances

Variance reports might apply the principle of management by exception. Some variance from the budget is inevitable, but it is only large or potentially significant variances that matter for control purposes. With exception reporting, only large and potentially significant items are reported to management and drawn to their attention. Exception reporting means that managers do not have to read through large amounts of insignificant cost data to find the information that really matters.

The amount of detail included in reports will vary according to the needs of management. As a guide, they should be in sufficient detail to motivate the individual manager to take the most appropriate action in all the circumstances. If a report lacks the required amount of detail, then an individual manager should request this from the management accountant.

Cost versus benefit

For some variances, especially small variances, the cost of investigating the causes might be more than the likely benefit from any control measures. In such circumstances, investigation of the variance is not worthwhile.

However, not all significant controllable variances will necessarily lead to control action. Managers should also consider:

- what it would cost to implement control action
- what would be the benefits from taking control action.

Control action is only worthwhile if the expected benefits from the control measures exceed the cost of implementing them.

The benefits from control action are not the same as the amount of the variance.

e.g

Illustration 13

A variance report indicates that there have been adverse material variances of $5,000 last month. Investigation has shown that the problem is due to a high wastage rate in a particular process. The wastage rate could be reduced, but only if the work force spends more time on the process, and this would add $6,000 a month to labour costs.

The control action is not worthwhile unless monthly savings exceed $6,000. Management should investigate if it is possible to source better quality material to reduce wastage or is an improvement to the process can be made.

Likelihood of successful correction

Measures to correct a variance might not be successful. The likelihood of control action having the desired effect should therefore be taken into consideration as well.

e.g **Illustration 14**

Investigation of the adverse material variances of $5,000 last month suggests that the variance will continue at this level in the future unless control measures are taken.

Control action would cost an extra $3,500 a month in labour costs. However, there is only a 50% chance that the corrective action would succeed in reducing the variance.

Here, the extra costs will be $3,500 each month, and the expected benefits either $0 or $5,000 (weighted average value = 0.50 × $0 + 0.50 × $5,000 = $2,500.) It is questionable whether the control measures will be worthwhile.

11 Chapter summary

The purposes of standard costing

- Provide 'targets'
- Useful for planning, control and decision making
- Essential for calculating and analysing variances
- Variances provide 'feedback' to management
- Easier method of accounting
- Standards may be on marginal or absorption costing basis

STANDARD COSTING

Standard costs per unit

- Collected on standard cost card
- Allow variances to be calculated
- In marginal costing includes variable costs only
- In absorption costing includes a fixed cost per unit also

Variance calculation and analysis

You need to know how to calculate and interpret the following variances

SALES VARIANCES

MATERIAL COST VARIANCES

LABOUR COST VARIANCES

VARIABLE OVERHEAD VARIANCES

FIXED OVERHEAD VARIANCES

Operating statements

- Variances summarised in operating statement
- Reconcile budgeted profit (or contribution) with actual profit
- Marginal costing operating statements do not have fixed overhead volume variances (and therefore capacity and efficiency variances)
- Marginal costing operating statements calculate a sales volume variance using standard contributions per unit
- Absorption costing operating statements calculate a sales volume variance using standard profit per unit

Test your understanding answers

Test your understanding 1

(a) **Standard cost per unit under absorption costing**

	$
Direct materials	150,000
Direct labour	200,000
Production overhead	
Variable	50,000
Fixed	25,000
Total production cost	425,000

Budgeted production units = 5,000

Standard cost per unit – absorption costing = $425,000/5,000 units = $85

(b) **Standard cost per unit under marginal costing**

	$
Direct materials	150,000
Direct labour	200,000
Variable overhead costs	50,000
Total variable cost	400,000

Budgeted production units = 5,000

Standard cost per unit – marginal costing = $400,000/5,000 units = $80

Test your understanding 2

Sales price variance	=	($2.00 – $2.50) × 500	=	$250 (A)
Sales volume variance (MC)	=	(500 – 400) × $0.70*	=	$70 (F)
Sales volume variance (AC)	=	(500 – 400) × $0.50**	=	$50 (F)

*Standard contribution per unit = $(2.50 – 1.80) = $0.70

**Standard profit per unit = $(2.50 – 1.80 – 0.20) = $0.50

Test your understanding 3

Price variance	=	($61 – $60) × 6,000	=	$6,000 (F)
Volume variance	=	(6,000 – 6,500) × $5*	=	$2,500 (A)
				$3,500 (F)

* Standard profit per unit

Test your understanding 4

Actual quantity × Actual price		$20,900	
	Price variance		$1,100 (F)
Actual quantity × Standard price			
2,200 hours × $10		$22,000	
	Usage variance		$2,000 (A)
Standard quantity × Standard price			
1,000 × 2 × $10		$20,000	
	Total variance		$900 (A)

Test your understanding 5

		$	$
Actual quantity purchased × Actual price		= 91,520	
	Price variance		8,320 A
Actual quantity purchased × Standard price 20,800 × 90,000 ÷ 22,500		= 83,200	
	Value of closing inventory 500 × $4		2,000
Actual quantity used × Standard price 20,300* × 90,000 ÷ 22,500		= 81,200	
	Usage variance		3,200 A
Standard quantity × Standard price 6,500 × 22,500 ÷ 7,500 × 90,000 ÷ 22,500		= 78,000	

* 20,800 kg were purchased but there were 500 kg of closing inventory therefore 20,300 kg must have been used.

Test your understanding 6

Labour variances		$	$
Actual hours × Actual rate		$17,680	
	Price variance		**$680 (A)**
Actual hours × Standard rate			
3,400 hours × (15,000/3,000)		$17,000	
	Efficiency variance		**$500 (A)**
Standard hours × Standard rate			
1,100 × (3,000/1,000) × $5		$16,500	
	Total variance		**$1,180 (A)**

Test your understanding 7

Actual hours × Actual rate		$5,544	
	Expenditure variance		**$396 (F)**
Actual hours × Standard rate			
1,980 hours × $3		$5,940	
	Efficiency variance		**$540 (A)**
Standard hours × Standard rate			
900 × 2 hours × $3		$5,400	
	Total variance		**$144 (A)**

Test your understanding 8

A

	$
Actual hours × FOAR per hour	
38,000 × $250,000/40,000 hours	$237,500
Budgeted expenditure	$250,000
Capacity variance	$12,500 (A)

Test your understanding 9

Actual quantity × 11,280	Standard price $4.10 **(W1)**	= $46,248
		Usage variance = $492 A
Standard quantity × ? **(W3)**	Standard price $4.10	= $45,756 **(W2)**

(W1) Standard price per kg = $46,248/11,280 kg = $4.10.

(W2) Adverse usage variance means that the actual quantity was greater than the standard quantity.

(W3) Standard quantity = $45,756/$4.10 = 11,160 kg.

Test your understanding 10

	$	$
Actual hours × Actual rate	182,000	
Rate variance		nil
Actual hours × Standard rate		
= ? × $8 = 4	182,000	
Efficiency variance		26,000 (A)
Standard hours × Standard rate		
= 6,500 × Standard hours × $8 =	156,000	

Standard labour hours per unit = $\frac{\$156{,}000}{6{,}500 \times 8}$ = 3 hours

Test your understanding 11

D

Standard contribution on actual sales	$44,000
Add: Favourable sales price variance	$2,000
Less: Adverse total variable costs variance	($6,500)
Actual contribution	$39,500

Test your understanding 12

Material variances

1 The actual number of brake discs manufactured was **11,500 units**

2 The material usage variance was **$2,500 F**

3 The actual price paid per kg of material was **$5.50**

Actual quantity × **Actual price** 22,500 kg × **$5.50**	$123,750	
		Price $11,250 A
Actual quantity × Standard price 22,500 kg × $5	$112,500	
		Usage $2,500 F
Standard quantity × Standard price 2 kg × **11,500 units** × $5	$115,000	

Labour variances

4 The standard rate per labour hour was **$7**

5 The labour rate variance was **$6,000 F**

Actual hours × Actual rate 6,000 hours × $6	$36,000	
		Rate $6,000 F
Actual hours × **Standard rate*** 6,000 hours × **$7**	$42,000	
		Efficiency $1,750 A
Standard hours × **Standard rate*** 0.5 hours × 11,500 units × **$7**	$40,250	

* Standard rate is calculated as follows:

Standard hours = 0.5 × 11,500 = 5,750 hours

Actual hours – standard hours = 250 hours more being worked.

This is causing an efficiency variance of $1,750A therefore the standard rate per hour = $1,750/250 = $7

Fixed overhead variances

6 The fixed overhead expenditure variance was **$20,000 A**

Actual fixed overhead – Budgeted fixed overhead

$260,000 – $240,000 = **$20,000 A**

7 The overhead absorption rate was **$48 per labour hour**

$$\frac{\text{Overhead cost}}{\text{Overhead activity}} = \frac{\$240{,}000}{10{,}000 \text{ units} \times 0.5 \text{ hours}} = \$48 \text{ per labour hour}$$

8	The fixed overhead capacity variance was **$48,000 F**	
	Actual hours × OAR = 6,000 hours × $48	$288,000
	Budgeted hours × OAR = 0.5 hours × 10,000 units × $48	$240,000
	Capacity variance	**$48,000 F**
9	The fixed overhead efficiency variance was **$12,000 A**	
	Standard hours × OAR = 0.5 hours × 11,500 units × $48	$276,000
	Actual hours × OAR = 6,000 hours × $48	$288,000
	Efficiency variance	**$12,000 A**
10	The fixed overhead volume variance was **$36,000 F**	
	Capacity variance	$48,000 F
	Efficiency variance	$12,000 A
	Volume variance	**$36,000 F**

Test your understanding 13

Budgeted profit	**$300,000**
Sales price variance	+$2,100 (F)
Sales volume variance	+$1,800 (F)
Materials price variance	–$6,000 (A)
Materials usage variance	–$2,000 (A)
Labour rate variance	–$1,000 (A)
Labour efficiency variance	+$1,500 (F)
Fixed overhead expenditure variance	–$2,800 (A)
Fixed overhead volume variance	–$2,100 (A)
Actual profit	**$291,500**

Test your understanding 14

C

The actual contribution earned by R Limited last month was $31,360.

$(32,000 – 800 – 880 + 822 + 129 + 89) = $31,360.

Test your understanding 15

(a) **Variances**

Sales price

[(63,000/10,600) – $6] × 10,600 = $600 (A)

Sales volume

(10,600 – 10,000) × [$6 – (450/100)] = $900 (F)

Materials price and usage

Actual quantity × Actual price		$42,500	
	Price variance		**$60 (F)**
Actual quantity × Standard price			
53,200 × $0.80		**$42,560**	
	Usage variance		**$160 (A)**
Standard quantity × Standard price			
10,600 × (500/100) × $0.80		**$42,400**	

Labour rate and efficiency

Actual hours × Actual rate		$3,100	
	Rate variance		**$40 (A)**
Actual hours × Standard rate			
2,040 × $1.50		**$3,060**	
	Efficiency variance		**$120 (F)**
Standard hours × Standard rate			
10,600 × (20/100) × $1.50		**$3,180**	

Fixed overhead expenditure

The standard fixed overhead cost is $20 per 100 cylinders. Monthly production is budgeted at 10,000 cylinders. Therefore the budgeted fixed overhead cost is:

10,000 × $20/100 = $2,000.

The actual cost was $2,200.

The extra cost of **$200** is an **adverse** fixed overhead expenditure variance.

Fixed overhead volume

	$
Actual units × FOAR per unit = 10,600 × 20/100	2,120
Budgeted units × FOAR per unit = 10,000 × 20/100	2,000
Volume variance	**120 (F)**

(b)

Chapel Ltd – Operating statement for November

	F	A	
Budgeted profit **(W1)**			15,000
Sales volume variance			900 F
Sales price variance			600 A
			15,300
	F	A	
Materials price	60		
Materials usage		160	
Labour rate		40	
Labour efficiency	120		
Fixed overhead expenditure		200	
Fixed overhead volume	120		
Total	300	400	100 A
Actual profit **(W2)**			15,200

(W1) Budgeted profit

	$
10,000 cylinders @ $6.00	60,000
Less: total cost	(45,000)
Profit	15,000

(W2) Actual profit

		$	$
Sales			63,000
Less:	Materials	42,500	
	Labour	3,100	
	Fixed overheads	2,200	
			47,800
			15,200

Chapter

16

Performance measurement

Chapter learning objectives

Upon completion of this chapter you will be able to:

- discuss the purpose of mission statements and their role in performance measurement
- discuss the purpose of strategic and operational and tactical objectives and their role in performance measurement
- discuss the impact of economic and market conditions on performance measurement
- explain the impact of government regulation on performance measurement
- explain the impact of sustainability on performance measurement
- discuss and calculate measures of financial performance (profitability, liquidity, efficiency and gearing) and non-financial measures
- Perspectives of the balanced scorecard
  - discuss the advantages and limitations of the balanced scorecard
  - describe performance indicators for financial, customer, internal business process and innovation and learning
  - discuss critical success factors and key performance indicators and their link to objectives and mission statements
  - establish critical success factors and key performance indicators in a specific situation

- Economy, efficiency and effectiveness
  - explain the concepts of economy, efficiency and effectiveness
  - describe performance indicators for economy, efficiency and effectiveness
  - establish performance indicators for economy, efficiency and effectiveness in a specific situation
  - discuss the meaning of each of the efficiency, capacity and activity ratios
  - calculate the efficiency, capacity and activity ratios in a specific situation
- Resource utilisation
  - describe measures of performance utilisation in service and manufacturing environments
  - establish measures of resource utilisation in a specific situation
- Profitability
  - calculate return on investment and residual income
  - explain the advantages and limitations of return on investment and residual income
- Quality
  - distinguish performance measurement issues in service and manufacturing industries
  - discuss the measurement of performance in service industry situations
  - explain total quality management (TQM) as a quality management technique
- compare cost control and cost reduction
- describe and evaluate cost reduction methods
- describe and evaluate value analysis
- discuss the importance of non-financial performance measure
- discuss the relationship between short-term and long-term performance
- describe performance measures appropriate for service industries
- discuss the measurement of performance in non-profit seeking and public sector organisations

- discuss measures that may be used to assess managerial performance and the practical problems involved
- discuss the role of benchmarking in performance measurement
- Produce reports highlighting key areas for management attention and recommendations for improvement.

PER

One of the PER performance objectives (PO1) is to take into account all relevant information and use professional judgement, your personal values and scepticism to evaluate data and make decisions. You should identify right from wrong and escalate anything of concern. You also need to make sure that your skills, knowledge and behaviour are up-to-date and allow you to be effective in your role. Working through this chapter should help you understand how to demonstrate that objective.

PER

One of the PER performance objectives (PO13) is to plan business activities and control performance, making recommendations for improvement. Working through this chapter should help you understand how to demonstrate that objective.

PER

One of the PER performance objectives (PO14) is to measure and assess departmental and business performance. Working through this chapter should help you understand how to demonstrate that objective.

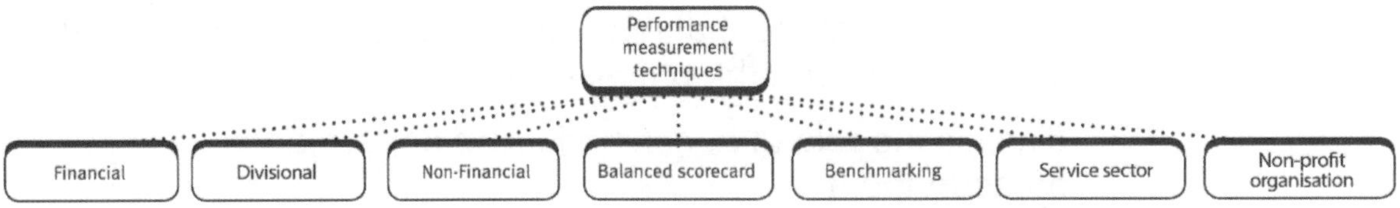

1 The purpose of performance measurement

Performance measurement is the monitoring of budgets or targets against actual results to establish how well the business and its employees are functioning as a whole and as individuals.

Performance measurements can relate to short-term objectives (e.g. cost control) or longer-term measures (e.g. customer satisfaction).

Objectives and goals of a business will vary depending on the type of business that is being operated. For example:

- A profit seeking company's overall goal will be to maximise their shareholders wealth so they will want to monitor profitability (based on increasing sales and reducing costs) and growth or market share compared to competitors.
- A not for profit organisation, for example a government department, will want to provide the best service possible for the lowest cost so that the residents being cared for achieve value for money from the taxes they pay.

What these businesses have in common is that they will have long term (strategic) goals or objectives. These long term goals will be broken down into tactical and operational targets which will need to be monitored. To be able to do this they will identify critical success factors and key performance indicators to monitor to ensure targets are met.

Performance measurement is very important as it can affect behaviour, so it is crucial when setting performance targets that we consider what behaviour we are looking to encourage. Setting poor performance targets can lead to dysfunctional behaviour, behaviour that is not in the best interests of the organisation as a whole.

The mission statement and the corporate plan

You will recall that a mission statement, as discussed in chapter 1, should describe the overall goal of the organisation and that objectives may be developed at strategic, operational and tactical levels in order to allow an organisation to measure progress towards the overall goal.

The different elements of the mission statement can be used as a guide for producing performance measures for the business.

- **Purpose** – is the business meeting its main aims? Maximisation of shareholder wealth? Maintaining customer satisfaction? Producing innovative products/services?

- **Strategy** – is the business providing the products and services it planned to? Is the product or service being provided in the manner it intended?
- **Policies and culture** – are the staff behaving in the manner expected of them? Is customer service at an appropriate level?
- **Values** – are the core principles of the business being maintained and not compromised? Is staff morale being maintained at a suitable level? What is the level of staff turnover?

Suitable performance measures need to be set to monitor the achievement of each objective. Measures will differ according to the type of objective.

As seen in chapter 1 there are three different planning levels:

- **Strategic** or corporate planning – often the responsibility of the senior management and will be measured by indicators that reflect the performance of the whole organisation over the longer term.
- **Tactical** – often the responsibility of middle management and measures may be used that summarise the performance of a department or division, breaking the strategic plan into manageable chunks for each business unit or department.
- **Operational** – often concerned with the day-to-day running of the organisation and are often physical measures turning the strategic and tactical plans into the day to day running of the business.

Suitable measures may include:

- **Strategic** – measurement of the overall profitability of the business and/or the return made on investing surplus cash. Return on investment (ROI), operating profit margin produced monthly.
- **Tactical** – comparison of the actual costs and revenues with the budgeted costs and revenues for each business unit or department. Actual profit compared to budget produced monthly.
- **Operational** – measurement of day to day targets such as meeting production requirements, meeting sales targets and reducing wastage. Quantity of rejects, number of customer complaints produced daily.

This means there are short term objectives and long term goals and objectives. The short term objectives will enable the businesses to monitor progression towards the ultimate long term goal and to enable performance of employees to be measured along the way. Suitable performance measures therefore need to be set to monitor the achievement of each objective.

Type of business

There are many different types of business which can broadly be placed into one the following groups:

- Manufacturing industry
- Service provider
- Non-profit organisation (charities)
- Public sector organisation (government departments).

Each of these business sectors will have different objectives, for example:

- Manufacturing – reduce the cost of the product
- Service provider – improve the quality of the service
- Non-profit organisation – to meet the demands of the 'customer'
- Public sector organisation – to stay within a tight budget.

Each business will need to monitor the performance of their objectives to ensure they are able to succeed in their chosen field but each will face their own difficulties in deciding on appropriate measures to use. For example, as seen in a previous chapter, measurement of a service providers output can be difficult due to:

- Intangible nature of the service
- The variability of the service
- Simultaneous production and consumption of the service
- Perishability of the service.

Non-profit and public organisations will have difficulties deciding on performance measures as the usual financial performance measures will not be applicable.

Responsibility centres

Performance measures will also differ according to the type of centre a manager is responsible for:

Responsibility centre	Example	Examples of measures used to assess performance
Cost centre	Production line in a manufacturing business Costs only	• total cost and cost per unit • cost variances • non-financial performance indicators (NFPIs) related to quality, productivity and efficiency

Revenue centre	Sales team for a car show room Revenues only	• total sales and market share • sales variances • NFPIs related to customer satisfaction
Profit centre	Retail division of a carpet manufacturer Costs and revenues	All the above plus: • profit percentages • working capital ratios
Investment centre	The European business unit in an international organisation Costs, revenues and authority to invest in new assets and dispose of old ones	All of the above plus: • Return on Investment (ROI) • Residual Income (RI)

Other factors affecting performance measurement

External factors may be an important influence on an organisation's ability to achieve objectives. In particular market conditions and government policy will be outside of the control of the organisation's management and will need to be carefully monitored to ensure forecasts remain accurate.

Economic and market conditions

Any performance measure that is used by a business will need to be flexible to allow for peaks and troughs in economic and market conditions that are beyond the control of the business or the specific employee or manager.

The actions of competitors must also be considered. For example, demand may decrease if a competitor reduces its prices or launches a successful advertising campaign.

Government regulation

The government can have a direct effect on the workings of a private sector organisation by introducing regulations or by having departments that monitor business activity. Examples in the UK include:

- The Competition Act which prohibits anticompetitive agreements and any abuse of a dominant market position.
- The Office of Fair Trading who investigates any businesses suspecting of breaching the Competition Act.

Other regulations that the government can enforce include:

- Taxation – tax on alcohol and petrol with the intention of reducing consumption
- Subsides – subsides given to firms providing training for employees
- Fines and quotas – quotas or maximums are set to limit production and if exceeded fines are imposed. For example fishing quotas are set to prevent over fishing of the seas and if a trawler brings in too much then a fine is incurred.

If a private sector organisation is affected by government regulation then the performance measures should take account of this externally imposed limitation i.e. a sales team target should not exceed a quota or exceed/undercut a price set by the government.

Public Sector organisations are owned and controlled by the government (or local government). They aim to provide public services, often free at the point of delivery. Their purpose is to provide a quality service to the public, for example a state school, the provision of water and sewerage services, refuse collections. The measurement of performance is much harder for public sector organisation the standard of the service will be based on opinions or feelings and not necessarily fact.

If we are trying to compare the performance of a private organisation with that of a public organisation the differences in strategy need to be considered. This can be seen in the summarised table below showing the differences between a private school and a state school.

Comparing strategy in private and public-sector organisations

Strategic feature	**Private school**	**State school**
General strategic goal	Competitiveness	Achievement of mission
General financial goals	Profit; growth; market share	Cost reduction; efficiency
Values	Innovation; creativity; good will; recognition	Accountability to public; integrity; fairness
Desired outcome	Customer satisfaction	Customer satisfaction
Stakeholders	Fee payers	Taxpayers; inspectors; legislators
Budget defined by	Customer demand	Leadership; legislators; planners
Key Success Factors	Growth rate; earnings; market share Uniqueness Advanced technology	Best management practices Standardisation; economies of scale Standardised technology

Sustainability in performance measurement

Accountants could encourage a business to switch to triple bottom line (TBL) reporting. TBL reporting expands the traditional company reporting framework to take into account environmental and social performance in addition to financial (economic) performance.

A key aspect of TBL is that it relates to both performance measurement and decision making. Once targets are set for these aspects and performance is measured, then firms will incorporate the effects into decision making.

The concept is often explained using the triple 'P' headings of 'Planet, People and Profit'.

e.g

Illustration 1 – Triple bottom line reporting

Planet

- A TBL company will try to reduce its 'ecological footprint' by managing resource consumption and energy usage and limiting environmental damage.

  For example, production processes will be efficient in terms of resource use and environmentally-damaging outputs such as toxic waste eliminated.

- The drive for environmental sustainability also means that TBL companies will not be involved in resource depletion.

  For example, fish stocks are maintained at sustainable levels and timber use is balanced by replanting to retain the resource into the future.

People

- A TBL business will ensure workers' rights are respected.

  For example, it will pay its workers fair wages, maintain a safe working environment and not use child labour.

- Similarly, the company would promote its surrounding community, for example by providing educational opportunities or a safe community to live in.

  For example, the Bourneville estate established by Cadbury, a chocolate maker in England.

Profit

- A TBL company will try to balance the profit objective with the other two elements of the TBL.

The problem with TBL is that it can be difficult to measure the three factors concerned.

e.g

Illustration 2 – Measuring performance using TBL reporting

Typical measures include the following:

Planet

- Electricity consumption
- Fossil fuel consumption
- Water usage
- Amount of greenhouse gases and other pollutants produced
- Percentage of resources recycled compared with dumped as landfill.

People

- Jobs created/unemployment rates
- Average pay levels
- Health and safety measures, such as accident rates
- Equality measures such as the diversity of employees.

Profit

- Profitability of individual businesses/divisions
- Taxes paid.

Critical success factors

Critical success factors (CSFs) are the essential areas of the business that must be performed well if the mission, objectives and goals of the business are to be achieved.

CSFs act as a common point of reference to measure the success of the business. CSFs help everyone in the team to know exactly what they need to do to ensure the success of the business. This helps employees perform their own work in the right context and so pull together towards the same overall aims to achieve goal congruence.

CSFs are related to the mission and goals of the business:

- The mission focuses on the overall long term aims and what is ultimately to be achieved
- Objectives break down the mission into quantifiable goals
- CSFs are the essential areas that must be perfected to achieve the objectives and therefore the mission of the business.

Measurement of CSFs is possible by the creation of key performance indicators (KPIs). KPIs can be based on financial and non-financial information.

Examples of CSFs and KPIs

The table below shows a number of performance indicators grouped against CSFs. The organisation will formulate its own, specific KPIs which best suit its business.

CSFs	KPIs
Competitiveness	• sales growth by product or service • measures of customer base • relative market share and position
Resource utilisation	• efficiency measurements of resources • measurements of resources available against those used • productivity measurements
Quality of service	• quality measures in every unit • evaluate suppliers on the basis of quality • number of customer complaints received • number of new accounts lost or gained
Customer satisfaction	• speed of response to customer needs • informal listening by calling a certain number of customers each week • number of factory and non-factory manager visits to customers
Quality of working life	• days absent • labour turnover • overtime • measures of job satisfaction
Innovation	• proportion of new products and services to old one • new product or service sales levels
Responsiveness (lead time)	• order entry delays and errors • wrong blueprints or specifications • long set-up times

Quality of output	•	returns from customers
	•	reject rates
	•	reworking costs
	•	warranty costs
Flexibility (ability to react to changing demand and a changing environment)	•	product/service introduction flexibility
	•	product/service mix flexibility
	•	volume flexibility
	•	delivery flexibility
	•	time to respond to customer demands

2 Financial performance measures

Financial performance measures are used to monitor the inflows (revenue) and outflows (costs) and the overall management of money in the business. These measures focus on information available from the Statement of profit or loss and Statement of financial position of a business.

Financial measures can be used to record the performance of cost centres, profit centres and investment centres within a responsibility accounting system but they can also be used to assess the overall performance of the organisation. For example, if cost reduction or cost control is identified as a critical success factor, cost based performance measures might be an appropriate performance indicator to be used.

Cost based performance measures can be calculated as a simple cost per unit of output. The organisation will have to determine its policy for establishing cost per unit for performance measurement purposes. The chosen method should then be applied consistently.

Measuring profitability

The primary objective of a profit seeking company is to maximise profitability. A business needs to make a profit to be able to provide a return to any investors and to be able to grow the business by re-investment.

Note: In the following calculations operating profit is profit before interest and tax and after non-production overheads have been charged.

Return on capital employed (ROCE)

Return on capital employed (ROCE) = operating profit ÷ (non-current liabilities + total equity) %

This is a key measure of profitability as an investor will want to know the likely return from any investment made.

ROCE is the operating profit as a percentage of capital employed. It provides a measure of how much profit is generated from each $1 of capital employed in the business.

Operating profit is being compared to long term debt (non-current liabilities) plus the equity invested in the business.

Operating profit represents what is available to pay interest due to debt and dividends to shareholders so the figures used are comparing like for like.

A high ROCE is desirable. An increase in ROCE could be achieved by:

- Increasing profit, e.g. through an increase in sales price or through better control of costs.
- Reducing capital employed, e.g. through the repayment of long term debt.

Operating profit margin (OPM)

Operating profit margin = operating profit ÷ revenue %

This is the operating profit as a percentage of revenue.

A high return is desirable. It indicates that either sales prices and or volumes are high or that costs are being kept well under control.

Asset turnover

Asset turnover = Revenue ÷ Capital employed

The asset turnover measures how much revenue is generated from each $1 of capital employed in the business.

A high asset turnover is desirable. An increase in the asset turnover could be achieved by:

- Increasing revenue, e.g. through the launch of new products or a successful advertising campaign.
- Reducing capital employed, e.g. through the repayment of long term debt.

ROCE, OPM and the Asset turnover ratios can be used together:

$$\textbf{ROCE} = \textbf{OPM} \times \textbf{Asset turnover}$$

$$\frac{\text{Operating profit}}{\text{Capital employed}} = \frac{\text{Operating profit}}{\text{Revenue}} \times \frac{\text{Revenue}}{\text{Capital employed}}$$

This can be useful if only partial information is available. For example if the OPM and Asset turnover ratios are known then the ROCE can be calculated.

e.g

Illustration 3 – ROCE, OPM and asset turnover

Companies X and Y are both involved in retailing.

Relevant information for the year ended 30 September 20X5 was as follows:

	X	Y
	$000	$000
Revenue	80,000	200,000
Operating profit	10,000	10,000
Capital employed	50,000	50,000

It is possible to calculate ROCE, OPM and Asset turnover from the above information to examine the relationship between these 3 ratios.

Company X

ROCE = 10,000 ÷ 50,000 × 100 = 20%

OPM = 10,000 ÷ 80,000 × 100 = 12.5%

Asset turnover = 80,000 ÷ 50,000 = 1.6

ROCE = OPM × Asset turnover = 0.125 × 1.6 = 0.2 = 20%

Company Y

ROCE = 10,000 ÷ 50,000 × 100 = 20%

OPM = 10,000 ÷ 200,000 × 100 = 5%

Asset turnover = 200,000 ÷ 50,000 = 4

OPM = ROCE ÷ Asset turnover = 0.2 ÷ 4 = 0.05 = 5%

Gross profit margin

Gross profit margin = gross profit ÷ revenue %

The gross profit margin focuses on the trading activity of a business as it is the gross profit (revenue less cost of sales) as a percentage of revenue.

A high gross margin is desirable. It indicates that either sales prices and or volumes are high or that **production** costs are being kept well under control.

Measuring liquidity

A business can be profitable but at the same time encounter cash flow problems. Cash at the bank and profit are not the same thing (as discussed in Chapter 14).

There are two liquidity ratios that are used to give an indication of a company's ability to manage and meet short term financial obligations.

Current ratio

This is the current assets divided by the current liabilities.

$$\text{Current ratio} = \frac{\text{Current assets}}{\text{Current liabilities}}$$

The ratio measures the company's ability to meet its short term liabilities due within one year with the current assets than should be converted into cash within one year.

A ratio in excess of 1 is desirable but the expected ratio varies depending on the type of industry.

A decrease in the ratio year on year or a figure that is below the industry average could indicate that a company has liquidity problems. The company should take steps to improve liquidity, e.g. by paying payables as they fall due or by better management of receivables in order to convert the money owed into cash more efficiently.

Equally a high ratio could indicate that any surplus cash is not being made efficient use of. Cash does not provide a return so it should be re-invested in the business.

Acid test (Quick ratio)

This is a similar to the current ratio but inventory is removed from the current assets due to its poor liquidity (time taken to convert into cash) in the short term.

$$\text{Quick ratio} = \frac{\text{Current assets} - \text{inventory}}{\text{Current liabilities}}$$

The comments are the same as for the current ratio.

Measuring efficiency

Efficiency ratios look at how well a business manages to convert statement of financial position items into cash. They are used to investigate how efficiently current assets are managed.

Inventory holding period

Inventory holding period (days) = inventory ÷ cost of sales × 365

This indicates the average number of days that inventory items are held for before they are sold.

Cost of sales is used in this calculation as opening inventory plus purchases less closing inventory equals the inventory being held. Sometimes a business might want to look at a specific line of inventory so more detailed information will be required.

An increase in the inventory holding period could indicate that the company is having problems selling its products and could also indicate that there is an increased level of obsolete inventory. The company should take steps to increase inventory turnover, e.g. by removing any slow moving or unpopular items of inventory and by getting rid of any obsolete inventory.

A decrease in the inventory holding period could be desirable as the company's ability to turn over inventory has improved and the company does not have excess cash tied up in inventory. However, any reductions should be reviewed further as the company may be struggling to manage its liquidity and may not have the cash available to hold the optimum level of inventory.

Receivables collection period

Receivable collection period (days) = receivables ÷ credit sales × 365

This is the average period it takes for a company's receivables to pay what they owe.

Sometimes the breakdown of revenue into cash and credit sales is not available, in which case revenue is used in place of credit sales and it is assumed that all sales are on credit.

An increase in the receivable collection period indicates that the company is struggling to manage its debts. Possible steps to reduce the ratio include:

- Credit checks on customers to ensure that they will pay on time
- Improved credit control, e.g. invoicing on time, chasing up debts.

A decrease in the receivable collection period may indicate that the company has improved its management of receivables. However, a receivables collection period well below the industry average may make the company uncompetitive and profitability could be impacted as a result.

Payables payment period

Payable payment period (days) = payables ÷ credit purchases × 365.

This is the average period it takes for a company to pay suppliers for purchases.

If the value of credit purchases is not available then cost of sales can be used in its place.

An increase in the company's payable payment period could indicate that the company is struggling to pay its debts as they fall due. However, it could simply indicate that the company is taking better advantage of any credit period offered to them.

A decrease in the company's payable payment period could indicate that the company's ability to pay for its purchases on time is improving. However, the company should not pay for its purchases too early since supplier credit is a useful source of finance.

Test your understanding 1

The following figures are extracted from the accounts of Super Soups, a company selling gourmet homemade soups.

	20X9	20X8
	$	$
Total production costs	6,538,000	5,082,000
Gross profit	3,006,000	2,582,000
Operating profit	590,000	574,000
Total capital employed	6,011,000	5,722,000

Required:

Using appropriate ratios, comment on the profitability of Super Soups.

Test your understanding 2

Calculate the activity and liquidity ratios for P for the year ended 31 December 20X9.

	$m
Revenue	1,867.5
Gross profit	489.3
Inventory	147.9
Trade receivables	393.4
Trade payables	275.1
Cash	53.8
Short-term investments	6.2
Other current liabilities	284.3

Measuring risk

In addition to managing profitability, liquidity and efficiency it is also important for a company to manage its risk. How 'geared' a business is can be calculated to assess financial risk. Gearing indicates how well a business will be able to meet its long term debts.

Capital gearing (leverage)

This ratio calculates the relationship between borrowed capital (debt) and owner's capital (equity):

Capital gearing = non-current liabilities (debt) ÷ ordinary shareholders funds (equity) %

or

Capital gearing = non-current liabilities (debt) ÷ (non-current liabilities + ordinary shareholders funds (debt + equity)) %

The level of gearing indicates how much a business relies on long term debt finance. The higher the percentage the higher the level of risk as any debt finance must be paid back through interest and capital repayments. There is a legal obligation to make these payments. Repayment of equity finance is through dividends and there is no legal obligation to make these payments to shareholders.

There is no 'correct' level of gearing but if debt exceeds equity then gearing is too high.

Interest cover (income gearing)

Interest cover = Operating profit ÷ Interest expense.

This shows how many times the interest cost (interest payments) could be paid out of the operating profit. The higher the figure the better.

A decrease in the interest cover indicates that the company is facing an increased risk of not being able to meet its finance payments as they fall due.

The ratio could be improved by taking steps to increase the profit, e.g. through better management of costs, or by reducing finance costs through reducing the level of debt.

3 Divisional performance measurement

Measuring managerial performance

There are practical problems involved in isolating managerial performance from the performance of the division being managed. The personal performance of the manager is not the same as the overall performance of the division due to external factors which are outside of the control of the organisation. For example:

- a manager may be in control of a division which faces fierce competition and difficult operating conditions and therefore will not be able to grow the business easily
- another manager may be given a division which faces less competition and an easier business environment.

Measures which reflect the performance of the division as a whole, therefore, may not reflect the performance of the manager.

There are two main ways of measuring managerial performance.

1 **Set specific managerial objectives**

   Individual managers can be set specific objectives against which their performance can be measured at regular intervals. These objectives will be linked to the overall objectives of the organisation as a whole.

   For example, the organisation may have an objective to increase overall sales by 5% per annum. The specific objective for a manager operating in a very competitive environment may be to maintain sales at the current level rather than try to increase them. This objective should be agreed with the individual manager as being set at a level which is tough but achievable in order to provide motivation. The payment of bonuses or other performance-related pay may also be linked to the achievement of the agreed objectives.

2 **Use measures based on controllable costs and revenue i.e. controllable profit**

Budget targets can distinguish between controllable and uncontrollable costs and revenue. The divisional performance can be measured against the total budget using traceable costs and revenues whereas managerial performance can be measured based on what the controllable element is.

The major problem is the difficulty in deciding what is controllable or traceable. If we are assessing the performance of a manager we should only consider those factors that are capable of being controlled by that manager. In assessing the success of the division, our focus should be on costs and revenues that are traceable to the division and hence judge the division on traceable profit. For example, depreciation on divisional machinery would not be included as a controllable cost in a profit centre. This is because the manager has no control over investment in non-current assets. It would, however, be included as a traceable fixed cost in assessing the performance of the division.

The traditional performance indicator for a division is the controllable profit statement. A typical pro-forma statement is given below.

Proforma of a controllable profit statement

	$	$
Sales		
External	X	
Internal	X	
		X
Controllable divisional variable costs		(X)
Controllable divisional fixed costs		(X)
Controllable divisional profit		X
Other traceable divisional variable costs		(X)
Other traceable divisional fixed costs		(X)
Traceable divisional profit		X
Apportioned head office cost		(X)
Profit		X

Return on investment (ROI)

This is a similar measure to ROCE but is used to appraise the investment decisions of an individual division.

$$\text{ROI \%} = \frac{\text{Controllable profit}}{\text{Controllable capital employed}} \times 100$$

- Controllable profit is usually taken after depreciation but before tax.
- Capital employed is total assets less current liabilities or total equity plus long term debt.
- Non-current assets might be valued at cost, net replacement cost or carrying amount. The value of assets employed could be either an average value for the period as a whole or a value as at the end of the period. An average value for the period is preferable.

e.g

Illustration 4 – ROI

The following data has been collected in respect of investment centre A:

Controllable profit $50,000

Controllable assets $250,000

Required:

Calculate the ROI for investment centre A.

Solution

$$\text{ROI \%} = \frac{50{,}000}{250{,}000} \times 100 = 20\%$$

This means that the centre has made a rate of return of 20% on the assets under its control.

Test your understanding 3

The following data relate to the operational performance of the four divisions of Questor plc.

Division	A	B	C	D
	$000	$000	$000	$000
Profit	250	400	320	80
Net assets	1,300	2,500	1,600	320

Using ROI to evaluate performance, which division has been most successful?

A Division A

B Division B

C Division C

D Division D

Residual Income (RI)

Residual income is the net operating income that an investment centre or division earns above the minimum required return on its operating assets.

RI = Controllable profit – Notional interest on capital

- Controllable profit is calculated in the same way as for ROI.
- Notional interest on capital = the capital employed in the division multiplied by a notional cost of capital or interest rate.
  - Capital employed is calculated in the same way as for ROI.
  - The selected cost of capital could be the company's average cost of funds (cost of capital). However, other interest rates might be selected, such as the current cost of borrowing, or a target ROI.

Illustration 5 – RI calculation

An investment centre's statement of financial position shows assets under its control amounting to $300,000. The profit of the centre, in its statement of profit or loss amounts to $50,000. The notional cost of capital of 10%.

Required:

Calculate the RI for this centre.

Solution

The residual income calculation of the investment centre would show:

Controllable profit	$50,000
Less notional cost of capital $300,000 × 10%	($30,000)
Residual income	$20,000

Test your understanding 4

An investment centre has net assets of \$800,000 and operating profits of \$160,000. The notional cost of capital is 12%.

Required:

Calculate and comment on the RI for the period.

Illustration 6 – ROI versus RI

A division currently has:

Controllable profit of \$20m

Controllable assets of \$100m

Cost of capital 10%.

An investment opportunity has arisen that would increase the controllable profit by \$10m and increase the controllable assets by \$50m.

Required:

Should the manager of the division take advantage of the opportunity?

Solution

The investment does not change the ROI of the division:

Current ROI = \$20m/\$100m × 100 = 20%

With investment ROI = \$30m/\$150m × 100 = 20%

The investment improves the RI of the division:

Current RI = \$20m – (10% × \$100m) = \$10m

With investment RI = \$30m – (10% × \$150m) = \$15m

Based on RI the investment should be accepted as it produces a higher absolute level of income.

This suggests that the use of ROI as a performance measure may lead to sub-optimal decisions which do not maximise profit (and therefore wealth) generated by the organisation.

Test your understanding 5

A division has a residual income of $280,000 and a controllable profit before interest of $740,000.

If it uses a notional rate of 10% for interest on its invested capital, what is its return on investment to the nearest whole percentage?

A 4%

B 10%

C 16%

D 27%

Evaluation of ROI as a performance measure

ROI is a popular measure for **divisional performance** but has some serious failings which must be considered when interpreting results.

Advantages	Disadvantages
• familiar and simple calculation • uses readily available information • widely used measure • gives result in percentage terms so can be used to compare business units of different sizes	• based on accounting information • open to manipulation • may be distorted by inflation • may discourage investment in new assets • use of a percentage comparison can be misleading • may lead to non-goal congruence

Advantages and disadvantages of ROI

Advantages

- It is a familiar and simple calculation – everyone with a basic knowledge of accounting will be familiar with the return on capital concept.
- It uses readily available information taken from the investment centres normal accounting system. It is therefore a low cost measure – no additional information is usually required in order to be able to carry out the calculations.

- It is a widely used measure, so comparisons with other organisations should be readily available.
- As ROI gives a result in percentage terms, it can be used to compare units which differ in size – their performance is reduced to a common base as a result of the percentage calculation.

Disadvantages

- The measure is based on accounting information (profit figures and asset figures). Different accounting policies, such as the depreciation policy, may impact on the figure calculated.
- It may be open to manipulation. Managers may be tempted to massage the figures to present a better picture of their performance, especially if bonuses are at stake.
- The measure may be distorted by inflation as historical cost accounts does not reflect the current value of the assets.
- ROI may discourage investment in more technologically up to date assets. Old assets, almost fully depreciated will give a low asset base in the ROI calculation, which will result in an increased figure for ROI and give the impression of an improved level of performance.
- ROI gives a percentage value – useful for making comparisons as we have mentioned above. However, the use of comparatives can also be misleading.
- Importantly, ROI may lead managers to take decisions which are to their advantage but which do not benefit the organisation as a whole. In technical terms, ROI may lead to dysfunctional decision making.

Evaluation of RI as a performance measure

Compared to using ROI as a measure of performance, RI has several advantages and disadvantages:

Advantages	Disadvantages
• encourages new investment • interest charge • absolute measure	• not comparable with different size business units • based on accounting measures • determination of the appropriate cost of capital

Advantages and disadvantages of RI

Advantages

- It encourages investment centre managers to make new investments if they add to RI. A new investment might add to RI but reduce ROI. In such a situation, measuring performance by RI would not result in dysfunctional behaviour, i.e. the best decision will be made for the business as a whole.
- Making a specific charge for interest helps to make investment centre managers more aware of the cost of the assets under their control.
- RI gives an absolute measure, not a percentage measure – it therefore avoids some of the problem of ROI.

Disadvantages

- It does not facilitate comparisons between divisions since the RI is driven by the size of divisions and of their investments.
- It is based on accounting measures of profit and capital employed which may be subject to manipulation.
- There is a major problem inherent in the RI calculation – that is, the determination of an appropriate notional cost of capital.

Test your understanding 6

An organisation is divided into a number of divisions, each of which operates as a profit centre. Which of the following would be useful measures to monitor divisional performance?

(i) Contribution

(ii) Controllable profit

(iii) Return on investment

(iv) Residual income

A (i) only

B (i) and (ii) only

C (iii), (iv) only

D All of them

4 Problems with using only financial performance indicators

All of the ratios reviewed so far have concentrated on the financial performance of the business. Many of these ratios, e.g. ROCE, gross margin, may be used to assess the **performance of a division** and of the **manager** in charge of that division.

Achievement of these target ratios (financial performance indicators) may be linked to a reward system in order to motivate managers to improve financial performance.

However, there are a number of problems associated with the use of financial performance indicators to monitor performance:

Short-termism vs long term performance

Linking rewards to financial performance may tempt managers to make decisions that will improve short-term financial performance but may have a negative impact on long-term profitability. E.g. they may decide to cut investment or to purchase cheaper but poorer quality materials.

As mentioned at the start of this chapter any targets that are set at the different planning levels should all aim towards achieving the overall aim or mission of the business. There should be goal congruence to reduce the risk of a short termist view being taken by the managers.

e.g

Illustration 7 – Short termism

In order to achieve cost savings and to boost annual profit there are a limited number of things that a manager can do easily. One of these is to cut back on discretionary costs such as:

- advertising and marketing
- training
- maintenance
- research and development.

All these cuts may produce a short-term profit improvement; the problem comes with long-term profitability. Cut advertising and future sales may fall, cut training and staff may leave or become less efficient, cut maintenance and plant and machinery will become less productive. Cut backs on research and development can be particularly damaging in the long-term – the organisation may fall behind its competitors in developing new products and taking advantage of new technology.

Manipulation of results

In order to achieve the target financial performance and hence their reward, managers may be tempted to manipulate results.

For example:

- **Accelerating revenue** – revenue included in one year may be wrongly included in the previous year in order to improve the financial performance for the earlier year.
- **Delaying costs** – costs incurred in one year may be wrongly recorded in the next year's accounts in order to improve performance and meet targets for the earlier year.
- **Understating a provision or accrual** – this would improve the financial performance and may result in the targets being achieved.
- Manipulation of **accounting policies** – for example, closing inventory values may be overstated resulting in an increase in profits for the year.

Do not convey the full picture

The use of only financial performance indicators has limited benefit to the company as it does not convey the full picture regarding the factors that will drive long-term profitability, e.g. customer satisfaction, quality.

Therefore, when monitoring performance, a broader range of measures should be used.

5 Non-financial performance indicators (NFPIs)

Although profit cannot be ignored as it is the main objective of commercial organisations, critical success factors (CSFs) and key performance indicators (KPIs) should not focus on profit alone. The view is that a range of performance indicators should be used and these should be a mix of financial and non-financial measures.

Examples of Non-Financial Performance Indicators (NFPI) include:

- measurements of customer satisfaction e.g. returning customers, reduction in complaints
- resource utilisation e.g. are the machines being operated for all the available hours and producing output as efficiently as possible?
- measurement of quality e.g. reduction in conformance and non-conformance costs.

The large variety in types of businesses means that there are many NFPIs. Each business will have its own set of NFPIs that provide relevant measures of the success of the business. However, NFPIs can be grouped together into 2 broad groups:

- Productivity
- Quality.

Measuring productivity

A productivity measure is a measure of the efficiency of an operation, it is also referred to as **resource utilisation**. It relates the goods or services produced to the resources used, and therefore ultimately the cost incurred to produce the output. The most productive or efficient operation is one that produces the maximum output for any given set of resource inputs or alternatively uses the minimum inputs for any given quantity or quality of output.

Examples of resource utilisation:

- Hotel – the cost of the bed linen used in each room compared to the number of times the linen can be used before it needs to be disposed of, time taken to clean and set fair a room.
- Car sales team – Sales per employee, Sales per square metre of available floor space, average length of time a second hand car (e.g. taken as part exchange) remains unsold.

Types of productivity measures

Productivity measures are usually given in terms of labour efficiency. However productivity measures are not restricted to labour and can also be expressed in terms of other resource inputs of the organisation such as the machine hours used for production.

Productivity is often analysed using three control ratios:

Production-volume ratio

The production/volume ratio assesses the overall production relative to the plan or budget. A ratio in excess of 100% indicates that overall production is above planned levels and below 100% indicates a shortfall compared to plans.

The production/volume ratio =

$$\frac{\text{Actual output measured in standard hours}}{\text{Budgeted production hours}} \times 100$$

Capacity ratio

The capacity ratio provides information in terms of the hours of working time that have been possible in a period.

The capacity ratio =

$$\frac{\text{Actual production hours worked}}{\text{Budgeted production hours}} \times 100$$

A ratio in excess of 100% indicates that more hours have been worked than were in the budget and below 100% less hours have been worked than in the budget.

Efficiency ratio

The efficiency ratio is a useful indicator of productivity based on output compared with inputs.

The efficiency ratio =

$$\frac{\text{Actual output measured in standard hours}}{\text{Actual production hours worked}} \times 100$$

A ratio in excess of 100% indicates that the workforce have been more efficient than the budget predicted and below 100% less efficient than in the budget.

e.g

Illustration 8 – Productivity measures

Suppose that the budgeted output for a period is 2,000 units and the budgeted time for the production of these units is 200 hours.

The actual output in the period is 2,300 units and the actual time worked by the labour force is 180 hours.

Required:

Calculate how productive the work force has been.

Solution

Production/volume ratio

$$\frac{\text{Actual output measured in standard hours}}{\text{Budgeted production hours}} \times 100$$

$$\text{Standard hours per unit} = \frac{200 \text{ hours}}{2{,}000 \text{ units}} = 0.1 \text{ hours per unit of output}$$

Actual output measured in standard hours	=	2,300 units × 0.1 hours	=	230 standard hours

$$\text{Production/volume ratio} = \frac{230}{200} \times 100 = 115\%$$

This shows that production is 15% up on planned production levels.

Capacity ratio

$$\frac{\text{Actual production hours worked}}{\text{Budgeted production hours}} \times 100$$

$$\text{Capacity ratio} = \frac{180}{200} \times 100 = 90\%$$

Therefore this organisation had only 90% of the production hours anticipated available for production.

Efficiency ratio

$$\frac{\text{Actual output measured in standard hours}}{\text{Actual production hours worked}} \times 100$$

$$\text{Efficiency} = \frac{230}{180} \times 100 = \mathbf{127.78\%}$$

The workers were expected to produce 10 units per hour, the standard hour.

Therefore, in the 180 hours worked it would be expected that 1,800 units would be produced. In fact 2,300 units were produced. This is 27.78% more than anticipated.

NB: Production/volume ratio = capacity ratio × efficiency ratio

Examples of productivity measures

Productivity measures are not restricted to use in manufacturing industries but can be adapted for use in both the service and public sectors.

Public sector

A nurse in a fracture clinic should be able to complete the plastering of an average broken bone in 45 minutes.

The data on one nurse showed the following:

Hours worked in one week	55 hours
Actual number of casts completed	70

Each nurse is expected to work a 10 hour shift 5 days a week.

Calculate the production/volume ratio, capacity ratio and efficiency ratio for this nurse.

$$\text{Production/volume ratio} = \frac{70 \times 45/60}{50} \times 100 = \mathbf{105\%}$$

$$\text{Capacity ratio} = \frac{55}{50} \times 100 = \mathbf{110\%}$$

$$\text{Efficiency ratio} = \frac{52.5}{55} \times 100 = \mathbf{95.45\%}$$

Service sector

It should be possible to deliver a fast food meal in 1 minute 30 seconds. The information for one fast food restaurant is as follows:

Opening hours	8.30am to 7pm
Actual meals in one day	380 meals
Budgeted meals in one day	420 meals

Calculate the production/volume ratio, capacity ratio and efficiency ratio for this day.

$$\text{Production/volume ratio} = \frac{380 \times 1.5/60}{10.5} \times 100 = \mathbf{90.5\%}$$

$$\text{Capacity ratio} = \frac{10.5}{10.5} \times 100 = \mathbf{100\%}$$

$$\text{Efficiency ratio} = \frac{9.5}{10.5} \times 100 = \mathbf{90.5\%}$$

Test your understanding 7

The budgeted output for a period is 1,500 units and the standard time allowed per unit is 30 minutes. The actual output in the period was 1,400 units and these were produced in 720 hours.

Required:

Calculate the production/volume ratio, capacity ratio and efficiency ratio. Explain the meaning of your answer.

Measuring quality

Quality is an issue whether manufacturing products or providing a service. Poor quality products or services will lead to a loss of business and damage to the businesses reputation. Targets of an appropriate level need to be set.

Examples of NFPIs that could be used to monitor quality both from an internal and external (customer) perspective includes:

- Wastage levels
- Internal re-working of finished products

- Customer complaints
- Speed of delivery
- Accuracy of delivery
- Number of returns
- Repeat sales
- New customers
- Growth in sales
- Labour turnover
- Staff absences
- Evaluation of development plans
- Job satisfaction
- Overtime working
- Product improvements
- Sales from new products
- Cost of research and development
- Cleanliness
- Tidiness
- Meeting staff needs
- Meeting government targets on emissions.

Total quality management (TQM)

Total quality management (TQM) is a philosophy of quality management and cost management that has a number of important features.

- **Total** – means that everyone in the value chain is involved in the process, including employees, customer and suppliers
- **Quality** – products and services must meet the customers' requirements
- **Management** – quality is actively managed rather than controlled so that problems are prevented from occurring.

There are three basic principles of TQM:

1 **Get it right, first time**

TQM considers that the costs of prevention are less than the costs of correction. One of the main aims of TQM is to achieve zero rejects and 100% quality.

2 **Continuous improvement**

The second basic principle of TQM is dissatisfaction with the status-quo. Realistically a zero-defect goal may not be obtainable. It does however provide a target to ensure that a company should never be satisfied with its present level of rejects. The management and staff should believe that it is always possible to improve next time.

3 **Customer focus**

Quality is examined from a customer perspective and the system is aimed at meeting customer needs and expectations.

Quality related costs

Failing to satisfy customers' needs and expectations, or failing to do so first time, costs the average company between 15% and 30% of sales revenue.

A quality-related cost is the 'cost of ensuring and assuring quality' as well as the loss incurred when quality is not achieved. Quality costs are classified as prevention costs, appraisal cost, internal failure cost and external failure cost.

1 **Prevention cost**

Prevention costs represent the cost of any action taken to prevent or reduce defects and failures. Examples include:

- customer surveys
- research of customer needs
- field trials
- quality education and training programmes
- supplier reviews
- investment in improved production equipment
- quality engineering.

2 **Appraisal costs**

Appraisal costs are the costs incurred, such as inspection and testing, in initially ascertaining the conformance of the product to quality requirements. Examples might be:

- the capital cost of measurement equipment
- inspection and testing
- product quality audits
- process control monitoring
- test equipment expense.

3 **Internal failure cost**

Internal failure costs are the costs arising from inadequate quality where the problem is discovered before the transfer of ownership from supplier to purchaser. Examples include:

- rework or rectification costs
- net cost of scrap
- disposal of defective products
- downtime or idle time due to quality problems.

4 **External failure cost**

The cost arising from inadequate quality discovered after the transfer of ownership from supplier to purchaser. Examples include:

- complaint investigation and processing
- warranty claims
- cost of lost sales
- product recalls.

Conformance costs and non-conformance costs

Appraisal and prevention costs may also be referred to as conformance costs, whilst internal and external failure costs may be referred to as non-conformance costs.

Test your understanding 8

Which of the following are examples of prevention costs of quality?

(i) Inspection of raw materials

(ii) Routine repairs and maintenance of machinery

(iii) Returns of faulty products

(iv) Training costs of operational staff

Options:

A (ii) and (iii) only

B (i) and (iv) only

C (ii) and (iv) only

D (i) and (iii) only

Test your understanding 9

Which of the following statements about costs of quality are correct?

(i) Conformance costs include prevention costs and appraisal cost

(ii) As a company invests in preventing errors, cost of conformance will increase, and cost of non-conformance will fall

(iii) Internal failure costs are costs of conformance

(iv) External failure costs arise before the product is shipped to the customer

Options:

A (i) and (ii) only

B (iii) and (iv) only

C (i) and (iv) only

D (ii) and (iii) only

Problems with non-financial performance indicators

The use of NFPI measures is now common place, but it is not without problems:

- Setting up and operating a system involving a wide range of performance indicators can be time-consuming and costly
- It can be a complex system that managers may find difficult to understand
- There is no clear set of NFPIs that the organisation must use – it will have to select those that seem to be most appropriate
- The scope for comparison with other organisations is limited as few businesses use precisely the same NFPIs as the organisation under review.

6 The balanced scorecard

To get an effective system of performance appraisal a business should use a combination of financial and non-financial measures.

One of the major developments in performance measurement techniques that have been widely adopted is the balanced scorecard.

The concept was developed by Kaplan and Norton in 1993 at Harvard. It is a device for planning that enables managers to set a range of targets linked with appropriate objectives and performance measures.

The four perspectives

The framework looks at the strategy and performance of an organisation from four points of view, known in the model as four perspectives:

- financial
- customer
- internal business process
- innovation and learning.

The approach is shown in the following diagram:

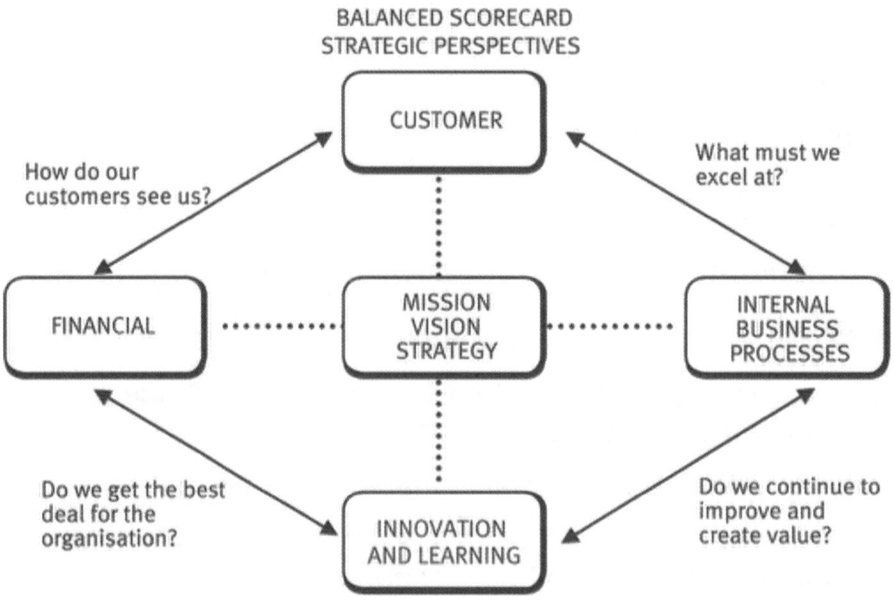

Financial perspective

This focuses on satisfying shareholder value.

Appropriate performance measures would include:

- return on capital employed
- return on shareholders' funds.

Customer perspective

This is an attempt to measure the customers view of the organisation by measuring customer satisfaction. Examples of relevant performance measures would include:

- customer satisfaction with timeliness
- customer loyalty.

Internal business process perspective (process efficiency)

This aims to measure the organisation's output in terms of technical excellence and consumer needs. Indicators here would include:

- unit costs
- quality measurement.

Innovation and learning perspective

This focuses on the need for continual improvement of existing products and techniques and developing new ones to meet customers' changing needs.

- A measure would include the percentage of revenue attributable to new products.

e.g

Illustration 9 – The balanced scorecard

For each perspective of the balanced scorecard, suggest and explain one performance measure that could be used by a company that provides a passenger transport service, e.g. a taxi company or a train company.

Customer perspective

Performance measure: percentage of services arriving on time

Reason for monitoring: on-time service is important to the customer

Internal business process perspective

Performance measure: percentage of time for which vehicles are unavailable due to breakdown, maintenance etc.

Reason for monitoring: maximising vehicle availability is important for achievement of service targets

Innovation and learning perspective

Performance measure: Training days per employee

Reason for monitoring: Need to keep employees updated with safety regulations, first aid and emergency procedures, etc.

Financial perspective

Performance measure: Operating profit per month

Reason for monitoring: Achievement of budgetary profit target

Note: other performance measures for each perspective would be equally acceptable.

Test your understanding 10

The following is Horn Ltd's statement of profit or loss for year ended 20X3, together with additional analysis of revenue and costs.

Horn Ltd

Statement of profit or loss for the year ended X3

	$m
Revenue	1.35
Cost of sales	0.83
Gross profit	0.52
Admin and distribution costs	0.15
Operating profit	0.37
Taxation	0.04
Profit after tax	0.33
Dividends	0.13
Profit for the period	0.20
Total assets less current liabilities	2.40

An analysis of revenue and costs show:

Revenue	$m
Existing products	1.03
New products	0.32
Sales to existing customers	0.82
Sales to new customers	0.53

Included in the cost structure is:	$m
Research and development	0.08
Training	0.14
Customer support costs	0.04
Quality assurance	0.03

Required:

Suggest and calculate 2 suitable indicators for each of the 4 balanced scorecard perspectives.

Advantages and disadvantages of the balanced scorecard

The model can be seen as an extension of the use of a range of performance indicators, including non-financial measures and a move away from the traditional over-reliance on profit based and other financial measures.

Advantages	Disadvantages
• uses four perspectives • less able to distort the performance measure • harder to hide bad performance • long term rather than short term • focuses on KPIs • KPIs can be changed as the business changes	• large numbers of calculations required • subjective • comparison with other businesses is not easy • arbitrary nature of arriving at the overall index of performance

Advantages and disadvantages of the Balanced Scorecard

The advantages of the approach include the following:

- It looks at performance from the point of view of the four perspectives outlined above, not just from the narrow view of the shareholders as traditional analysis would.
- Managers are unlikely to be able to distort the performance measure.
- Bad performance is more difficult to hide as more performance indicators are being measured.
- It should lead to the long-term success of the business rather than focusing on short-term improvements.
- It focuses on key performance indicators. The process of identifying these indicators can make senior managers question strategy and focus on the core elements of the business.
- As the core elements of the business change, the performance indicators can be changed accordingly. It is therefore a flexible measure.

The disadvantages of the model include the following:

- It can involve a large number of calculations which may make performance measurement time-consuming and costly to operate.
- The selection of performance indicators under each of the four perspectives is subjective.
- This in turn will make comparisons with the performance of other organisations difficult to achieve satisfactorily.
- The weighting used to arrive at an overall index of performance are arbitrary and may need to be arrived at by trial and error.

Test your understanding 11

Faster Pasta is an Italian fast food restaurant that specialises in high quality, moderately priced authentic Italian pasta dishes and pizzas. The restaurant has recently decided to implement a balanced scorecard approach and has established the following relevant goals for each perspective:

Perspective	**Goal**
Customer	• To increase the number of new and returning customers • To reduce the % of customer complaints
Internal business process	• To reduce the time taken between taking a customer's order and delivering the meal to the customer • To reduce staff turnover
Innovation and learning	• To increase the proportion of revenue from new dishes • To increase the % of staff time spent on training
Financial	• To increase spend per customer • To increase gross profit margin

The following information is also available for the year just ended and for the previous year.

	20X8	20X9
Total customers	11,600	12,000
– of which are new customers	4,400	4,750
– of which are existing customers	7,200	7,250
Customer complaints	464	840
Time between taking order and customer receiving meal	4 mins	13 mins
% staff turnover	12%	40%
% time staff spend training	5%	2%
Revenue	$110,000	$132,000
– revenue from new dishes	$22,000	$39,600
– revenue from existing dishes	$88,000	$92,400
Gross profit	$22,000	$30,360

Required:

Using appropriate measures, calculate and comment on whether or not Faster Pasta has achieved its goals.

7 Benchmarking

Benchmarking is a technique that is increasingly being adopted as a mechanism for continuous improvement.

Benchmarking is the establishment, through data gathering, of targets and comparators, that permit relative levels of performance (and particular areas of underperformance) to be identified. The adoption of identified best practices should improve performance.

It therefore requires organisations to:

- identify what they do and why they do it
- have knowledge of what the industry does and in particular what competitors do
- be fully committed to achieving best practice.

Any activity can be benchmarked and an organisation should focus on those:

- that are central to business strategy
- where significant improvement is required without increasing resources
- where staff are committed and eager for improvement.

The basic idea of benchmarking is that performance should be assessed through a comparison of the organisation's own products or services, performance and practices with 'best practice' elsewhere. The reasons for benchmarking may be summarised as:

- To receive an alarm call about the need for change
- Learning from others in order to improve performance
- Gaining a competitive edge (in the private sector)
- Improving services (in the public sector).

Types and levels of benchmarking

There are several types and levels of benchmarking, which are mainly defined by whom an organisation chooses to measure itself against.

These include:

Internal benchmarking. With internal benchmarking, other units or departments in the same organisation are used as the benchmark. This might be possible if the organisation is large and divided into a number of similar regional divisions. Internal benchmarking is also widely used within government. In the UK for example, there is a Public Sector Benchmarking Service that maintains a database of performance measures. Public sector organisations, such as fire stations and hospitals, can compare their own performance with the best in the country.

Competitive benchmarking. With competitive benchmarking, the most successful competitors are used as the benchmark. Competitors are unlikely to provide willingly any information for comparison, but it might be possible to observe competitor performance (for example, how quickly a competitor processes customer orders). A competitor's product might be dismantled in order to learn about its internal design and its performance: this technique of benchmarking is called reverse engineering.

Functional benchmarking. In functional benchmarking, comparisons are made with a similar function (for example selling, order handling, despatch) in other organisations that are not direct competitors. For example, a fast food restaurant operator might compare its buying function with buying in a supermarket chain.

Strategic benchmarking. Strategic benchmarking is a form of competitive benchmarking aimed at reaching decisions for strategic action and organisational change. Companies in the same industry might agree to join a collaborative benchmarking process, managed by an independent third party such as a trade organisation. With this type of benchmarking, each company in the scheme submits data about their performance to the scheme organiser. The organiser calculates average performance figures for the industry as a whole from the data supplied. Each participant in the scheme is then supplied with the industry average data, which it can use to assess its own performance.

The benchmarking process

The following steps are required in a systematic benchmarking exercise:

- planning
- analysis
- action
- review.

Planning includes selecting the activity to be benchmarked, involving fully the staff engaged with that activity and identifying the key stages of the activity relating to inputs, outputs and outcomes. It is important to establish the benchmark to a level of 'best practice'.

Analysis includes identifying the extent to which the organisation is under performing and to stimulate ideas as to how this can be met.

This may include whether new processes or methods are required. Implementation concerns the use of an action plan to achieve the improvement or the maintenance of the pre-determined standards. Management should ensure that resources are made available to meet the objectives set.

Action involves putting an appropriate plan into force in order to improve performance in the benchmarked areas.

Review includes monitoring progress against the plan and reviewing the appropriateness of the performance measure.

In practice, businesses establishing benchmarks will use a variety of information sources for their programmes. The most relevant and useful information would be that from a benchmarking partner. Such partnerships can be organised through trade associations and inter-firm comparison links.

All organisations can benefit with comparisons with others. Ideally, it should be judged against best practice wherever that may be found. Benchmarking analysis can provide such comparisons of the resources, competences in separate activities and overall competence of the organisation.

8 The service sector

Many of the basic principles will apply in service industries – CSFs, KPIs etc, but their application will require special attention if they are to be useful in assessing performance.

The service sector of the economy

In many western economies one of the major changes that has taken place in recent years has been a change in the structure of those economies – the manufacturing sector has declined in size and significance and the service sector has grown in importance. The service sector consists of banks, airlines, transport companies, accountancy and consultancy firms and service shops.

We shall consider two main aspects of performance in relation to service organisations:

- financial performance
- service quality. Quality is seen to be a particularly important nonfinancial performance indicator in the service sector.

Financial performance

Conventional financial analysis distinguishes four types of ratio: profitability, liquidity, gearing and activity ratios. Analysis of a company's performance using accounting ratios involves comparisons with past trends and/or competitors' ratios. Typical ratios that could be used by a service organisation include:

- revenue per 'service'
- revenue per 'principal' or partner in, for example, a management consultancy
- staff costs as a % of revenue
- space costs as a % of revenue
- training costs as a % of revenue
- profit %
- current ratio
- quick asset ratio
- market share
- market share increase year by year.

Financial ratio analysis is of use but due to the 'human' nature of a service provider – the quality of the service also needs to be considered.

e.g

Illustration 10 – Service sector examples

Barclays Bank plc (a major UK based banking group)

Barclays Bank has split its business between individuals, corporate and retail customers. The bank has many products and services, most of which are variants on borrowing or lending, whose profitability is tied to borrowing and lending rates as affected by transactions with the Bank of England and government economic policy. Individual retail customers can make use of a mix of these services – albeit in most cases a limited sample of the total range – via several possible 'service delivery processes': by post, telephone, automatic teller machines (ATMs), cashiers or the branch manager. Whilst the gross margins of individual services are known, no attempt is made to trace costs, even labour costs, to them.

> **Commonwealth Hotels**
>
> Each hotel has a general manager and a number of responsibility centres: rooms, food, bar, reception (including telephones) and marketing. Individual customers can use any mix of these services. Here gross margins (after deducting all direct costs) are known, but indirect costs are not allocated to the responsibility centres. The management team is rewarded by a bonus system related to the hotel's total profit.

Service quality

BAA plc

BAA (British Airports Authority) is a large company which operates many of the UK's major airports. The company uses regular customer surveys for measuring customer perceptions of a wide variety of service quality attributes, including, for example, the cleanliness of its facilities, the helpfulness of its staff and the ease of finding one's way around the airport.

The quality measure and the mechanisms used to gather information will depend on the 'quality issue'.

Quality	Measures	Mechanisms
Access	Walking distance/ease of finding way around	Surveys operational data
Aesthetics	Staff appearance/airport appearance, quality of catering	Surveys inspection
Availability	Equipment availability	Internal fault monitors
Cleanliness	Environment and equipment	Surveys/inspection
Comfort	How crowded it is	Surveys/inspection
Communication	Information clarity/clarity of labelling and pricing	Surveys/inspection
Competence	Staff efficiency	Management Inspection
Courtesy	Courtesy of staff	Surveys/inspection
Friendliness	Staff attitude	Surveys/inspection
Reliability	Equipment faults	Surveys/inspection
Responsiveness	Staff responsiveness	Surveys/inspection
Security	Efficiency of security checks/number of urgent safety reports	Surveys/internal data

Internal quality measurement

Inspection and monitoring of the inputs to the service process is important for all organisations. The quality of the solicitors in a practice or the number and grades of staff available in a consultancy organisation are crucial to the provision of service quality. BAA monitors the availability and condition of equipment and facilities.

Many service companies use internal mechanisms to measure service quality during the process of service delivery. BAA has advanced systems to monitor equipment faults and the terminal managers are expected to report any problems they see.

The quality of the service may be measured after the event, that is by measuring the results by outputs of the service.

9 Non-profit seeking and public sector organisations

There are said to be two main problems involved in assessing performance of these organisations:

- the problem of identifying and measuring objectives
- the problem of identifying and measuring outputs.

Objectives

One of the issues in performance evaluation, in any sector, is defining organisational objectives. Once that is done, performance indicators can be devised that indicate the extent to which such objectives have been achieved.

In non-profit seeking organisations the objectives may be much more varied, reflecting the variety of organisations included in the sector:

- charities
- professional institutions
- educational establishments
- government bodies.

Although the detail will vary depending on the organisation involved, we could suggest that the general objective of non-profit seeking organisations is to provide the best possible service within a limited resource budget:

- **Charities** will have a limited amount of funds available – they will seek to use these funds to provide services to as many of their beneficiaries as possible. It will be important not to waste money or any other resources.
- A central **government department** (health or education for example) or a local authority typically has a limited amount of finance available. Its objective will be to provide the best possible service to the community with the financial constraints imposed upon it.

The problems of output measurement

Outputs of organisations in these sectors are often not valued in a money terms. How do we measure the output of a school or hospital?

Output targets can be set in these situations, but they will always be open to debate and argument.

e.g

Illustration 11 – Schools

In the UK, the Government sets targets for schools in the form of examination pass rates/grades – a form of output for the school. League tables are then published but:

There are many people who argue that the output of a school cannot be measured by examination results. They argue the output is a wider concept than this – and one which is not so easily measured – the concept of value added education. This would look at the improvement in knowledge and ability of pupils over their life at the school. But how do we measure this?

Comparing schools performance by publishing league tables of examination results is also open to question. It is of course an attempt to carry out comparative analysis of performance – one school against another. But, many people make the point that the tables do not compare like with like. Different schools have children from different social backgrounds, which may be reflected in examination results.

Value for Money (VFM)

The value for money (VFM) concept has been developed as a useful means of assessing performance in an organisation which is not seeking profit.

VFM concept revolves around the 3Es, as follows:

- **Economy** (an input measure) – measures the relationship between money spent and the inputs. Are the resources used the cheapest possible for the quality required?
- **Efficiency** (link inputs with outputs) – is the maximum output being achieved from the resources used?
- **Effectiveness** (links outputs with objectives) – to what extent the outputs generated achieve the objectives of the organisation.

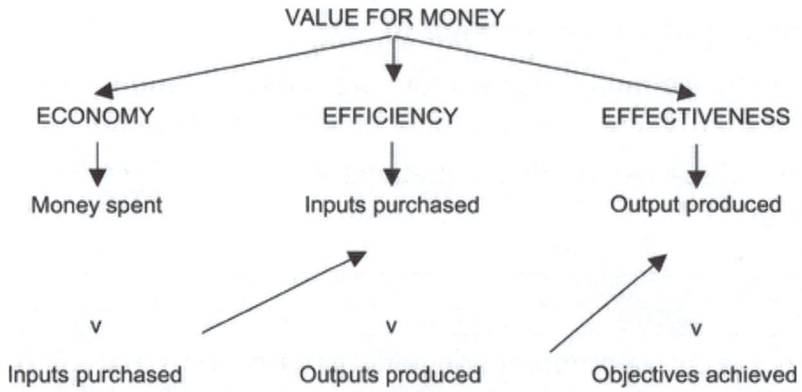

If you follow through the diagram, you will see that, ultimately, VFM relates money spent to objectives achieved.

You should note that VFM still focuses on financial performance. Non-profit seeking organisations will also need to consider non-financial performance, particularly quality.

Value for money

The non-profit sector incorporates a diverse range of operations including national government, local government, charities, executive agencies, trusts and so on. The critical thing about such operations is that they are not motivated by a desire to maximise profit.

Many, if not all, of the benefits arising from expenditure by these bodies are non-quantifiable (certainly not in monetary terms, e.g. social welfare). The same can be true of costs. So any cost/benefit analysis is necessarily quite judgemental, i.e. social benefits versus social costs as well as financial benefits versus financial costs. The danger is that if benefits cannot be quantified, then they might be ignored.

Another problem is that these organisations often do not generate revenue but simply have a fixed budget for spending within which they have to keep. Value for money is often quoted as an objective here but it does not get round the problem of measuring 'value'.

Illustration 12 – Value for money

Value for money in a university would comprise the three element of:

Economy – this is about balancing the cost with the quality of the resources. Therefore, it will review areas such as the cost of books, computers and teaching compared with the quality of these resources. It recognises that the organisation must consider its expenditure but should not simply aim to minimise costs. e.g. low cost but poor quality teaching or books will hinder student performance and will damage the reputation of the university.

Efficiency – this focuses on the efficient use of any resources acquired. For example:

- How often are the library books that are bought by the university taken out on loan by students?
- What is the utilisation of IT resources?
- What amount of their working time do lecturers spend teaching or researching?

Effectiveness – this measures the achievement of the organisation's objectives. For example:

- The number of students achieving a target grade.
- The number of graduates who find full time employment within 6 months of graduating.

The 3E's

Below are the calculations for economy, efficiency and effectiveness:

1 **Economy**

$$\frac{\text{Standard input}}{\text{Actual input}} \times 100$$

2 **Efficiency**

$$\frac{\text{Actual output}}{\text{Actual input}} \times 100$$

3 **Effectiveness**

$$\frac{\text{Actual output}}{\text{Standard output}} \times 100$$

e.g

Illustration 13 – Examples of performance measures using the 3Es

Hospitals

1 **Economy**

Comparing the standard cost of drugs used in treatments with the actual cost of drugs.

2 **Efficiency**

Comparing the number of beds in use in a ward with the number of beds available in the ward.

3 **Effectiveness**

Comparing the current waiting time for patients with the desired waiting time for patients.

A College

1 **Economy**

Comparing the standard cost of tutors with the actual cost of the tutors.

2 **Efficiency**

Comparing actual tutor utilisation in hours with planned tutor utilisation in hours.

3 **Effectiveness**

Comparing actual exam results (% over a certain grade or percentage passes) with desired exam results.

Test your understanding 12

St Alice's Hospice is a charity which collects funds and donations and utilises these in the care of terminally ill patients. The governing body has set the manager three performance objectives for the three months to 30 June 20X7:

- to achieve a level of donations of $150,000 over the 3 month period
- to keep administration costs to no more than 8% of donations per month
- to achieve 80% of respite care requested from the community. Actual results were as follows:

	April	May	June
Donations($)	35,000	65,000	55,000
Administration costs ($)	2,450	5,850	4,400
Respite care requests (days)	560	570	600
Respite care provided (days)	392	430	510

Required:

Calculate appropriate performance measures to evaluate the managers performance.

Test your understanding 13

A government is looking at assessing state schools by reference to a range of both financial and non-financial factors, one of which is average class sizes.

Which of the three E's best describes the above measure?

A Economy

B Effectiveness

C Efficiency

D Externality

Test your understanding 14

A government is looking at assessing the performance of teachers in a state school by reference to a range of both financial and non-financial factors, one of which is pass rates.

Which of the three E's best describes the above measure?

A Economy

B Effectiveness

C Efficiency

D Externality

10 Cost control and cost reduction

Cost control

Cost control involves the setting of targets for cost centre managers and then monitoring performance against those targets.

Performance can be measured using standard costing and variance analysis.

Cost reduction

Cost reduction is the reduction in unit cost of goods or services without impairing suitability for the use intended i.e. without reducing value to the customer.

Cost reduction has rather negative connotations. It is perceived as being about cutting back, about saving money, even about penny pinching. Profit improvement is about accepting the possibility that costs may go up but because they add further value to the product, and make the product more attractive to the customer, profit goes up even further.

Note the important point here – any reduction in cost should not be seen as a reduction in value in the eyes of the consumer.

Cost reduction techniques

A number of techniques are widely used as a means of attempting to achieve cost reduction, particularly in manufacturing organisations.

Value analysis

Value analysis is a systematic examination of factors affecting the cost of a product or service, in order to devise means of achieving the specified purpose most economically at the required standard of quality and reliability.

Value analysis is a method of improving profitability by reducing costs without necessarily increasing prices; it is particularly useful to manufacturers or suppliers who are unable to fix their own price because of, for example, a competitive market. However it can be used in all circumstances to try to improve profitability.

Value analysis resulted from a realisation by manufacturers that they were incorporating features into their product which the user of the product did not require and was not prepared to pay for. For example, for a car manufacturer are customers really willing to pay for upholstery or trim which is relatively expensive for the manufacturer to buy? If customers would pay the same price for a car produced with slightly cheaper trim, the company could modify the specification.

Value analysis takes a critical look at each feature of a product, questioning its need and its use, and eliminating any unjustifiable features.

One of the problems with value analysis is placing a meaning on the word 'value'.

It is useful to distinguish two types of value:

- **Utility value** is the value an item has because of the uses to which it can be put.
- **Esteem value** is the value put on an item because of its beauty, craftsmanship, etc.

An individual who wants a basic, functional car to get from A to B will be considering utility value of the car and will not be too concerned with its colour, image or top speed. Other individuals may be looking more at the esteem value of a car than its utility value. They will be concerned about the image of the car, its design, its specification and so on.

The value analysis method

Value analysis can be carried out in five key steps:

Step 1 Establish the precise requirements of the customer. By a process of enquiry it should be possible to discover precisely why customers want an item, whether the item has any esteem value, etc. Only in this way can the manufacturer be certain that each function incorporated into the product contributes some value to it.

Step 2 Establish and evaluate alternative ways of achieving the requirements of the customers. There may be methods of producing the item which have not been considered e.g. replacing metal panels with plastic. Each alternative method must be costed out in units of:

(i) Materials – amount required, acceptable level of wastage (can it be improved?), alternative, cheaper materials.

(ii) Labour – can the cost be reduced by eliminating operations or changing production methods?

(iii) Other factors – can new, cheaper processes be found? Would a cheaper finish be acceptable?

Step 3 Authorise any proposals put forward as a result of step 2. The assessment in step 2 may be carried out by middle management and, if so, it will require ratification by top management before implementation.

Step 4 Implementation of proposals.

Step 5 Evaluate feedback from new proposals to establish the benefits from the change.

Several benefits will result from value analysis;

- many customers will be impressed by the interest shown in their requirements and this will lead to increased sales
- a firm which adopts this approach is likely to attract better staff, due both to the prospects for an outlet for their ideas and the higher morale resulting from the team approach
- there are economic and financial benefits arising from the elimination of unnecessary complexity and the better use of resources.

Value engineering

A useful principle which can be employed in a target costing context is that of value engineering. It takes the approach of value analysis right back to the design stage of the business process.

Value engineering attempts to design the best possible value at the lowest possible cost into a new product. This cost can then be used in a target costing system.

Work Study

Work study is a systematic examination of the methods of carrying out activities in order to improve the effective use of resources and to set up standards of performance for the activities carried out.

Work study is the body of knowledge concerned with the analysis of the work methods and the equipment used in performing a job, the design of an optimum work method and the standardisation of proposed work methods.

There are two areas of work study:

- **Method study** – the analysis of current and new work methods to enable more effective techniques to be used and to reduce costs.
- **Work measurement** – identifying the time it should take to complete a specific task by an experienced and qualified member of staff.

Objectives of work study

1 To analyse the present method of doing a job, systematically in order to develop a new and better method.

2 To measure the work content of a job by measuring the time required to do the job for a qualified worker and hence to establish standard time.

3 To increase the productivity by ensuring the best possible use of human, machine and material resources and to achieve best quality product/service at minimum possible cost.

4 To improve operational efficiency.

Other cost reduction techniques

Standardisation of materials and components

This relates to a policy of reducing, so far as is possible, the range and variety of materials and components purchased by the manufacturer and of components produced. If the manufacturer is producing a number of models of the product, it is often possible for one component to be used throughout the range. For example, where there is a series of car models it may be possible to use one type of door handle on all models.

The advantages of such a policy are:

(i) the manufacturer can buy, or make, large quantities, gaining the benefit of reduced unit cost

(ii) having proved the efficiency of a material or component, the manufacturer knows that the quality and content will not change

(iii) because of the reduction in variety, inventory control will be easier

(iv) better service can be provided to customers in the provision of spare parts

(v) less time will be needed to train operatives who handle the component.

The possible disadvantages are:

(i) if there is only one supplier of the material or component, the manufacturer will be at risk if supplies are interrupted

(ii) there may be restrictions on the design of a new model if the manufacturer wishes to continue the policy for economic reasons

(iii) for the same motive, a standard component may be used in one model when it would be better technically if a special component was used.

As an example, many of the major car manufacturers now design vehicles in such a way as to ensure that as many components as possible are common to as wide a range of models as possible.

Standardisation of product

This refers to the production of articles to the same standard, or a range of products each of which is standardised.

The advantages are as follows:

(i) the manufacturer derives the benefit of long runs of production with reduced unit cost

(ii) tooling is simpler because it is geared to one method of production

(iii) because of the uniformity of the production method, mechanisation can be extensive

(iv) the consequent buying of large amounts of the same materials and parts results in a reduction of unit cost

(v) production management is simpler, being confined to standard processes

(vi) less training of operatives is required because the processes do not change

(vii) there are fewer demands on the design staff

(viii) inspection costs are low

(ix) customers know they are buying a proven product and that the quality will not change.

A range of products may be basically standardised but with minor differences between models. Again, using the car industry as an example, a particular model of a car may be available in, say, 20 different colours – but apart from this all of the cars are identical.

The policy can produce disadvantages, such as the following:

(i) The manufacturer may feel safe in doing what he/she knows best and may become complacent about the success of the product, so that when the product faces new competition or the public becomes disloyal, he/she is too slow to recognise it.

(ii) If the product has to be altered because of the above circumstances, then equipment, technical knowledge and managerial experience may be too fixed to adapt successfully.

(iii) If production is continued to a level beyond the reduced demand and that demand does not rise, there will be surplus components, materials and finished goods.

Using a cost reduction team

A cost reduction team can be used to identify scope for achieving cost reductions but care must be taken so that costs saved are not outweighed by the costs of the team itself. A well-defined programme must be instituted so that the cost reduction teams spend their time in fields where there is scope for savings. Furthermore, it is important that a fixed time is allocated to a particular exercise. There may well be a request to continue the exercise in order to complete the study and obtain extra savings, but these may be quite marginal, and the law of diminishing returns will begin to operate. A cost/benefit approach to a cost reduction programme is essential.

Another aspect is the time and trouble taken by line management to accommodate changes brought about by a cost reduction scheme.

Departments and whole functions must be given time to adjust and consolidate agreed changes. A permanent state of change may harm morale and upset the proper working of departments. It is important to recognise that cost reduction implies a specific programme aimed at reducing costs at a given time. The concept does not relate to a continuous situation; it should have a definite start and finish and should incorporate well-defined targets. The activity of cost control is a continuous function of management.

11 Performance measurement reports

General criteria may be laid down for such reports:

(a) Reports should be **relevant** to the information needs of their recipients. They should highlight key areas for management attention. This means that the report should contain all relevant information to the decisions to be made, and responsibilities exercised by the manager who receives the report. Generally, other information should be excluded although there is an argument for including background information on divisional/company performance.

(b) Reporting should be linked to **responsibility**.

(c) Reports should be **timely**. One of the most frequent reporting problems is that reports are received after the decision for which they are required. In such cases managers must often rely on informal information sources outside the budget system. This may be less efficient and also reduces the credibility of the budgetary control system in the eyes of that manager.

(d) Reports should be **reliable**. The reports should be regarded as containing reliable information (though not necessarily exact to the penny). There may be a conflict between reliability and timeliness, and often an assessment must be made of what is an acceptable error rate and/or degree of approximation.

(e) Reports should be designed to **communicate effectively**, often with managers who are not professional accountants. Reports should avoid jargon, be concise, but contain sufficient detail (often in supporting schedules). Maximum use should be made of graphical presentation.

(f) Reports should be **cost-effective**. A report is only worthwhile if the benefits from its existence exceed the cost of producing it.

(g) Reports should include any **recommendations** for improvement.

12 Chapter summary

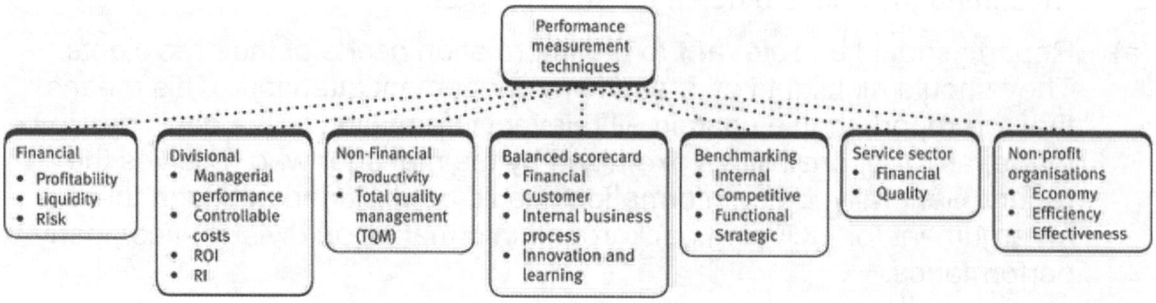

Test your understanding answers

Test your understanding 1

Profitability ratios

	20X9	**20X8**
Gross profit margin = gross profit ÷ revenue (%)	31.50%	33.69%
Operating profit margin = operating profit ÷ revenue (%)	6.18%	7.49%
ROCE = operating profit ÷ CE (%)	9.82%	10.03%
Asset turnover = revenue ÷ CE	1.59	1.34

Note: Revenue = total production cost + gross profit 9,544,000 7,664,000

Comment

Overall, profitability has deteriorated slightly year on year.

Gross profit margin – Despite an increase in revenue of 24.6%, the gross margin has fallen by over 2% to 31.5%. Although revenue has shown a significant increase, the production costs have increased at a faster rate of 28.7% year on year. The falling gross margin may indicate that the company is unable to achieve the same level of sales prices as it was in 20X8 or is not as efficient at controlling its production costs.

Operating profit margin – Again, despite an increase in revenue of 24.6%, the OPM has fallen from 7.49% to 6.18%. The falling return may indicate that the company is unable to achieve the same level of sales prices as it was in 20X8 or is not as efficient at controlling all of its costs.

Asset turnover – this has actually shown a small improvement year on year from 1.34 in 20X8 to 1.59 in 20X9. This shows that the company is getting better at generating revenue from the capital employed within the business.

ROCE – Despite the improvement in asset turnover, the ROCE has actually fallen slightly from 10.03% in 20X8 to 9.83% in 20X9. This means that the company is not as good at generating profit from its capital employed. The decrease in the ROCE is due to the fall in the profit margin.

It would be useful to obtain a further breakdown of revenue and costs, in order to fully understand the reasons for the changes and to prevent any further decline in the ratios discussed. It would also be useful to obtain the average ratios for the industry in order to gauge Super Soups performance against that of its competitors.

Test your understanding 2

Current ratio	(147.9 + 393.4 + 53.8 + 6.2)/ (275.1 + 284.3) = 601.3/559.4	= 1.07
Quick ratio	(601.3 – 147.9)/559.4	= 0.81
Receivables collection period (days)	393.4/1,867.5 × 365	= 77 days
Inventory holding period (days)	147.9/(1,867.5 – 489.3) × 365	= 39 days
Payables payment period (days)	275.1/(1,867.5 – 489.3) × 365	= 73 days

Test your understanding 3

D

Division	**A**	**B**	**C**	**D**
	$000	$000	$000	$000
Profit	250	400	320	80
Net assets	1,300	2,500	1,600	320
ROI	19%	16%	20%	25%

Test your understanding 4

If performance is measured by RI, the RI for the period is:

	$
Operating profit	160,000
Notional interest (12% × $800,000)	96,000
RI	64,000

(**Note:** Capital employed is not available in this question and therefore net assets should be used as a substitute value).

Investment centre managers who make investment decisions on the basis of short-term performance will want to undertake any investments that add to RI, i.e. if the RI is positive.

Test your understanding 5

C

RI = Controllable profit – Notional interest on capital

$280,000 = $740,000 – (10% × invested capital)

$740,000 – $280,000 = 10% × invested capital

$460,000 = 10% of the capital invested

Capital invested = $460,000/10 × 100 = $4,600,000

ROI = Controllable profit/controllable capital employed × 100

ROI = $740,000/$4,600,000 × 100

ROI = 16%

Test your understanding 6

B

The manager of a profit centre can exercise control over revenues and controllable costs, but has no influence concerning the capital invested in the centre.

Contribution (i) would be a useful performance measure because a profit centre manager can exercise control over sales revenue and variable costs. Controllable profit (ii) would also be useful as long as any overhead costs charged in deriving the profit figure are controllable by the profit centre manager. Apportioned central costs would not be deducted when calculating controllable profit. Return on investment (iii), and residual income (iv) would not be useful because they require a measure of the capital invested in the division.

Test your understanding 7

Output per standard hour is 2 units as each unit has a standard time allowance of 30 minutes.

Budgeted labour hours are 1,500/2 = 750

The actual output measured in standard hours is 1,400/2 = 700 standard hours

The production/volume ratio = 700/750 × 100% = 93.3%

The capacity ratio = 720/750 × 100% = 96%

The efficiency ratio = 700/720 × 100% = 97.2%

Production is 6.7% less than planned. This is due to a shortfall in capacity available of 4% and lower productivity of 2.8%.

Test your understanding 8

C

Prevention costs are those incurred in order to prevent poor quality.

Inspection of raw materials is an appraisal cost.

Returns from customers are an external failure cost.

Test your understanding 9

A

Internal failure costs are costs of non-conformance.

External failure costs arise after the goods have been sent to the customer.

Test your understanding 10

Balanced scorecard

Potential Horn Ltd performance indicators

- **Financial perspective**

  Return on capital employed = 0.37/2.40 × 100 = 15.42%

  Operating profit margin = 0.37/1.35 × 100 = 27.41%

- **Customer perspective**

  Customer support as % of revenue = 0.04/1.35 × 100 = 2.96%

  % of business from existing customers = 0.82/1.35 × 100 = 60.74%

- **Innovation and learning perspective**

  Training costs as % of total costs = 0.14/(0.15 + 0.83) × 100 = 14.29%

  % of revenue from new products = 0.32/1.35 × 100 = 23.70%

- **Internal business process perspective**

  Quality assurance % of revenue = 0.03/1.35 × 100 = 2.22%

  Admin and distribution costs % of revenue = 0.15/1.35 × 100 = 11.11%

This list is not exhaustive – there will other indicators that Horn Ltd could calculate for each of the four perspectives.

To be useful these performance indicators would need to be compared with benchmarked or target levels for the current period and undergo analysis with previous years.

Test your understanding 11

Customer perspective

Goal: To increase the number of new and returning customers

Measure: The number of new customers has increased year on year from 4,400 to 4,750. This is an 8.0% increase. The number of returning customers has also increased slightly from 7,200 to 7,250, i.e. a 1.0% increase.

Comment: The company has achieved its goal of increasing the number of new and existing customers. It is worth noting that the proportion of customers who are returning customers has fallen slightly from 62.1% to 60.4% of the total customers. This could indicate a small drop in the level of customer satisfaction.

Goal: To decrease the % customer complaints

Measure: The percentage of customer complaints has increased from 4% (464 ÷ 11,600) to 7% (840 ÷ 12,000).

Comment: Faster Pasta should investigate the reasons for the increase in customer complaints and take the required action immediately in order to ensure that it can meet this goal in the future.

Internal business process perspective

Goal: To reduce the time taken between taking the customer's order and delivering the meal to the customer

Measure: The time taken has more than tripled from an average of 4 minutes in 20X8 to an average of 13 minutes in 20X9.**Comment:** Customers may place a high value on the fast delivery of their food. The increase in time may be linked to the increased number of customer complaints. If this continues customer satisfaction, and therefore profitability, will suffer in the long-term. The restaurant should take steps now in order to ensure that this goal is achieved going forward.

Goal: To reduce staff turnover

Measure: This has risen significantly from 12% to 40% and hence the business has not achieved its goal.

Comment: The reasons for the high staff turnover should be investigated immediately. This may be contributing to longer waiting times and the increase in customer complaints. This will impact long-term profitability.

Innovation and learning perspective

Goal: To increase the proportion of revenue from new dishes

Measure: This has increased year on year from 20% ($22,000 ÷ $110,000) in 20X8 to 30% ($39,600 ÷ $132,000) in 20X9. Therefore, the restaurant has achieved its goal.

Comment: This is a favourable increase and may have a positive impact on long-term profitability if the new products meet the needs of the customers.

Goal: To increase the % of staff time spent on training

Measure: This has fallen significantly from 5% to only 2% and hence the company is not achieving its goal.

Comment: Staff may be unsatisfied if they feel that their training needs are not being met. This may contribute to a high staff turnover. In addition, staff may not have the skills to do the job well and this would impact the level of customer satisfaction.

Financial perspective

Goal: to increase spend per customer

Measure: Spend per customer has increased from $9.48 ($110,000 ÷ 11,600) to $11.00 ($132,000 ÷ 12,000), i.e. a 16.0% increase.

Comment: This is a favourable increase. However, the issues discussed above must be addressed in order to ensure that this trend continues.

Goal: To increase gross profit margin

Measure: The gross profit margin has increased year on year from 20% ($22,000 ÷ $110,000) to 23% ($30,360 ÷ $132,000).

Comment: This is a favourable increase. However, the issues discussed above must be addressed in order to ensure that this trend continues.

Test your understanding 12

	April	May	June
Administration costs as a % of donations	7%	9%	8%
Respite care provided	70%	75.4%	85%

Total donations of $155,000 have been received which exceeds the target for the period. Administration costs have been within the target of 8% in April and June but exceeded the target in May.

There has been a steady improvement in the level of respite care provided and in June the target was exceeded.

Test your understanding 13

C

Class sizes are the result of the number of pupils educated (output), the number of teachers employed (input) and how well the timetable is organised in using those teachers. Therefore this is a measure of efficiency.

Test your understanding 14

B

Pass rates (objective) are the result of how well the teachers educate the pupils (output). Therefore this is a measure of effectiveness.

Chapter

17

Presenting information

Chapter learning objectives

Upon completion of this chapter you will be able to:

- prepare written reports representing management information in suitable formats according to purpose
- use data visualisation to present information using tables, charts and graphs (bar charts, line graphs, pie charts and scatter graphs)
- construct scatter diagrams and lines of best fit
- interpret information (including the tables, charts and graphs) presented in management reports.

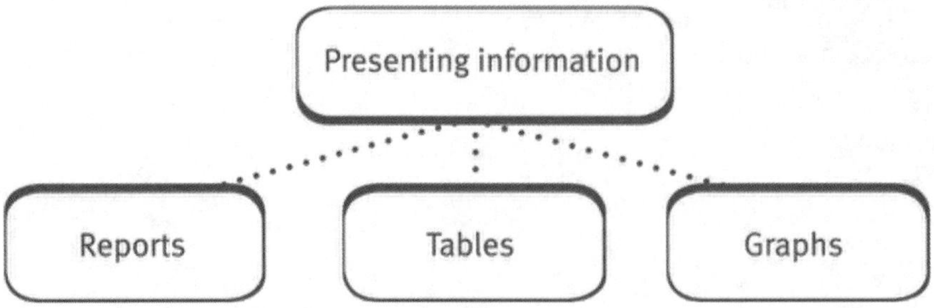

1 Writing reports

The four-stage approach to report writing

When producing written reports, the management accountant needs to carry out four steps.

Prepare

- determine the type of document required: detailed report, short memo, discussion notes, etc.
- establish the user of the information: the type of language used and the level of knowledge assumed will be largely determined by the end user.
- find out what the report will be used for: the report will often be aimed at providing information to help management make a decision.

Plan

- select the relevant data: summarise, analyse, illustrate (if appropriate) to turn the raw data into useful information. This will often involve the use of management accounting techniques.
- produce a logical order for the material.

Write

- determine the writing style that is appropriate.
- take care over spelling, use of language and arithmetic – your meaning must be clear and logical.

Review

- re-read what you have written.
- check that it meets the requirements of the document.
- ensure that it is complete and clear.

The structure of a report

A typical report structure will be as follows:

- **Title** – At the top of your report show who the report is to, who it is from, the date and a heading.
- **Introduction** – showing what information was requested, the work done and where results and conclusions can be found.
- **Analysis** – presenting the information required in a series of subsections.
- **Conclusion** – including, where appropriate, recommendations. Never introduce new material into a conclusion.
- **Appendices** – containing detailed calculations, tables of underlying data, etc. If you use appendices refer to them in your report.

Numbered headings and cross referencing between sections make reports easier to follow (or navigate).

Use of English

English is technically a complicated language – if you try to write lengthy complex sentences or paragraphs, it may go wrong.

The single most important point is to make sure that the reader can understand what you are saying.

Some specific guidelines are:

- avoid excessively long sentences
- avoid over-long words
- do not use jargon, clichés, metaphors – the aim is to communicate in a professional manner
- if acronyms (e.g. ACCA) are used – they should be explained the first time they are introduced into the report
- take care with punctuation and grammar to make sure your ideas are communicated clearly.

2 Tables

Tabulation is the process of presenting data in the form of a table – an arrangement of rows and columns.

The purpose of tabulation is to summarise the information and present it in a more understandable way.

Rules of tabulation

The following rules or principles of tabulation should be considered when preparing tables:

(a) Title: the table must have a clear and self-explanatory title.

(b) Source: the source of the material used in drawing up the table should be stated (usually by way of a footnote).

(c) Units: the units of measurement that have been used must be stated e.g. 000s means that the units are in thousands.

(d) Headings: all column and row headings should be clear and concise.

(e) Totals: these should be shown where appropriate, and also any subtotals that may be applicable to the calculations.

(f) Percentages and ratios: these should be shown, if meaningful, with an indication of how they were calculated.

Columns and rows

A table is set up in the form of a number of columns headed up across the page and then a number of rows of information moving down the page. A typical table would be set up as follows:

	Column 1	**Column 2**	**Column 3**
Row 1			
Row 2			
Row 3			

A key element of setting up a good table is to decide upon the optimal arrangement of columns and rows.

Three general rules apply here:

1 Try to ensure that the table fits on one page.

2 The columns should be arranged so that related information is shown alongside each other.

3 The information shown in the rows should be arranged so that there is a logical progression through the information and any meaningful totals or subtotals can be clearly made.

3 Graphs and charts

Data visualisation

The major theme underlying management accounting is information. The processes involved in collecting that information has been dealt with in previous chapters – this can be seen as the input into the management accounting process.

One of the desirable qualities of information is that it should be understandable to the user. Management accountants have been criticised in the past for presenting information in a form which is unclear to the non-expert. Very often, graphical methods of presentation are clearer to the user than written or numerical presentation.

The provision of information to help support the efficient and effective running of all functions within a business and the business overall is the fundamental purpose of the finance function.

Key benefits of data visualisation include:

- Accessibility – traditional spreadsheets and financial reports can be both difficult to understand and unappealing to look at. Modern data visualisation graphics and dashboards are designed to be user friendly and intuitive.
- Real-time synchronising – real time data with data visualisation tools gives live up-to-date numbers in a clear, informative style. This allows a quicker response to business changes rather than waiting for weekly or monthly reports.
- Performance optimisation – the immediacy and clarity of the information being displayed supports better decision-making and proactive, efficient utilisation of resources as problems are identified promptly.
- Insight and understanding – combining data and visualising it in a new way can lead to improved understanding and fresh insights about the cause and effect relationships that underpin performance.

e.g

Illustration 1 – Visualisation

Key performance indicators (KPIs) are a set of metrics used by a business to monitor performance in areas where things must go according to plan for the business to be successful. These critical areas must first be identified, and then suitable metrics established to monitor performance, before finally setting targets for the desired performance.

Companies are increasingly using dashboards (a collection of key infographics displayed together) to display KPIs to staff in real time and to flag areas requiring improvement in order to hit the pre-determined targets and drive success. This instant feedback allows for action to be taken quickly to highlight and fix potential problems.

For instance, an IT service desk within a business will use KPI dashboards to monitor and display performance for all staff and the department as a whole.

Metrics such as the number of support tickets logged, time taken to open support tickets, time taken to resolve support tickets and customer satisfaction would all be displayed clearly using graphics.

If performance in any of the areas is falling below target levels the graphics will clearly display this, prompting action to resolve the poor performance.

In the majority of businesses, graphs and charts are very important parts of presentations, reports, and website pages. They also play a key role in monitoring profits and investigating business opportunities. Bar charts and column graphs seem to be used the most; however pie charts and line graphs are also encountered.

Graphs are extremely important in sales, marketing and finance. The sales team will use graphs extensively to monitor and analyse sales into volume sold over time or to compare the sales of different products. Placing information into a graph can clearly reveal where the most money is coming from, what products are selling well and what products are not making enough money. Businesses also aim to make a profit and different types of graphs can clearly display profits and losses.

A graph or chart should be clear and unambiguous. In order to help to achieve this aim a number of rules should be followed:

- give each graph or chart a name or a title
- state the source of any data that has been used
- state the units of measurement that have been used
- give a scale so that the graph or chart can be properly interpreted
- ensure that the presentation is neat
- use a key to explain the contents
- if axes are used, they should be properly labelled.

These guidelines are similar to those suggested above for the construction of tables.

The types of graphs and charts which are covered in your syllabus are:

- bar charts
- line graphs
- scatter graphs
- pie charts.

Bar charts

Bar charts are a type of graph that are used to display and compare the number, frequency or other measure, for different discrete categories of data. Bar charts are one of the most commonly used types of graph because they are simple to create and very easy to interpret. They are also a flexible chart type and there are several variations of the standard or simple bar chart that can be used to illustrate data in different ways:

- component (or stacked) bar charts
- percentage component bar charts
- compound (or multiple) bar charts.

Bar charts are useful for displaying data that are classified into categories.

Nominal data are categorised according to descriptive or qualitative information such as type of product, geographical area or business type.

Ordinal data are similar but the different categories can also be ranked, for example in a survey people may be asked to rank a product or service between 1 and 5, with 1 being very poor and 5 being excellent.

Bar charts are also useful for displaying data that include categories with negative values, because it is possible to position the bars below and above the x-axis.

The chart is constructed such that the lengths of the different bars are proportional to the size of the category they represent. The x-axis represents the different categories and so has no scale. In order to emphasise the fact that the categories are discrete, a gap is left between the bars on the x-axis. The y-axis does have a scale and this indicates the units of measurement.

Simple bar charts

A simple bar chart is where only one variable is being illustrated. The bars on a simple bar chart should be of equal widths as the height or length of the bar represents the 'value' of the variable.

The simple bar graph below shows sales units (data) per product (category).

Component bar chart

A component bar chart is a bar chart which shows information about different sub-groups of the main categories. For example the total product sales figures can be broken down into each area or sector of the business that has achieved the sales. It is still possible to interpret the total sales from the graph but it is now also possible to see the sales from each area. This would allow managers to analyse the progress of sales in each area.

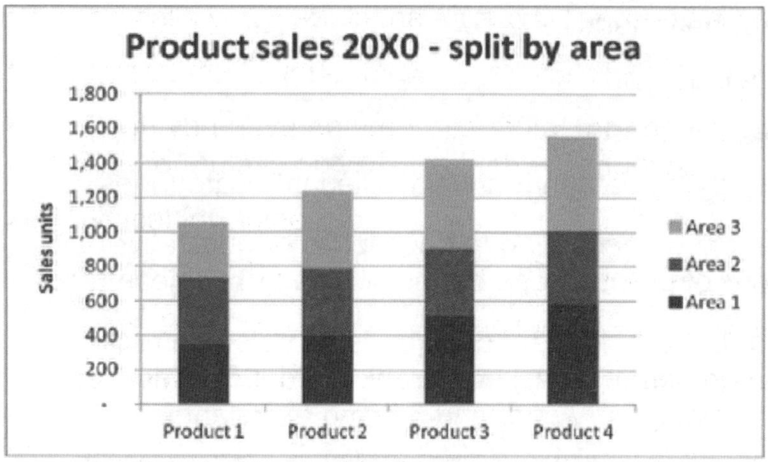

Percentage component bar chart

A percentage component bar chart shows the data for each category as a percentage of the whole. Each bar is the same height (100%) and each component is represented by a section proportional in size to its representation in the total of each bar. It is not possible to interpret total sales for each product but you are able to see the proportion of the sales units that each area contributes.

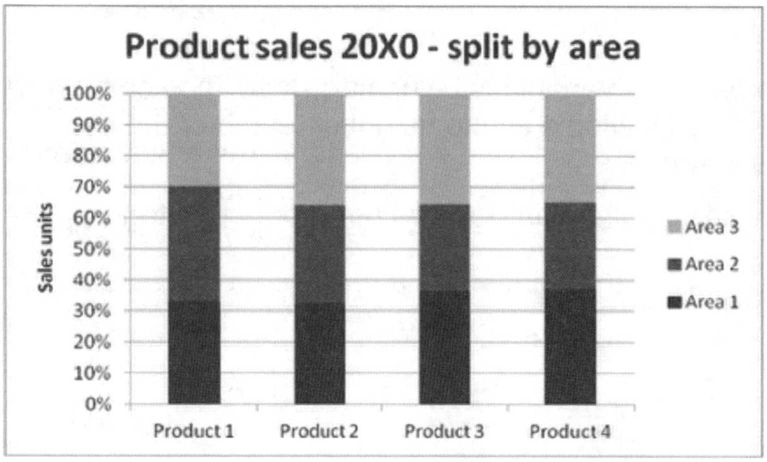

Compound (multiple) bar charts

A compound (multiple) bar chart can show the same information as a component bar chart but instead of the data being stacked into one column a separate bar is used for each sub-group. Compound bar charts can be used to show several sub-groups of each category but care needs to be taken to ensure that the chart does not contain too much information making it complicated to read and interpret.

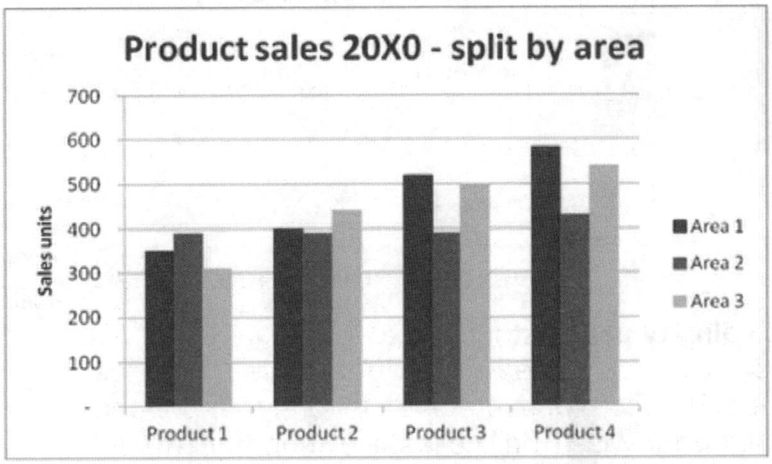

All of the different bar charts could also be used to see how the different products are selling in the different areas if the x-axis category was changed to 'Area'.

Component bar chart

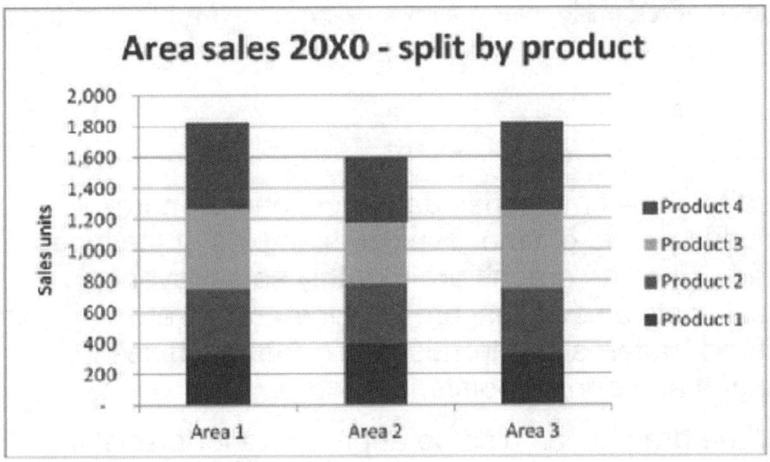

Percentage component bar chart

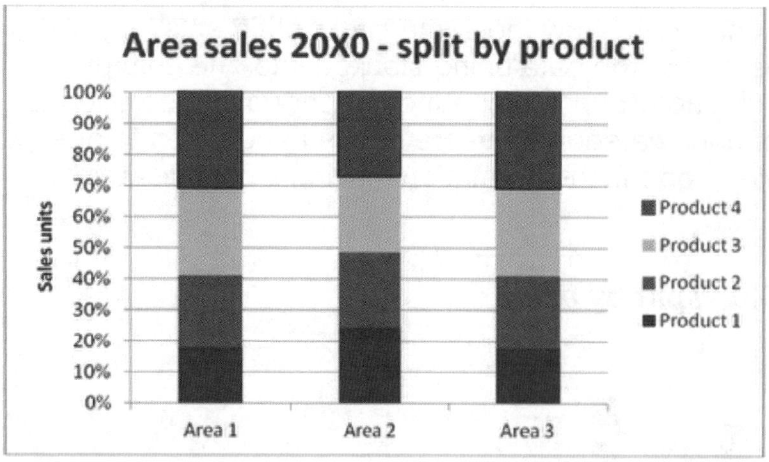

Compound bar chart

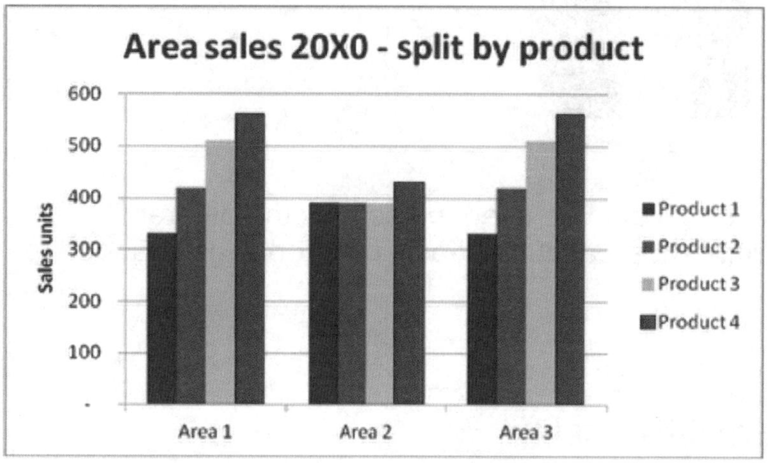

Line graphs

Line graphs are usually used to show time series data, how one or more variables vary over a continuous period of time. Typical examples of the types of data that can be presented using line graphs are monthly sales revenue, monthly sales volume, annual costs and annual profits. Line graphs are particularly useful for identifying patterns and trends in the data such as seasonal effects, large changes and turning points.

As well as time series data, line graphs can also be appropriate for displaying data that are measured over other continuous variables such as distance. For example, a line graph could be used to show how delivery costs changes in relation to distance travelled.

It is important to consider whether the data have been collected at sufficiently regular intervals so that estimates made for a point lying half-way along the line between two successive measurements would be reasonable.

In a line graph the x-axis (independent variable) represents the continuous variable (for example year or distance from the initial measurement) whilst the y-axis (dependent variable) has a scale and indicates the measurement.

Several data series can be plotted on the same line chart and this is particularly useful for analysing and comparing the trends in different datasets.

For example we can represent the total sales for Business X over the four quarters of the year as a single line graph.

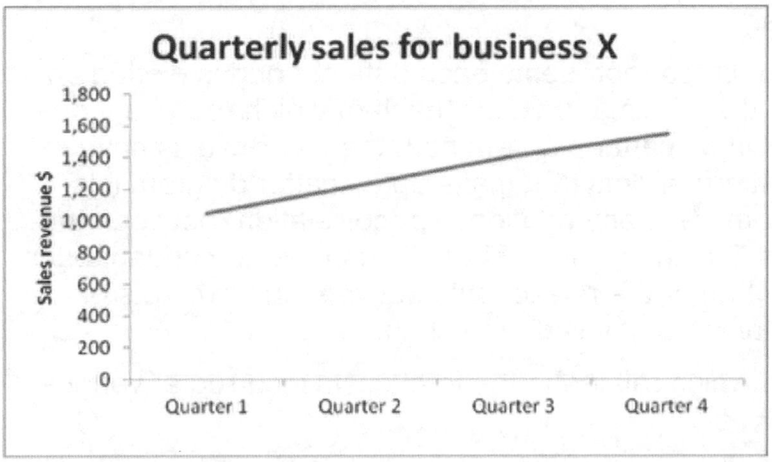

If we wanted to show the split between products then a multiple line graph could be used.

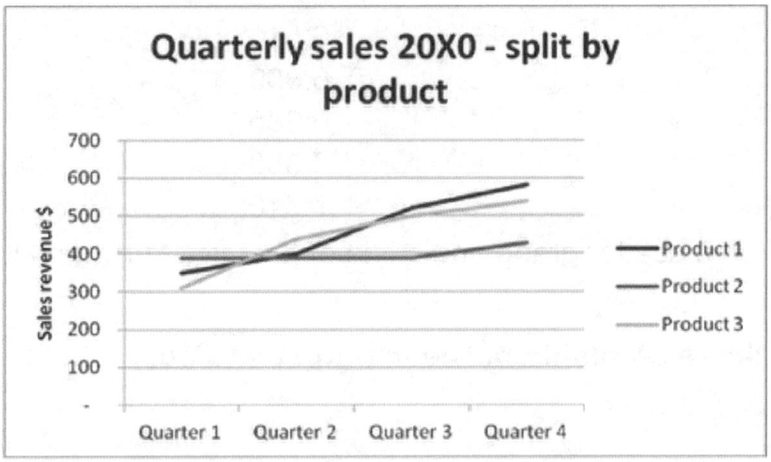

It may also be useful to combine a bar and line graph to illustrate information more clearly. Here we can see Sales (bar) and gross profit from those sales (line).

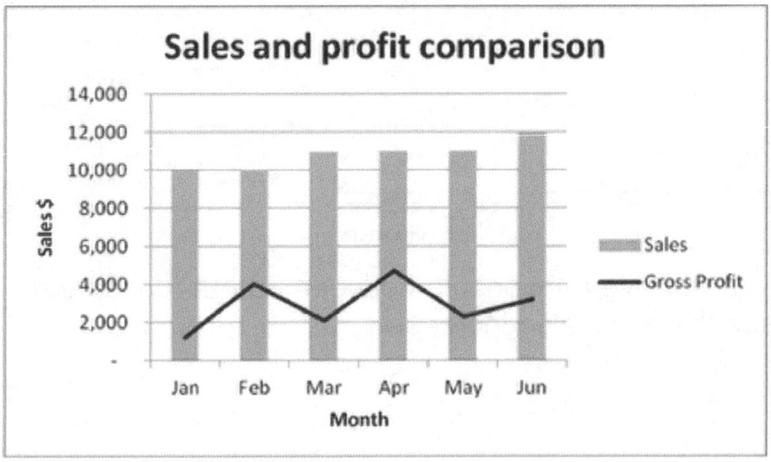

Scatter diagram

Scatter diagrams are used to show the relationship between pairs of quantitative measurements made for the same object or individual. For example, a scatter diagram could be used to present information about the production levels and costs.

In a scatter diagram a dot or cross represents each data set and is plotted on the graph with reference to the x-axis and y-axis, each of which represent one of the two measurements. On a scatter diagram both the x and y-axis have scales. By analysing the pattern of dots that make up a scatter diagram it is possible to identify whether there is any relationship (correlation) between the two measurements. Regression lines, lines of best fit, can also be added to the graph and used to decide whether the relationship between the two sets of measurements can be explained or if it is due to chance.

Consider the following data which relates to the total costs incurred at various output levels in a factory:

Output (units)	**Total cost** ($)
26	6,566
30	6,510
33	6,800
44	6,985
48	7,380
50	7,310

If the data shown is plotted on a scatter graph and a line of best fit is drawn on it would look like this:

A scatter graph showing the relationship between output and cost

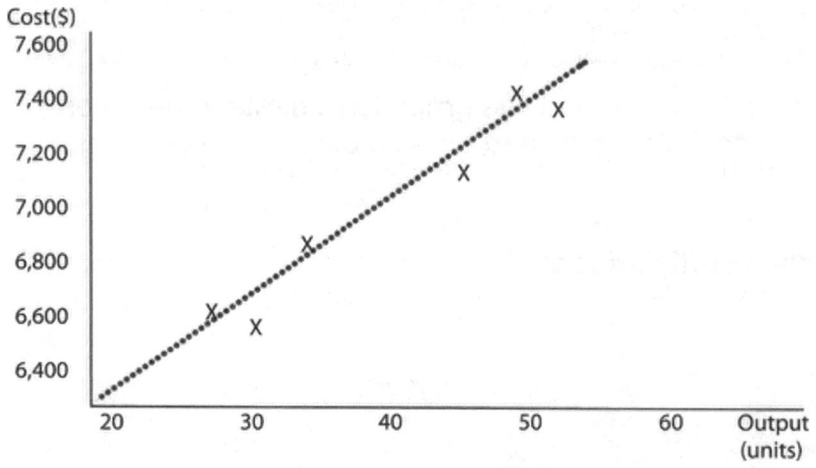

It is clear to see that there is a positive relationship between output (units) and costs ($). As output increases the costs also increase.

Pie charts

A pie chart is a circular graph that shows the relative contribution that different sub-groups contribute to an overall category. A wedge of the circle represents each sub-groups contribution. Every 1% contribution that a subgroup contributes to the total corresponds to an angle of 3.6 degrees.

Pie charts are similar to percentage component bar charts, in that they are generally used to show percentage or proportional data, but they can only represent one category split into its sub-groups. This makes it harder to draw any comparisons between either products or areas without producing multiple pie charts. It is also not possible to 'read off' the actual data unless data labels are added, which is possible with other forms of graphical representation.

Pie charts are good for displaying data for around 6 sub-groups or fewer. When there are more sub-groups it is difficult for the eye to distinguish between the relative sizes of the different sectors and so the chart becomes difficult to interpret.

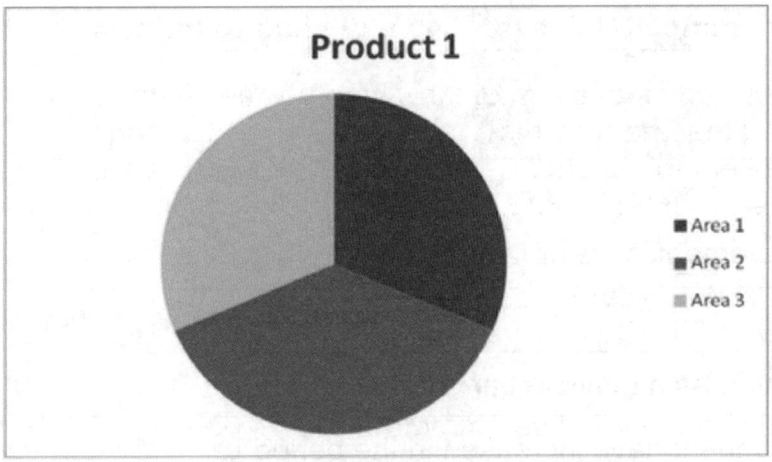

Interpretation of tables, charts and graphs

Although the information presented in diagrammatic form should be easy to understand, part of the role of the management accountant may involve interpreting the information, perhaps in the form of a brief report to management.

It will generally be the case that the better prepared the diagram is the less interpretation that will be required to assist management to understand the information.

Your objective in carrying out this sort of interpretation exercise is to bring out the meaning in the information and, perhaps, to help management reach conclusions based on the information presented. As a result of your interpretation, you may also be able to make suitable recommendations to management.

Test your understanding 1

The following diagram illustrates staff numbers at X Ltd for the period April to June:

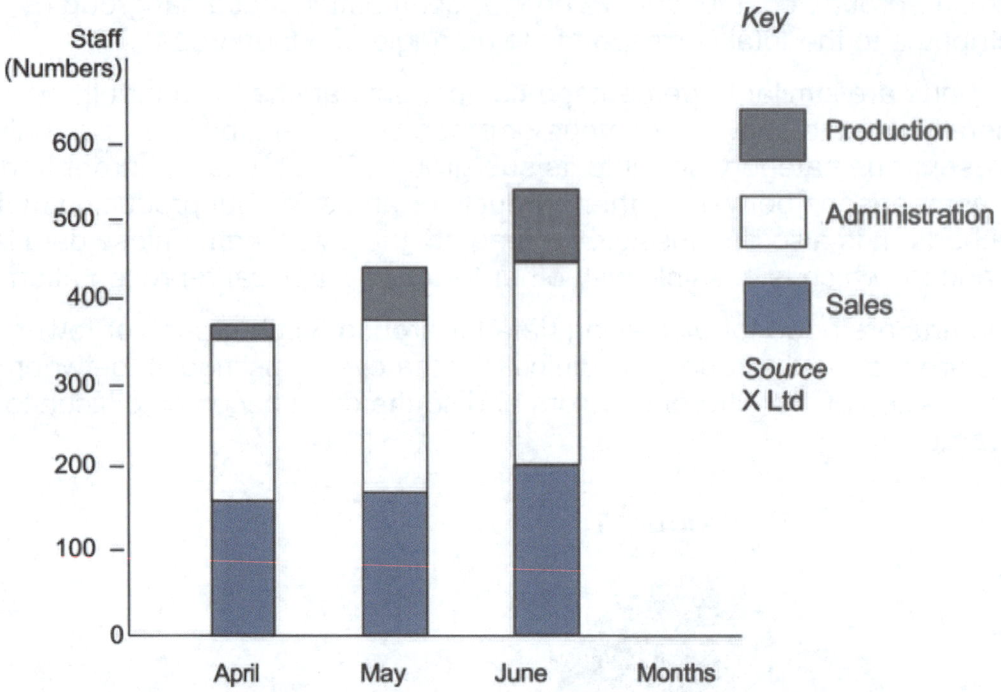

Are the following statements true or false?

	True	False
The data is presented as a multiple bar chart		
Production staff numbers have increased in the period		
Total staff numbers have increased in the period		

Test your understanding 2

Which of the following charts/graphs could be used to represent the relationship between sales volume and sales revenue?

(i) simple bar chart

(ii) line graph

(iii) multiple bar chart

(iv) scatter graph

A (i) only

B (i) and (ii)

C (ii) and (iii)

D (iv) only

Test your understanding 3

Which of the following charts/graphs could be used to represent the findings of a survey regarding the quality of service?

(i) scatter graph

(ii) pie chart

(iii) line graph

(iv) percentage component bar chart

A (i) and (ii)

B (ii) and (iii)

C (iii) and (iv)

D (ii) and (iv)

4 Chapter summary

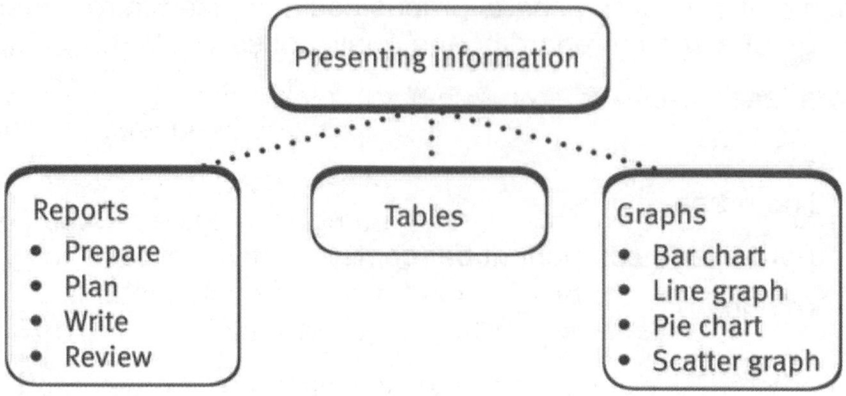

Test your understanding answers

Test your understanding 1

	True	False
The data is presented as a multiple bar chart		✓
Production staff numbers have increased in the period	✓	
Total staff numbers have increased in the period	✓	

Test your understanding 2

D

Sales volume and sales revenue are both quantitative data and a scatter graph is the only type of graph that has quantitative data on both the x and y axis. A line of best fit could be plotted to show the relationship.

Test your understanding 3

D

Both a pie chart and a percentage component bar chart show proportional data so could be used to illustrate how people rated a service on a scale of, for example, 1 to 5. A scatter graph requires two sets of quantitative data, a line graph requires one set of data to be continuous for example time or distance rather than separate ratings.

Chapter

18

Spreadsheets

Chapter learning objectives

Upon completion of this chapter you will be able to:

- explain the role and features of a computer spreadsheet system.
- identify applications for computer spreadsheets and their use in data analysis, cost and management accounting.

Most of this chapter has been included as expandable text as many students will already have detailed knowledge of such software through practical experience.

1 Uses of spreadsheets

Introduction

A spreadsheet is a computer package that is used to manipulate data. Much of the data of a company is likely to be held on spreadsheets. Spreadsheets can be used for anything with a rows and columns format. One of the most useful functions of a spreadsheet is being able to input formulae to enable calculation to happen automatically when data is input in specific cells.

Practical application of spreadsheets in the workplace

Spreadsheets are a convenient way of setting up all sorts of charts, records and tables. Uses include:

- 'what if?' analysis
- budgeting and forecasting
- reporting performance
- variance analysis
- inventory valuation.

'What if?' analysis

- The power of spreadsheets is that the data held in any one cell can be made dependent on that held in other cells by the use of formulae.
- This means that changing a value in one cell can set off a chain reaction of changes through other related cells.
- This allows 'what-if?' analysis to be quickly and easily carried out, e.g. 'what if sales are 10% lower than expected?'

Budgeting and forecasting

Preparing budgets and forecasts are classic applications of spreadsheets, as they allow estimates to be changed without having to recalculate everything manually.

Here is an extract from a cash flow forecast:

	A	B	C	D	E
1	**Revised cashflow forecast for 05/06**				
2	**£000**	**Jul-05**	**Aug-05**	**Sep-05**	**Oct-05**
3					
4	**Sales receipts**	**1867**	**1828**	**1893**	**1939**
5					
6	**Payments**				
7	Purchases	1691	1644	1701	1798
8	Overheads	57	57	57	57
9	Capex	50	50	50	25
10	Bank loan	12	12	12	12
11	VAT	160			171
12	CT				
13	Bank o/d interest	2	2	2	1
14		**1972**	**1765**	**1822**	**2064**
15					
16	Net cash in/out flow	**-105**	**63**	**71**	**-125**
17					
18	Bal b/f *	-134	-239	-176	-105
19	Bal c/f	-239	-176	-105	-230
20					

The key formulae are as follows:

- Total payments e.g. B14: = SUM(B7:B13)
- Net cash flow: e.g. B16: = B4-B14
- Bal c/f: e.g. B19: = B18+B16

Reporting performance

Performance appraisal usually involves calculating ratios, possibly involving comparatives between companies and from one year to the next.

- A neat way of doing this is to input the raw data, such as financial statements on one sheet and calculate the ratios on another.
- For example, here is an extract from the five years results for a company called Parkland, input on a sheet titled "historic data":

	A		Formula Bar	D	E	
1						
2					**Rutwater**	
3	£000		2005	2004	2003	2
4						
5	Revenue		319,361	316,197	309,119	3C
6	Cost of sales		-81,428	-84,627	-83,039	-8
7	Gross profit		237,933	231,570	226,080	22
8						
9	[illegible]		[illegible]	[illegible]	[illegible]	[illegible]

- Here are some ratios that have been set up on a separate sheet (titled "current and historic ratios") in the same workbook:

	A	B	C	D	E
1					
2	**Historic ratio analysis**				**Rutwater**
3			**2005**	**2004**	**2003**
4					
5	RoC		11.7%	12.5%	12.5%
6	Margin		27.8%	27.8%	26.8%
7	Asset turnover		£0.42	£0.45	£0.47
8	Gross margin		74.5%	73.2%	73.1%
9	EBITDA margin		49.2%	48.1%	47.2%
10					

- Taking just one as an example, gross profit margin – this is calculated as gross profit divided by revenue. The answer has been formatted to show as a percentage to one decimal place and the formula for cell C8 is as follows: ='Historic data'!C7/'Historic data'! C5
- The 'historic data'! part indicates which worksheet the information came from. While this looks complex, setting up the formula was simply a matter of clicking on the correct cells in the first place:
  - On the sheet "current and historic ratios" click on cell C8 and press "="
  - Switch to sheet "historic data" and click on cell C7 – Type "/"
  - Click on cell C5 while still on sheet "historic data"
  - Press enter and you will automatically return to the "current and historic ratios" sheet.

Variance analysis

Variance analysis involves management comparing actual results with budget and then investigating the differences. A relatively simple statement could be along the lines of the following:

	A	B	C	D	E	F	G
1	**Variance Report**						
2	**Project Name:**						
3	**Employee Name:**						
4							
5	**ID#**		**Task Name**	**Planned Effort** (Baseline)	**Actual Effort** (or Estimated Completion)	**Variance / Slippage**	**Comments**
6						0.0	
7						0.0	
8						0.0	
9						0.0	
10						0.0	
11						0.0	

2 Statistical functions

The basic commands for statistical functions that operate on lists of values are also very similar throughout the range of spreadsheet packages. Examples of these are:

- SUM – the total of the values in the list
- AVERAGE – the average of the values in the list
- MAX – the highest value in the list
- MIN – the lowest value in the list.

Entering formulae

- A formula always starts with an equal sign (=) in Excel.
- Formulae consist of numbers, cell co-ordinates (e.g. A2, F7), operators and functions. Operators perform actions on numbers and coordinates. Examples of operators are plus, minus, divide and multiply. Functions perform more advanced actions on numbers and coordinates.

The arithmetic operations and method of writing the basic formulae are very similar in all packages. The **BODMAS (Brackets, Order, Division, Multiplication, Addition, Subtraction)** rule must be used to evaluate an arithmetic problem:

- evaluate expressions within the brackets first
- deal with any orders, or 'power of' functions
- perform division and multiplication before addition and subtraction
- work from left to right if the expression contains only addition and subtraction.

BODMAS, BIDMAS, BEDMAS

You may also have seen the O in BODMAS being referred to as Operation

Other mnemonics are also used when remembering the order calculations should be carried out:

BIDMAS – Brackets, Indices, Divide, Multiply, Add and Subtract

BEDMAS – Brackets, Exponential, Divide, Multiply, Add and Subtract

The only difference is the name given to the 'power of' function.

Steps involved in entering formulae

To enter a formula:

- select the cell where you want to enter the formula
- press the equal sign (=) on the keyboard (or click on the sign in the formula bar, if one is shown)
- key in the formula directly from the keyboard or use the mouse to select the cells you want in the formula. There are no spaces in a formula
- press the <Enter> key
- when you have entered a formula, the resulting value appears in that cell. The formula is only visible in the formula bar
- typical formulae:

= (A6 + C10) – E25	Adds A6 with C10 and subtracts E25
= (H19*A7)/3	Multiplies H19 with A7 and divides the total by 3
= SUM(L12:L14)	A quick way of adding L12 + L13 + L14

3 Advantages and disadvantages of spreadsheets

Many users use spreadsheets to store data, even though the data could be better managed in a database. This confusion stems from the basic similarity that the key function of both spreadsheets and databases is to store and manipulate data.

- A database is designed to store and manipulate large amounts of data.
- A spreadsheet is designed mainly to run formulas and reports on numbers.

Advantages of spreadsheets

Spreadsheets are designed to analyse data and sort list items, not for long term storage of raw data. A spreadsheet should be used for 'crunching' numbers and storage of single list items. Advantages of spreadsheets include the following:

- Spreadsheet programs are relatively easy to use.
- Spreadsheet functions enable data to be processed more quickly.
- They include graphing functions that allow for quick reporting and analysis of data.
- Spreadsheets are often easier to read than hand written tables.
- They should reduce calculation errors.

Disadvantages of spreadsheets

- Data must be re-copied over and over again to maintain it in separate data files.
- Spreadsheets are not able to identify data input errors.
- Spreadsheets lack detailed sorting and querying abilities.
- There can be sharing violations among users wishing to view or change data at the same time.
- Spreadsheets are restricted to a finite number of records.
- Spreadsheets are open to cyber-attack through viruses, hackers and general system failure.

Using a spreadsheet package

The content of this expandable text is to help those unfamiliar with spreadsheet packages, this section will provide the basic introduction needed to feel confident to use Microsoft Excel and carry out simple information analysis tasks. The Test your understanding questions that follow are similar to what you should expect in the examination.

- This package has been chosen because it is the most popular and therefore the most likely to be used in your college or work environment.
- The editions and programs that you are using may not be the same as those used in this section. In that case, the screens you produce will not be identical to those shown here.
- However, all spreadsheet packages will have the basic features described in this section and access to a different package will not cause too many problems.
- If you are at all unsure, you should read the manual that accompanies your chosen spreadsheet.

In order to explain the role, features and uses of a spreadsheet package, the following instructions should be read and attempted in full if you are unfamiliar with the use of spreadsheets. If you are confident with using spreadsheets check through the notes for any areas you may not have covered previously.

What is a spreadsheet?

A spreadsheet could be defined as a table of rows and columns that intersect to form cells.

- Each row is identified by a number.
- Each column is identified by a letter (or letters).
- Each cell has a unique identifier formed by a letter (or letters) and a number.
- Numbers, text or formulae may be entered into these cells.
- A formula normally involves a mathematical calculation on the content of other cells, the result being inserted in the cell containing the formula. These are not visible when you are entering data but reside in the background.
- Some or all of a spreadsheet can be printed out directly or saved on disk for insertion into reports or other documents using a word processing package.

Basic spreadsheet terms

Make sure you learn the following basic spreadsheet terms if you don't know them already.

- **Worksheet:** a worksheet or spreadsheet is the basis of all the work you do. It could be considered to be the electronic equivalent of an accountant's ledger.
- **Workbook:** is a collection of worksheets. The workbook is simply a folder that binds together your worksheets.
- **Columns:** each column is referenced by one or two letters in the column heading. The whole worksheet consists of 256 columns, labelled A through IV.
- **Rows:** each row is referenced by the row number shown in the row heading to the left of a row. There are 65,536 rows in Excel.
- **Cells:** The intersection of a column and a row is known as a 'cell'. To refer to a particular cell, use its column and row location. This is called a 'cell address', for example A1, B22, etc.
- **Sheet tabs:** these are between the worksheet and the status bar and are used to move between worksheets in your workbook.
- **Window:** you can only see part of the worksheet at any time; you could consider the screen to be a window onto the worksheet. You have the facility to move this window, so that you can view any part of the spreadsheet.
- **Cell pointer:** indicates the active cell on by highlighting the border around the cell.

A good way of testing your understanding of spreadsheets in an examination is to ask you to select the correct definition of one of the basic spreadsheet terms from a list of possible options.

Running a spreadsheet program

The way to gain access to a spreadsheet package depends upon the type of computer system in use.

- A **menu** may be available to allow access to the chosen software by entering a single number or letter or by use of a cursor or mouse.
- If you are working in a **Windows** environment, you will access the spreadsheet package using the mouse.
- Click on the Start button in the bottom left hand corner of the Window.
- Keep the mouse button depressed and highlight the 'Programs' and then the package that you want to use. Click on the icon.
- The opening screen in Microsoft Excel might look like this.

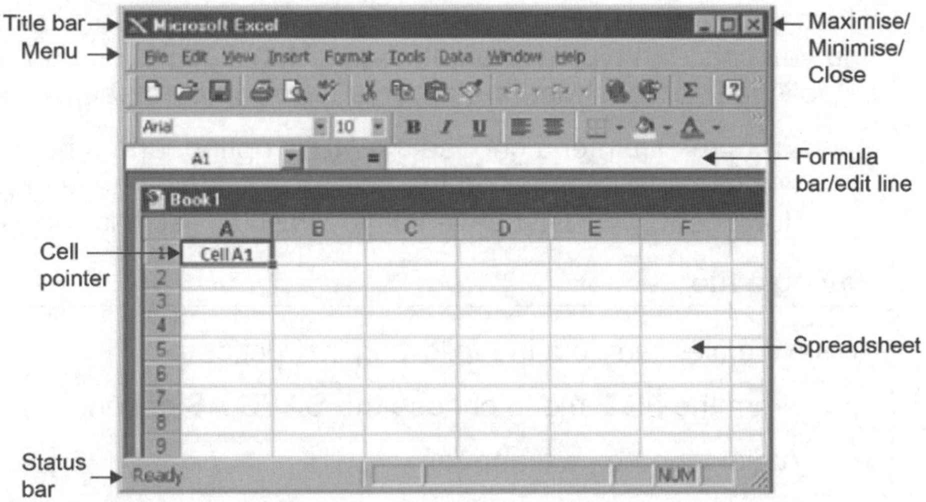

(Yours might look a little different if you have a different version of Excel).

- On the screen you will see the **title bar**, the **menu bar, the function tool bar** and in the top right corner the buttons to **minimise**, **maximise**/restore and close the worksheet. As with most Windows programs you can change the size and move the Excel Window.
- If your screen does not have a formula bar, a formatting bar or a toolbar you can show these by accessing **View** and then **Toolbars** from the menu at the top of the screen. You can then select (or deselect) what you want to show on the screen. A tick signifies that it is switched on.

- The toolbars are below the menu bar. Clicking on any of these buttons provides a shortcut to selecting options from the menu bar. If you hover the pointer over a button a label will appear and, in the **status bar**, Excel will tell you what that button does.
- The **formula bar** is between the spreadsheet and the toolbar. This provides you with information about the contents of the active cell. The co-ordinates of the active cell are displayed on the left-hand side of the formula bar.
- The **status bar** is at the bottom of the screen. It gives you information about your spreadsheet, such as when you are opening or saving a file and whether you have CAPS LOCK, NUM LOCK or SCROLL LOCK on.
- **Scroll bars** are used to move your spreadsheet both up and down and left to right. The vertical scroll bar (on the right hand side of the spreadsheet) is used to move up and down. The horizontal scroll bar (below the spreadsheet and above the status bar) is used to move left and right.

Creating a new file

When you first open Excel, a blank spreadsheet appears on the screen and you can start typing straight away. At this point you can work on an established spreadsheet or start on a new one by creating a file.

- From the file menu choose the NEW option, and a new Excel workbook will appear on the screen. Once you have created a document, you must save it if you wish to use it in the future.

Saving a file

To save a file, carry out the following instructions:

- From the **FILE** menu choose the **SAVE AS** option.
- A dialogue box will appear.
- If necessary, use the **DRIVE** drop down menu to select the relevant drive.
- In the **FILE NAME** text box type in the name you wish to use. All spreadsheet packages automatically add an extension to your filename.
- Click on the **OK** button.
- When you have saved a file once, you do not need to choose the **SAVE AS** option again, but simply choose **SAVE** from the **FILE** menu or click on the icon on the tool bar (picture of a floppy disk).

Closing a file/Quitting

When you have finished working on a spreadsheet and you have saved it, you will need to close it down.

- You can do this by either pressing the button at the top right hand side of the worksheet with a cross on it or by choosing the CLOSE or EXIT option from the FILE menu.
- If you only want to exit Excel briefly and prefer not to close down the whole package you can switch to another application or back to the Windows Program Manager by pressing <Alt><Tab> repeatedly. This allows you to step through all the opened packages in rotation.
- If you have changed the file, Excel will ask if you wish to save the changes you made before closing. Click on the appropriate button.

Moving directly to a cell: the GOTO command

Sometimes you may want to move to a specific address in the spreadsheet that is too far from your present position to warrant using the arrow keys to get there. On the top of the keyboard you can see a row of keys labelled F1 through to F12; these are known as 'function keys'.

- When the function keys are pressed, a special function is invoked. For example, the F5 key is the GOTO key in Excel.
- If you wish to go to cell D19, press F5 and a dialogue box will appear. You are prompted to enter an address or range. Enter D19 and the cell pointer will go directly to cell D19.

The help facility

Excel has a comprehensive help facility, which provides both **general** help and **context sensitive** help.

- To invoke the help command press the 'Help' button on the menu bar, the? box on the toolbar or the shortcut key F1.
- To obtain information on any particular subject shown, move the mouse pointer over the required topic and click, or you may be prompted to type in a question.
- Context sensitive help is available either when a help button is displayed in a dialogue box or when an error message is flashed onto the screen.
- Asking for help at this stage by either clicking on the help button,? box or by pressing F1 will result in the help window appearing at the topic relevant to the problem encountered.

Putting data onto a worksheet

Entering data on a worksheet is very easy. You simply type your entry, press return and whatever you typed will be placed in the current cell, i.e. where the cell pointer is.

- As you type, each character will be displayed on the edit line at the top of the screen. The entry is not put onto the worksheet until you press the return key.
- When you have finished entering data you can either press the <Enter> key on the keyboard or click on the Enter Box (a green tick) on the formula bar.
- If you change your mind about entering the data then either press the <Esc> key on the keyboard or click on the Cancel Box (a red cross) on the formula bar.
- If you have made a mistake, you can press the 'backspace key' (the key above the ENTER key) to delete what you have done one character at a time. If you have already pressed the ENTER key, you can delete it by highlighting the cell or cells and pressing the Delete key.
- There are three types of data that can be entered into your worksheet – text, numbers and formulae.

Entering text

Text is entered by simply typing into a cell. Typing any letter at the beginning of a cell entry causes it to be accepted as a 'label', rather than a 'value'.

- If the text you enter is longer than the width of the cell then the text will 'run over' into the next cell. But if the next cell also contains data/information then you will only see part of the text you entered, i.e. the label will be truncated.
- There will be times when you want a spreadsheet to treat a number or a formula as text. To do this you must type an apostrophe in front of the number or formula you are entering, e.g. '01707 320903 or '=A4+D5.

Entering numbers

Numbers can be entered on a spreadsheet by simply typing into a cell.

- If the space in the cell is insufficient, the number will be shown in an exponential form on the spreadsheet, but the number will still be retained in full in the formula bar.
- If you want to see the contents of cells in full, the columns can be widened to accommodate the number (or text).

- It is not necessary to put the commas in manually when entering large numbers (1,000 or more), because it is easy to format the data to display commas and decimal places to make the data easier to understand. For example:
  - if you wish to enter 123,456, enter 123456 into a cell and press Enter
  - move the cursor back onto that cell, click on 'Format' in the menu bar, then 'Cells'
  - choose the 'Number' tab and then 'Number' from the category list
  - now reduce the decimal places to '0' by clicking on the down arrow and tick the 'Use 1000 separator' box
  - press OK. Your number should now be shown as 123,456
  - you can also use the 'Currency' option from the category list to put $s in front.

Cut, Copy and Paste

- **Cut** then **paste** is used to **move** cells from one area of the spreadsheet to another.
- **Copy** then **paste** is used to **copy** cells from one area to another.
- Copying and pasting or cutting and pasting operations always have two parts:
  - define the range you want to copy or cut **from**; then
  - define the range that you want to copy or move to.

  You can copy formulae to different cells by the same method. Note that the cell references change automatically when formulae are copied – this is known as relative copying.

  If you do not wish for cell references to be changed automatically when copying formulae to different cells you can insert $ signs before the column reference, or the row reference or both. This is known as absolute referencing.

Formatting numbers

To make monetary data 100% clearer it should be formatted into monetary amounts. For columns with a '$' at the top:

- highlight the column of figures to be formatted
- click on 'Format' on the menu bar, then choose 'Cells'
- on the category list choose 'Currency'. It will probably automatically assign a '$' and 2 decimal places. Click OK.

Formatting text

Making a spreadsheet look good is more than just a cosmetic exercise. Proper formatting, underlining and emboldening can make the spreadsheet easier to follow, draw attention to important figures and reduce the chance of errors.

- For example, to change the font to Times New Roman throughout a spreadsheet: click on the first cell with an entry in it and drag the mouse to the last cell with an entry in it. The area covered should be shaded. Go to the Format menu and select Cells. Select the Font tab and then the chosen style.
- For example, to put titles in bold: click and drag the cursor over them, then click on the **B** button (**B**old) on the tool bar. Alternatively, all entries in a row or column can be selected by clicking on the letter at the head of the column or the number at the very left of the row.
- For example, to change the width of a column: place the mouse pointer in the column heading at the intersection and a two headed arrow should appear. Drag this to the right until the column is wide enough. Adjust the width of the other columns to accommodate the entries comfortably.
- For example, to align column headings use the align buttons on the formatting toolbar (to the right of the underline U).
- For example, to underline totals by highlighting the cells containing the totals: click on 'Format' on the menu bar, then click on 'Cells' then 'Border' tab, and a window similar to the following will appear.

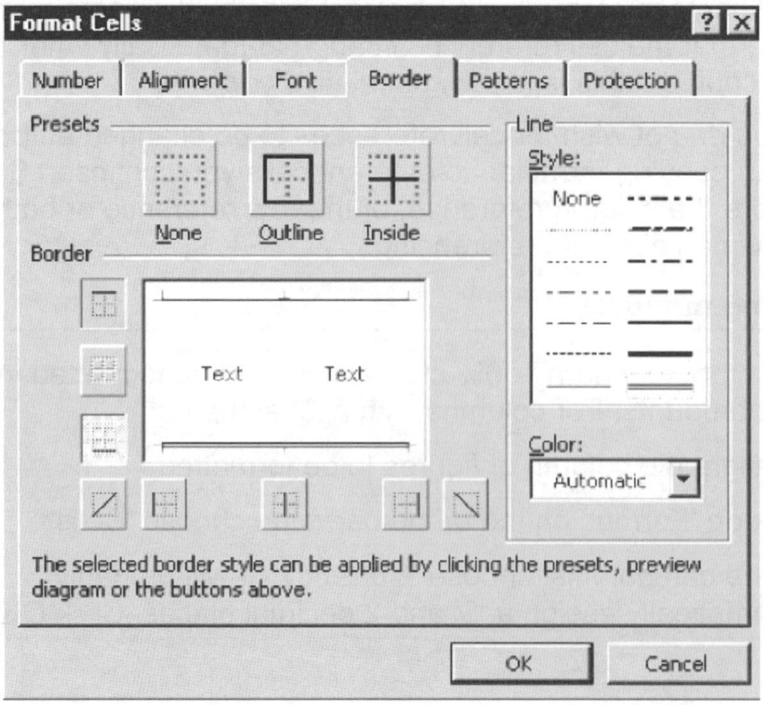

- The box on the left shows the edges of the cell or selection of cells, which will have a border.
- The box on the right shows the types of lines that are available.
- Click on the top line on the left-hand list and then on the single, non-bold line (probably already selected) in the right hand options.
- The top of the 'totals' cells should now have a single underlining.
- Now click on the bottom line and then on the double under-lining style. Click on OK.

Test your understanding 1

Which of the following is not an advantage of spreadsheet software over manual approaches?

A Security

B Speed

C Accuracy

D Legibility

Test your understanding 2

Angelina wants to calculate the expected value of the following cash flows using a spreadsheet

	A	B	C
1	Cash flow	Probability	CF × probability
2	250	0.3	
3	350	0.2	
4	450	0.4	
5	600	0.1	
6	Total	1	

What should the formulae be in

A Cell C3

B Cell C6?

Test your understanding 3

The following spreadsheet has been set up to look at the relationship between 20 sets of data relating to production volume (x) and costs (y).

	A	B	C	D	E	F
1		x	y	xy	x^2	y^2
2						
24						
25	Totals					

What formula is required to calculate the variable cost per unit?

Test your understanding 4

A company manufactures a single product. In a computer spreadsheet, the cells C1 to C12 contain the budgeted monthly sales units for the twelve months of next year in sequence with January sales in cell C1 and finishing with December sales in cell C12. The company policy is for closing inventory of finished goods each month to be 10% of the budgeted sales units for the following month.

Which of the following formulae will generate the budgeted production (in units) for May next year?

A = [(C5 + (0.1 * C6)]

B = [(C5 – (0.1 * C6)]

C = [(1.1 * C5) – (0.1 * C6)]

D = [(0.9 * C5) + (0.1 * C6)]

Test your understanding answers

Test your understanding 1

A

A computer-based approach exposes the firm to threats from viruses, hackers and general system failure.

Test your understanding 2

A C3 = A3*B3

B C6 = SUM(C2:C5)

Test your understanding 3

The variable cost per unit is the gradient ("b") of the linear regression line, given in this case by:

$$b = \frac{n\sum xy - \sum x\sum y}{n\sum x^2 - (\sum x)^2} = (20*D25 - B25*C25)/(20*E25 - B25^2)$$

Test your understanding 4

D

	April	May	June
Sales	C4	C5	C6
Less opening inventory		–C5 × 0.1	
Closing inventory		C6 × 0.1	
Production		(C5 × 0.9) + (C6 × 0.1)	

Chapter

19

Questions

Chapter 1: Accounting for management

Test your understanding 1

Data is information that has been processed in such a way as to make it meaningful for use by management in making decisions.

Is this statement TRUE or FALSE?

A True

B False

Test your understanding 2

Which of the following is not a fundamental attribute of good information?

A Complete

B Concise

C Timely

D Accurate

Test your understanding 3

Good information should be:

(i) Relevant

(ii) Timely

(iii) Accurate

(iv) Motivating

A (i) only

B (i) and (iii)

C (iii) and (iv)

D (i) (ii) and (iii)

Test your understanding 4

Which of the following steps does not form part of the planning process?

A Set objectives for achievement

B Identify ways in which objectives can be achieved

C Compare actual results and expected results

D Make a decision as to how objectives can be achieved based on information provided

Test your understanding 5

Which of the following is the appropriate name for planning which considers how the functional heads within a business unit will coordinate employees on a day-to-day basis?

A Strategic planning

B Tactical planning

C Operational planning

D Forecast planning

Test your understanding 6

The manager of a division is responsible for costs and revenues as well as capital invested?

Which is the appropriate classification for the division?

A Revenue centre

B Investment centre

C Profit centre

D Cost centre

Test your understanding 7

The following assertions relate to financial accounting:

(i) The main purpose of financial information is to provide a true and fair view of the financial position of an organisation at the end of an accounting period.

(ii) Financial information may be presented in any format deemed suitable by management.

Which of the following statements are true?

A Assertions (i) and (ii) are both correct

B Only assertion (i) is correct

C Only assertion (ii) is correct

D Neither are correct

Chapter 2: Cost classification

Test your understanding 8

Which of the following costs should not be included in the inventory valuation of a manufacturing business?

A Depreciation on the plant and machinery

B Salary of salesman

C Factory supervisor's salary

D Electricity for factory

Test your understanding 9

A shop carries out repairs on customers' electrical items, e.g. televisions, DVD players, etc.

Which of the following is an example of an indirect variable cost?

A Business rates for repair shop

B Salary of repair shop supervisor

C Repair person paid per hour worked

D Electricity for recharging repair tools

Test your understanding 10

The following diagram represents a cost behaviour pattern.

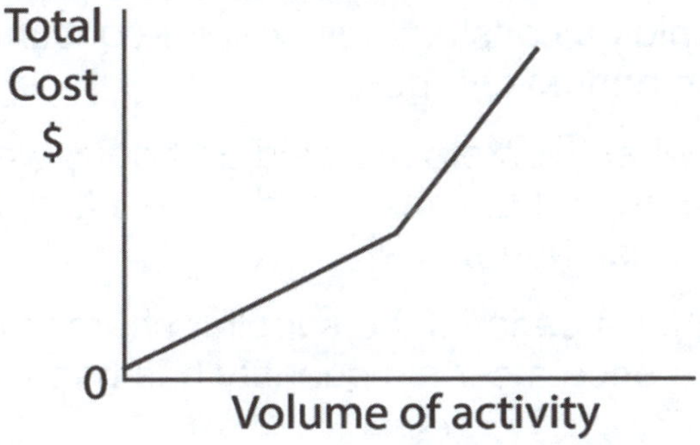

Which of the following statements is consistent with the above diagram?

A Annual factory costs when the electricity supplier sets a tariff based on a fixed charge plus a constant unit cost for consumption but subject to a maximum annual charge.

B Weekly total labour cost when workers are paid an hourly wage during normal working hours and a higher hourly rate if they are required to work outside those hours.

C Total direct material cost for a period if the supplier charges a lower unit cost on all units once a certain quantity has been purchased in that period.

D Total direct material cost for a period if the supplier has agreed to a maximum charge for that period.

Test your understanding 11

The following diagram represents a cost behaviour pattern.

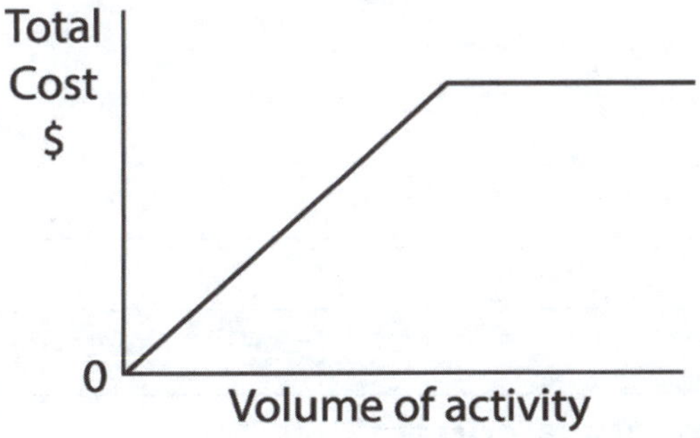

Which of the following statements is consistent with the above diagram?

A Annual factory costs when the electricity supplier sets a tariff based on a fixed charge plus a constant unit cost for consumption but subject to a maximum annual charge.

B Weekly total labour cost when workers are paid an hourly wage during normal working hours and a higher hourly rate if they are required to work outside those hours.

C Total direct material cost for a period if the supplier charges a lower unit cost on all units once a certain quantity has been purchased in that period.

D Total direct material cost for a period if the supplier has agreed to a maximum charge for that period.

Test your understanding 12

The telephone costs of a business are likely to be classified as a stepped fixed cost.

Is this statement TRUE or FALSE?

A True

B False

Test your understanding 13

A company has a performance related pay scheme in operation.

What is the most appropriate cost classification for the salaries of the managers?

A Fixed cost

B Stepped fixed cost

C Semi-variable cost

D Variable cost

Test your understanding 14

Which of the following statements is correct?

A Only direct production costs should be included in inventory valuation

B All indirect costs should be treated as non-production costs

C The sum of direct costs is known as prime cost

D Indirect costs per unit are always larger than direct costs per unit

Test your understanding 15

The costs and output of a business for the last quarter of the year were as follows:

	Output (units)	Cost ($)
Oct	1,800	8,850
Nov	2,000	8,750
Dec	800	3,950

Using the high low method which of the following represents the estimated cost in January of producing 1,500 units if the monthly fixed costs are expected to increase by $100 at the start of next year?

A $6,750

B $6,850

C $7,380

D $7,480

Test your understanding 16

A business has experienced the following labour costs:

Output (units)	Cost ($)
7,000	86,000
12,000	141,000
9,000	102,000

Fixed costs increase by $15,000 for output in excess of 10,000 units.

Using the high low method what is the estimated cost of producing 14,000 units?

A $142,000

B $157,000

C $163,000

D $178,000

Test your understanding 17

A manufacturing company has four types of cost (identified as Z1, Z2, Z3 and Z4).

The cost per unit for each type at two different production levels is:

Cost type	Cost per unit 120 units	Cost per unit 150 units
	$	$
Z1	12.00	12.00
Z2	12.50	10.00
Z3	8.00	8.50
Z4	7.50	6.00

Which two cost types could be classified as being fixed?

A Z1 and Z3

B Z1 and Z4

C Z2 and Z3

D Z2 and Z4

Chapter 3: Accounting for materials

Test your understanding 18

The following represent the materials transactions for a company for a year:

	$000
Materials purchases	240
Issued to production	215
Materials written off	12
Returned to stores	6
Returned to suppliers	2

The material inventory at 31 December 20X1 was $42,000.

What was the opening balance on the materials inventory account at 1 January 20X1?

A $1,000

B $25,000

C $33,000

D $59,000

Test your understanding 19

Continuous stocktaking is the process of checking the balance of every item of inventory on the same date, usually at the end of an accounting period.

Is this statement TRUE or FALSE?

A True

B False

This information is relevant for TYUs 20–25.

A business has inventory of material A of 400 units valued at $2.20 per unit at 1 September. During the month of September, the movements of material A were as follows:

5 September	Issue	250 units
10 September	Receipt	500 units @ $2.50 per unit
15 September	Issue	340 units
18 September	Receipt	400 units @ $2.70 per unit
27 September	Issue	600 units

Test your understanding 20

What is the cost of issues using the FIFO method?

A $2,913

B $2,980

C $2,975

D $2,990

Test your understanding 21

What is the value of the closing inventory using the FIFO method?

A $242

B $251

C $286

D $297

Test your understanding 22

What is the value of issues using the LIFO method?

A $2,913

B $2,924

C $2,980

D $2,968

Test your understanding 23

What is the value of closing inventory using the LIFO method?

A $242

B $251

C $286

D $297

Test your understanding 24

What is the cost of issues using the weighted average cost method?

A $2,913

B $2,924

C $2,980

D $2,968

Test your understanding 25

What is the value of closing inventory using the weighted average cost method?

A $242

B $251

C $286

D $297

Test your understanding 26

The objective of holding buffer inventory is to take advantage of quantity discounts.

Is this statement TRUE or FALSE?

A True

B False

Test your understanding 27

Which of the following is not a stockholding cost?

A The opportunity cost of capital tied up

B The cost of insurance

C Shipping and handling costs

D Inventory obsolescence

Test your understanding 28

A manufacturer uses 100,000 components costing $1 each at a constant rate throughout the year. The cost of making a single order for more components is $10 and the holding costs for each component are 0.5% of the average inventory value.

What is the EOQ?

A 1,411

B 2,000

C 14,142

D 20,000

Test your understanding 29

A retailer has a steady demand for rugby balls at 50 a month. Each ball costs $6 from the supplier. The costs involved in placing an order are $10 and the stockholding costs are 20% of the stockholding value per annum.

How many orders will be placed per annum?

A 1.73

B 6

C 8.48

D 100

Test your understanding 30

Annual demand for raw material is 1,000,000 units. Each unit costs 15 cents. Procurement costs for each order are $20 and lead time has been estimated as 2 days. There are 250 working days per annum, the carrying cost of inventory is 10 cents per unit and the cost of a stock out is 20 cents per unit.

What is the optimal reorder level?

A 50

B 8,000

C 20,000

D 4,000

Test your understanding 31

The adoption of Just in Time normally requires which one of the following factors to increase?

A Inventory levels

B Work-in-progress levels

C Batch sizes

D Quality standards

Chapter 4: Accounting for labour

Test your understanding 32

Which of the following should be classified as direct labour?

A The site foreman of a building company

B Workers assembling components on a production line

C The store man handling parts requisitions in a factory

D Human resources in a car manufacturing plant

Test your understanding 33

A company employs 100 direct workers in the factory, who are paid a basic rate of $5 per hour for a 35-hour week. In addition to working their normal hours last month, each worker was asked to work an additional 5 hours overtime per week to meet general production requirements. All overtime hours are paid at time and a half. As a result of some faulty material, 150 hours of direct labour time were registered as idle.

What is the indirect labour cost for last month, assuming a 4-week period?

A $750

B $2,000

C $5,750

D $15,750

Test your understanding 34

An employee receives a bonus. The employee's basic rate of pay is $6 per hour. The allowed time for the job was 1 hour and the employee completed it in 40 minutes.

The Rowan scheme is calculated as

$$\text{Bonus} = \frac{\text{Time taken}}{\text{Time allowed}} \times \text{Time rate} \times \text{Time saved}$$

What is the total payment for the job (to the nearest cent)?

A $1.33

B $4.00

C $5.00

D $5.33

Test your understanding 35

At 31 March 20X1 an organisation had 5,400 employees. During the previous year 750 had left the organisation, although the management had decided that only 600 needed replacing and had recruited accordingly.

What was the labour turnover rate for the year to 31 March 20X1 (to 2 decimal places)?

A 10.96%

B 11.11%

C 11.27%

D 13.89%

Test your understanding 36

The data below relates to last month's production of product Z:

Standard time allowed per unit = 20 minutes

Budgeted hours available = 210 hours

Actual output = 600 units in 220 hours

Which of the following is the correct labour capacity and efficiency ratio?

	Labour capacity	Labour efficiency
A	95.24%	90.91%
B	95.24%	104.76%
C	104.76%	90.91%
D	104.76%	95.24%

Chapter 5: Accounting for overheads

Test your understanding 37

A company manufactures two products, E and F, in a factory divided into two production cost centres, Primary and Finishing. In order to determine a budgeted fixed overhead cost per unit of product, the following budgeted data are relevant.

	Primary	Finishing
Allocated and apportioned fixed costs	$84,000	$93,000
Direct labour – minutes per unit		
E	36	25
F	30	40

Budgeted production is 9,000 units of E and 6,000 units of F. Fixed overheads are to be absorbed on a direct labour hour basis.

What is the budgeted fixed overhead cost of a unit of product E?

A $10

B $11

C $12

D $13

Test your understanding 38

Billecarte Ltd manufactures two products, Zonk and Tink, in a factory divided into two production cost centres, Machining and Assembly. In order to find a fixed overhead cost per unit, the following budgeted data are relevant.

	Machining	Assembly
Direct and allocated fixed costs	$120,000	$72,000
Labour hours per unit		
Zonk	0.50 hours	0.20 hours
Tink	1.00 hours	0.25 hours

Budgeted production is 4,000 units of each product and fixed overheads are to be absorbed by reference to labour hours.

What should be the budgeted fixed overhead cost of a unit of Zonk?

A $28

B $24

C $20

D $18

Test your understanding 39

Products alpha and beta are made in a factory that has two production cost centres: assembly and finishing. Budgeted production is 8,000 alpha and 10,000 beta. Fixed overheads are absorbed on a labour hour basis.

The following budgeted information is available:

	Production	Finishing
Allocated and apportioned fixed costs	$ 55,000	$ 63,000
Direct labour hours per unit		
Product alpha	1.5 hrs	2 hrs
Product beta	1 hr	0.5 hrs

What is the budgeted fixed cost per unit for product beta?

A $3.46

B $4.00

C $9.75

D $10.425

Test your understanding 40

Here are three statements on the determination of overhead absorption rates:

1 Costs can be allocated where it is possible to identify the department that caused them.

2 Costs need to be apportioned where they are shared by more than one department.

3 Service centre costs should not be included in unit overhead costs.

Which of these statements are correct?

A 1 and 2 only

B 1 and 3 only

C 2 and 3 only

D 1, 2 and 3

Test your understanding 41

The following statements refer to overhead absorption:

1 Factory rent and rates are typically allocated to departments rather than apportioned.

2 A single product firm does not need to apportion overheads to find a cost per unit.

3 If departmental overhead recovery rates are similar it makes little difference if overheads are applied on a departmental or business wide basis.

Which of these statements are correct?

A 1 and 2 only

B 1 and 3 only

C 2 and 3 only

D 1, 2 and 3

Test your understanding 42

A manufacturing company has the following budgeted and actual results for the year:

Budgeted fixed overhead expenditure	$504,000
Budgeted activity	42,000 machine hours
Actual fixed overhead expenditure	$515,000
Actual activity	45,000 machine hours

What is the result of using the pre-determined fixed overhead rate for the year?

A $11,000 under-absorbed

B $25,000 under-absorbed

C $25,000 over-absorbed

D $36,000 over-absorbed

Test your understanding 43

A manufacturing organisation has two production departments (Machining and Finishing) and two service departments (Quality control and Maintenance). After primary apportionment the overheads for the factory are as follows:

	Total	Machining	Finishing	QC	Maintenance
Overheads	$633,000	$220,000	$160,000	$140,000	$113,000
Work done by QC		45%	35%	–	20%
Work done by Maint'ce		30%	40%	30%	–

What is the total overhead to be apportioned to the Finishing department?

A $124,750

B $284,750

C $285,821

D $348,250

Chapter 6: Absorption and marginal costing

Test your understanding 44

The following statements relate to costing and overheads:

(i) Products create a demand for support activities in service cost centres in direct proportion to the volume of each product manufactured

(ii) Where overheads form a large proportion of total costs, then the arbitrary nature of apportionment is more of an issue

(iii) When closing inventory levels are lower than opening inventory levels, marginal costing gives a lower profit than absorption costing

(iv) Only fixed and variable production costs should be included in unit costs for inventory valuation purposes under absorption costing

Which TWO of the statements are correct?

A Statements (i) and (iii)

B Statements (i) and (iv)

C Statements (ii) and (iii)

D Statements (ii) and (iv)

Test your understanding 45

The number of units of finished goods inventory at the end of a period is greater than at the beginning.

What would the effect be of using the marginal costing method of inventory valuation?

A less operating profit than the absorption costing method

B the same operating profit as the absorption costing method

C more operating profit than the absorption costing method

D more or less operating profit than the absorption costing method depending on the ratio of fixed to variable costs

Test your understanding 46

Accounting standards support the use of the marginal costing approach to inventory valuation when preparing the published accounts of a company, as it achieves a better matching of sales and expenses for the period.

Is this statement TRUE or FALSE?

A True

B False

Test your understanding 47

A business has just completed its first year of trading. The following information has been collected from the accounting records.

		$
Variable cost per unit		
Manufacturing		6.00
Selling and administration		0.20
Fixed costs		
Manufacturing	90,000	
Selling and administration	22,500	

Production was 75,000 units and sales were 70,000 units. The selling price was $8 per unit throughout the year.

What is the difference in profit using marginal costing for inventory valuation, rather than absorption costing?

A $8,500

B $7,500

C $6,000

D $2,500

Chapter 7: Job, batch and process costing

Test your understanding 48

The cost of output goods is found by calculating the net costs of the manufacturing process and dividing by the number of units produced.

What is this approach known as?

A Job costing

B Batch costing

C Process costing

D Service costing

Test your understanding 49

Which one of the following organisations is most likely to use batch costing as the method for establishing the cost of products?

A Car repairs

B Clothing

C Oil refining

D Charity shop

Test your understanding 50

The following data relates to a process for the month of May:

	$
Input materials (500 litres)	3,000
Labour and overhead	2,670

Normal output is expected to be 9 litres for every 10 litres input.

Actual output was 460 litres.

Identify the quantity of the abnormal loss/gain in the process?

A 50 litres abnormal loss

B 410 litres abnormal gain

C 40 litres abnormal loss

D 10 litres abnormal gain

Test your understanding 51

Normal losses are expected to be 10% of input. Actual output was 3,550 kg and there was an unexpected extra loss of 50 kg.

How many kg were input into the process?

A 3,944

B 3,889

C 4,000

D 5,000

Test your understanding 52

Chemicals X, Y and Z are produced from a single joint process. The information below relates to the period just ended:

Input costs $153,280

Output from process:	Chemical X	1,440 litres
	Chemical Y	864 litres
	Chemical Z	576 litres

Selling prices:	Chemical X	$100 per litre
	Chemical Y	$80 per litre
	Chemical Z	$60 per litre

What is the share of the joint process costs charged to Chemical X, using the volume of output method of apportionment?

A $76,640

B $89,116

C $63,867

D $51,093

Test your understanding 53

The following data relates to a joint product – Product G

	Quantity produced	Sales price at split-off point	Further processing costs	Sales price after further processing
	kg	$ per kg		$ per kg
Product G	1,200	7	$400 plus $2.00 per kg	10.00

Common costs prior to the split-off point are $900.

Should product G be sold at the split-off point, or processed further before sale?

A At split-off point

B After further processing

Test your understanding 54

Which of the following is not a possible method of apportioning the joint costs of a manufacturing process?

A Physical quantity

B Market value at point of separation

C Carrying amount

D Net realisable value

Chapter 8: Service and operation costing

Test your understanding 55

The principles used to calculate unit costs in manufacturing industries can equally be applied to service industries.

Is this statement TRUE or FALSE?

A True

B False

Test your understanding 56

Which of the following would not be an appropriate situation for the use of service costing?

A Power supply industry

B Oil refinery

C Restaurant in a factory

D Haulage business

Test your understanding 57

Which of the following statistics is unlikely to be used by the Rooms department of a hotel business?

A Room occupancy

B Cleaning cost per room

C Meals served per guest

D Average cost per occupied bed

Test your understanding 58

Many service applications involve high fixed costs and the higher the number of cost units produced the higher the fixed costs per unit.

Is this statement TRUE or FALSE?

A True

B False

Test your understanding 59

A transport business has 6 lorries in operation, 5 days a week for 50 weeks of the year.

Each vehicle is expected to make 4 journeys a day, delivering an average load of 5 tonnes to each customer. The average customer is located 25 kilometres from the transport headquarters. Fuel and other variable running costs per kilometre travelled (laden or unladen) are budgeted to be $0.50. Other fixed running costs amount to $225,000 per annum.

What is the standard running cost per tonne kilometre?

A $0.45

B $0.50

C $0.77

D $1.25

Chapter 9: Alternative costing principles

Test your understanding 60

Which ONE of the following is an advantage of Activity Based Costing?

A It provides more accurate product costs

B It is simple to apply

C It is a form of marginal costing and so is relevant to decision making

D It is particularly useful when fixed overheads are very low

Test your understanding 61

In calculating the life cycle costs of a product, which of the following items would be excluded?

(i) Planning and concept design costs

(ii) Preliminary and detailed design costs

(iii) Testing costs

(iv) Production costs

(v) Distribution and customer service costs

A (iii)

B (iv)

C (v)

D None of them

Test your understanding 62

As part of a process to achieve a target cost, GYE Inc are interviewing prospective customers to determine why they would buy the product and how they would use it.

What term best describes this process?

A Value analysis

B Operational research

C Value engineering

D Lifecycle costing

Chapter 10: Sources of data

Test your understanding 63

If you choose the 10th or the 100th unit after the first has been chosen. This type of sampling is known as:

A Simple random

B Stratified

C Cluster

D Systematic

Test your understanding 64

Which of the following is an example of external information?

A Payroll system

B Government statistics

C Accounting system

D Strategic planning system

Test your understanding 65

If you select a sample for a national opinion poll prior to a general election. The process would start by dividing the country into areas and a random sample of areas is taken. Next divide the country into town and cities and a sample is taken again. Then perhaps a sample of streets and a random sample of houses are then chosen.

What type of sampling is this?

A Simple

B Random

C Multi-stage

D Cluster

Test your understanding 66

Here are possible reasons why sampling is used over other methods of gathering data.

(i) The whole population may not be known

(ii) Testing all items in a population may not be possible

(iii) Items may be destroyed in the testing process

Which of the statements are correct?

A (i), (ii) and (iii)

B (ii) and (iii)

C (i) and (ii)

D (iii) only

Test your understanding 67

When sampling a population if there are several well defined groups which method would be used?

A Random sampling

B Systematic sampling

C Stratified sampling

D Multi-stage sampling

Test your understanding 68

Which concept is not part of the 5Vs of Big Data?

A Volume

B Variety

C Viability

D Velocity

Chapter 11: Analysing data

Test your understanding 69

A project may result in profits of \$20,000 or \$12,000, or in a loss of \$5,000, with probabilities 0.3, 0.5 and 0.2, respectively.

What is the expected profit of the project?

A \$11,000

B \$27,000

C \$9,000

D \$12,000

Test your understanding 70

FGH stocks a weekly magazine which advertises local second-hand goods. The owner can buy the magazines for 15c each and sell them at the retail price of 25c. At the end of each week unsold magazines are obsolete and have no value.

The owner has estimated a probability distribution for weekly demand as follows:

Weekly demand in units	Probability
10	0.20
15	0.55
20	0.25

Calculate the expected value of demand.

Test your understanding 71

A company has a normally distributed sales pattern for one of its products, with a mean of $110. The probability of a sale worth more than $120 is 0.0119.

Using normal tables, the standard deviation, to two decimal places, associated with sales is:

A $4.41

B $4.42

C $4.43

D $4.44

Test your understanding 72

The weights of a certain mass-produced item are known, over a long period of time, to be normally distributed with a mean of 8 kg and a standard deviation of 0.02 kg.

Required:

(a) If items whose weight lies outside the range 7.985 – 8.035 kg are deemed to be faulty, what percentage of products will be faulty?

(b) If it is required to reduce the percentage of items that are too heavy (with weight over 8.035 kg) to 2%, to what value must the mean weight be decreased, leaving all other factors unchanged?

(c) If it is required to reduce the percentage of items that are too light (with weight below 7.985 kg) to 2%, to what value must the standard deviation be decreased, leaving other factors unchanged?

Test your understanding 73

A company is analysing the number of orders placed by its 10 main customers. The median was calculated as 29 from the following values:

13, 42, x, 7, 51, 69, 28, 33, 14, 8

What is the value of x?

A 25

B 29

C 30

D 32

Test your understanding 74

A company is analysing the number of complaints received each day over a period.

Complete the missing entries in the following table and calculate the arithmetic mean (to two decimal places).

Complaints (x)	Frequency (f)	fx
0	10	?
1	15	?
2	25	?
3	5	?
Totals	?	?

Test your understanding 75

Which ONE of the following statements about the mode is true? Select all that apply.

A It is the most widely used average

B It is a measure of dispersion

C It gives the most common value

D It is the middle point of a set of values

Test your understanding 76

Match the following terms to the correct definition.

Mean	the value which occurs most often in a data set
Median	the answer derived by dividing the sum of a set of values by the number of values
Mode	the middle of a set of values

Chapter 12: Analytical techniques in budgeting and forecasting

Test your understanding 77

Regression analysis has been used to find the line of best fit for two variables, x and y and the correlation coefficient has then been calculated to assess the reliability of the line as a forecasting tool.

What is the value of the correlation coefficient for the line that will provide the most reliable forecast?

A –0.9

B 0

C +0.2

D –0.4

Test your understanding 78

Using the data below, calculate the price index for 2003.

Year	Selling price $	Index
2000	22	100
2001	23	
2002	26	
2003	25	
2004	28	

A 105

B 118

C 114

D 127

Test your understanding 79

Using the information below, restate the 2006 revenue to 2008 prices.

Year	Revenue ($000)	Index
2004	1,150	100
2005	1,250	115
2006	1,200	130
2007	1,250	115
2008	1,300	140

A 1,610

B 1,522

C 1,400

D 1,292

The following data relate to Questions 80 and 81

H is forecasting its sales for next year using a combination of time series and regression analysis models. An analysis of past sales units has produced the following equation for the quarterly sales trend:

$y = 26x + 8,850$

where the value of x represents the quarterly accounting period and the value of y represents the quarterly sales trend in units. Quarter 1 of next year will have a value for x of 25.

The quarterly seasonal variations have been measured using the multiplicative (proportional) model and are:

Quarter 1 – 15%

Quarter 2 – 5%

Quarter 3 + 5%

Quarter 4 + 15%

Production is planned to occur at a constant rate throughout the year. The company does not hold inventories at the end of any year.

Test your understanding 80

The difference between the budgeted sales for quarter 1 and quarter 4 next year are:

A 78 units

B 2,850 units

C 2,862 units

D 2,940 units

Test your understanding 81

The number of units to be produced in each quarter of next year will be nearest to:

A 9,454 units

B 9,493 units

C 9,532 units

D 9,543 units

Test your understanding 82

Z plc has found that it can estimate future sales using time series analysis and regression techniques.

The following trend equation has been derived:

$$y = 25{,}000 + 6{,}500x$$

where:

y is the total sales units per quarter

x is the time period reference number

Using the above model, what is the forecast for sales units for the third quarter of year 7, assuming that the first quarter of year 1 is time period reference number 1.

A 194,000 units

B 200,500 units

C 207,000 units

D 213,500 units

Test your understanding 83

Regression analysis has been used to calculate the line of best fit from a series of data. Using this line to predict a value which lies between the two extreme values observed historically is known as extrapolation.

Is this statement TRUE or FALSE?

A True

B False

Test your understanding 84

Regression analysis has produced the following results from the batch production costs for each of the past 5 months.

$\Sigma x = 540$, $\Sigma y = 755$, $\Sigma x^2 = 61{,}000$, $\Sigma xy = 83{,}920$

Which of the following is the appropriate value for b in the regression line to 2 decimal places?

A –1.40

B 0.01

C 0.89

D 1.40

Test your understanding 85

A company is preparing its budgets for next year. The following regression equation has been found to be a reliable estimate of XYZ's deseasonalised sales in units:

$y = 10x + 150$

Where y = total sales units and x refers to the accountancy period.

What is the expected figure for actual sales in accounting period 19?

A 255

B 315

C 340

D 190

Chapter 13: Budgeting

Test your understanding 86

The following statements relate to budgeting:

(i) A forecast is an attempt to predict what will happen

(ii) A budget is a plan of what is intended to happen

(iii) All budgets are prepared in financial terms

(iv) The master budget consists of a budgeted statement of profit or loss and budgeted statement of financial position

(v) A flexible budget adjusts both fixed and variable costs for the level of activity

Which of the following is true?

A All statements are correct

B Statements (i) and (ii) are correct

C Statements (ii), (iii) and (iv) are correct

D Statements (i), (iii) and (v) are correct

Test your understanding 87

Which of the following statements is true?

A The principal budget factor is the person who is responsible for controlling and coordinating the budget process

B A business must always produce its sales budget first, before any other budgets can be decided on

C The budget committee consists of managers with final responsibility for agreeing the budget

D A business will always produce a labour budget based on the material it can purchase

Test your understanding 88

An organisation is preparing its quarterly budget. It has consistently maintained inventory levels at 10% of the following month's sales. Budgeted sales for January are 2,000 units and sales are expected to increase by 500 units per month for the following three months.

What is the budgeted production in units for February?

A 2,050

B 2,450

C 2,500

D 2,550

Test your understanding 89

The management accountant is preparing the master budget for his/her retail firm. The following information has been supplied

Sales	$300,000
Opening inventory	$40,000
Closing inventory	$60,000
Required profit	20%

What amount should be budgeted for purchases?

A $220,000

B $225,000

C $240,000

D $260,000

Test your understanding 90

An extract from next year's budget for a manufacturing company is shown below.

	Month 3	**Month 4**
Sales	100,000 units	120,000 units
Closing inventory of finished goods	6,000 units	8,000 units
Closing inventory of raw materials	22,000 kg	8,000 kg
Each unit requires 2 kg material		

What is the budgeted material usage for month 4?

A 230,000 kg

B 234,000 kg

C 240,000 kg

D 244,000 kg

Test your understanding 91

The following information has been supplied in connection with an organisation's labour and overhead budget:

	Product alpha Cost per unit $	**Product beta** Cost per unit $
Unskilled labour (@$5/hr)	15	10
Skilled labour (@ $8/hr)	16	24
	—	—
Total labour cost	31	34
	—	—
Budgeted production	8,000 units	12,000 units

What is the total amount of skilled labour hours required in the period?

A 40,000 hours

B 48,000 hours

C 52,000 hours

D 60,000 hours

Test your understanding 92

Performance-related pay involves:

A rewarding employees with a proportion of total profits

B rewarding employees with a proportion of total profits in excess of a target minimum level

C rewarding employees on the basis of the amount of work they have done

D rewarding employees for achieving agreed personal targets

Test your understanding 93

In the context of budget preparation, the term 'goal congruence' is:

A the alignment of budgets with objectives using feed-forward control

B the setting of a budget which does not include budget bias

C the alignment of corporate objectives with the personal objectives of a manager

D the use of aspiration levels to set efficiency targets

Test your understanding 94

Which of the following statements about imposed budgets are correct?

(i) Imposed budgets are likely to set realistic targets because senior management have the best idea of what is achievable in each part of the business.

(ii) Imposed budgets can be less effective than budgets set on a participative basis, because it is difficult for an individual to be motivated to achieve targets set by someone else.

(iii) Imposed budgets are generally quicker to prepare and finalise than participative budgets.

A (i) and (ii) only

B (i) and (iii) only

C (ii) and (iii) only

D (iii) only

Test your understanding 95

A flexible budget is

A a budget for semi-variable overhead costs only

B a budget which, by recognising different cost behaviour patterns, is designed to change as volume of activity changes

C a budget for a twelve-month period which includes planned revenues, expenses, assets and liabilities

D a budget which is prepared for a rolling period which is reviewed monthly, and updated accordingly

Test your understanding 96

The purpose of a flexed budget is:

A to cap discretionary expenditure

B to produce a revised budget by changing the original budget when actual activity is known

C to control resource efficiency

D to communicate target activity levels within an organisation by setting a budget in advance of the period to which it relates

Test your understanding 97

A fixed budget is:

A a budget for a single level of activity

B used when the mix of products is fixed in advance of the budget period

C a budget which ignores inflation

D an overhead cost budget

Test your understanding 98

In a responsibility accounting system for which of the following should the production line manager be held responsible?

A Raw material prices and labour wage rates

B Raw material usage and labour wage rates

C Raw material prices and labour hours worked

D Raw material usage and labour hours worked

Chapter 14: Investment appraisal

Test your understanding 99

A company is evaluating a new product proposal that will last 6 years.

The initial outlay is $2 million. The proposed product selling price is $220 per unit and the variable costs are $55 per unit and sales are planned to be 2,750 units each year. The incremental cash fixed costs for the product will be $3,750 per annum.

What is the NPV of this project if the cost of capital is 10%?

A $40,250

B –$40,250

C $190,600

D –$190,600

Test your understanding 100

The details of an investment project are as follows:

Cost of asset bought at the start of the project $80,000

Annual cash inflow $25,000

Cost of capital 5% each year

Life of the project 8 years

The present value of the cash flows that occur in the second year of the project is:

A $23,800

B $22,675

C $21,000

D $20,575

The following data relates to Questions 101 and 102.

Year	Item	Cash flow
0	Cost of machine	(50,000)
1	Net cash flow from sales	22,000
2	Net cash flow from sales	22,000
3	Net cash flow from sales	20,000

A company uses a cost of capital of 10%. Assume all cash flows accrue evenly through the year.

Test your understanding 101

What is the payback period of the data above?

A 1 year 4 months

B 1 year 10 months

C 2 years 4 months

D 2 years 10 months

Test your understanding 102

What is discounted payback of the data above?

A 1 year 4 months

B 1 year 10 months

C 2 years 4 months

D 2 years 10 months

Test your understanding 103

An education authority is considering the implementation of a CCTV (closed circuit television) security system in one of its schools. Details of the proposed project are as follows:

Life of project 5 years

Initial cost $75,000

Annual savings:

Labour costs $20,000

Other costs $5,000

The project should be appraised using cost of capitals of 15% and 20%.

What is the internal rate of return for this project?

A 20.1%

B 19.9%

C 19.1%

D 18.9%

Test your understanding 104

The details of an investment project are:

Life of the project 10 years

Cost of asset bought at the start of the project $100,000

Annual cash inflow $20,000

Cost of capital 8% each year

What is the payback of the cash flows that occur?

A $34,200

B $100,000

C 5 years

D 6 years and 8 months

Test your understanding 105

A company has determined that the net present value of an investment project is $12,304 when using a 10% discount rate and $(3,216) when using a discount rate of 15%.

What is the internal rate of return of the project to the nearest 1%?

A 13%

B 14%

C 16%

D 17%

Test your understanding 106

An investment project with no residual value has a net present value of $87,980 when it is discounted using a cost of capital of 10%. The annual cash flows are as follows:

Year	$
0	(200,000)
1	80,000
2	90,000
3	100,000
4	60,000
5	40,000

Calculate the Internal Rate of Return (IRR) of the project (us 20% as the other discount rate).

A 11.6%

B 16.4%

C 17.3%

D 25.7%

The following data relates to Questions 107 to 109.

M plc is evaluating three possible investment projects and uses a 10% discount rate to determine their net present values.

Investment	**A**	**B**	**C**
	$000	$000	$000
Initial investment	400	450	350
Incremental cash flows			
Year 1	100	130	50
Year 2	120	130	110
Year 3	140	130	130
Year 4	120	130	150
Year 5	100	150	100
Net present value	39	55	48

Test your understanding 107

What is the payback period of investment A?

A 3 years

B 3 years 4 months

C 4 years

D 4 years 4 months

Test your understanding 108

What is the discounted payback period of investment B?

A 3 years 1 month

B 3 years 6 months

C 4 years 5 months

D 4 years 8 months

Test your understanding 109

What is the Internal Rate of Return (IRR) of investment C (calculate the alternative NPV using a 20% discount rate)?

A 12.3%

B 13.5%

C 14.9%

D 15.2%

Chapter 15: Standard costing

Test your understanding 110

A company's standard labour rate for its factory workers is set at $5 per hour.

The standard time allowed for producing one unit is 20 minutes.

During the period 4,800 units were produced and the factory workers were paid $5.25 per hour. The actual hours worked were 1,560.

What was the total labour cost variance?

A $390 adverse

B $190 adverse

C $190 favourable

D $390 favourable

Test your understanding 111

Which of the following would explain an adverse materials usage variance?

A The volume of activity was more than originally expected

B A higher quality of materials than anticipated was used

C There was a major spillage resulting in the loss of raw materials

D The material cost more than the standard

The following information relates to questions 112 and 113:

The materials budget for producing 5,000 units of product is 25,000 litres at $3.30 per litre. In the first month of production the company purchased 30,000 litres at a cost of $105,000, of which 28,000 litres were used to produce an actual output of 5,900 units.

Test your understanding 112

What was the material usage variance?

A $9,900 adverse

B $650 adverse

C $4,950 favourable

D $5,250 favourable

Test your understanding 113

What was the material price variance?

A $6,000 adverse

B $12,600 adverse

C $6,000 favourable

D $12,600 favourable

The following information relates to questions 114 and 115:

A company's product results for the month are as follows:

	Actual	Budget
Sales units	9,500	9,000
	$	$
Sales revenue	104,500	108,000
Manufacturing costs at standard	76,000	72,000
Contribution	28,500	36,000

Test your understanding 114

What was the sales price variance?

A $3,500 adverse

B $9,000 adverse

C $9,500 adverse

D $9,500 favourable

Test your understanding 115

What was the sales volume contribution variance?

A $1,500 favourable

B $2,000 favourable

C $6,000 favourable

D $7,500 adverse

Test your understanding 116

A company's standard variable overhead rate for manufacturing is $7 per hour and the standard time allowed for production is 2.5 hours per unit.

During the period 3,200 units were produced in 8,320 hours. The variable overhead expenditure variance was $1,664 favourable.

What was the actual variable overhead rate per hour?

A $6.53

B $6.80

C $6.93

D $7.20

Test your understanding 117

If a manufacturing organisation is absorbing fixed overheads on a labour hour basis, the fixed overhead volume variance can be split into expenditure and efficiency variances.

Is this statement TRUE or FALSE?

A True

B False

Test your understanding 118

A company's budgeted fixed overhead for the last quarter of the financial year was $280,000 for 7,000 units of output. It actually spent $284,400 manufacturing 7,200 units.

What was the fixed overhead volume variance?

A $ 8,000 adverse

B $ 4,400 adverse

C $ 7,900 favourable

D $ 8,000 favourable

Test your understanding 119

A company uses standard marginal costing. Last month, when all sales were at the standard selling price, the standard contribution from actual sales was $85,600 and the following variances arose:

Total variable costs variance	$12,600 Adverse
Total fixed costs variance	$10,500 Favourable
Sales volume contribution variance	$20,500 Favourable

What was the Actual contribution for last month?

A $62,500

B $73,000

C $83,000

D $93,000

Chapter 16: Performance measurement

Test your understanding 120

A division has a residual income of $240,000 and operating profit of $640,000.

If it uses a rate of 10% for computing imputed interest on its invested capital, what is its return on investment (ROI) to the nearest whole number?

A 4%

B 10%

C 16%

D 27%

The following information is for questions 121–123

The budgeted output for a period is 1,500 units and the standard time allowed per unit is 30 minutes. The actual output in the period was 1,400 units and these were produced in 720 hours.

Test your understanding 121

Calculate the production/volume ratio

A 97.2%

B 93.3%

C 96.0%

D 95.8%

Test your understanding 122

Calculate the capacity ratio

A 97.2%

B 93.3%

C 96.0%

D 95.8%

Test your understanding 123

Calculate the efficiency ratio

A 97.2%

B 93.3%

C 96.0%

D 95.8%

Test your understanding 124

HH plc monitors the % of total sales that derives from products developed in the last year. Which part of the balanced scorecard would this metric be classified under?

A Financial perspective

B Customer perspective

C Internal perspective

D Learning perspective

Test your understanding 125

If the current ratio for a company is equal to its acid test ratio, then:

A the current ratio must be greater than one

B the company does not carry any inventory

C trade receivables plus cash is greater than trade payables minus inventory

D working capital is positive

Test your understanding 126

A government is looking at assessing hospitals by reference to a range of both financial and non-financial factors, one of which is survival rates for heart by-pass operation.

Which of the three E's best describes the above measure?

A Economy

B Effectiveness

C Efficiency

D Externality

Test your understanding 127

An organisation is divided into a number of divisions, each of which operates as a profit centre.

Which of the following would be useful measures to monitor divisional performance?

(i) Contribution

(ii) Controllable profit

(iii) Return on investment

(iv) Residual income

A (i) only

B (i) and (ii) only

C (iii) and (iv) only

D All of them

Test your understanding 128

Quality control costs can be categorised into internal and external failure costs, appraisal costs and prevention costs.

In which of these four classifications would the following costs be included?

– The costs of a customer service team

– The cost of equipment maintenance

– The cost of operating test equipment

	Customer service team	Equipment maintenance	Test equipment
A	Prevention costs	Appraisal costs	Internal failure costs
B	Prevention costs	Internal failure costs	Appraisal costs
C	External failure costs	Internal failure costs	Prevention costs
D	External failure costs	Prevention costs	Appraisal costs

Chapter 17: Presenting information

Test your understanding 129

What type of graph is this?

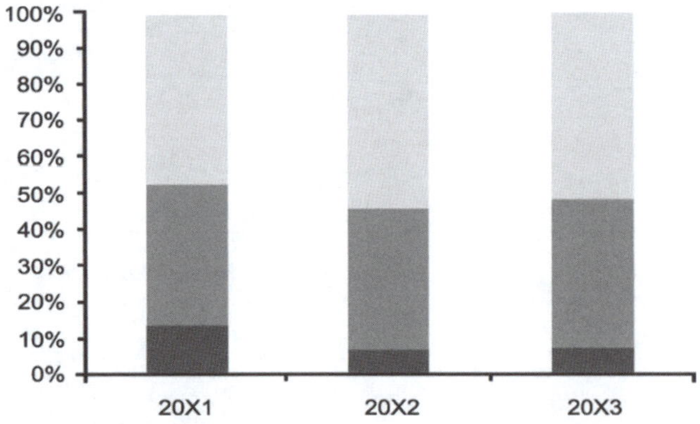

A line graph

B compound bar chart

C percentage compound bar chart

D percentage component bar chart

Test your understanding 130

Below is a pie chart showing the colours of shirts ordered by one shop.

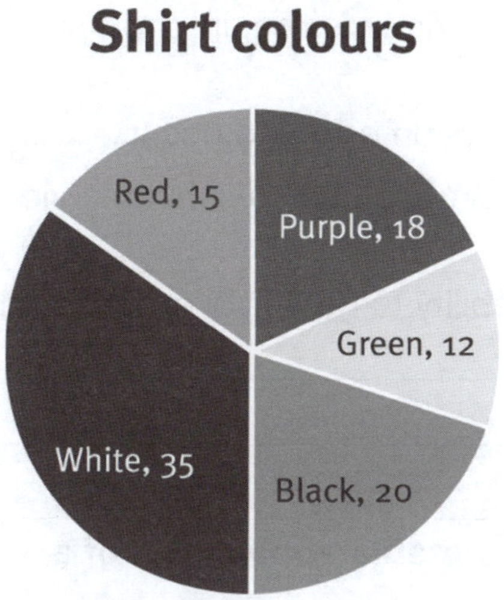

What is the angle of the wedge showing black shirts ordered?

A 44°

B 54°

C 65°

D 72°

Chapter 18: Spreadsheets

Test your understanding 131

The benefit of using a spreadsheet to prepare a budget is that estimates can be varied without everything having to be recalculated manually.

Is this statement TRUE or FALSE?

A True

B False

Test your understanding 132

A spreadsheet is more useful than a database when the primary objective is to store large amounts of raw data that needs to be accessed by multiple users.

Is this statement TRUE or FALSE?

A True

B False

Test your understanding 133

Which of the following is a disadvantage of using spreadsheets?

A Using spreadsheets can increase the time required to analyse data

B Using spreadsheets cause calculation errors to occur

C There can be sharing violations among users wishing to view or change data at the same time

D Spreadsheets do not have the ability to generate graphs and charts for the analysis of data

Test your understanding 134

Which of the following is the least suitable application of a spreadsheet package?

A Budgeting and forecasting

B Maintenance of customer records

C Inventory valuation

D Variance analysis

Chapter

20

Answers

Chapter 1: Accounting for management

Test your understanding 1

B FALSE

Data consists of numbers, letters and raw facts that have been recorded but not yet processed into a suitable form. Data that has been processed so as to make it meaningful is known as information.

Test your understanding 2

B

Test your understanding 3

D

Test your understanding 4

C

Test your understanding 5

C

Test your understanding 6

B

Test your understanding 7

B

Chapter 2: Cost classification

Test your understanding 8

B

B is a non-production cost and as such should not be used to value inventory.

Test your understanding 9

D

A Indirect and fixed

B Indirect and fixed

C Direct and variable

D Indirect and variable

Test your understanding 10

B

Test your understanding 11

D

Test your understanding 12

B FALSE

Telephone costs are likely to consist of a fixed element for line rental and a variable element for calls, hence are semi-variable.

Test your understanding 13

C

Test your understanding 14

C

Test your understanding 15

B

Take the highest and lowest output and associated costs.

	Output (units)	**Cost** ($)
High	2,000	8,750
Low	800	3,950
Change	1,200	4,800

Hence VC = $4,800/1,200 = $4 per unit.

FC = 3,950 – (800 × 4) = 750 this year and therefore 850 next.

So cost of 1,500 units = 850 + (1,500 × 4) = 6,850

Test your understanding 16

B

Take the highest and lowest output and associated costs when fixed costs are constant.

	Output (units)	**Cost** ($)
High	9,000	102,000
Low	7,000	86,000
Change	2,000	16,000

Hence VC = $16,000/2,000 = $8 per unit.

FC = 102,000 – (9,000 × 8) = 30,000 at output under 10,000 units.

So cost of 14,000 units = 30,000 + 15,000 + (14,000 × 8) = 157,000

Test your understanding 17

D

Cost type	**Total cost 120 units**	**Total cost 150 units**
	$	$
Z1	1,440	1,800
Z2	1,500	1,500
Z3	960	1,275
Z4	900	900

Z2 and Z4 have a constant total cost over different levels of activity so could be assumed to be fixed.

Chapter 3: Accounting for material

Test your understanding 18

B

Material inventory account

	$000		$000
Opening balance (bal fig)	25	Issued to production	215
Purchases	240	Materials returned to suppliers	2
Materials returned to stores	6	Written off	12
		Closing balance	42
	271		271

Test your understanding 19

FALSE

The statement refers to periodic stocktaking.

In continuous stocktaking a business counts and values selected items of inventory on a rotating basis. Specialist teams count and check certain inventory items on each day.

Test your understanding 20

A

				$
Issue on 5th Sept	250	$2.20	=	550
Issue on 15th Sept	150	$2.20	=	330
	190	$2.50	=	475
Issue on 27th Sept	310	$2.50	=	775
	290	$2.70	=	783
				2,913

Test your understanding 21

D

Closing inventory	110	$2.70	=	$297

Test your understanding 22

D

				$
Issue on 5th Sept	250	$2.20	=	550
Issue on 15th Sept	340	$2.50	=	850
Issue on 27th Sept	400	$2.70	=	1,080
	160	$2.50	=	400
	40	$2.20	=	88
				2,968

Test your understanding 23

A

Closing inventory 110 × $2.20 = $242

Test your understanding 24

B

			$
Issue on 5th Sept ($880/400 = $2.20)	250	$2.20	550
Issue on 15th Sept ($1,580/650 = $2.43077)	340	$2.43	826
Issue on 27th Sept ($1,834/710 = $2.5831)	600	$2.58	1,548
			2,924

Test your understanding 25

C

Closing inventory 110 × $2.58 = $286

Test your understanding 26

B FALSE

The objective of holding buffer inventories is to reduce the risk of a stock out occurring e.g. where supplier lead times are uncertain (the time taken between placing and receiving an order).

The availability of quantity discounts would affect the order quantity not the reorder level.

Test your understanding 27

C

This is a cost of ordering and obtaining the inventory.

Test your understanding 28

D

EOQ = $\sqrt{(2C_0D/C_h)}$

C_0=10, D =100,000, C_h= \$0.005

EOQ = $\sqrt{(2 \times 10 \times 100{,}000/0.005)}$ = 20,000

Test your understanding 29

B

C_0=10, D = 50 × 12 = 600, C_h= 0.2 × \$6

EOQ = $\sqrt{(2C_0D/C_h)} = \sqrt{(2 \times 10 \times 600/1.20)}$

EOQ = 100

Therefore place 6 orders p.a. (600/100).

Test your understanding 30

B

ROL = demand in the lead time

Demand per day = 1,000,000/250 = 4,000 units (answer D).

So expected demand in the lead time and hence ROL is 8,000

C is the EOQ and A the number of orders that would be placed p.a.

Test your understanding 31

D

An increase in quality standards is one of the key factors that allows the other items listed to be reduced.

Chapter 4: Accounting for labour

Test your understanding 32

B

Test your understanding 33

C

Idle time = 150 hours @ $5 = $750

Overtime (premium only) = 100 × 5 × 4 @ $2.50 = $5,000

Total indirect labour element = $5,750

Test your understanding 34

D

Basic rate = 40/60 × $6 = $4

Bonus = 40/60 × $6/60 × 20 = $1.33

Total payment = $5.33

Test your understanding 35

A

No of leavers requiring replacement = 600

Employees at 1 April 20X0 = 5,400 + 750 – 600 = 5,550

Average number of employees = (5,550 + 5,400) ÷ 2 = 5,475

Labour turnover rate = 600 ÷ 5,475 × 100 = 10.96%

Test your understanding 36

C

Labour capacity ratio = 220/210 × 100 = 104.76%.

Expected hours to produce actual output (standard hours):

600 units × 20/60 = 200 hours

Labour efficiency ratio = 200/220 × 100 = 90.91 %

Chapter 5: Accounting for overheads

Test your understanding 37

B

Product	Units	Hours per unit	Hours in the Primary department	Hours per unit	Hours in the Finishing department
E	9,000	× 36 ÷ 60	5,400	× 25 ÷ 60	3,750
F	6,000	× 30 ÷ 60	3,000	× 40 ÷ 60	4,000
			8,400		7,750

Rate per hour in the Primary department = $8,4000 ÷ 8,400 = $10

Rate per hour in the Finishing department = $93,000 ÷ 7,750 = $12

E = ($10 × 36 ÷ 60) + ($12 × 25 ÷ 60) = $11

Test your understanding 38

D

Machining hours
= 4,000 × 0.5 hours + 4,000 × 1.0 hours = 6,000 hours

Assembly hours
= 4,000 × 0.2 hours + 4,000 × 0.25 hours = 1,800 hours

$$\text{Machine absorption} = \frac{\$120,000}{6,000 \text{ hours}} = \$20 \text{ per hour}$$

$$\text{Assembly absorption rate} = \frac{\$72,000}{1,800 \text{ hours}} = \$40 \text{ per hour}$$

Fixed overhead per unit of Zonk
= (0.5 hours × $20) + (0.2 hours × $40) = $18

Test your understanding 39

B

	Production	**Finishing**
Allocated and apportioned fixed costs	$55,000	$63,000
Total Direct labour hours:		
Product alpha	1.5 × 8,000	2 × 8,000
Product beta	1 × 10,000	0.5 × 10,000
	22,000 hrs	21,000 hrs
Fixed overhead per labour hour	$2.50	$3.00

Product beta: (1 hr @ $2.5) + (0.5 hrs @ $3) = $4

Test your understanding 40

A

Test your understanding 41

C

Test your understanding 42

C

Pre-determined overhead rate = $504,000/42,000 = $12 per hour

	$
Overhead absorbed (45,000 hours @ $12)	540,000
Overhead incurred	515,000
Fixed overhead over-absorbed	25,000

Test your understanding 43

B

	Machining	**Finishing**	**QC**	**Maintenance**
Primary apportionment	220,000	160,000	140,000	113,000
Re-apportion QC	63,000	49,000	(140,000)	28,000
Re-apportion Maintenance	42,300	56,400	42,300	(141,000)
Re-apportion QC	19,035	14,805	(42,300)	8,460
Re-apportion Maintenance	2,538	3,384	2,538	(8,460)
Re-apportion QC	1,142	888	(2,538)	508
Re-apportion Maintenance	152	204	152	(508)
Re-apportion QC	69	53	(152)	30
Re-apportion Maintenance	9	12	9	(30)
Re-apportion QC	5	4	(9)	–
Total overhead	348,250	284,750		

Alternative working:

1 Q = 140,000 + 0.3M

2 M = 113,000 + 0.2Q

Substitute (1) in equation (2):

M = 113,000 + 0.2 (140,000 + 0.3M)

M = 113,000 + 28,000 + 0.06M

0.94M = 141,000

M = 150,000

Substituting this into equation (1)

Q = 140,000 + 0.3(150,000) = 185,000

Total overheads for departments

	Machining	Finishing
Primary apportionment	220,000	160,000
Share of QC	185,000 × 45% = 83,250	185,000 × 35% = 64,750
Share of maintenance	150,000 × 30% = 45,000	150,000 × 40% = 60,000
TOTAL	348,250	284,750

Chapter 6: Absorption and marginal costing

Test your understanding 44

D

(i) Incorrect. Smaller volume products often cause a disproportionate amount of cost

(ii) Correct

(iii) Incorrect. Marginal costing gives a higher profit.

(iv) Correct

Test your understanding 45

A

Test your understanding 46

B FALSE

The absorption costing approach charges fixed overheads to units produced and as a result achieves a better matching of sales and costs during a period and a more realistic measure of profit.

Test your understanding 47

C

Closing inventory = 5,000 units

Under full absorption costing a proportion of the fixed manufacturing overhead will be carried forward in this inventory.

$$\frac{\$90{,}000}{75{,}000} \times 5{,}000 = \$6{,}000$$

This is the difference in profit.

Chapter 7: Job, batch and process costing

Test your understanding 48

C

Test your understanding 49

B

Test your understanding 50

D

Normal loss = 1 ÷ 10 × 100 = 10%

Normal loss = 500 × 10% = 50 litres

Input = Output + NL

500 = 460 + 50 therefore AG of 10 litres

Test your understanding 51

C

Input = Output + NL + AL

Output + AL = 90% of input

3,550 kg + 50 kg = 3,600 kg

Input = 3,600 kg ÷ 90 × 100 = 4,000 kg

Test your understanding 52

A

$153,280 × 1,440 ÷ 2,880 = $76,640

Test your understanding 53

B

Sales value after split-off point = 1,200 × \$7 = \$8,400

Sales value after further processing = 1,200 × \$10 = \$12,000

Incremental sales value = \$12,000 – \$8,400 = \$3,600

Further processing costs = 1,200 × \$2 + \$400 = \$2,800

Incremental sales value is greater than the further processing costs so Product G should be sold after further processing.

Common costs are not relevant to this decision.

Test your understanding 54

C

Chapter 8: Service and operation costing

Test your understanding 55

A TRUE

Test your understanding 56

B

This would use process costing to establish the cost of a physical product.

Test your understanding 57

C

Which would be of use to the Restaurant/Kitchen

Test your understanding 58

B FALSE

Many service applications do involve high fixed costs but a higher number of cost units will result in a lower fixed cost per unit.

Test your understanding 59

B

Total km travelled p.a. = 200km × 5 days × 50 weeks × 6 vehicles = 300,000 km

Total VC = 300,000 km @ $0.50 = $150,000

Total Running costs = $150,000 VC + $225,000 FC = $375,000 p.a.

Total tonne km p.a. = 4 journeys × 25 km × 5 tonnes × 5 days × 50 weeks × 6 vehicles = 750,000 tonne/km

Standard cost per tonne km = $375,000/750,000 = $0.50

Chapter 9: Alternative costing principles

Test your understanding 60

A

ABC is fairly complicated, is a form of absorption (not marginal) costing and is particularly useful when fixed overheads are high and not primarily volume driven.

Test your understanding 61

D

A product's life cycle costs are very inclusive; none of these would be excluded.

Test your understanding 62

A

Value analysis involves identifying why and how customers value a product to enable cost savings to be made without compromising the value to the customer.

Chapter 10: Sources of data

Test your understanding 63

D

Data collection can be simplified by selecting say every 10th or 100th unit after the first unit has been chosen randomly. Such a procedure is called systematic random sampling.

Test your understanding 64

B

Test your understanding 65

C

This method is often applied if the population is particularly large, for example all TV viewers in the UK.

Test your understanding 66

A

Test your understanding 67

C

Test your understanding 68

C Viable

Chapter 11: Analysing data

Test your understanding 69

A

Expected profit = ($20,000 × 0.3) + ($12,000 × 0.5) – ($5,000 × 0.2) = $11,000

Test your understanding 70

EV of demand = (10 × 0.20) + (15 × 0.55) + (20 × 0.25) = **15.25 units per week**.

Test your understanding 71

B

P(sale > 120)	=	0.0119
P(110 < sale < 120)	=	0.5 – 0.0119
	=	0.4881

which corresponds to z = 2.26 from normal tables.

$$z = \frac{x - \mu}{\sigma}$$

2.26 = (120 – 110) ÷ σ

σ = (120 – 110) ÷ 2.226 = **$4.42**

Test your understanding 72

(a) **26.67% of products will be faulty**

If weight is 7.985 kg:

$$z = \frac{x - \mu}{\sigma}$$

Z = (7.985 – 8) ÷ 0.02 = –0.75

If weight is 8.035 kg:

Z = (8.035 – 8) ÷ 0.02 = 1.75

So we want P(–0.75 < z < 1.75) = TE(0.75) + TE(1.75) = 0.2734 + 0.4599 = 0.7333

Faulty items are outside this range so the probability that an item is faulty is 1 – 0.7333 = 0.2667.

(b) **The mean weight must be decreased to 7.994 kg.**

The tail-end probability of 2% corresponds to the table entry 48% = 0.48, and so to the z-value 2.05.

Use the formula to work back to calculate the mean:

2.05 = (8.035 – μ)/0.02

μ = 8.035 – (2.05 × 0.02) = 7.994.

(c) **The standard deviation must fall to 0.0073 kg.**

From the logic above, the z-value must now be –2.05

Use the formula to work back to calculate the standard deviation:

–2.05 = (7.985 – 8)/σ

σ = –0.015 ÷ –2.05 = 0.0073

Test your understanding 73

C

In order of magnitude, without x, the values are:

7, 8, 13, 14, 28, 33, 42, 51, 69

Including x, there are ten values so the median of 29 is the average of the fifth and sixth. The only possible solution is that x lies between 28 and 33 and has a value such that (28 + x)/2 = 29. Hence, x = 30.

Test your understanding 74

The arithmetic mean is **1.45**

The complete table is:

x	**f**	**fx**
0	10	0
1	15	15
2	25	50
3	5	15
Totals	55	80

Arithmetic mean = 80/55 = 1.45

Test your understanding 75

C

It is the most widely used average. This is false as the most widely used average is the mean.

It is a measure of dispersion. This is false as mode is an averaging measure. Measures of dispersion are range, variance and standard deviation.

It is the middle point of a set of values. This is false as it describes the median.

Test your understanding 76

The correct match is:

Mean	the answer derived by dividing the sum of a set of values by the number of values
Median	the middle of a set of values
Mode	the value which occurs most often in a data set

Chapter 12: Analytical techniques in budgeting and forecasting

Test your understanding 77

A

The correlation coefficient measures the strength of the connection between two variables. A correlation coefficient of 0 suggests that the two variables are unrelated and as a result there is no linear relationship between them. The closer the value to +1 or –1 the greater the correlation and the more reliable the line of best fit.

Test your understanding 78

C

The calculation of the index for 20X3 is as follows:

25/22 × 100 = 114

Test your understanding 79

D

Year	Revenue ($000)	Index adjustment	Adjusted revenue ($000)
2006	1,200	140/130	1,292

Test your understanding 80

D

Quarter	Value of x	Trend units	Forecast sales units
1	25	26×25+8,850=9,500	9,500×85%=8,075
2	26	26×26+8,850=9,526	9,526×95%=9,050
3	27	26×27+8,850=9,552	9,552×105%=10,030
4	28	26×28+8,850=9,578	9,578×115%=11,015

Difference between Q1 and Q4 budgeted sales = 11,015 – 8,075 = 2,940 units

Test your understanding 81

D

Budgeted production each quarter = 38,170/4

= 9,542.5 units rounded to 9,543 units.

Test your understanding 82

B

X is the time period reference number and for the first quarter of year 1 is 1. The time period reference number for the third quarter of year 7 is 27.

y = 25,000 + 6,500 × 27 = 200,500 units

Test your understanding 83

B FALSE

Using the line to predict values within the range observed is known as interpolation.

Test your understanding 84

C

$$b = \frac{(5 \times 83{,}920) - (540 \times 755)}{(5 \times 61{,}000) - (540^2)} = 0.89$$

Test your understanding 85

C

Y = (10 × 19) + 150 = 340

Chapter 13: Budgeting

Test your understanding 86

B

(i) Correct

(ii) Correct

(iii) Incorrect, e.g. budget for number of employees required

(iv) Incorrect. Master budget also includes budgeted cash flow

(v) Incorrect. Adjusts variable costs. Fixed are fixed

Test your understanding 87

C

Test your understanding 88

D

	Jan	Feb	Mar
Sales	2,000	2,500	3,000
– Opening inventory	(200)	(250)	(300)
+ Closing inventory	250	300	350
Production	2,050	2,550	3,050

Test your understanding 89

D

Required profit = $300,000 × 0.2 = 60,000

Cost of sales = Sales – Required profit = $240,000

Cost of sales = opening inventory + purchases (P) – closing inventory

240,000 = 40,000 + P – 60,000

P = 240,000 – 40,000 + 60,000

P = $260,000

Test your understanding 90

D

Month 4 production = 120,000 + 8,000 – 6,000 = 122,000 units

Month 4 usage = 122,000 units @ 2 kg = 244,000 kg

Test your understanding 91

C

Total hours required = 16,000 + 36,000 = 52,000

	Alpha	Beta
Skilled Hours per unit	2	3
Units	8,000	12,000
Total hours	16,000	36,000

Test your understanding 92

D

Answers A and B refer to profit-related pay and answer C describes either piece work payment or payment by the hour/day.

Test your understanding 93

C

Where there is goal congruence, managers who are working to achieve their own personal goals will automatically also be working to achieve the organisation's goals. Although the use of aspiration levels to set targets (option D) is likely to help in the achievement of goal congruence, it is not of itself a definition of the term.

Test your understanding 94

C

Statement (i) is incorrect. Managers at an operational level are more likely to know what is realistically achievable than a senior manager imposing budget targets from above. Statement (ii) is arguably correct: participation in budgeting could improve motivation. Statement (iii) is correct: imposed budgets should be much quicker to prepare, because less discussion time and negotiation time is required than with participative budget-setting.

Test your understanding 95

B

Option C is a fixed budget and option D is a rolling budget. Option A is incorrect as a flexible budget includes all costs.

Test your understanding 96

B

A flexed budget is prepared at the end of the budget period and is based on actual level of activity by recognising cost behaviours.

Test your understanding 97

A

A fixed budget is a budget prepared for a planned single level of activity. It does not ignore inflation (option C is incorrect) and it includes direct costs as well as overhead costs (option D is incorrect). A fixed budget can be prepared for a single product as well as a mix of products (option B is incorrect).

Test your understanding 98

D

The production-line manager does not control prices or rates.

Chapter 14: Investment appraisal

Test your understanding 99

B

	Cash flow	Discount rate	Present value
	$	10%	$
Year 0 Initial outlay	(2,000,000)	1.000	(2,000,000)
Year 1–6 Annual cash flow	450,000	4.355	1,959,750
Net present value			(40,250)

Test your understanding 100

B

Year	Cash flow	Discount factor	Present value
	$	5%	$
0	(80,000)	1.000	(80,000)
1	25,000	0.952	23,800
2	25,000	0.907	22,675

Test your understanding 101

C

Year	Cash flow	Cumulative cash flow
	$	$
0	(50,000)	(50,000)
1	22,000	(28,000)
2	22,000	(6,000)
3	20,000	14,000

2 years and 4 months

Months calculated = 6,000/20,000 × 12 = 3.6 months

Test your understanding 102

D

Year	Cash flow	Discount factor 10%	PV	Cumulative cash flow
	$		$	$
0	(50,000)	1.000	(50,000)	(50,000)
1	22,000	0.909	19,998	(30,002)
2	22,000	0.826	18,172	(11,830)
3	20,000	0.751	15,020	3,190

Test your understanding 103

B

Year	Cash flow	Discount factor 15%	Present value	Discount factor 20%	Present value
	$		$		$
0	(75,000)	1.000	(75,000)	1.000	(75,000)
1 – 5	25,000	3.352	83,800	2.991	74,775
NPV			8,800		(225)

IRR = 15 + [8,800/(8,800 – –225) × 5] = 19.9%

Test your understanding 104

C

$100,000/$20,000 = 5 years

Test your understanding 105

B

IRR = 10 + [12,304/(12,304 – –3,216) × 5] = 13.96% therefore 14%

Test your understanding 106

D

Year	Cash flow	Discount factor 20%	Present value
	$		$
0	(200,000)	1.000	(200,000)
1	80,000	0.833	66,640
2	90,000	0.694	62,460
3	100,000	0.579	57,900
4	60,000	0.482	28,920
5	40,000	0.402	16,080
		NPV	32,000

IRR = 10 + [87,980/(87,980 – 32,000) × 10] = 25.7%

Test your understanding 107

B

Investment	Cash flows	Cumulative cash flow
	$000	$000
Initial investment	(400)	(400)
Incremental cash flows		
Year 1	100	(300)
Year 2	120	(180)
Year 3	140	(40)
Year 4	120	80

Months = 40 ÷ 120 × 12 = 4 months

Test your understanding 108

C

Investment	Cash flows	Discounted cash flows	Cumulative cash flow
	$000	$000	$000
Initial investment	450	450	(450)
Incremental cash flows			
Year 1	130	118.17	(331.83)
Year 2	130	107.38	(224.45)
Year 3	130	97.63	(126.82)
Year 4	130	88.79	(38.03)
Year 5	150	93.15	55.12

Months = 38.03 ÷ 93.15 × 12 = 4.899 = 5 months

Test your understanding 109

D

Investment	Cash flows	Discounted cash flows (20%)
	$000	$000
Initial investment	(350)	(350)
Incremental cash flows		
Year 1	50	41.65
Year 2	110	76.34
Year 3	130	75.27
Year 4	150	72.30
Year 5	100	40.20
Net present value		(44.24)

IRR = 10 + [48/(48 – –44.24) × 10] = 15.2%

Chapter 15: Standard costing

Test your understanding 110

B

Aq × Ap =	
1,560 × $5.25 =	$8,190
Sq × Sp =	
4,800 × 20/60 × $5 =	$8,000
	$190A

Test your understanding 111

C

Test your understanding 112

C

Actual materials used × standard rate		
28,000 × $3.30	92,400	
Standard cost of actual production		
5,900 × 5 × $3.30	97,350	
	4,950	favourable

Test your understanding 113

A

$105,000 – 30,000 × $3.30 = $6,000 adverse

Test your understanding 114

C

Budget selling price = $108,000/9,000 = $12

$104,500 – 9,500 × $12 = $9,500 adverse

Test your understanding 115

B

Standard contribution = $36,000/9,000 = $4 per unit

Volume variance = 500 × $4 = $2,000 favourable.

Test your understanding 116

B

	$
Actual hours × standard rate 8,320 × $7	58,240
Less favourable expenditure variance	(1,664)
Actual expenditure	56,576

Therefore actual rate per hour = $56,576/8,320 = $6.80

Test your understanding 117

B FALSE

The fixed overhead volume variance can be subdivided into a capacity and an efficiency variance.

Test your understanding 118

D

Standard fixed overhead rate per unit = $280,000/7,000 = $40 per unit

Fixed overhead volume variance = 200 units × $40 = $8,000 favourable (over-absorbed)

Test your understanding 119

B

Standard contribution on actual sales	$85,600
Less: Adverse total variable costs variance	($12,600)
Actual Contribution	$73,000

Chapter 16: Performance measurement

Test your understanding 120

C

RI = Operating profit – (10% × invested capital)

Therefore \$240,000 = \$640,000 – (10% × invested capital)

So 10% × invested capital = \$400,000

Therefore, invested capital = \$4m

ROI = Operating profit/Invested capital

ROI = \$640,000/\$4,000,000 × 100 = 16%

Test your understanding 121

B

Output per standard hour is 2 units as each unit has a standard time allowance of 30 minutes.

Budgeted labour hours are 1,500/2 = 750

The actual output measured in standard hours is 1,400/2 = 700 standard hours

The production volume ratio = 700/750 × 100% = 93.3%

Test your understanding 122

C

The capacity ratio = 720/750 × 100% = 96%

Test your understanding 123

A

The efficiency ratio = 700/720 × 100% = 97.2%

Test your understanding 124

D

Test your understanding 125

B

The current ratio is all current assets including inventory divided by current liabilities, while the acid test is the current asset figure less inventory divided by current liabilities. These can only be equal if a firm carries no inventory.

Test your understanding 126

B

Reducing mortality rates is likely to be a stated objective of the hospital and as such is a measure of output, or effectiveness.

Test your understanding 127

B

The manager of a profit centre can exercise control over revenues and controllable costs, but has no influence concerning the capital invested in the centre.

Contribution (i) would be a useful performance measure because a profit centre manager can exercise control over sales revenue and variable costs. Controllable profit (ii) would also be useful as long as any overhead costs charged in deriving the profit figure are controllable by the profit centre manager. Apportioned central costs would not be deducted when calculating controllable profit. Return on investment (iii), residual income (iv) would not be useful because they require a measure of the capital invested in the division.

Test your understanding 128

D

A customer service team deals with customer queries and complaints from outside the organisation, typically after goods have been delivered to the customer. The costs of this team arise from quality failures and are preventable. They are external failure costs. Maintenance is intended to prevent machine breakdowns and so to prevent quality failures, and they are therefore prevention costs. Test equipment is used for inspection.

Chapter 17: Presenting information

Test your understanding 129

D

Test your understanding 130

D

The black shirts are 20% of the order therefore will be 20% of the degrees in a circle.

360° × 20% = 72°

Chapter 18: Spreadsheets

Test your understanding 131

A TRUE

Test your understanding 132

B FALSE

A database would be more useful.

Spreadsheets are designed to analyse data and sort list items, not for long-term storage of raw data.

Test your understanding 133

C

Spreadsheets should speed up data analysis, reduce calculation errors and they do include a graphical function.

Test your understanding 134

B

Where a database would be more suitable.